CW01645430

FORMAL AND TRANSCENDENTAL LOGIC

EDMUND HUSSERL

FORMAL AND TRANSCENDENTAL LOGIC

Translated by

DORION CAIRNS

1969
MARTINUS NIJHOFF
THE HAGUE

PRINTED IN THE NETHERLANDS

The publication of this English translation by Dorion Cairns of *Formale und transzendentale Logik* fulfills a desire expressed by Edmund Husserl. Husserl himself, in the last years of his life, entrusted the translation of this work to Dorion Cairns, whom he counted among his best students. For various reasons, it is only now that this translation can be published. In the meantime, Dorion Cairns's translation into English of Husserl's *Cartesianische Meditationen* has been acknowledged everywhere as a work of the highest scientific quality. The present translation of the *Formale und transzendentale Logik* is a very important further step for making Husserl's thought known in the English-speaking world. In the name of the Husserl-Archives, I wish to express my sincere thanks to Professor Dorion Cairns for his self-sacrificing work.

H. L. Van Breda
Director of the Husserl-Archives
Louvain

CONTENTS

PART II / FROM FORMAL TO TRANSCENDENTAL LOGIC

INTRODUCTION <1>

What we today call science, in our pregnant sense of the word, is not science in the historically oldest sense, that of a naïvely straightforwardly effected work of theoretical reason. Only in a loose sense do we still refer to the philosophies of the pre-Platonic age, or similar cultural formations of other peoples and times, as sciences. Only as preliminary forms, as stages preliminary to science, do we accept them. Science in a new sense arises in the first instance from *Plato's establishing of logic*, as a place for exploring the essential requirements of "genuine" knowledge and "genuine" science and thus discovering norms, in conformity with which a science consciously aiming at thorough justness, a science consciously justifying its method and theory by norms, might be built. In intention this logical justification is a justification deriving entirely from pure principles. Science in the Platonic sense intends, then, to be no longer a merely naïve activity prompted by a purely theoretical interest. Every step that it takes, it also demands to justify as genuine, as necessarily valid, according to principles. Thus the original sense here is that logical insight into principles, the insight drawn from the pure idea of any possible cognition and method of cognition whatever, precedes the method factually employed and the factual shaping of science, and guides them in practice; whereas the fact of a method and of a science, which have grown up somehow in naïveté, must not pass itself off as a norm for rightly shaping scientific production.

Plato's logic arose from the reaction against the universal denial of science by sophistic skepticism. If / skepticism denied <2>
the essential possibility of any such thing as "philosophy", as science, then Plato had to weigh, and establish by criticism, precisely the *essential possibility* of such a thing. If all science was

called in question, then naturally no fact, science, could be presupposed. Thus Plato was set on the path to the pure idea. Not gathered from the de facto sciences but formative of pure norms, his dialectic of pure ideas — as we say, his logic or his theory of science — was called on to make genuine[1] science possible now for the first time, to guide its practice. And precisely in fulfilling this vocation the Platonic dialectic actually helped create sciences in the pregnant sense, sciences that were consciously sustained by the idea of logical science and sought to actualize it so far as possible. Such were the strict mathematics and natural science whose further developments at higher stages are our modern sciences.

But the original relationship between logic and science has undergone a remarkable reversal in modern times. The sciences made themselves independent. Without being able to satisfy completely the spirit of critical self-justification, they fashioned extremely differentiated methods, whose fruitfulness, it is true, was practically certain, but whose productivity was not clarified by ultimate insight. They fashioned these methods, not indeed with the everyday man's naïveté, but still with a *naïveté of a higher level,* which abandoned the appeal to the pure idea, the justifying of method by pure principles, according to ultimate apriori possibilities and necessities. In other words: logic, which was originally the torchbearer for method and claimed to be the theory of the pure principles of possible cognition and science, lost this historical vocation and lagged far behind in its development. The grand reshaping of the natural sciences in the seventeenth century was still determined by logical reflections concerning the essence and requirements of a genuine cognition of Nature and the essential aims and methods of such cognition. These reflections found their place in the nexus of efforts, so characteristic of that age, to establish a new logic, the true one. Here belongs not only Galileo but also, as should be emphasized, Descartes. The very title, *Discours de la Méthode,* is characteristic; and, in his *Meditationes,* "first philosophy" is itself only an expression for a completely radical, and at the same time universal, theory of science. But while logic, in these modern
<3> beginnings, still led the way for the sciences, / this essential

[1] *Translator's note: Reading* echte *instead of* faktische.

relationship became altered in the following age, precisely as the age during which the sciences became self-sufficient special sciences, no longer caring about a logic — indeed, thrusting logic aside almost scornfully. Logic itself, however, has strayed utterly away from its own sense and inalienable task in recent times. Instead of seeking out the pure essential norms of science in all its[1] essential formations, to give the sciences fundamental guidance thereby and to make possible for them genuineness in shaping their methods and in rendering an account of every step, logic has been pleased to let itself be guided by the de facto sciences, particularly the much-admired natural sciences, in conceiving its ideal of science and in setting its own problems.

Perhaps this evinces a tragedy of modern scientific culture, deeper and more telling than the one usually deplored in scientifc circles: that the list of special sciences has become so long that nobody is able any more to derive full advantage from all this wealth, to survey and enjoy all these treasures of cognition. The defect in our scientific situation seems to be much more essential, more radical in the literal sense. It concerns, not the collective unifying and appropriating of the sciences, but their *rootedness in principles* and their unification as springing from these roots. It is a defect that would remain, even though an unheard-of mnemonics and a pedagogy guided thereby were to make possible for us an encyclopedic knowledge of what has at any particular time been ascertained with theoretical Objectivity[2] in all the sciences. Science, in the form of special science, has become a sort of theoretical technique, which, like technique in the usual sense, depends on a "practical experience" accruing from many-sided and often-exercised practical activity itself — on what, in the realm of practice, is called "intuition", a knack, or a good practical eye — much more than on insight into the *ratio* of its accomplished production.

Thus modern science has abandoned the ideal of genuine science that was vitally operative in the sciences from the time of

[1] *Translator's note: Perhaps* their.

[2] *Translator's note:* In this essay *Gegenstand* and *Objekt* do not usually express the same sense. Having found no acceptable alternative to translating them both as *object*, I differentiate by spelling the word with a small letter when it represents *Gegenstand* and with a capital when it represents *Objekt*. All this applies, *mutatis mutandis*, in the case of any word derived from *Gegenstand* or from *Objekt*. If *object*, or a word derived from it, stands first in a sentence, the German word is given in brackets.

Plato; and, in its practice, it has abandoned radicalness of scientific self-responsibility. No longer is its inmost driving force that radicalness which unremittingly imposes on itself the demand to accept no knowledge that cannot be accounted
<4> for by originarily first principles, which are at the same time matters of perfect insight / — principles such that profounder inquiry makes no sense. Science as actually developing may have been very imperfect in this respect. But the essential thing was that this radical demand guided a corresponding practical striving toward perfection, and that logic accordingly was still assigned the great function of exploring, in their essential universality, the possible avenues to ultimate principles and, by displaying in detail the essence of genuine science as such (and therefore its pure possibility), giving to actual science its norm and guidance. Nothing was more remote, therefore, than to aim at a sort of merely technical productivity, the naïveté of which sets it in extremest contrast to the productivity of a radical self-testing by normative principles.

But this matter of principles (as all the giants of the past, from Plato on, have seen) gains its full force, its full apodictic evidentness on every side, from the universality with which all sciences are inseparably connected as branches of one *sapientia universalis* (Descartes). The emancipated special sciences fail to understand the essential one-sidedness of their productions; they fail to understand that they will not encompass in their theories the full being-sense of their respective provinces until they lay aside the blinders imposed by their method, as an inevitable consequence of the exclusive focusing of each on its own particular province: in other words, until they relate their combined researches to [*ihre Forschungen hineinlenken in*] the universality of being and its fundamental essential unity. For this situation, as we have said, logic itself shares the blame — because, as may be added here, instead of keeping its eye unfalteringly on its historical vocation and developing as the pure and universal theory of science, logic itself became a special science. Its own final sense demanded that, reflectively, it make that final sense a theme for radical considerations and master the essentially differentiated strata of problems in the theory of science that predelineate the hierarchy of logical disciplines, in which alone the idea of a theory of science — and science itself — can become actualized. But logic did not satisfy this, its own essential sense.

The present condition of European sciences necessitates radical investigations of sense. At bottom these sciences have lost their great belief in themselves, in their absolute significance. The modern man of today, unlike the "modern" man of the Enlightenment, does not behold in science, and in the new culture formed by means of science, the self-Objectivation of human reason or the universal activity mankind has devised for itself in order / to make possible a truly satisfying life, an individual <5>
and social life of practical reason. The belief that science leads to wisdom — to an actually rational self-cognition and cognition of the world and God, and, by means of such cognition, to a life somehow to be shaped closer to perfection, a life truly worth living, a life of "happiness", contentment, well-being, or the like — this great belief, once the substitute for religious belief, has (at least in wide circles) lost its force. Thus men live entirely in a world that has become unintelligible, in which they ask in vain for the wherefore, the sense, which was once so doubtless and accepted by the understanding, as well as by the will.

Now, however critical and skeptical our attitude toward our scientific culture as it has developed historically, we cannot simply abandon it, with no more reason than that we lack an ultimate understanding of it and are unable to manage it by virtue of such an understanding — because, in other words, we are unable to explicate its sense rationally, to determine the true range of its sense, the range within which we can self-responsibly[1] justify the sense of our culture and, with our continued labor, make this sense actual. If we are not satisfied by the joy of creating a theoretical technique, of contriving theories with which one can do so much that is useful and win the admiration of the world — if we cannot separate genuine humanity and living with radical self-responsibility, and therefore cannot separate scientific self-responsibility from the whole complex of responsibilities belonging to human life as such — then we must place ourselves above this whole life and all this cultural tradition and, by radical sense-investigations, seek for ourselves singly and in common the ultimate possibilities and necessities, on the basis of which we can

[1] *Translator's note: Reading* selbstverantwortlich *instead of* selbst verantwortlich.

take our position toward actualities in judging, valuing, and acting. True, in that manner we gain nothing but *universalities* for which we can give an ultimate accounting, "principles"; whereas life, after all, consists in decisions of the "moment", which never has time to establish anything with scientific rationality. But if science, with radical responsibility, has reached decisions, they can impress on life habitual norms as volitional bents, as predelineated forms within which the individual decisions ought in any case to confine themselves, and can confine themselves so far as those universal decisions have become actually appropriated. For a rational practice, theory a priori can be only a delimiting form; it can only plant fences, the crossing of which indicates absurdity or aberration. What
<6> problems / arise in this connexion for self-education and the education of mankind, is a separate question; and, by the way, in its universal form, it is itself a question to be dealt with by an all-embracing science, which considers all possibilities and truths. About that, however, we need not say anything further here; we need only make clear to ourselves, by observing our present scientific and cultural situation, the necessity of radical and universal investigations of sense. These investigations, concerning the possible sense and possible method of genuine science as such, are naturally directed first of all to what is essentially common to all possible sciences. They should be followed secondarily by corresponding sense-investigations for particular groups of sciences and single sciences.

Problems in the theory of science are a chief theme for the philosophy of our age; and therefore it naturally occurs to us to conduct our sense-investigations in the form of a criticism of contemporary philosophic efforts. But that would be quite a hopeless undertaking in our confused philosophic situation, where indeed the literature of philosophy not only has swollen beyond all measure but is so lacking in uniformity of method that there are almost as many philosophies as philosophers. Our scientific situation having in fact become similar to that encountered by Descartes in his youth, an all-embracing sense-investigation can attempt the bold *path of the Cartesian meditations.* With a radicalness that cannot be surpassed and is, for that very reason, exemplary for philosophy, the idea of genuine science as

science grounded on an absolute foundation — the old Platonic idea — is renewed in full earnest; and the intrinsically primary basis already presupposed by any cognition, and therefore by the cognition belonging to the positive sciences, is sought. The first attempt at such an absolutely radical grounding of science, Descartes' own attempt, miscarried. The steadfast will, not to accept any cognition unless it is justified absolutely, is not sufficient to the deed; an absolutely good conscience — and therefore, in particular, an absolutely good intellectual conscience — is an infinite idea. But even a best possible conscience and a method of practical approximation to that idea are a theme for meditations far more extensive and difficult than Descartes supposed. Unnoticed prejudices directed his meditations, so that, viewed as a whole, they lacked the power to convince even his contemporaries. However greatly his going back to the *ego cogito* affected the whole of modern philosophy, the style of those meditations — starting from absolute cognitive / subjectivity, to <7>
undertake an absolute grounding of the sciences in their all-embracing unity, or (this being the same thing to Descartes) an absolute grounding of philosophy — that style was never resumed, up to the time of transcendental phenomenology.[1]

Other paths are possible for sense-investigations with a radical aim; and the present work attempts to open up, at least in main sections, one suggested precisely by the historically given relation of the idea of genuine science to logic as its antecedent norm.

Logic, which originated in the struggles of Platonic dialectic, had already, with Aristotle's analytics, crystallized off within

[1] *Author's note:* See my *Ideen;* also the new work, *Cartesianische Meditationen, eine Einleitung in die transzendentale Phänomenologie* [*Cartesian Meditations, an Introduction to Transcendental Phenomenology*] (Halle a. S., Max Niemeyer), which is to appear in the Autumn [of 1929].

[The full title of the work referred to here as *Ideen* is *Ideen zu einer reinen Phänomenologie und phänomenologischen Philosophie, Erstes Buch, Allgemeine Einfuhrung in die reine Phänomenologie* [*Ideas pertaining to a Pure Phenomenology and to a Phenomenological Philosophy*, "Book One, General Introduction to Pure Phenomenology"]. It was first published in 1913. A new edition, "enlarged on the basis of the author's manuscript additions" by Walter Biemel, was published as *Husserliana, Band III* (Haag, Martinus Nijhoff, 1950). Meanwhile an English translation by W. R. Boyce Gibson had appeared under the title, *Ideas: General Introduction to Pure Phenomenology* (London, Unwin, and New York, Macmillan, 1931). It will be cited hereafter as "English translation". The "new work" also referred to was published only posthumously, in *Husserliana, Band I* (*idem*), though a French translation had appeared in 1931. An English translation by Dorion Cairns has been published (The Hague, Martinus Nijhoff, 1960).]

itself a rigidly formed systematic theory, which has defied milleniums almost as successfully as Euclid's geometry. There is no need here of recalling Kant's well-known opinion, which greatly over-estimated the completeness of this logic; but every glance at the world's philosophic literature, and even at the chaos of modern logical efforts, shows that "formal logic" has had an invincible strength. Even through such widely divergent presentations and, indeed, distorting caricatures it has prevailed, with an essentially identical core of unrelinquishable content. Though the specific sense of its formalness may have remained undifferentiated, this formal logic was, according to its sense, the first historical attempt at a universal theory of science, a theory relating to the essential conditions for any possible science whatever. To be sure, it was confined to a one-sidedness that is natural, nay, even rooted in essential grounds; while, on another side, an Apriori belonging to the theory of science was indeed continually touched on but, in its depths (which are hidden from natural thinking), not only remained for thousands of years inaccessible to a systematically theoretical investigation, but did not even come within this logic's range of vision.

If, however, we restrict ourselves to that which, thanks precisely to this naturally motivated one-sidedness, enters our experience as a solid intellectual formation, namely the *core* of theories that actually remains visible and unchanging in the different temporary appropriational forms and modes of interpretation, we may venture the attempt to explicate, step by step, its sense as theory of science, while directing our regard con-
<8> tinually to the projects / of ancient and modern positive sciences, back to which in ancient and modern times this sense has related, as it still relates today. Thus we are presupposing the sciences, as well as logic itself, on the basis of the "experience" that gives them to us beforehand. Because of this, our procedure seems not to be at all radical, since the genuine sense of all sciences — or, equivalently, the essential possibility of their existence as genuine and not merely supposed sciences — is the very thing in question. And this applies in the case of logic itself, which is said to be the science of science, taken universally, and to bring out with its theories — or, as existing historically, to have ostensibly brought out — precisely that essential possibility. Nevertheless, whether

sciences and logic be genuine or spurious, we do have experience of them as cultural formations given to us beforehand and bearing within themselves their meaning, their "sense": since they are formations produced indeed by the practice of the scientists and generations of scientists who have been building them. As so produced, they have a final sense, toward which the scientists have been continually striving, at which they have been continually aiming. Standing in, or entering, a community of empathy with the scientists, we can follow and understand — and carry on "sense-investigation".

Sense-investigation [*Besinnung*] signifies nothing but the attempt actually to produce the sense "itself", which, in the mere meaning, is a meant, a presupposed, sense; or, equivalently, it is the attempt to convert the "intentive sense [*intendierenden Sinn*]" (as it was called in the *Logische Untersuchungen* [1]), the sense "vaguely floating before us" in our unclear aiming, into the fulfilled, the clear, sense, and thus to procure for it the evidence of its clear possibility. Precisely this possibility is genuineness of sense and is, accordingly, the aim of our investigative search and discovery. Sense-investigation, we may also say, is radically conceived *original sense-explication,* which converts, or at first strives to convert, the sense in the mode of an unclear meaning into the sense in the mode of full clarity or essential possibility.

Accordingly, for purposes of radical sense-investigation, we may let ourselves be guided by our empathic experience of the sciences, taking them as produced formations through which there runs the unity of an aiming "meaning". Similarly we may let ourselves be guided by such an experience of traditional logic, in its relation to the experientially given sciences. In so doing, we are chiefly intent on *the genuine sense of a logic as theory of science,* a logic that would necessarily have as its own task / the <9>
clearing up and the clear theoretical explicating of the genuine sense of all science as such. That on which we fix our regard initially, in our experiencing, is the aforesaid "core" of formal logic and, in our correlative viewing of the sciences given before-

[1] *Author's note: Logische Untersuchungen* [*Logical Investigations*], *2. Aufl., II. Band, I. Teil* [(Halle, Niemeyer, 1913)], pp. 50ff. [*Cf.* Marvin Farber, *The Foundation of Phenomenology* (Cambridge, Harvard University Press, 1943), pp. 230ff.]

hand, the thing about them that this logic (supposedly) lays hold of as an essential possibility and a norm. From there the investigation of sense proceeds at first with the *one-sidedness* conditioned by this relation back <to the given sciences> and by this line of regard, a one-sidedness that determines the specific sense of traditional logic as essentially an "Objective" logic.

Radical sense-investigation, as such, is at the same time criticism for the sake of original clarification. Here original clarification means shaping the sense anew, not merely filling in a delineation that is already determinate and structurally articulated beforehand. Nowhere indeed is such a quite determinate predelineation of sense essentially possible, except as a secondary consequence of clarity previously obtained. After the living evidence of clarity has passed, the effect this evidence produced in the realm of habit persists, along with the possibility of a restoration, which at first is empty but contains, in empty form, the determinate sense-predelineation. This predelineation brings with it, then, the certainty of possible clear restoration, as renewal of the evidence. If, as in our case, such clarification is out of the question, then original sense-investigation signifies a combination of determining more precisely the vague indeterminate predelineation, distinguishing the prejudices that derive from associational overlappings, and cancelling those prejudices that conflict with the clear sense-fulfilment [*mit der besinnlichen Erfüllung*] — in a word, then: critical discrimination between the genuine and the spurious.

So much by way of a most general characterization of the aim and method of this essay. It is, accordingly, an *intentional explication of the proper sense of formal logic.* The explication begins with the *theoretical formations* that, in a survey, are furnished us by historical experience — in other words: with what makes up the traditional Objective content of formal logic — and puts them back *into the living intention of logicians,* from which they originated as sense-formations. And, this being inseparable from such a restoration, the explication turns back to the intentionality of the *scientists,* from whom the Objective stock of concrete scientific theory originated — since, indeed, the logician directs his attention to the sciences that are given him beforehand. The intentionality that comes to life in any actual following and understanding is asked what it is properly aiming at. Reflective sense-explication [*Die besinnliche Auslegung*], as critical clarification, must yield the answer.

In the systematic execution of our task we shall begin quite simply, and not directly with consideration of the logic given us beforehand; / rather we shall relate our first universal distinctions <10>
to the significations of the word logos and to the question of the extent to which these significations can indicate themes for a theory. By such "Preparatory Considerations" we shall acquire a preliminary understanding of the theme to which the historically given logic directs its interest; and that understanding will provide the line of vision for our subsequent analyses of sense.

In "Part I" these lead first of all to a *three-fold stratification of the fundamental concepts — and therefore of the disciplines — of formal logic.* This stratification, which was not yet completely recognized in my *Logische Untersuchungen*, is of the greatest significance, not only for actual understanding of the genuine sense of logic as one particular science, but also for the whole of philosophy. The substantiating investigations, as necessarily going back to noetic intentionality (since, after all, logical formations originate from categorial activity), are directed to the subjective. Whether they should be called psychological, or how else they should be characterized, is quite beside the question, so long as they retain their initial, purely ancillary, significance.

But other great problems are connected with the demonstrated three-fold stratification. They concern a radical *clarification of the relationship between formal logic and formal mathematics*, and the deeper vindication of their indissoluble union in the idea of a *formal mathesis universalis* (vindication on a primary level having already been effected in my *Logische Untersuchungen*). With this, however, there emerges as an essential advance the long-desired and, I hope, *definitive clarification of the sense of pure formal mathematics* (including formal syllogistics, as correspondingly purified), according to the prevailing intention of mathematicians: its sense, namely, as a *pure analytics of non-contradiction*, in which the concept of truth remains outside the theme.

Again, connected therewith is the genuine sense of a *formal ontology*, the concept of which was introduced (in the *Logische Untersuchungen*) with the fundamental essential distinction between formal ontology and material ontology (ontology that has material content) and, correlatively, between the realm of an "analytic" Apriori and that of a "synthetic" (material) Apriori.

It appears to me that these clarifications of sense, accomplished in "Part I", should be of enduring use to philosophers; at all events, the problems mentioned have disturbed and greatly occupied me for decades. /

<11> For those who may be interested in a more detailed statement on this point, I should like to remark also that the problem guiding me originally in determining the sense of, and isolating, a pure logic of "non-contradiction" was a problem of evidence: namely, the problem of *the evidence of the sciences making up formal mathematics*. It struck me that the evidence of truths comprised in formal mathematics (and also of truths comprised in syllogistics) is entirely different from that of other apriori truths, in that the former do not need any intuition of objects or of predicatively formed affair-complexes as concrete examples, even though they do relate to these, albeit with the universality of empty forms. Though it seemed obvious that a science relating with this universality to anything and everything — to everything possible, everything imaginable — deserves to be called a formal *ontology*, still, if it is to be one actually, then the *possibility* of objectivities belonging in its sphere must be established by intuition. It is now easy to solve this problem decisively, on the basis of the isolation (legitimated in "Part I") of a pure "logic of *Konsequenz* (consistency)" or "non-contradiction" [1]; though the investigations carried out in the text do not themselves begin with this line of inquiry.

In "Part II" of this work the *subjective-logical* becomes the chief theme, still within the nexus of our continued sense-investigations concerning a formal logic as a theory of science; and the natural path from formal to transcendental logic is marked out. The spectre of psychologism emerges at the very beginning; and, first of all, the particular sense of the much-discussed attack on psychologism in the first volume of the *Logische Untersuchungen* undergoes a new and sharper clarification — this being essential as a preparation for our clarification of "transcendental psycholo-

[1] *Translator's note:* On the sense of the terms "logic of *Konsequenz*" and "logic of non-contradiction" see "Appendix III", § 1, pp. 330–334, *infra*.

gism", which comes much later. A series of *presuppositions* involved in logical cognition, and pointed back to by the themes of logic, is then uncovered; and gradually this awakens the insight that *none of the sense-problems relating to the subjective* that are, and must be, raised in such an investigation of science and logic is a *problem of natural human subjectivity* — that is to say, a *psychological* problem; rather that all of them are problems of *transcendental subjectivity*, in the sense introduced by me and peculiar to *transcendental phenomenology*. As we continue to penetrate more deeply, there is opened to us the insight that an *actually philosophic logic*, a theory of science that / explicates on <12>
all sides the essential possibility of genuine science as such and is therefore able to guide the development of genuine science, *can grow up only in the nexus of a transcendental phenomenology.* Historically existing logic, with its naïve positivity, its way of obtaining truths as objects of naïve straightforward evidence, proves to be a sort of philosophic puerility. An *independently developed logic* of ideal signification-formations is just as *unphilosophic* as any other positive science; it lacks in itself that originary genuineness by virtue of which it might achieve ultimate self-understanding and self-justification. It therefore has no norms with which to help the positive sciences over their positivity. The *unphilosophic character of this positivity* consists precisely in this: The sciences, because they do not understand their own productions as those of a productive intentionality (this intentionality remaining unthematic for them), are unable to clarify the genuine being-sense of either their provinces or the concepts that comprehend their provinces; thus they are unable to say (in the true and ultimate sense) what sense belongs to the existent of which they speak or what sense-horizons that existent presupposes — horizons of which they do not speak, but which are nevertheless co-determinant of its sense.

In connexion with the dogmatic naïveté of an allegedly self-sufficient formal *logic* based on adequate evidence, we find the *naïveté of an externally appended and ex post facto theory of cognition*, asking and allegedly answering universal questions about origins and validity in logic's behalf, but in a manner that cannot alter, in any respect, the <presupposed> absoluteness of Objective logic's validity. The *true theory of cognition*, after all, is clarification of the "genuine" sense belonging to logical concepts and to logic itself — not an antecedent sense already existing in fact, but a sense yet to be created by the theory of cognition, yet to be explored with regard to the horizons of its range: created and explored, however, under the guidance of the sense merely supposed beforehand. The case of logic is like that of any other positive science: So far as positive sciences already exist as historical facts, they are projects, claims; as such they are *clues* to guide transcendental researches, the aim of which is to create sciences for the very first time as genuine.

Our investigations will expose at ever new levels the ***radical defect of historically existing logic*** and modern logic in particular:
<13> that it could not in any manner fulfil the great tasks / set by the idea of science ***with respect to the subjective***, with respect, namely, to judicative, cognitive, investigative thinking. The psychology of cognition, beginning with Locke, has completely failed — even as properly psychological investigation — because of its countersensical sensualism. But — and this is particularly important to a philosophic theory of science (that is: one that retains the historically original, the only genuine, sense of a theory of science) — it has failed also because Locke and all later psychologizing logicians and epistemologists have been unable to distinguish between a ***psychological*** and a ***transcendental*** investigation of cognition. Fundamentally essential problems, which presented themselves as manifestly tending toward a radical theory of science, and therefore as specifically philosophic, have been displaced to the level of an anthropological psychology, and an empirical one at that. When we add to this the fact that Kant's transcendental investigation of cognition took effect afterwards in a manner that remained far removed from any actually and concretely explicative analysis of cognition, the result is the immense defect in modern theory of Objective science: It has not been able to make understandable, even as a ***problem***, the deepest clarification and establishment of the possibility of genuine sciences (and, with that, the possibility of an Objectivity itself which is true in itself), its clarification and establishment, namely, by investigating the universality of the consciousness that, whithin itself, constitutes Objective sense — to say nothing of its having been able to develop and pursue the method of solution.

What science has before it as a province, given in advance for theoretical work, is, in respect of its sense and being, a province for the investigators (singly and in communion) by virtue of sources belonging to the (likewise separate and communalized) productivity of the investigators' own consciousnesses; anything further that, as a theory of that province, has at any time become a finished result is the result of an active productivity, which has made the whole sense of the theory, including its truth-sense. A theory can be naïvely-straightforwardly accepted; by virtue of evidence, by virtue of repeated critical confirmation, it can "be" for us (an "actual" theory), just as truly as a physical thing, by virtue of experience and experiential verification, is for us an existent actuality, naïvely accepted as a matter of course. But that is not to say that the being-for-us of the theory is understandable transcendentally; any more than the being-for-us of the physical thing is understandable in such a manner: namely as constituted by virtue of sources belonging to the subjectivity of the single individual and to intersubjectivity, constituted as what it is for us, for "everyone" — as the only being that has sense for us. Any sense in which we philosophers ask about a sense of the world (the real world or no matter what ideal one) / presupposes <14>
clarification of the transcendental origin; and "the question" itself pertains to the field of transcendental science.

Lotze, in a famous aphorism, designated as the highest task of cognition, not merely to calculate the course of the world, but to understand it. We must appropriate this saying and apply it, *mutatis mutandis*, in the case of logic and the realm of logical formations: in the sense, namely, that it is not enough that logic, in the manner characteristic of positive sciences, methodically fashion Objective theories and reduce the forms of possible genuine theory to principles and norms. We must rise above the self-forgetfulness of the theorizer who, in his theoretical producing, devotes himself to the subject-matter, the theories, and the methods, and accordingly knows nothing of the inwardness of that producing — who lives in producing,[1] but does not have. this productive living itself as a theme within his field of vision. Only by virtue of a fundamental clarification, penetrating the depths of the inwardness that produces cognition and theory, the

1 *Translator's note: Reading* ihm (it) *instead of* ihnen (them).

transcendental inwardness, does what is produced as genuine theory and genuine science become understandable. Only by virtue of such a clarification, moreover, does the true sense of that being become understandable, which science has labored to bring out in its theories as true being, as true Nature, as the true cultural world. Therefore: *only a science clarified and justified transcendentally* (*in the phenomenological sense*) *can be an ultimate science; only a transcendentally-phenomenologically clarified world can be an ultimately understood world; only a transcendental logic can be an ultimate theory of science, an ultimate, deepest, and most universal, theory of the principles and norms of all the sciences.*

If we conceive the idea of logic as greatly, as large-mindedly, as it requires according to its original intention, and if we animate it with the transcendental spirit, we shall have to say: What the modern sciences lack is the true logic, which includes all the problems and disciplines of "theory of science" (in the broadest, but still an essentially unitary, sense), a logic that, as transcendental logic, lights the way for the sciences with the light of a deepest self-cognition of cognition and makes them understandable in all their doings. This logic, then, does not intend to be a mere pure and formal logic — conceived most broadly, in the Leibnizian sense, a *mathesis universalis:* a logical science of idealities, but still only a "positive" science. On the other hand,
<15> it intends even less / to be a merely empirical technology for a sort of intellectual productions having the greatest practical utility and going by the name "science" — a technology adjusted empirically to practical results. Rather, as the highest functioning of our operative purely theoretical interest, it intends to bring to light the system of transcendental principles that gives to sciences the possible sense of genuine sciences.

How much the sciences need such a logic, how little they are fit to present themselves in naïve positivity as self-sufficient and to persist in such a self-sufficiency, is shown by the controversy in every science, no matter how exact, about the true sense of its fundamental concepts. Such controversy is a symptom of the fact that the sciences are indeed completely in the dark about their own sense. But then transcendental logic alone makes it fully understandable that the positive sciences can bring about only a relative, one-sided, rationality, which leaves a complete irrationality on necessary opposite sides; and that a mere systematic connecting of all the particular sciences can never yield that universal ontological cognition, in the highest sense, to which the ancient philosophy originally aspired.

So much on the sense of the investigations presented in this essay. It lies in the nature of the subject-matter that the investigations of "Part I" have a certain completeness and self-containedness inevitably lacking in "Part II", which suggests more than it carries through to a finish. For there we are drawn into the prodigious expanses of intentional phenomenology, of which even the part already in actual existence is by no means common property. Moreover, I am preparing an exposition of a number of very comprehensive investigations, carried on for many years and intended to supplement those pertaining to the formal theory of science by those, of a wholly different sort, pertaining to a material theory of science — as well as, on the other hand, predelineative and concretely founding investigations, which attempt to prepare and carry out systematically the other possible courses, besides the above-described first (or, so to speak, Cartesian) course of radical sense-investigation.

In closing, let me mention with warm thanks the efficient help of Dr. Ludwig Landgrebe, who, through the generosity of the *Deutsche Notgemeinschaft,* was provided with a stipend for such purposes. Indefatigably he assisted me in preparing this work for publication.

<16>
PREPARATORY CONSIDERATIONS

§ 1. Outset from the significations of the word logos: speaking, thinking, what is thought.

The word logos, from which the name logic is derived, has a great many significations, which, by easily understood metaphors, arose from the more original significations of λέγειν — namely: "to lay together", "to set forth", and then, to set forth by means of the word, by means of speech.

1. In the developed language, λόγος sometimes signifies word, or *speech*, itself; sometimes, that spoken about, the *affair-complex referred to in speaking*; but also, on the other hand, the propositional thought produced by the speaker for purposes of communication or else for himself: the mental *sense*, as it were, of the assertoric sentence, that which the speaker means by the expression. Furthermore, in many locutions logos points to the *mental act* itself: the predicating, the asserting, or other thinking, in which such a sense-content is generated as concerning the objects or affair-complexes in question.

2. But, particularly where a scientific interest is active, all these significations of the word logos take on a pregnant sense, because the idea of a *rational norm* enters into them. Logos then signifies: sometimes *reason* itself, as an ability, and sometimes rational thinking — that is, thinking that has the quality of insight, or thinking directed to a truth given in insight. Logos signifies also, more specifically, the ability to form legitimate concepts; furthermore it signifies the corresponding rational concept-forming and likewise the resultant correct concept itself.

Now, if we take this multiplicity of visibly interrelated significations of the word logos as a guide in forming our initial idea of a science of logos, it discloses fruitful and interconnected themes for theoretical research and normative application. At the same time, a natural course of inquiry is easy to find.

If we start with the second group of significations, then the

theme of reason as the ability to think correctly and in a manner justifiable by insight — especially to think scientifically — leads us, by way of / the general question of how the transient acts of an <17>
Ego[1] establish corresponding habitual abilities, directly to the question: What sort of acts are the "rational" acts of thinking that are in question here? But naturally, before the specific nature of their rationality can reach consideration, the specific nature of thinking itself must become our theme — *prior*, that is, to any distinction between rational and irrational.

The sense of the word logos leads us predominantly to assertive thinking — judging, in the usual sense of the word — and, correlatively, to judgments as thoughts. But judging does not embrace all "thinking", at least not in the widest conceivable sense of this word. Therefore we come back to *thinking in the broadest sense*, as the theme to be examined first of all. Now human thinking is normally done in language, and all the activities of reason are as good as entirely bound up with speech. Furthermore, so far as it is intersubjective, all the criticism from which the rationally true should emerge employs language and, in the end, leads always to statements. Our first concern, therefore, is not with bare acts of thinking and bare thoughts, but is above all with statements, stated thoughts. This leads us back to the first group of significations of the word logos. Accordingly the researches to be carried out concern three topics: *speaking, thinking,* and *what is thought.* Naturally the corresponding abilities must then become thematic too: the ability to speak; in union with speaking, to think; and, in thinking, to refer to something thought.

§ 2. The ideality of language. Exclusion of the problems pertaining to it.

But the three stated topics are still very multifarious. They need further differentiation and, because of the fluid obscurity of the words used, clarification. To begin with, let us note concerning the topic *speech* a certain distinction that we must not overlook. The uttered word, the actually spoken locution, taken

[1] *Translator's note:* Sometimes Husserl uses *Ego* and *Ich* to express different senses. Because the homophony of *I* and *eye* makes the English noun *I* intolerable, *Ich* has been translated as *Ego* (spelled with a capital) and *Ego* has been translated as *ego* (spelled with a small letter).

as a sensuous, specifically an acoustic, phenomenon, is something that we distinguish from the word itself or the declarative sentence itself, or the sentence-sequence itself that makes up a more extensive locution. Not without reason — in cases where we have not been understood and we reiterate — do we speak precisely of a reiteration of the *same* words and sentences. In a treatise or a novel every word, every sentence, is a one-time
<18> affair, which does not become multiplied / by a reiterated vocal or silent reading. Nor does it matter who does the reading; though each reader has his own voice, his own timbre, and so forth. The treatise itself (taken now only in its lingual aspect, as composed of words or language) is something that we distinguish, not only from the multiplicities of vocal reproduction, but also, and in the same manner, from the multiplicities of its permanent documentations by paper and print, parchment and handwriting, or the like. The one unique language-composition is reproduced a thousand times, perhaps in book form: We speak simply of the *same* book with the same story, the same treatise. And this self-sameness obtains *even with respect to the purely lingual composition;* while, in another manner, it obtains also with respect to the sharply distinguishable significational contents, which we shall shortly take into account.

As a system of habitual signs, which, within an ethnic community, arises, undergoes transformation, and persists in the manner characteristic of tradition — a system of signs by means of which, in contrast to signs of other sorts, an expressing of thoughts comes to pass —, language presents altogether its own problems. One of them is the just-encountered *ideality of language,* which is usually quite overlooked. We may characterize it also in this fashion: *Language has the Objectivity proper to the objectivities making up the so-called spiritual* [*geistige*] *or cultural world, not the Objectivety proper to bare physical Nature.* As an Objective product of minds, language has the same properties as other mental products: Thus we also distinguish, from the thousand reproductions of an engraving, the engraving itself; and this engraving, the engraved picture itself, is visually abstracted from each reproduction, being given in each, in the same manner, as an identical ideal object. On the other hand, only in the form of reproduction does it have factual existence in the real world. The situation is just the same when we speak of the Kreutzer Sonata, in contrast to its reproductions *ad libitum.* However much it itself consists of sounds, it is an ideal unity; and its constituent sounds are no less ideal. They are obviously not the sounds dealt with in physics; nor are they the sounds pertaining to sensuous acoustic perception, the sounds that come from things pertaining to the senses and are really extant only in an actual reproduction and the intuiting of it. Just as the one sonata is reproduced many times in the real reproductions, each single sound belonging to the sonata is reproduced many times in the corresponding sounds belonging to the reproductions. Like the whole, its part is something ideal, which becomes real, *hic et nunc*, only after the fashion of real singularization. / Now it <19> is quite the same in the case of all verbal formations; and the ideality in their case is not solely an ideality of what is expressed in them — however great a rôle the expressed may also play. To be sure, our ascertainments do concern verbal formations *also* as sense-filled locutions, concrete unities of verbal body and expressed sense. But they concern such formations even with respect to the verbal corporeality itself, which is, so to speak, a *spiritual corporeality*. The word itself, the sentence itself, is an ideal unity, which is not multiplied by its thousandfold reproductions.

The fundamental treatment of the great problems that concern clarification of the sense and constitution of Objectivities belonging to the cultural world, with respect to all their fundamental types, including language, makes up a realm by itself. Here it is to be noted only that, for the logician, language is of primary importance solely in its ideality, as the identical lingual word, the identical lingual sentence or complex of sentences, in contrast to the actual or possible reifications: precisely as the aesthetician's theme is the particular work of art, the particular sonata, the particular picture, not as the transient physical complex of sounds or as the physical picture-thing, but as the picture itself, the sonata itself — the properly aesthetic object, corresponding to the properly linguistic object in the parallel case.

This whole group of problems will be left out of consideration in our further investigations, which, by their own content and coherence, will sufficiently justify the omission.

§ 3. Language as an expression of "thinking". Thinking, in the broadest sense, as the sense-constituting mental process.

We shall now consider the second topic mentioned: *thinking* — a word the sense of which must be gathered from the often-used combination, "*die Sprache und das Denken* [language and thinking]". In this context the word has an enormously broad sense, one that, it might almost seem, embraces the whole of man's psychic life: For indeed it is often said also that "*in der Sprache drücke der Mensch sein Seelenleben aus* [in language man expresses his psychic life]". But here we must be more cautious. Actually man does not "express" *all* his psychic life in language; nor is he ever able to do so. If usage is frequently to the contrary, that is owing to the multisignificance of the word "expressing"
<20> and defective clarification of the / relations obtaining here. To begin with, we can limit this use of the word by taking heed that, with every word and every combination of words so arranged that they make up the unity of a locution, the speaker means something. Stated more precisely: where speech proceeds in its natural function, actually as speech in which "such and such is uttered", the speaker's practical intention is obviously not directed ultimately to the mere words, but is directed "through" them to their signification. The words carry significative intentions; they serve as bridges leading over to the significations, to what the speaker means "by" them. This is true wherever speech is normally functioning and actual speech. Naturally, a parrot does not actually speak. We are now excluding mendacious speech too, which says something other than what is believed. To the *unity of the locution* there corresponds a *unity of sense or meaning;* and to the verbal articulations and forms of the locution there correspond articulations and formations of the sense or meaning. The latter, however, does not lie externally beside the words; rather, in speaking we are continously performing an internal act of meaning, which fuses with the words and, as it were, animates them. The effect of this animation is that the words and the entire locution, as it were, *embody* in themselves a meaning, and bear it embodied in them as their sense.[1]

[1] *Author's note:* On this and what follows *cf. Logische Untersuchungen, II. Bd., I. Teil, I. Unters.*, "*Ausdruck und Bedeutung* [Expression and Signification]." [*Cf.* Farber, *op. cit.*, Chap. VII, pp. 222–243.]

We need go no further to delimit, as a preliminary, *a first and broadest, concept of thinking,* one that shall embrace all the psychic processes in which this *act of meaning* consists — this act in which there is constituted for the speaking subject (or, on the other hand, for the hearing and understanding subject) the *meaning* — that is, the *signification,* the sense — expressed in the locution. For example, if we utter a judgment, we have effected, in union with the words of our assertive statement, a unity of judging, of inwardly "thinking" asserting. No matter what other psychic producings may also be effected, whereby the words themselves come about, and no matter what others may play a rôle with respect to the fusion that generates the "expression", we shall pay attention only to what is fused on, namely the acts of judging that function as sense-bestowing acts, i.e., that bear in themselves the judicial meaning or opinion that finds its expression in the assertoric sentence. We are leaving out of consideration the *pointing tendencies* belonging to words (as well as to all other signs): the phenomenon of pointing, away / from <21>
themselves, to the opinion. We are leaving out of consideration also other psychic processes that combine with the acts of judging — for example: those psychic processes in which we turn to our interlocutor, in which we will to make our judgment known to him, and so forth. But naturally we are leaving them out of consideration, only in so far as the character of address is not expressed in the locution — for example: in the form, "I tell you".

What we have learned from the example of the assertive statement holds good universally. When we utter a wish, like "Heaven help me!", we have, united with the structurally articulated producing of the words, a certain wishing, expressed in the verbal articulation and having, for its part, a correspondingly articulated content. The like is true when we utter a command or a question. Conceived with such breadth, *thinking* includes every mental process appertaining in this fashion to the chief function of the expression (namely, to express something) and going on simultaneously with speaking: that is to say, every mental process in which the sense that is to become expressed becomes constituted in the manner peculiar to consciousness — the sense that, if it does become expressed, is called the signification of the expression, particularly of the locution as used on the particular occasion. The process is called thinking, whether it is a judging, a wishing, a willing, an asking, or an uncertain presuming.

But we must not overlook here that alteration of attitude which makes it possible at any time to give expression to wishing and wish, asking and question, or the like, not immediately but mediately, after the fashion of a judgment — that is to say: through the mediation of a judicial positing by which the direct wish, for example, becomes changed into a judicial statement concerning that wish. In its modified expression, which indicates the mediation, the wish is now a moment in a judgment-expression, as when we say, "I wish that S might be p", instead of saying, "May S be p!". Such modification (because of which the phrase "expression of a wish" is often ambiguous) assumes importance owing to the circumstance that, with this mediation, the realm of judicial significations absorbs all other significations, and consequently the logic of judgments is able to include the logic of all other significations as, in a certain fashion, part of itself. But it is unmistakable here that the above-mentioned changes of attitude yield statements that give expression in the primary and proper sense, not to the wishes, the questions, the uncertain presumptions, and so forth, but always and exclusively to judgments. Unmodified properly optative statements, properly interrogative statements, and the like, have become judicial statements with a special sense. When that is taken into consideration, the multifariousness of the acts capable of the expressional function proper is maintained; and so is that concept of "thinking" which is adjusted to the universe of this function. /
<22> Thus we retain at the same time the universality of the coincidence between speech and thinking. These terms now designate for us, accordingly, two parallel realms, corresponding to one another as the realm of possible verbal expressions (locutions) and the realm of possible senses, possibly expressible meanings. In their intentionally combined unity they yield the two-sided realm of actual and concrete, sense-filled locutions. Thus any assertion is truly both a locution and an actual meaning or sense, more specifically an actual judicial meaning or actual opinion; every stated wish is both an optative locution and an actual wish

itself, an actual wish-meaning or wish-sense; and so forth. But, with more precise observation, it is apparent that more than a duality is involved. A sharp distinction must be made between the mental process of meaning and the meaning intended, the sense [*zwischen Meinen und Meinung*]: between judging and judgment [*Urteilen und Urteil*] [1], wishing and wish, and so forth; so that, in fact, there turns out to be a triality, to which the distinction between thinking and what is thought (the thought) has already pointed.

§ 4. The problem of ascertaining the essential limits of the "thinking" capable of the significational function.

The broadest concept of thinking does not have only an adventitious delimitation, as the empirical sphere embracing processes of consciousness that can take on a significational function in connexion with languages. Nor does it have the — indeed essential, but much too broad — delimitation implicit in the obvious fact that only what is psychic, only processes of consciousness, can bestow a sense. For these do not all have this ability. Mental processes appertaining to original passivity — functioning associations, the processes of consciousness in which originary time-consciousness (the constitution of immanent temporality) goes on, [2] and the like — are unable to bestow a sense. Thus we encounter here the significant and difficult *problem of ascertaining the essentially determined limits of this "thinking" in the most universal sense* — the problem of a delimitation, which, as acquired from intuitions of examples with essential universalization, will yield an essential genus, and do so with the insight that universally, for all particularizations of this "thinking", it is possible to form expressions on which they would bestow significations.

The question is: What universal essential character must a process of consciousness have, in order to be capable of taking on

[1] *Translator's note:* Nevertheless in numerous later passages *Urteil* must signify *judging* and not *what is judged*, and in numerous others it probably signifies *judging* but may signify *what is judged*. In almost every case it has been translated here as *judgment* — with a corresponding ambiguity in many contexts. In the few cases where it has been translated as *judging*, the original word is given in brackets. Unless the original word *Urteil* is given, the substantive *judging* represents the gerundial infinitive *Urteilen*.

[2] *Translator's note: Cf.* Appendix II, § 2, *c*, pp. 318f., *infra*.

a significational function? Must it not have the character of an Ego-act in the specific sense (a position-taking act), or else that of a variant mode corresponding to all such acts (secondary
‹23› passivity — for example: passively emerging / judgment, as something that comes to mind)? And furthermore: How is the sought-for essential concept of "thinking" essentially differentiated into its species? The investigative answering of these questions cannot be undertaken here. We content ourselves with pointing to the unity that can be noted in a survey of examples; and we take the broadest concept of thinking as the frame within which the specifically logical must be isolated.

§ 5. Provisional delimitation of logic as apriori theory of science.

We shall attempt a first delimitation of the province that should be assigned to logic, by keeping to the most universal part of the original historical sense of that science, the part which has been, on the whole, its guiding sense up to within our own time. Significations and signification-bestowing acts can be divided into visibly heterogeneous classes, such that concrete "senseful" locutions are grouped accordingly: statements (in the specific sense of assertive statements), as expressions of judgments and their modalities; expressions of affective acts such as wishes; of volitional acts such as commands. Obviously connected with the differences among these sorts of acts is the differentiation of sorts of reason: judicative reason (including specifically theoretical reason), valuing reason, and practical reason.

If we follow the signification of the word logos which is the richest in content and has been, so to speak, raised to a higher power, namely reason, and if we also give pre-eminence to *scientific reason*, we have thereby delimited at the same time a distinctive sphere of acts and significations, precisely as a sphere to which science, as a rational activity, relates particularly. Scientific thinking, the continual activity of the scientist, is *judicative* thinking: not just any judicative thinking, but one that is formed, ordered, connected, in certain manners — according to final ideas of reason. The *formations* generated in the course of such thinking — in science, formations expressed in language and permanently documented — have a coherence

that is "logical" in the sense specific to theoretical reason: the coherence of theories and, at a higher level, the coherence of "systems". They are built up in determinate forms, out of fundamental propositions or principles, theorems, arguments, proofs, and so forth; lingually they are built up in multi-membered locutions, which, in any one science, all belong together as making up the unity of a locution that is internally connected by the rational sense of all the significations. By virtue of the fact that this significational unity is Objectively documented and /
can be regenerated by anyone, the generated formations become <24>
common property for mankind. Each science, in its theoretical work, has aimed exclusively at "logical" formations, formations produced by the theoretical logos. In this sense, each is itself a "logic". But logic as usually conceived is the science of all that is logical: first, in the sense applicable to all such formations produced by judicative reason — but then, on the other hand, in the sense applicable to judicative reason itself and consequently to any judicative subjectivity whatever as generating such formations.

Language is taken into consideration here secondarily, because in science there is combined with the primary purposes of theoretical reason, which lie on the significational side and consist in the attainment of truths, an epistemo-technical purpose, namely that of furthering the work of judging by a suitable scientific language. A maximally durable documentation of the results, in the Objective cultural world, is also relevant to this purpose.

In our further considerations pertaining to the systematic clarification of the idea of logic, we shall address ourselves exclusively to the significational side of scientific locutions — that is to say: purely to judicative reason itself and the formations it produces. That the cognitive subject's primary and true aim lies on this side becomes apparent in the fact that, although the statement-formations are the first to make their appearance in his field of consciousness among its prominences (in the so-called *Blickfeld der Aufmerksamkeit* [field of possible attentive regard]), still his thematizing regard is never directed to the locutions as sensuous phenomena, but always "clear through them" to what is meant. They are not thematic ends but theme-indicators, pointing beyond themselves to the true themes of logic.

Following the historical logical tradition, we have framed the concept of logic as the science of logos in a pregnant sense: as the science of logos in the form of science, or as the science of the essential parts that make up genuine science, as genuine. We could, however, have left the concept of a science of logos in its broader universality from the start; in other words, we could have framed this concept as the concept of a science that, with absolute universality, explores all judicative thinking and its products — including, therefore, rationally judicative thinking and its rational products (among them, those of the sub-scientific level). But, because *scientifically* judicative reason, in the manner characteristic of a highest level, presupposes all the lower levels of productions effected by thinking and, when taken concretely as a theme, includes them all, the reference to science,
<25> and therefore / the conception of *logic as theory of science*, involves no restriction; it simply has the advantage of directing attention to the highest final idea of judicative reason.

As a theory of science concerned with principles, logic intends to bring out *"pure" universalities*, *"apriori" universalities*. As already said in the Introduction, it does not intend to investigate empirically the so-called sciences that are given beforehand — the cultural formations, going by that name, which have in fact come into existence — and abstract their empirical types; on the contrary, free from every restriction to the factual (which supplies it only with points of departure for a criticism of examples), it intends to make completely clear the final ideas that hover dimly before us whenever we are actuated by a purely theoretical interest. Constantly investigating the pure possibilities of a cognitive life, as such, and those of the cognitional formations, as such, attained therein, logic intends to bring to light the essential forms of genuine cognition and genuine science in all their fundamental types, as well as the essential presuppositions by which genuine cognition and genuine science are restricted and the essential forms of the true methods, the ones that lead to genuine cognition and genuine science.

We have spoken of *genuine* cognition, *genuine* science, *genuine* method. Without exception the ideas with which logic is concerned are ideas of "genuineness". The genuine is what reason aims at ultimately — even in its decadent mode, the mode of unreason. The genuine is what is "missed" in obscurity or confusion; whereas, with clarity of goal and way and in the essential forms pertaining to such clarity, it is attained.

§ 6. The formal character of logic. The formal Apriori and the contingent Apriori.

The universality of logic, as concerned with principles, is not simply an apriori or eidetic universality; rather it is, more particularly, a *formal* universality. Not only the narrow and vaguely bounded discipline usually called formal logic (a discipline restricted by a particular concept of the formal, with which we shall have to occupy ourselves greatly), but all logic whatever, in its universal and (as universal) its only philosophic sense, is "formal" throughout all its disciplines. We could say equally well: *Reason itself*, including theoretical reason in particular, *is a form-concept*.

To characterize the most universal and most important concept of form which is involved in these propositions, we may state the following. In a certain sense every eidetic cognition is a product of "pure" reason — *pure from all empeiria* (a characteristic likewise / indicated, from another side, by the word apriori); but <26> not every eidetic cognition is pure in a *second sense*, the one pertaining to *form as a principle*. An apriori proposition about all *sounds* as such, about sounds meant with "pure" universality, is pure only in the first sense; it is, as we may say for certain reasons, a *"contingent" Apriori*. It has in the eidos *sound* a materially determinate core, which goes beyond the realm of the universality of "principles" in the most radical sense, and restricts it to the "contingent" province of ideally possible sounds. *"Pure" reason is not only above everything empirically factual, but also above every sphere of hyletic, materially determinate, essences*. It is the title for the self-contained system of pure principles that precede every hyletic, materially determinate, Apriori and all the sciences concerned with such an Apriori, but that, on the other hand, govern these sciences themselves as rational products — govern them, that is, with respect to form.

To acquaint us more closely with the concept of the contingent Apriori, the following exposition will suffice within the bounds of our present, merely anticipatory, observations: A subjectivity

as such (whether solitary or in communication) is thinkable only as having an essential form, whose highly multifarious constituents we obtain with progressive evidence when we uncover to intuition our own concrete subjectivity and then, with the aid of a free changing of its actuality into "other" possibilities of any concrete subjectivity as such, direct our regard to the invariable that can be seen throughout — that is to say: the essentially necessary. If we stipulate, from the beginning of this variation, that the subjectivity shall always have the capacity to be and remain a "rational" and, in particular, a judicatively cognizing subjectivity, we encounter restrictive essential structures that fall under the heading of pure reason and, in particular, pure judicative reason. Such a subjectivity also involves as a presupposition a continual and essentially necessary relatedness to some hyletic components or other: as apperceptional foundations for the possible experiences that judging necessarily presupposes.[1] Therefore, if we define the concept of form, as a principle, by the essentially necessary components of any rational subjectivity whatever, the concept *hyle* (exemplified by every "Datum of sensation") is a form-concept and not what we shall define as the opposite of this, a contingent concept. On the other hand, there
<27> is / no essential requirement that a judicatively cognizing subjectivity (or a rational subjectivity of any kind) be capable of sensing colors or sounds, that it be capable of sensuous feelings having just such and such a differentia, or the like — though the concepts of such matters too can be framed as apriori (as freed from everything empirically factual). Accordingly they too have their Apriori, which, however, is contingent and not an Apriori of pure reason; or, as we may also say, introducing an old word that tended blindly in the same direction, it is not an "innate" Apriori.

If we restrict ourselves to judicative reason, then, as pure reason, as the complete system of this *formal Apriori in the most fundamental sense*, it designates at the same time the highest and widest conceivable theme of logic, of "theory of science". Consequently we may say that logic is the *self-explication of pure reason* itself or, ideally, the science in which pure theoretical

[1] *Author's note:* On the relatedness of all judging to experience, see Part II, Chap. 4, §§ 83–87, [pp. 204–214], *infra*. On the concept of hyle, see also my *Ideen*, pp. 171ff. [English translation, pp. 246ff.]

reason accomplishes a complete investigation of its own sense and perfectly Objectivates itself in a system of principles. In this system pure reason or, correlatively, logic is related reflexively to itself; the self-explication of pure reason is itself a purely rational activity and comes under the very principles that thereby attain explication.

§ 7. THE NORMATIVE AND PRACTICAL FUNCTIONS OF LOGIC.

The pre-eminent normative function of logic is obvious. Any apriori science is called on to exercise normative functions, with respect namely to those sciences of matters-of-fact that are subordinate to it. But logic alone is a universal norm in the highest sense and with the greatest conceivable universality. The norms applied by logic are the principles of pure reason itself and the tests of rationality as such. Its formal cognitions are the standards for measuring the extent to which ostensible science conforms to the idea of genuine science, the extent to which the single cognitions of ostensible science are genuine cognitions and its methods genuine methods — methods that, so far as their essential form is concerned, square with the formally universal norms of pure reason.

In taking on normative functions, logic also assumes functions pertaining to the practical shaping of science; and accordingly it can also be included in a logico-practical technology and perhaps combined with an empirical anthropological component. In exercising such functions, logic is related reflexively to itself, not only as a science but also normatively: as a science because, as has already been said, logic is the apriori science / of all science as ‹28›
such and is at the same time itself a science; normatively because, in its progressive practical work, it must utilize its already-gained results as norms, going back, perhaps, to apply them to what it has already fashioned in naïve evidence.

Logic *becomes* normative, it becomes practical; with a suitable change of attitude, one can convert it into a normative-technological discipline. But intrinsically it is itself not a normative discipline but precisely a science in the pregnant sense, a work of purely theoretical reason — like all the other sciences. As we were saying, apriori sciences, by virtue of being apriori, always *function* normatively and technologically; but, for that reason, they *are* sciences and not technologies. The attitude of the technologist (not the technician but the person devising a technology) is essentially different from that of the scientist. It is a practical and not a theoretical attitude — even when the technologist incidentally runs into scientific problems and solves them in the interest of technology. His theorizing is then but a means to some (extra-theoretical) practice. It makes no essential difference that here the problem concerns, not an individual instance of practice, but a universal *sort* of practice, which is to be examined, subjected to rules, and furthered — universally, by practical reason. The situation is the same if we consider by itself the mere applying of the norm, prior to any question of a corresponding refashioning of practice. The aim is to help oneself or others "practically" in a certain manner, and not to satisfy purely theoretical interests.

To be sure, the distinction is after all a relative one: because even purely theoretical activity is indeed activity — that is to say, a practice (when the concept of practice is accorded its natural breadth); and, as a practice, it is part of the universal nexus comprising all practical activities and is subject to formal rules of universal practical reason (the principles of ethics), rules with which a *science pour la science* can hardly be compatible. But then there remains the essential difference that all sciences come under the *idea* of an interest of theoretical reason that operates *ad infinitum*. This idea, moreover, is conceived relatively to the idea of a community of scientific investigators, which goes on working *ad infinitum*, a community united in respect of activities and habitualities of theoretical reason. Here we shall mention only the working of investigators for and with one another and their criticizing of one another's results, those obtained by one investigator being taken over as works that pave the way for others, and so forth. But a life lived by single individuals and by the many according to this
<29> idea / is a life compatible, for example, with the conviction that all the theoretical results thus acquired in common, and the infinite science itself, have a hypertheoretical human function; just as, in the case of the single individual, his abiding scientific vocation, with the always-intermittent excercising of it, is compatible with his other, extra-theoretical, purposes as a father,

a citizen, and so forth, and must find its place within the highest practical idea, that of an all-embracing ethical life, the individual's own and the life of the open community of human beings.

§ 8. The two-sidedness of logic; the subjective and the Objective direction of its thematizing activity.

Logic, as the science of all the logical as such and — in its highest form, which embraces all other forms of the logical — as the science of all science as such, inquires *in two opposite directions*. Everywhere it is a matter of rational productions, in a double sense: on one side, as *productive activities and habitualities*; on the other side, as *results* produced by activities and habitualities and afterwards persisting.

On the side where the results lie, we have as the theme of logic the manifold forms of judgment-formations and cognitional formations, which accrue to cognitive subjects during the performance of their thinking activities and do so, moreover, in the particular manner characteristic of a "theme". The formations accruing on the particular occasion are indeed what the thinking subject is aiming at and intends to make his abiding acquisition; while at the same time they are meant to serve him as means for gaining similar new acquisitions. At any particular time, something has come into being, not just somehow or other, but rather as the thing aimed at in his thinking action: In a particular manner the thinking subject *"directs himself" to it*; he has it before him *"Objectively"*. In their higher forms, to be sure, these formations transcend the current sphere of presence to consciousness. But they remain nevertheless component parts of a more extensive, thematically encompassed "field", a peculiar realm of products generated by practice, products to which one can always "return" and by means of which one can always generate new formations: new concepts, judgments, arguments, proofs, and theories. In the *unity of a science* all such formations, and the whole field of products that have arisen within the unity pertaining to a theoretical interest, are *unitarily combined to make up an all-embracing theory*, the systematically continuous development of which, *ad infinitum*, is the common aim of the scientists, as they work with / and for one another in open community. <30>
By means of this theory the particular scientific "province" is

to be made a province of systematic *cognition*, in an all-inclusive unity of cognitional formations, called theoretical truths, which are built one upon another to produce the unity-form of a truth-system.

These Objective affairs all have more than the fleeting factual existence of what comes and goes as a formation actually present in the thematic field. They have also the being-sense of abiding validity; nay, even that of Objective validity in the special sense, reaching beyond the subjectivity now actually cognizing and its acts. They remain identical affairs when repeated, are recognized again in the manner suitable to abiding existents; in documented form they have Objective factual existence, just like the other objectivities of the cultural world: Thus they can be found in an Objective duration by everyone, can be regeneratively understood in the same sense by everyone, are intersubjectively identifiable, are factually existent even when no one is thinking them.

The opposite direction of logic's thematizing activity is *subjective*. It concerns the deeply hidden subjective forms in which theoretical "reason" brings about its productions. The first question here concerns *reason in its present activity* — in other words: that intentionality, as it flows on during its living execution, in which the aforesaid Objective formations have their "origin". Stated more particularly, the effect produced by this intentionality is that, in the executing subject's thematic field, the formations generated on the particular occasion, the judgment-objectivities and cognitional objectivities, make their appearance "Objectively", with the character of generated products. While the corresponding intentionality is being executed, while it is flowing in this manner as an Objectivatingly productive living, it is "unconscious" — that is to say: it *makes* thematic, but it itself is, for that very reason and as a matter of essential necessity, non-thematic. It remains hidden, as long as it has not been uncovered by a reflection and has not thus itself become a theme, the theoretical theme of that logical research which is directed to the subjective. The subject who is straightforwardly judging or thinking in any manner (for example: generating conceptual formations, no matter how complicated) has "consciously" before him, thematically, only the formations

undergoing production at that time. Everything that by itself is, in this sense, Objectively logical has, as its "subjective" correlate, the intentionalities constituting it; and, as a matter of essential necessity, there corresponds to each form of the formations a system of productive intentionality, a system that may be called a subjective form. But there is also involved the *further subjective production* by virtue of which the affair *now* actually constituted / is, for the cognitive subjects (thanks to sources pertaining to their <31>
habituality), more than this momentarily thematic affair of the actual present. This production makes it possible for the constituted to be consciously intended to as something *Objective*, something abidingly valid for the corresponding subjectivity, and makes the constituted take on, in and for the cognitive community, the sense of an ideal Objectivity existing *"in itself"*.

The two-sidedness of everything logical, in consequence of which the problem-groups become separated and again combined, places in the way of an explication of their true sense, and in the way of their correct organization, quite extraordinary difficulties. These, one can say, account for the fact that logic, after thousands of years, has not yet entered the steady course of a truly rational development — that it has not become, as its peculiar vocation unconditionally demanded, a science that has pressed onward to a clear consciousness of its goals and, progressing surely from stage to stage, made them actual. Nearly everything that concerns the fundamental sense of logic, of its problems and method, is infected with incomprehensibilities from this turbid source, this perpetually uncomprehended and never rightly examined Objectivity deriving from subjective production. Everything is therefore disputed; but in the dispute nothing is clarified. Even the ideal Objectivity of logical formations and the apriori character of the logical doctrines relating to them specifically, and then again the sense of this Apriori, are stricken with this same obscurity: since the ideal does indeed appear as located within the subjective sphere; it does indeed arise from this sphere as a produced formation.

Accordingly, what we have said so far about logic expresses a precursory survey and an insight yet to be confirmed by more concrete explications and, so far as appears useful, by coming to terms with historical motivations and with interpretations of logic that have arisen from them.

§ 9. The straightforward thematizing activity of the "Objective" or "positive" sciences. The idea of two-sided sciences.

As is already plain, even from our first elucidations, the two-sidedness of everything logical *does not signify a parity of the two sides*, the Objective and the subjective. To think with simple devotedness to the matters in question is to create a coherent thematic field, which contains exclusively the pertinent products of thinking. They are what the thinkers aim at; they are results of thinking and at the same time bases for new thinking
<32> actions. The thinking itself — understood concretely as / the intentionality, qualified one knows not how, in whose "synthesis" the products of thinking become constituted as "unities of sense" — still requires uncovering, which would take place in a new thinking.

The thinking of scientists is — actionally and habitually, privately and intersubjectively — coherent thinking. It has coherence by virtue of the unity of a theoretical interest and the correlative unity of the scientific province that is to be systematically explored and cognized. Whatever accrues in the process of scientific thinking, as judgment-results or cognitional results pertaining to that province, makes up an openly endless *thematic field by itself*, the expanding unity of the *science as theory*, a multiplicity of themes belonging together and thematically combined.

This thematic field is *overstepped* by reflections turned toward the subjective. In general, therefore, the scientist, because of the exclusiveness of his theoretical interest in his particular province, will not introduce the investigation of any subjective theme into his research. Thus the geometer, for example, will not think of exploring, besides geometrical shapes, geometrical thinking. It may be that shifts to the subjective focus are occasionally helpful or even necessary to what he truly has in view, namely the theory of his province; as in other far-seeing actions, so in theoretical actions the need may arise to deliberate reflectively and ask, "What method shall I try now? What premises can serve me?" But the subjective that then comes into view does not itself belong to what the science is aiming at, its proper theme, which, as a universal theory, embraces all its separate themes. The same is true of other cases where subjects and their acts are brought into scientific discourse; the subjective — the thinking or the subjects themselves who think — is not thereby introduced into the theme, into the particular scientific province and its theory. Thus it is in all *"Objective" or "positive" sciences*, which are, as a rule, the only ones we think of when speaking simply of sciences. This is because the idea of *sciences that have systematically two-sided themes*, themes that combine the theory of the scientific province systematically with a theory of the cognition of that theory, has emerged only in modern times and, moreover, so obscurely that it must still contend for its peculiar sense and its legitimacy. /

The positive sciences operate exclusively on the plane of the <33>
theory that can be fashioned straightforwardly, when the theorizer directs himself to the province of cognition as his theme — fashioned, that is, by the continuous categorial forming of experiential objectivities belonging to the province, as they come within the scope of determining processes of thinking, and by the systematic connecting of the formations thus acquired, to make cognitional formations at higher and higher levels: the openly endless, and yet systematically unitary, edifice of the scientific theory of the province.

This plane of theory delimits the themes of science, and does so to such a degree that the positive sciences make a conscious effort to frame the concept of theoretical Objectivity even more rigorously: in such a manner that positive sciences will exclude, as merely subjective, many a thing that the pre-scientifically experiencing and thinking subject finds as an Objective theme. In this manner the scientific investigator of Nature excludes "sensuous qualities". The single experiencing subject finds natural Objects as sensuously qualified, but nevertheless as Objects, as existing in and by themselves, not affected in their existence by the reflectively apprehensible acts of experiencing and of experiential thinking, neither determined nor determinable by the contents of those acts. Yet, with the effecting of an intersubjective communion of experiencing and thinking, the contents of sensuously experienced Objectivity and the descriptive concepts fitted to its contents show a dependence on the experiencing subjects; though the identity of the Objects in question nevertheless remains intersubjectively cognizable and determinable. A purely Objective science aims at a theoretical cognizing of Objects, not in respect of such subjectively relative determinations as can be drawn from direct sensuous experience, but rather in respect of strictly and purely Objective determinations: determinations that obtain for everyone and at all times, or in respect of which, according to a method that everyone can use, there arise theoretical truths having the character of "truths in themselves" — in contrast to mere subjectively relative truths.

§ 10. Historically existing psychology and scientific thematizing activity directed to the subjective.

Though the positive sciences shut themselves off in this manner from all that belongs to the merely subjective of the experiencing and thinking of the matters in question, and do so in order to satisfy the requirements imposed by the idea of pure Object as their exclusive theme, nevertheless a particular positive science of subjects makes its appearance among them, the science
<34> of men / and brutes — namely *psychology* — that makes the psychic, the specifically subjective, in these its chief theme. If this psychology were in fact the science of everything subjective, it would stand in a remarkable relationship of perfect correlation with all the sciences. All of them are subjectively produced formations; all of them get their Objective themes from hidden producings. Even the object-provinces of the sciences are there pre-theoretically, for persons investigating them, as provinces that come from subjective sources comprised in the harmonious experience that gives "those provinces" beforehand; as experienced or experienceable, they arouse the theoretical interest and take on categorial forms — among these, the forms of scientific truth, given in scientific evidence. Accordingly the universal science of the subjective would embrace every conceivable existent, precisely as something experienceable and theoretically true. It would be the science of universal subjectivity, the science in which everything that is truth — deriving from an actual or possible living, with the possibilities of experience and theory predelineated within that living itself — would

receive the sense: true being. In relation to each science, as a developed and still developing production, it would be the perfectly correlative science of precisely that production. Since this psychology itself would be a science, it would be reflexively related to itself; as the science of everything subjective, it would include the science of those subjective sources by virtue of which it accomplished its own productions. And this would be repeated in it at an infinitude of levels.

Obviously none of the historically developed psychologies of ancient or modern times has ever satisfied this requirement of universality or even thought it through seriously as a problem. Without any question an anthropology and a zoology, including a psychology and a psychophysics of men and brutes, have a valid sense. But the extent to which they are capable of the indicated universal correlational tasks concerning all the sciences and all that ever exists for us — this may be characterized as the great enigma of the modern age, with its peculiar and always freshly reattempted transcendental philosophies, critiques of knowledge, theories of knowledge, theories of the understanding, theories of reason, or whatever the chosen names may be. We ourselves shall have to consider this question more precisely, on the basis of our structural researches concerning the idea of logic.[1] In the present context, all that matters is sharp illumination of the contrast between the "straightforward" thematizing activity of the positive / sciences, which is determined by a particular <35>
object-province given beforehand by (intersubjective) experience — a province to which that activity is devoted with an exclusive interest — and, on the other hand, the thereby-excluded but still openly possible reflective thematizing, which would concern experiencing-cognizing-producing subjectivity.

§ 11. The thematizing tendencies of traditional logic.

a. Logic directed originally to the Objective theoretical formations produced by thinking.

From consideration of the sciences we now pass on to *logic*, which indeed, as theory of science, has adjusted itself to the sciences as examples; and we ask how the above-described

[1] *Author's note:* See Part II, § 79, pp. 196 ff., *infra*.

essential relationships between the Objective and the subjective work out in the historical development of logic.

Obviously, from the beginning and, indeed, up to within our times, logic had none but Objective, none but "positive", sciences — though at very different stages of development — before its eyes to guide it. Accordingly it could find, as its *first universal theme,* nothing but the *realm of thematic formations* produced by scientific thinking in relation to some Objective provinces or other that were somehow given beforehand — that is to say: judgments (with the "concepts" occurring in them), arguments, proofs, complete theories, with their modalities and the normative differences between truth and falsity. To explore all these actual and ostensible knowledge-formations with respect to their formal types and the conditions for possible truth involved by their formal types, was the first task presented.

To be sure, the logicians' naturally predominant epistemo-practical interest, their aiming at a rational production by cognitional strivings and actions, directed their regard precisely to these. But that in no way involved a revelatory penetration of constitutive intentionality, which takes place out of sight in the cognitionally striving and acting subjects; on the contrary, it involved only "a viewing of" what — in this case, as in that of any other volitive aiming and acting — goes on in the field of consciousness, as it were visibly and outstandingly, in union with the goal-setting and with the realizing genesis of the results: namely what goes on under the heading, "I am striving for such and such; I generate it; it is coming into being by the volition of my Ego". In this connexion the produced formations, with their
<36> multiform constituents / and articulations and the intermediate formations at various stages, are, as in any other case, what can be properly described, rather than the uniform and unvarying "I am aiming at it and realizing it member by member".

We shall discuss this important point in more detail. Here we point out, first of all, the following essential difference. Theoretical formations offer themselves, not as Ego-acts do (as transient and merely reiterable), but as *Objects* do; and that signifies: as, so to speak, seizable objectivities, steadfast under observation, always re-identifiable, and accessible to repeated observation, analysis, and description — not much otherwise than objectivities of external experience. Except that theoretical formations are not, like the latter, given beforehand and accepted passively, but rather are, as categorial objectivities, given in the first place only in consequence of theoretical action.[1] But then they too are strictly there: first of all, as in process of construction; and then, with a reiteration of the activity, as identifiable. Thus from each judging on one's own part, at every level of complication, theoretical formations can be taken, as its result; likewise from each actual or phantasied judging [*Urteil*] on another's part, which one performs in "following" him (and, in this case, depending on whether the judging is actual or phantasied, the formations are taken from it either as the judgments actually "made" or as possible judgments). As the objects of experience are given, in any other experiencing, so here, in "categorial experience", the categorial formations (the expression being taken very broadly in this context) are given evidently, in the manner that characterizes original intuition. Later, however, we shall learn that here, with different focusings of regard, different objectivities can become — and, for the logician, must become — identifiable, experienceable in corresponding evidences.

Thus the logician had steadfast objects as examples, to serve as substrates for "ideations"; consequently there arose the possibility of those "pure formalizations" that yield concepts of analytic-logical "forms". These forms, in turn, were similarly but even more thoroughly firm and steadfast objects, which could be described with respect to their elementary formal components and considered, moreover, operationally. Ways of modifying and of connecting forms — constructively, in reiterable operations — were given as open possibilities, ways in which one could always generate new forms from forms already given: as one does in the combinative constructing of complex judgment-forms out of simpler judgment-forms or in the free constructing of syllogistic forms out of judgment-forms. Accordingly the logician projected in advance, with formal universality, the /
conceivably possible forms of judgments, and of cognitions, that <37>
can be produced concretely in any conceivable province of cognition.

Understandably, therefore, even beginning logic, in its sense-

[1] *Author's note:* See Part II, § 46. *Translator's note:* Husserl probably meant § 63.

investigations concerning knowledge and science [*Wissen und Wissenschaft*], was attracted predominantly by the Objective theoretical formations; though at first, and for a long time afterward, there was no thought of limiting the theme quite consciously and expressely to pure judgment-formations and cognitional formations, which nevertheless made up the field in which the work of logic was actually being done. Once work had started in this manner, the internal consistency of the matters in question kept things going automatically. The situation, after all, is not essentially different from that obtaining in fields of research that come from any sort of experience. Once theoretical interest has become fixed on data of experience in some sphere or other, it carries on consistently. The data taken by logic, as we again emphasize, were *also*, after their own manner, data of experience, identifiable and viewable objects — whether or not it is customary to speak in this connexion of experience and, indeed, even if the essential analogy between the manner in which *they* are given originally and the manner in which objects are given originally in what is generally called experience has never been grasped. And this "experience" of logical data (with its modifications as memory, "possible" experience, and the like) functions like any other as a basis for the forming of descriptive concepts and the effecting of descriptive cognitions, including, in particular, eidetic cognitions.

b. Logic's interest in truth and the resultant reflection on subjective insight.

Now logic was focused, not on just any judgments, on supposed knowledge, but ultimately on *genuine* knowledge and its typical formations. In the first place, that unavoidably produced a sort of *turning toward the subjective*. The logician said something like this to himself: Genuine knowledge, truth, is seized upon in the activities of *"reason"*, in *insight* — which, once it has been exercised, can be repeated by the same subject, and likewise by any other rational subject, and remains as an intellectual possession. Propositions that are immediate objects of insight lead, in evident elementary arguments, to propositions that become evident therewith as consequent truths. A deductive theory, a genuine one, is a complex of elementary steps, built

entirely with steps of *insight* and thus making up a unity of truth. Also in the case of "concrete" arguments, starting from non-evident premises and having their hypothetical cognition-value. In their case, after all, / the includedness of the conclusions, as <38>
consequences, in the premises is seen; and at the same time it is seen that the consequences would become truths, *if* the premises were to show themselves in insight as truths. Thus, in genuine science, nothing in the way of propositions or proposition-complexes occurs on the Objective side, unless it has acquired its "cognition-value" — its validity-characteristic of trueness, of hypothetical consequence, or the like — from *insights*.

In such reflections — which, as initial, obviously determine logic originally — one cannot avoid speaking continually about the *subjective*, above all about *reason* and *insight* (a word, by the way, that usually connotes an enduring accessibility to insight — an accessibility originally acquired, to be sure, by virtue of an actually operative act of insight). But, although this subjective manner of speaking presupposes a turning of regard toward the psychic, still *everything* that becomes ascertained as a *result* in science lies purely on the Objective side; and accordingly what the logician intends to bring out thematically with such reflections and treat as theory of theory, is likewise only what is Objectively logical.

It must be particularly heeded here that *the "true", or "consequent", or "non-contradictory", acquired in insight, makes its appearance as a characteristic and predicate attached to the judgment-formations themselves*; that is to say, it makes its appearance on the Objective side, and is accordingly a theme in the formal theories that are to be treated by a pure logic of significations. Everything that is "logical" in the pregnant sense — the "rational" — has these characteristics attached to it as Objective characteristics; and logic must name them expressly and seek out the conditions under which they belong to something legitimately. "Truth" is the Objective locution; "insight", "reason", is the subjective and perfectly correlative one. Similarly in the case of each particular mode among the validity-predicates. Every unitarily self-contained and unqualified scientific statement has, or claims to have, this predicate truth, as a predicate derived from insight. In the sciences, since it goes without saying and its repetition would be burdensome and useless, it is not stated, except perhaps with reference to some previous doubt or controversy. In logic, however, it is, in its relation to the bare forms of judgments, precisely the chief thematic consideration.

Frequent reflection on subjective doing is, by the way, something the sciences have in common with the other provinces of technical action. The sense of thought-formations themselves, as formations that have sprung from actions of thinking, involves
<39> reference to the corresponding acts, in their / order and connexion. Accordingly one can describe the formations also from the side belonging to the agent and his doing. For example: instead of of saying "$a - b + b = a$", one can say, "Subtract *b* from *a* and then add *b* again", and so forth; or, instead of saying, "*Q* follows from the premises *M* and *N*", one can say, "*Q* can be concluded from the judgments *M* and *N*". But one has gained nothing essential by this: There is, to be sure, a reference to the more or less complex rhythm of the Ego's acts (the steps of *ego cogito*); but, properly speaking, no description of these acts themselves has been made. To count is to generate numbers, to substract is to generate differences, to multiply is to generate products, and so forth; and, in the same way, to conclude is to generate judgment-consequences from judgments. One has one's eye on the generated products, on what one strives for and generates, and here lies what is solid and seizable; whereas the empty I-count, I-conclude, signifies no more than the conative aiming and the allowing of the products to come into being [*und die Erzeugnisse in ihrem Werden ablaufen lassen*]. Naturally that is not to say that there can be no analyses or descriptions of the subjective; it is only to say that, over and above the generated products and their subjective initiation (?) [*Ablaufen*] in the mode of step-by-step actualization, an intentional subjectivity is to be explored, in which the products coming into being and those already generated are constituted as synthetic unities — a subjectivity that is not yet opened up at all by such a mere turning to the "I think".

c. Result: the hybridism of historically existing logic as a theoretical and normative-practical discipline.

After all this we understand why logic, throughout its whole development up to within recent times (as long as transcendental-philosophic motives had not become radically effective upon it), necessarily had as its principal thematic sphere the field of theory, the manifold judgment-formations and cognitional formations, and why the thematizing of subjective actions of thinking, though superficially it stood out in bold relief, was completely secondary.

Yet we must not overlook the following: While we were describing the thematizing tendencies of traditional logic and how they were motivated by taking the positive sciences as a guide, we, in our reflections, had to dissect the intentional interconnexions with an awareness and a sharpness that were still foreign to logic itself or to logicians who dealt with them. The thing to which we have paid particular attention, namely the Objectivity of theoretical formations as data of a specific "experience" / ("categorial experience", as we called it), was <40> far from gaining acceptance in the tradition; and even today it still has to fight for its legitimacy. One must not shun the indispensable broadening of the Object-concept to cover not only real but also irreal ("ideal") Objects; to it there corresponds the broadening of the concept of experience, which, with this amplification, retains precisely the essential property: seizing upon something itself (having of something itself, giving of something itself).[1]

The logicians' naturally predominant focusing on norms and on techniques of cognition, as we said above, brought thinking, as a mental doing, into the foreground for them; and thus it gave prominence to the real psychic process in which the irreal object, the ideal formation produced by thinking, makes its appearance at a particular time. Rules for this doing, or for the psychic subject as a subject who is active in thinking, were to be ascertained. The intrusive interest in providing norms tended understandably *to mask the ideal Objectivity of the produced formations themselves* and also to prevent the rise of a theoretical thematizing activity relating to them consciously and *purely*. And this was the case, even though the logician's work, as we saw above, dealt

[1] *Author's note: See* Part II, Chap. 1, §§ 57–59, [pp. 153–159, *infra*]; also *Logische Untersuchungen, II. Bd., II. Teil,* pp. 142ff., the passage introducing the concept of categorial intuition. [*Cf.* Farber, *op. cit.*, p. 455.]

continually with these ideal formations, identifying them, subsuming them under form-concepts, and so forth. In spite of this, they remained thematically unseparated from the subjective. In this connexion — we shall have to speak of this again — there are also objective difficulties; because the matters dealt with are not external products, but products generated inside the psychic sphere itself.

Now, however, our only concern is to gain an understanding of the essential character of historically existing logic, by means of an explication of the intentionality determining the sense of logic most originally. Briefly summarized, the first requisite was to understand the historically existing logic in respect of its hybridism, as both a theoretical and a normative-practical discipline, and in respect of the consequent hybridism of its theme as, on the one hand, the ideal significations (the categorial formations) and, on the other hand, the actions of thinking and the regulation of these by norms. But it was further requisite to understand that the theoretically seizable and solid constituent of this hybrid, the part to be found in the historically existing syllogistic theories, was essentially nothing other than a *theory of theory*, though not grasped purely — a theory, therefore, of the produced *judgment-formations and cognitional formations* making up the field of ideal Objects. Whatever went beyond that, in
<41> locutions and / thoughts relating to the subjective, brought (as we pointed out) no essentially new content but only obvious subjective variants. To this were added, though not until a very late date (with the instituting of psychologistic or anti-psychologistic transcendental philosophy), actually new and substantial investigations of the subjective, over which, to be sure, no lucky star held sway and which, in any case, must still struggle for their true sense. These we left out of consideration; and, for the time being, we shall continue to do so. Meanwhile, guided by the insight that we have acquired for ourselves concerning the purely Objective theme of logic, and taking the original logical apophantics as our point of departure, we shall first explore the *essentially determined structures of an Objective apophantic logic* — one that is "analytic", "formal" — and shall then deal with the problems involved in ascertaining its essentially determined boundaries. Here we shall start with the modern mathematical

disciplines that should likewise be characterized as "analytic" and "formal" and direct our attention to the obscure questions that concern the relationship of this "analytic" mathematics to traditional formal logic, and consequently the relationship between the idea of formal ontology and the idea of formal apophantics.

<42> PART I.

THE STRUCTURES AND THE SPHERE OF OBJECTIVE FORMAL LOGIC.

A. THE WAY FROM THE TRADITION TO THE FULL IDEA OF FORMAL LOGIC.

CHAPTER I.

Formal logic as apophantic analytics.

§ 12. DISCOVERY OF THE IDEA OF THE PURE JUDGMENT-FORM.

From our general explanations it is already understandable that, as historically the first part of a systematically executed logic, Aristotelian analytics arose, a first commencement of a logic of theoretical formations. Within the limits imposed by focusing on this theme, it was a *"formal" logic in a particular sense*; though, even as that, it did not attain the full purity and breadth prescribed by its essence. In a survey of the (always materially determinate) judgments of life and science, the most universal groupings of judgments according to types, the perfect likenesses of form among judgments pertaining even to heterogeneous provinces, immediately came to the fore. Aristotle was the first to bring out the idea of form which was to determine the fundamental sense of a "formal logic", as we understand such a discipline today and as Leibniz already understood it in effecting his synthesis of formal logic (as apophantic) and formal analysis to make the unity of a *mathesis universalis*. Aristotle was the first, we may say, to execute in the *apophantic* sphere — the sphere of assertive statements ("judgments" in the sense expressed by the word in traditional logic) — that "formalization" or algebraization which makes its appearance in modern algebra with Vieta and distinguishes subsequent formal "analysis" from all material mathematical disciplines (geometry, mechanics, and the rest). In the materially determinate statements taken as examples, Aristotle substituted algebraic letters for the words (terms) indicating the material: that which is spoken about in the state-
<43> ments, that which determines judgments as / judgments relating to divers material provinces or single matters. As concerning the sense, this implied that he substituted the moment "anything whatever" for each materially filled "core" in the judgments,

while the remaining judgment-moments were held fast as moments of form, moments that persist without change when one changes the relatedness of the given judgment to matters — or interchanges judgments pertaining to different material spheres — at pleasure. With this taking of the materially filled cores as indeterminate optional affairs — lingually, as indeterminate terms, S, p, and the like — the exemplificative determinate judgment becomes converted into the universal and pure form-idea: the pure concept of any judgment whatever that has, as the case may be, the determinate judgment-form "S is p", the form "If S is p, then Q is r", or the like.[1]

To be sure, in Aristotle the variability of the terms is not completely free, and consequently the idea of form is not quite pure: since, as a matter of course, Aristotle relates his analytics to the real world and, in so doing, has not yet excluded from his analytics the categories of reality. For modern thinkers it was the emergence of algebra that made possible for the first time the advance to a purely formal logic; yet it seems that the Middle Ages, in the treatise *De modis significandi*, ascribed to Duns Scotus, had already attained the conception of the purely formal,[2] admittedly without making that insight prevail.

§ 13. The theory of the pure forms of judgments as the first discipline of formal logic.

a. The idea of theory of forms.

The possibility of subsuming all judgments under pure concepts of configuration or form immediately suggested the thought of a descriptive classification of judgments, exclusively from this formal point of view: regardless, that is, of all other distinctions and lines of inquiry, like those concerning truth or non-contradiction. Thus one distinguished, in respect of form, simple and / composite judgments; among simple forms, one distinguished <44>

[1] *Author's note: Cf.* Appendix I, pp. 294 ff., *infra*.

[2] *Author's note:* See Martin Heidegger, *Die Kategorien- und Bedeutungslehre des Duns Scotus* [*Duns Scotus's Theory of Categories and Signification* (Tübingen, 1916)], particularly p. 34. Also Martin Grabmann, "*Die Entwicklung der mittelalterlichen Sprachlogik* [The Development of Medieval Linguistic Logic] (*Tractatus de modis significandi*)", *Philosophisches Jahrbuch der Görresgesellschaft*, 1922, pp. 121ff. and 199ff., and the same article, revised and expanded, in Grabmann, *Mittelalterliches Geistesleben: Abhandlungen zur Geschichte der Scholastik und Mystik*, München, 1926. On the *Grammatica speculativa*, previously attributed to Duns Scotus, as in fact a work by Thomas of Erfurt, see *op. cit.*, particularly pp. 118–125.

those of the singular, the particular, and the universal judgment; and one went on to the complex configurations of the conjunctive, the disjunctive, the hypothetical, and the causal judgment — judgments among which the judgment-complexes called arguments or syllogisms also belonged. Furthermore one took into consideration the modalizations that judgments (as certainties) undergo and the judgment-forms arising from such modalizations.

Systematically consistent and clean execution of such a description would have permitted the sharp isolation of a peculiar discipline, first defined in the *Logische Untersuchungen* and characterized there as *theory of the pure forms of significations* (or *grammar of pure logic*). This theory of the pure forms of judgments is the intrinsically first discipline of formal logic, implanted as a germ in the old analytics but not yet developed. According to our explanations, it concerns the *mere possibility of judgments, as judgments*, without inquiry whether they are true or false, or even whether, merely as judgments, they are compatible or contradictory.[1]

b. Universality of the judgment-form; the fundamental forms and their variants.

To have grasped the idea of this theory of pure forms, one would have had to make clear to oneself that, when one aims at a classification of all possible judgments with regard to their forms, "fundamental forms" emerge, or a closed system of fundamental forms emerges, out of which, in accordance with a set of appertinent eidetic laws, ever new, ever more highly differentiated forms, and finally the system of all conceivable judgment-forms without exception, can be generated by construction, with the infinity of their differentiated and always-further-differentiable configurations. It is remarkable that neither this nor the fundamental logical task implicit in it was ever seen.

Stated more precisely, one would have had to make clear to oneself, first of all, that each judgment-form, no matter how it may have been acquired, is a generic universality, not only with regard to possible determinate judgments but also with regard to

[1] *Author's note:* For the thorough legitimation of the idea of this "grammar of pure logic" see *Logische Untersuchungen, II. Bd., I. Teil, Abschnitt IV*. [*Cf.* Farber, *op. cit.*, Chap. XI, pp. 313–332.]

pure forms subordinate to it. Thus, for example, the form "*Sp* is *q*" is subordinate to the form "*S* is *p*"; and the form "(*Sp*)*q* is *r*" is subordinate in turn to "*Sp* is *q*". But each judgment-form also bears within itself a universality with a wholly different sense, since each takes in / a multiplicity of possible forms as its <45> "modifications"; for example, the form "*S* is *p*" takes in the modifications "if *S* is *p*", "then *S* is *p*", and so forth, which can occur as component parts of whole judgment-forms. The like is true of each and every form. One would have to take heed expressly that the forms standing thus as differents under a universal form can be derived from it by *construction*. Furthermore, that not every form can be regarded as such a constructional differentiation of another form, but that, on the contrary, in every case we get back to *primitive forms*. Thus the form of the determining judgment, "*S* is *p*" (where *p* designates a determination, and *S* its substrate), is a primitive form, from which one can derive particularizations and modifications. It is a primitive form: more precisely, it is primitive within the highest genus of apophantic logic, "apophansis", if this genus is extended exclusively to predicative judgment-certainties, while judgment-modalities (which, in themselves, are not subsumed under this genus) become included in its scope by undergoing a transmutation into judgment-certainties with an altered content: namely certainties about possibilities, probabilities, and the like.

Naturally the genus apophansis, with its universality left without differentiation into particular forms, can likewise be designated as a form; and, with this universality, it can be included in form-constructions. Thus, letting the literal signs designate closed assertive statements, we might form "*A* and *A'* " (this being understood as the formation that a conjunctive judgment has; *in forma*, then, as the type pertaining to the corresponding generation of forms), likewise "if *A*, then *A'* ", and so forth. We might then determine the undetermined forms, *A* and *A'*, first of all by primitive forms of particularizations, and go on from these to new forms, continuing thus without limit, according to any of the principles of form-construction. Such universal formation-forms as the conjunctive and the hypothetical must likewise be called fundamental forms, since they indicate *fundamental kinds of "operations"* that we can undertake with any two judgments or judgment-forms.

c. Operation as the guiding concept in the investigation of forms.

If we have become attentive to the *point of view of "operation"* (with *laws of operation* in which, mathematically speaking,
<46> "existential propositions" are implicit), we shall / naturally choose the concept of operation as a guide in our investigation of forms; we shall have to conduct this research in such a way that it leads to an *exhibition of the fundamental operations and their laws*, and to the *ideal construction of the infinity of possible forms* according to these laws. Consequently the fundamental forms will not stand side by side, but will be graded one above another. Thus, for example, the form "S is p" is more original than the form "Sp is q", which is an operational transformation of it, namely by the operation of converting a predicate into an attribute. But the form "Sp is q" makes its appearance in the definition of this operation, and forthwith bears within itself a new principle for the construction of forms.

Finally one will be able to take the point of view of operation so broadly that one regards even the fundamental form "S is p" as an operation: the operation of determining a determinable substrate, S. Similarly, one will then regard every modalization as a form-productive operation that transmutes the sense in a certain manner, so that, relative to the series of modalities, the form of the apophansis (in the original sense: assertoric certainty) is characterized for essential reasons as the primitive form, and the other forms are characterized as its variants. To be sure, one then sees forthwith that operation, in the sense of a free changing of any judgment into another one, yields a norrower concept, since modalization is plainly not a matter of arbitrary transmutation.

This, moreover, should be emphasized expressly: *Every operative fashioning of one form out of others has its law*; and this law, in the case of operations proper, is of such a nature that the generated form can itself be submitted to a repetition of the same operation. *Every law of operation thus bears within itself a law of reiteration.* Conformity to this law of *reiterable operation* extends throughout the whole province of judgments, and makes it possible to construct reiteratively (by means of fundamental forms and fundamental operations, which can be laid down) the infinity of possible forms of judgments.

§ 14. CONSEQUENCE-LOGIC (LOGIC OF NON-CONTRADICTION) AS THE SECOND LEVEL OF FORMAL LOGIC.[1]

From the theory of the pure forms of judgments there is differentiated, as a higher level of the formal logic of judgments, the science of the *possible forms of true judgments*. It has / been <47>
developed at least in part as a historical fact, though not in a systematic context such as this, and not with purity. Indeed, the obvious procedure was to inspect the mere forms of judgments with a view to determining the extent to which, separately or as fashioned into complex forms, they involve eidetically universal conditions for possible truth or falsity, conditions that apply to all conceivable judgments with corresponding forms. Particularly in the case of argument-forms (complex proposition-forms in which valid and fallacious arguments proceed) it was evident that not all proposition-forms can be combined to make forms of genuine arguments, *actually "consequent"* arguments. It can be seen that certain argument-forms have, at the same time, the value of formal *eidetic laws*, namely as general truths about *judgment-consequence*: about the (*"analytic"*) *includedness* of judgments having such and such a form in premise-judgments having an appropriate form; likewise that other argument-forms have the value of eidetic laws of *analytic anti-consequence, analytic "contradictions"* — that properly they are forms, not of implicative arguments [*von Schlüssen*] but, so to speak, of "exclusions" [*von "Ausschlüssen*].

With deeper consideration of the sense of this analytic includedness and excludedness, logical research could have attained the cognition that the *traditional formal logic is not a pure "logic of non-contradiction"* and that, with the bringing out of such a logic in its purity, a most significant *division* would have to be made *within the complex of problems and the theory of logic.*

To seek out systematically the eidetic laws that govern *just the*

[1] *Translator's note:* For a clarification of the terms "consequence-logic" and "logic of non-contradiction" see Appendix III, § I, pp. 330–334, *infra.*

analytic includedness and excludedness, just the internal and external *analytic non-contradictoriness* of judgments, singly or in combination, is a *separate problem.* In such inquiry one is *not yet concerned with the truth* of judgments, but is concerned *merely* with whether the judgment-members included in a whole judgment, no matter how simple or how complex it may be, are *"compatible" with one another or contradict one another* and thereby make the whole judgment itself a contradictory judgment, one that cannot be made "properly". Reference to logical laws that, on the basis of form, govern the *mere non-contradictoriness* of judgments must be understood in a corresponding sense. It is an important insight, that questions concerning consequence and inconsistency can be asked about judgments *in forma,* without involving the least inquiry into truth or falsity and therefore without ever bringing the concepts of truth and falsity, or their derivatives, into the *theme.* In view of this possibility, we
<48> distinguish a level of / formal logic that we call *consequence-logic* or *logic of non-contradiction.*

The problem of non-contradiction naturally extends to the compossibility of quite arbitrarily assembled judgment-collections, so far as, in thinking of these, one normally thinks also of the connexion of the judgments to form the unity of one collective judgment — which, accordingly, is meant by one judging subject in one judging process of meaning. Equally it concerns the non-contradictory unifiability of judgments in other judgment-compounds: for example, judgments that have unity as judgment-members in any ostensible theory — such unity being indeed that of a single judgment, though a very complicatedly founded judgment, which belongs to a higher order. The like is true when we descend from complex judgments to judgments that are simple in the usual sense. Any self-contained apophansis whose members are not themselves judgments that likewise have an apophantic self-containedness is accepted as simple in this sense. But even such an apophansis still has members that must be called "judicial" unities, though they are not self-sufficient unities. Therefore the difference between non-contradictory unifiability and contradiction extends also to the "simple" apophansis; and so do the laws of formal analytics.

This determines a pregnant and self-contained concept of a

"*pure apophantic analytics*", an analytics in which belong not only the whole of syllogistics, so far as its essential content is concerned, but also (as we shall show) many other disciplines, namely those of formal-mathematical "analysis". Nevertheless, as may be emphasized forthwith, the original concept of analytics as an *analytics in the broader sense* will also be indispensible; and, as our investigations progress, we shall be able to determine its peculiar sense more strictly — precisely on the basis of the narrower concept.

The fundamental concepts of pure analytics in the pregnant sense include, *as fundamental concepts of validity* (norm-concepts), *only analytic consequence and analytic contradiction*; as already said, *truth and falsity*, along with their modalities, are *not present* among them. This must be rightly understood: They are not present as fundamental concepts pertaining to the *thematic* sphere. Therefore, in this pure analytics, they play only the rôle that is theirs in all the sciences, so far as all sciences strive for truths and consequently talk about truth and falsity; but that is not to say that truth and falsity / belong among the "funda- <49>
mental concepts" of every science, the concepts pertaining to the proper essence of its particular scientific *province.*

§ 15. Truth-logic and consequence-logic.

Inquiry for formal laws of possible *truth* and its modalities would be a higher logical inquiry, *after* the isolation of pure analytics. If a logic restricts itself to the bare forms of the significations of statements — that is, the judgment-forms — what means does it have of becoming a genuine logic of truth? One can see forthwith that *non-contradiction* is an essential condition for possible *truth*, but also that mere analytics becomes converted into a *formal truth-logic* only by virtue of a *connexion* between these intrinsically separable concepts, a connexion that determines an eidetic law and, in a logic, *must be formulated separately.* More about that later. For the present, let us restrict ourselves to the domain of pure apophantic analytics.

§ 16. THE DIFFERENCES IN EVIDENCE THAT SUBSTANTIATE THE SEPARATING OF LEVELS WITHIN APOPHANTICS. CLEAR EVIDENCE AND DISTINCT EVIDENCE.

a. Modes of performing the judgment. Distinctness and confusion.

Mere predelineation of the separations with which the last sections were concerned, separations that must be made in formal logic, is not enough. There is need of more penetrating substantiations, which explicate the correspondingly differentiated evidences; only with such substantiations, moreover, can an actual insight into the necessity and the scope of these separations be opened up.

A judgment can be given as evidently the same judgment in very different manners of subjective givenness. It can make its appearance as something completely vague that comes to mind or perhaps as the completely vague signification of a statement read, understood, and believingly accepted. In such cases not the slightest bit of an *explicit performance belonging to judicative spontaneity* need take place: not the slightest bit of an explicit subject-positing, of a positing-thereupon as predicate, of a passing on relatingly to another Object, which is posited separately, or of any like process. If the "vaguely", *"confusedly", judging process of meaning* something that comes to mind is followed by such a
<50> process of *explicit judging,* then we say, / on the basis of the synthesis of fulfilling identification that comes about: The confused meaning or opinion *"becomes distinct";* now, for the first time, something is *"properly judged";* and the judgment, which previously was meant only expectantly, now is *properly* and itself *given.*

Similarly in the case of *reading* or *hearing.* In this case we have, it is true, a *sensuous unity* and mutual congruity of the seen or heard *verbal signs* in their *sensuous configuration;* but, in ordinary reading, *we by no means have, combined with that, an accompanying articulation of actual thinking, of thinking produced from the Ego, member by member, in synthetic activity.* Rather, this course of thinking proper is *only indicated* (by the passively flowing synthesis of the sensuous verbal sounds) as a course of thinking *to be* performed.

Let us examine the situation somewhat more closely.

The verbal sounds have their indications, which, in themselves, refer interdependently to one another and are built one on another. The sounds conjoin to make the unity of a word-formation, which in turn consists of relatively self-contained formations. Each of these is bearer of a unity of indication; and the whole is a self-contained unity, which has noetically the phenomenological characteristic of associative self-containedness and on the parallel side (noematically) the phenomenological characteristic that consists in the self-containedness of an indicated "significational" unity, built correspondingly out of indicated formations.

Now, on the significational side, the indicated formations, *the judgments themselves*, can make their appearance in the *"evidence" of a progressive fulfilment of the indicating intentions* — that is, in the manner that distinguishes judgments proper, *judgments that are not only indicated but at the same time generated in originary activity*; *or*, as happens in passive reading, they can be *indicated in an empty manner.*

Here we have a particular case of a quite universal regularity. Within every species of *empty consciousness* the following difference in the empty intendedness can occur: The consciousness can flow in an internally unseparated manner, in such a manner that it does *not* have particular empty meanings as its members; or else as an articulated, articulatedly exercised, empty consciousness. For example, I may be non-intuitively conscious of, and even paying attention to, the street in front of my house "confusedly, all at the same time"; on the other hand, perhaps subsequently, I may be conscious of it in explicitly "going through" it, as, in an articulative manner, I become conscious of the windings of the street, the trees and houses along it — but still non-intuitively or perhaps with some points where members emerge momentarily as intuited. Thus a / non-articulated empty consciousness can <51> become converted into a "corresponding" articulated empty consciousness, the confusedly meant sense-content (while entering into identifying coincidence of the sort peculiar to "explication") becoming "spread out" as the *explicate*, the meaning proper of the previously confused unitary content.

The same is true in the particular case of indicated judicial significations, whether they are the significations of (one's own or another's) actually given judgings or those of judgings intended to in phantasy as possible. In this connexion the following is to be noted: In understanding another's judgings, I "follow"; and this,the mode understanding-in-following-another (and perhaps judging *with* him), is to be carefully distinguished from the judging that is originally one's own and from the different modes of this: from the judging that is now being done actively, and likewise from one's own past, but confusedly "reawakened", judging, which is only "still in force", and so on.

Accordingly we have to make a distinction that, in a certain manner, cuts across these: We have to distinguish, on the one hand, a *non-explicit judgment*, indicated by a sentence that makes its appearance explicitly, and, on the other hand, a corresponding *explicit judgment* or, as the case may be, a subsequent explication with identification of the meant.

But we have to distinguish two cases of making distinct: besides the one to which we have paid exclusive attention up to now — namely the case in which the distinct explicate is *non-contradictory* and simply identifiable ⟨with the confusedly meant⟩ — we must note the case in which the explicate is *contradictory*. In witnessing non-contradictory coincidence, I see that the explicated is the same as the unexplicated, or that what was meant by the judger in the earlier confused meaning is merely made distinct. In the contrasting case, that of contradiction, the unity of the confused total meaning, as a *unitary belief*, is presupposed. Now, as explication progresses, this or that newly appearing *particular belief* can undergo cancellation, annulment, by the particular beliefs that have already been exercised explicitly and remain firmly in force. When that occurs, the underlying total belief, the one that is being explicated, forthwith and necessarily assumes the characteristic of nullity. What has happened now to the coincidence of identity between the total explicand and the total explicate? Obviously we must say: With the cancellation, the belief that has suffered this cancellational modification is still there in a certain manner, as a belief having this sense — no longer, indeed, as a belief now actually exercised by the Ego or rooted in him as his continuingly accepted conviction, but still in his consciousness as his *earlier* belief, with the whole sense in its sense-articulations and the corresponding doxic positings. /

If it is a matter of another's judging, then, in case I do not <52> believe too, I have the "mere idea" of the other's belief that has such and such a content: I have a presentiation [*Vergegenwärtigung*] analogous to a memory of some past belief of my own "in which I no longer join" but which I nevertheless accept now, in memory, as my previously exercised believing. My judgment — which I made *just now* but must reject upon explication, which therefore, from this moment on, is no longer my judgment now but only my just-past judgment — now has, according to the explication, such and such an explicit sense; and the situation is the same in the case of my *earlier* past judgment and similar in the case of the other's appresented judgment. In this connexion it is to be noted that, throughout the cancellational change, there continues to be a coincidence of identity, which concerns the mere judgment-"material". The cancellation alters nothing in the judgment that is presentiated retentionally, or recollectively, or in the manner characteristic of empathy; and, if I explicate what is implicit in it, then the judgment presentiated in one of those manners coincides with the explicate, even though, while explicating, I make my cancellation. Naturally that is not to say that the other subject or I knew beforehand what explication would yield as a distinct proposition; otherwise no one could overlook contradictions, whether immediate or mediate.

After these clarifications we understand the essential difference between the *vague or "confused" manners of judging* [*Urteilsweisen*] and the *"distinct"* ones and can see at once that there is *no* question of whether judgings [*Urteile*] have *evidence* (intuitiveness) *with regard to their predicatively formed affair-complexes* [*hinsichthich ihrer Sachverhalte*] or not. On the one side, *within vagueness itself*, the difference that is so important in relation to verbal thinking emerged for us: Even the sensuousness of the verbal sounds and of their articulations can be vague; then again there can be sharp articulation in this respect and, with it, an *articulation of the indications*. But even then the very important *distinctness of the judicative meanings themselves is lacking*: They are indeed believings and to that extent judgings; yet they are not "proper" judgings.

In the case of verbal judging, an explicit performance of the judging, concurrent with the indications, is called with good

reason "*judging* actually and *properly*": because it alone has the essential characteristic of the originariness in which the judgment is given originaliter, given as the judgment itself — in that (this being the same thing here) the judgment is built up "syntactically"
<53> in the judger's actual action proper. / The following is only a different expression: Explicit judging, *"distinct" judging, is the evidence appropriate to the "distinct judgment"*, as the *ideal objectivity* that becomes constituted originarily in such a synthetic action, and identified in the repetition of such an action.

This evidence is an original emerging of the judgment as it itself, but not yet an evidentially experiencing ⟨act of⟩ *seizing upon and regarding it thematically*. Subsequently what has become constituted in this evidence, in this polythetic action, is graspable "monothetically", in one grasping ray; the polythetic formation becomes an object.[1]

Naturally confusion and distinctness of judging can be intermingled; as they are if, when we are reading, we actually and properly perform a few judgment-steps and -sequences, and then let ourselves be carried along for a while by the mere indications belonging to the word-formations — which in turn, as we said, can have their own distinctness or indistinctness, of quite a different sort.[2]

b. Distinctness and clarity.

But there is also a mingling of another sort and therefore, with appropriate purification, another important contrast for us to take into consideration: namely the mingling of "*distinctness*" and "*clarity*", and the purely apprehended difference between them.

Two evidences become separated here. First, the evidence wherein the *judgment itself, qua judgment,* becomes itself given — the judgment that, as itself given, is called also a distinct judgment, taken from the actual and proper judgment-performing. Second, *the evidence* wherein *that* becomes itself given *which the judger wants to attain "by way of" his judgment* — the judger, that is, as wanting to *cognize*, which is the way logic always conceives him.

[1] *Author's note: Cf. Ideen*, pp. 247f. [English translation, pp. 335ff.]
[2] *Author's note:* On this whole exposition *cf.* Appendix II, [pp. 313–329, *infra*].

To judge explicitly is not *per se* to judge with *"clarity"*: Judging with "clarity" has at once *clarity of the affairs*, in the performance of the judgment-steps, and *clarity of the predicatively formed affair-complex* in the whole judging [*im ganzen Urteil*]. An unclear and a clear judging can judge one and the same judgment; thus evidence of the self-identity of the judgment can extend throughout essentially different modes of givenness. But only a *judging with full clarity* can be *actual present cognition*; and, as such, it is a *new evidence*, pertaining to a / givenness <54>
originaliter of the affairs themselves, of the predicatively formed affair-complex itself, at which one aims in the judging that strives toward cognition — even where the judging is still quite unclear, intuitionally quite unfulfilled.

c. Clarity in the having of something itself and clarity of anticipation.

But here the differences are again ramified, since "clarity" may designate either judging in the mode of the judging that gives its meant affair-complex *itself* — that is, what one usually has in mind as *evident judging* — or else judging in the mode of a judging that makes intuited in that it *prefigures* the meant affair-complex. In the latter case, what is *itself* given is not the predicatively formed affair-complex but precisely a prefiguration, an *intuitional* anticipation, yet to be confirmed by the having of the affair-complex itself. Perfect clarity signifies, in the one case, clarity of "seeing", of "seizing upon", in the actual and proper sense: so that the predicatively formed affair-complex and the affairs entering into it — they themselves — are seized upon; in the other case, perfectly prefigurative clarity of the goal not yet actualized but only striven toward in judging. Here the cognitional striving tends *from "confusion" toward distinctness*; and, if the latter yields a still imperfectly intuitional judgment or, worse yet, a judgment completely devoid of intuition, despite being constituted explicitly, then the striving tends *through* this judgment, *perhaps at first toward only a prefiguration* of the cognitional goal. The phenomenon of transition to synthetic coincidence is then called, in the usual sense of the word, *clarification* of the judgment qua meaning or opinion (making one's meaning clear to oneself). The cognitional striving, however, has not thereby reached its goal; it tends farther, toward that *other clarity*, toward *evidence as the having of the meant itself*, the final goal.

These two modes of clarity have their degrees of perfection, with the appertinent ideas of perfect obscurity and perfect
<55> clarity.[1] Moreover, with the transition to / clarity — accordingly, among "clarifications" — those cases become isolated in which only single parts of what has become posited acquire clarity, or can acquire it: because, though they indeed combine to make up either a clear picture or an evidently given affair-complex "itself", they do so in such a fashion that this, which has become intuited, does not fulfil the judging intention but, on the contrary, annuls it — in the manner appropriate to an impossibility, or else (in the other case) to an "untruth", that becomes evident.

§ 17. The essential genus, "distinct judgment", as the theme of "pure analytics".

Pure apophantic analytics, in our pregnant sense, has as the superordinate concept determining its province the concept of the *judgment*: the judgment *proper*, which derives its being-sense originaliter from the explicit properness of the judgment-performing and from that alone. The cognitional striving — which often tends *through* a merely explicit judging and which the logician (with his interest in scientific judging — correlatively, scientific judgments as judgments aimed in the direction of truth as cognition) has pre-eminently in mind — remains quite

[1] *Author's note:* To speak of a "limit" rather than an idea of clarity would not always be appropriate, though limit is the word that first comes to mind. Not always should one think of something like a *limes*. Perfect evidence of external experience, for example, is a regulative idea in the Kantian sense. External experience is, a priori, never a perfect giving of anything itself; but, as long as external experience goes on with consistent harmony, it bears within itself, as an intentional implication, the idea of an infinite self-contained system of possible experiences that we, starting from *de facto* experience, could have gone through, or could go through now or in the future, — experiences such that, as harmonious continuations of *de facto* experience, they would have shown (or would show) what the physical thing is, "in and of itself", besides what it has already shown itself to be. As the correlate of this phenomenologically clarifiable infinite anticipation (which, *as* an infinite anticipation, has an evidence of its own) the physical thing existing in itself is, for its part, an idea, one that rightly guides the thinking done in natural science and enables such thinking to progress by degrees of approximation, each having its relative evidence. For our purposes we can content ourselves with a crude initial description of "clarity". (On the concept of the physical thing as an idea in the Kantian sense, *cf. Ideen*, pp. 390ff., [English translation pp. 411ff.].)

beside the question in the sphere of pure analytics; it is abstracted from. The identical judgment — whether clarified or even at all clarifiable, whether or not it can be converted into cognition, provided only that it is, or can be, derived actually *from distinct evidence* — *that* is the theme.

Like all logic as an apriori science, pure analytics has to do, not with actual judgments — that is to say, judgments actually made sometime and somewhere — but with apriori possibilities, to which all corresponding actualities are subordinated in an easily understood sense. If the logician, in order to obtain eidetic universality in pure analytics, must begin with examples, which he uses as a basis for seeing essences, he can take actual judgments of his own; on the other hand, he can take other persons' judgments, which he perhaps rejects entirely but which, in following and understanding them in a proper quasi-performing, he nevertheless grasps evidently as possible judgments. But he can likewise project himself into a phantasy-world and become immersed in a judging (his own or another's) within it — provided only that he / produces the variant of distinct evidence that has <56>
the significance of evidence of possible judgments as possible. Thus the *purely* analytic logician has the *essentical genus, distinct judgment*, with its sphere of possible judgments, as his *province*.

§ 18. THE FUNDAMENTAL QUESTION OF PURE ANALYTICS.

The question now is: While remaining *entirely within* this province, what can we state about possible distinct judgments *in forma*, after the antecedent logical discipline, the theory of pure forms (which, in any case, contains the forms of distinct judgments), has constructed the multiplicity of possible forms and placed it at our disposal?

Restricted as we are to what appertains to the own-essentiality of judgments — that is, the constituent properties belonging to them *as* judgments — we can expect, in addition to the own-essentiality explicated by the theory of forms, only relationships founded a priori on the own-essentiality of judgments. And we do in fact encounter here relationships with which we are acquainted and which belong a priori purely to distinct judgments as distinct: *consequence* (includedness); *inconsistency* (analytic contradiction, excludedness); and the *tertium*, judgment-compatibility, which is neither one nor the other — *empty non-contradiction,* as the unifiability of judgments that "have nothing to do with one another".

On closer inspection we discover that what has just been said applies even to the *judgment-members* of apophantic wholes — namely as members posited, or positable, with distinctness. They too, as we indicated in advance,[1] are *"judgments" in the broader sense* (but not self-sufficient ones), since, when cognition is the goal, they are destined to become judgment-members of apophantic wholes (judgments in the pregnant sense), and only thus do they acquire cognitional significance. These *judgments in an unusually amplified sense* — which shall henceforth determine our concept of the judgment — also stand in the above-indicated fundamental analytic relationships: As standing in consequence-relationships, they can demand or exclude one another; and, in case they are mutually exclusive, they are incompatible in the unity of a whole judgment.

Since, as closer consideration shows, all pure analytic relation-
<57> ships are relationships in which / different judgments — we are referring exclusively to judgments falling under the concept of the distinct judgment, the judgment proper — either go together to form the unity of one judgment or else are impossible in such a unity, the *fundamental question of pure analytics* can be formulated as follows:

When, and in what relations, are any judgments — as judgments, and so far as mere form is concerned — possible within the unity of one judgment?

Naturally they are thus possible, only as either standing in a consequence-relation or unrelated in respect of a possible consequence.

"Non-contradiction" therefore signifies the possibility that the judger can judge distinct judgments *within the unity* of a judgment performable with distinctness. In this connexion it should be noted that even mere judging *together* involves a judgment-unity, a unity of co-positedness.

In formal and pure analytics the inquiry concerns judgment-*forms*: Which forms can be known, and known a priori, to be *universal* forms pertaining to the performing of a distinct judging; and which can be known not to be such forms? In that question

[1] *Author's note:* See § 14, [pp. 53–55, *supra*].

the following is included: Which forms of judgment-combinations at any level are apriori forms of unitary judgments that are distinctly evident as properly performable?

§ 19. Pure analytics as fundamental to the formal logic of truth. Non-contradiction as a condition for possible truth.

In these researches, then, we must never go outside the proper essence of judgments or judgment-forms, never go beyond distinct evidence. But we go beyond this apriori sphere, as soon as we ask *questions concerning truth* or as soon as, with regard to the objects taken at first only as distinct judgments, we ask questions concerning their adequation to the affairs themselves: in short, as soon as we bring the concept of truth into our theme. The predicate truth does indeed relate to judgments and only to judgments, whether we take the above-characterized narrower judgment-concept (the concept of apophansis) or the broader one as our basis. But, as long as we restrict ourselves to merely distinct evidence and what is identifiable in it under the name judgment, although every contradiction (every *analytic countersense*) is indeed excluded, an opening remains for every *material countersense* and for every other untruth. After all, we are abstracting from every effect produced by clarification, by resorting to material possibility or to truth; we are abstracting, in other words from all questions of verification. /

What then does it signify, to seek formally universal eidetic <58>
insight concerning possible judicial truth? It obviously signifies phantasying possible judgments as possibly undergoing verification, as possibly standing in a relationship of adequation to the corresponding judgments that give the supposed affairs themselves. *Now* the judgments are thought of from the very beginning, not as mere judgments, but as judgments pervaded by a dominant *cognitional striving*, as meanings that have to become *fulfilled*, that are not objects by themselves, like the data arising from mere distinctness, but passages to the "truths" themselves that are to be attained.

If, in this manner, one exchanges the theoretical focusing on mere judgments for the *focusing on cognition*, on the predicatively formed affair-complexes that are judgingly cognized or, correlatively, on the verifying adequation, then one grasps forthwith, as an eidetic insight, that whatever is incompatible in the unity of a distinct judgment is incompatible also in the truth, or that a contradiction in the mere judgments of course excludes the possibility of adequation. *Truth* and falsity are predicates that can *belong only to a judgment that is distinct* or can be made distinct, *one that can be performed actually and properly*. Logic has never made clear to itself that *this* concept of the judgment is at the basis of the old thesis that truth and falsity (in the original sense) are predicates of judgments. *Thus, in a mediated fashion, a pure analytics*, by virtue of its essence, is at the same time *a fundamental part of a formal logic of truth.* The division of the universe of judgment-forms into those that are law-forms belonging to consequence, those that are law-forms belonging to inconsistency, and those that, as standing outside both classes, are non-contradictory in the "trivial" sense (as the mathematician would express it), acquires immediate significance for the possibility of adequation or truth. Any *consequence-relationship of judgments*, if it can be effected with intuitiveness, becomes a *consequence-relationship of truths* or of material possibilities. Any contradiction, on the other hand, excludes from the start all questions of adequation; it is *a limine* a falsity.[1]

§ 20. THE PRINCIPLES OF LOGIC AND THEIR ANALOGUES IN PURE ANALYTICS.

The separation of a pure consequence-logic from truth-logic
‹59› results in / a two-sidedness that also extends to the so-called principles of traditional logic — that is, the principles explicating the concepts truth and falsity.

The *double principle of contradiction and excluded middle*, as a principle of truth-logic, says the following:

"If a judgment is true, then its contradictory opposite is false"; and "of two contradictory judgments, one is necessarily true"; combining the two propositions: "any judgment is exclusively one or the other, true or false".

The *analogue* of these propositions in consequence-logic is a principle that appertains to the essence of judgments proper

[1] *Translator's note: Cf.* Appendix III, § 4, pp. 338–340, *infra.*

(judgments that are themselves given in distinct evidence). It reads:

If two judgments are contradictory, it is not the case that both are possible as judgments proper, that both can become given in distinct evidence; it is not the case that both have ideal "mathematical existence". Nevertheless one of them has it; one of them can become given in distinct evidence.[1]

The *principles that originally connect truth and consequence* must also be reckoned among the highest truth-principles of apophantic logic. Traditional logic offers them in the impure form of the *modus ponens* and the *modus tollens*. Here too we have the same analogy. Already, in the sphere of mere analytic consequence-relationships, there are a *modus ponens* and a *modus tollens*, which, naturally, say nothing about truth or falsity thematically, but rather appertain, as a particular consequence-law, purely to the essence of judgments proper and to the relationships of analytic consequence peculiar to these. Solely in this form are the *modus ponens* and the *modus tollens* a genuine ⟨purely analytic⟩ logical *principle*. This principle reads:

"*N*" follows analytically from two judgments of the forms, "If *M*, then *N*" and "*N*". In the same manner, "Not *M*" follows from two judgments of the forms, "If *M*, then *N*" and "Not *N*".

The corresponding *truth-principle* then reads:

If an immediate relationship of total analytic antecedent and total analytic consequent obtains between any two judgments, *M* and *N*, then the truth of the antecedent entails the truth of the consequent, and the falsity of the consequent entails the falsity of the antecedent.

We have introduced the phrases "total antecedent" and "total consequent" to indicate the *immediacy* of the relationship. We understand by these phrases nothing but the actual / members of <60>
a relationship of immediate consequence, no matter how they

[1] *Translator's note:* It may be that the intent of this paragraph would be indicated less misleadingly as follows.

> A judgment in which two mutually contradictory judgments are conjoined is not possible as a judgment proper; it cannot become given as a possible judgment in distinct evidence; it does not have ideal "mathematical existence". But at least one of any two mutually contradictory judgments has such "existence"; at least one of them can become given as a possible judgment in distinct evidence.

For a justification of the main changes involved in this rendering, see § 14, *supra*, the first sentence in the fourth paragraph.

may be divisible afterwards. It is only as parts of total antecedents and total consequents that the component premises and the component consequents determine consequence-relationships, which therefore are already *mediate.* If, in one of the consequent-wholes (which is the total consequent, only as being the complete whole), a single consequent is false, it immediately determines the falsity of the total consequent, and only thus the falsity of the total premise.

When applied to the above-stated *modus ponens* and *modus tollens*—understood as a principle of immediate pure consequence-relationships — the principle laid down by us yields immediately the correct modes belonging to truth-logic:

If the antecedent in a hypothetical judgment is true, its consequent is true; if the consequent is false, so is the antecedent. Or, put formally:

If, at the same time, "If *M*, then *N*" and "*M*" are true (if they "hold good" at the same time), then "*N*" is true. If, at the same time, "If *M*, then *N*" and "Not *N*" are true, then "Not *M*" is true (or, equivalently, "*M*" is false).

As for *mediacies* of analytic consequence: In the first place, it is a pure law of analytic consequence-relationships (pertaining therefore to "mere", but distinct, judgments and prior all questions concerning their possible truth), that *an immediate analytic consequent of an immediate analytic consequent is itself an analytic consequent of the antecedent*; whence it follows, as itself a consequence, that a consequent with any degree of mediacy is also a consequent of the antecedent. If we combine this law with our truth-principle concerning immediate analytic consequence-relationships then it follows — and, indeed, with mere analytic consequence — that this principle, when broadened, retains its validity for analytic consequences having any degree of mediacy.

§ 21. The evidence in the coinciding of "the same" confused and distinct judgment. The broadest concept of the judgment.

If we cast a backward glance at *"confused" judgments*, which we have contrasted with judgments in the pregnant sense belonging to analytics (judgments as distinct), we see that, in the identification of "confused" judgments, each with the corre-

sponding distinct judgment, yet a *third evidence* is concealed, by virtue of which a *third concept of the judgment* receives being-sense. With the transition, with the making distinct to oneself of what one / truly meant in the vague judging process of meaning <61>
(what was truly said by oneself or by another, what was truly thought in having something vaguely come to mind) — with this transition the distinct judgment becomes given as an *evident mere explication of the true sense or meaning*. There comes to pass a coincidence of identity belonging to an originally peculiar type, which indicates a *fundamental type of "evidence"*. This evidence, like any other (any "experience" in the widest conceivable sense), has its degrees of perfection and its idea — here indeed an ideal limit[1] of perfection, at which the synthetic coincidence would in fact be absolutely perfect.

These two manners of judging [*Urteilsweisen*] — with their respective correlates, the *confused judgment* and the *distinct judgment* themselves — obviously have *a relationship similar to that between distinct but empty* (or else imperfectly intuitive) judging and *distinct* judging *with insight*, the judging in which the possible being, or the true being, of the affairs aimed at in cognitional judging is itself given in insight. Confused judging bears within itself — not always, but (as we have already said) in the nexus of a theoretical interest — an *aiming*, which is directed to the distinct judgment and which, if it attains this, becomes *fulfilled* therein. Now, in the case of a clarifying fulfilment-synthesis, a focusing of regard and an identification are possible, by virtue of which an *empty* judgment and a *full* judgment become identified, *merely as judgments*, and gain an objectivity of their own as the *same* judgment; and the like is true of the parallel fulfilment-synthesis that effects the coincidence of a *confused* and a *distinct* judgment. Or, to put it differently: Just as the cognition, the having of the predicatively formed affair-complex itself, is *also* intrinsically a distinct judgment (as truly a distinct judgment as the corresponding empty judgment is), so the judgment with vagueness and the judgment with distinctness are "the same judgment". That is not to say that every confused judgment admits of being converted into "the same" distinct judgment — any more than every

[1] *Translator's note: Cf.* § 16 *c*, p. 62, note, *supra*.

distinct judgment admits of being converted into a material insight, whether as a possibility or as a truth.

The *broadest concept of the judgment* is therefore the one that is unaffected by the differences among confusion, distinctness, and clarity, or that consciously abstracts from these differences. When this concept is taken as a basis, there corresponds to each insightfully cognitive judgment, and to each distinct judgment (in view of the essential possibility — and, genetically, the constant necessity — of its becoming confused), a like judgment, or rather the same one, in the confused mode; and therefore the concept of the confused judgment embraces, in a certain manner, all judgments in the broadest sense, including those that can be made distinct and those that can be made clear. /

<62> § 22. THE CONCEPT DEFINING THE PROVINCE BELONGING TO THE THEORY OF APOPHANTIC FORMS, AS THE GRAMMAR OF PURE LOGIC, IS THE JUDGMENT IN THE BROADEST SENSE.

The importance of this discrimination of the third evidence and its correlative, the new and broadest concept of the judgment, lies in our having now acquired the basis for understanding the province belonging to the theory of the pure forms of judgments. Obviously the concept defining that province is the judgment in the broadest sense; and all the laws of form that go to make up the theory are tied to the proper essence of *these* judgments. As confused, every judgment is possible that, as distinct, is impossible; and again, as distinct, every judgment is possible that, as an evident cognition, is impossible. In the theory of forms, the free construction of forms knows as yet no restraining contradictions. The whole support of form-construction is *speech,* with its well-differentiated indications, its references to sense, which attach to the sensuously differentiated signs and their sensuous configurations. And it is therefore not without reason that the theory of the forms of significations was characterized in my *Logische Untersuchungen* as the "grammar of pure logic". In a certain manner, furthermore, it is also not without reason that people often say that formal logic has let itself be guided by grammar. In the case of theory of forms, however, this is not a reproach but a necessity — provided that, for guided by grammar (a word intended to bring to mind *de facto* historical languages and their grammatical description), guidance by the grammatical itself be substituted. Distinctly understanding a statement and framing it as a possible judgment — this can and often does signify a distinct grasping of the *word*-sequences (accompanied by an internal explicit following, in a quasi-speaking) and also of their *reference-articulations,* with which there accrues the unity of a judgment, confused and yet articulated in a definite form. Thus we can understand quite definitely and articulatedly: "No quadrangle has four angles", or "All *A*'s are *B*'s, including some that are not *B*'s", or the like. Such examples too pass muster in the "grammar of pure logic"; and thus all forms of contradictory judgments belong in the system of forms. Without the definite articulation of vague judgments by means of the sensuous articulation of verbal signs, no theory of forms, no logic whatever, would be possible — and, of course, no science either.

By these analyses the sense of the three-fold stratification of formal logic, briefly characterized in §§ 13–15, has been / clarified from the most original sources, and the essential <63>
necessity of this stratification has been established. Up to now, this stratification has remained foreign to logic; only the isolation of a theory of pure forms had already been effected in the *Logische Untersuchungen*; in the present context, however, the separation has been established on incomparably deeper grounds. Needless to say, our separation of the formal logic of non-contradiction from the formal logic of truth is something fundamentally and essentially new, however familiar its wording may be to everyone. For the words in question meant something entirely different, namely the distinction between, on the one hand, all the problems of formal logic, which, as formal, leave out all the non-formal "material of cognition", and, on the other hand, the somehow broader problems (broader in a sense that was not exactly clear) to be propounded by a logic — problems that take into account precisely this non-formal material: for example, questions concerning the possibility of a cognition of real actuality or the possibility of fashioning truths about the real world.

CHAPTER 2.

Formal apophantics, formal mathematics.

§ 23. THE INTERNAL UNITY OF TRADITIONAL LOGIC AND THE PROBLEM OF ITS POSITION RELATIVE TO FORMAL MATHEMATICS.

a. The conceptual self-containedness of traditional logic as apophantic analytics.

Formal logic in its delimitation up to now, as apophantic analytics in the broader sense, owes its apriori self-containedness to its concept (the Aristotelian concept) of the judgment-form. One can define this concept also as the determining of all judgments exclusively by their *"syntactical forms"*, the forms that they, as formations produced by *"syntactical operations"*, have by apriori necessity. The syntactical form of any judgment can be apprehended purely, in eidetic concepts. To say that it is apprehended purely is to say that the *"syntactical stuffs"* going into the syntaxes are thought of as indeterminately optional. Thus the pure form-concept of a judgment as such originates: that of a judgment as determined exclusively by syntactical forms that are given and conceptually determinate in the particular case.[1] As codeterminant ⟨of the judgment as such⟩ and therefore as pertaining to the form-concept in analytic logic, only the most
‹64› universal *"modal" / variations* may also be included, those that any judgment whatever can undergo, regardless of all the syntactical operations that build it or can be performed on it. The concept of modal variation employed here is far from being exhausted by the so-called judgment-modalities. Under it belongs also, for example, a variation that has hardly ever been understood, the variation represented by subjects of existential propositions and by propositions as subjects of truth-predications — as contrasted with the corresponding unmodalized subjects and apophantic propositions. In a systematic logic all these modalities must be defined separately as primitive formal concepts.

Now as long as logic remains bound to this concept of the formal — as long as all "terms" in the fundamental apophantic

[1] *Author's note: Cf.* Appendix I, [pp. 294 ff., *infra*].

forms (and in the forms that can be constructed out of these) are left as undetermined variables — it can acquire only such cognitions about possible truth as are annexed immediately to the pure analytics of non-contradiction and are therefore what might be called (except a few propositions) trivial versions of the formal theories of that discipline (which do enrich cognition significantly). For, when formal logic is actually developed with that radical purity which is necessary to its philosophic usefulness, and indeed gives it the highest philosophic importance, it lacks everything that makes possible a *differentiating* of truths or, correlatively, of evidences. Just as its concept of an object is the most universal (that of any substrate whatever in possible determining predications), so its concept of a predicatively formed affair-complex and its concept of evidence are the most universal concepts. Consequently it cannot make even such universal distinctions as that between individual and categorial objects, or that among "mere things", valuable objects, practical goods, and so forth; nor can it make any distinction between universalities drawn from individual objects — the universalities called genera and species in the usual sense — and other universalities. That being the case, we can already sense that this formal logic cannot be the whole of logic: the full and — in a new and richer sense — formal theory of science.

b. The emerging of the idea of an enlarged analytics, Leibniz's "*mathesis universalis*", and the methodico-technical unification of traditional syllogistics and formal mathematics.

But we must not begin here an intentional explication of the idea of logic along this line. For, no matter how certain we have become of the self-containedness of analytic formal logic, this discipline itself still presents us with great problems. The structural divisions that we have made within it pay no / heed to <65>
the great enlargements that, beginning with Leibniz, have been demanded in the case of traditional logic, with the conviction that only by them could it fully satisfy the idea of a formal analytics — formal in its own peculiar sense of the word. It is time now that we took these enlargements into consideration: that is to say, the already-mentioned synthesis of traditional

syllogistics and formal analysis in the Leibnizian idea of a *mathesis universalis*.

Out of continuity with Leibniz, whose genial intuition was denied historical effect, an incorporation of syllogistics into formal mathematics came to pass with the development of a syllogistic algebra. It was motivated, not by philosophic reflections on the fundamental sense and the necessity of a *mathesis universalis*, but by the needs of the deductive theoretical technique of mathematical science, and took place first in English mathematics after the beginning of the nineteenth century (De Morgan, Boole). With this incorporation, syllogistics at once had to submit to a doubtful reinterpretation as an "extensional logic" — a reinterpretation that, in its fundamental obscurity, has carried with it many a countersense and artifices of every sort to make them harmless, so far as the practice of mathematical theorization is concerned. On the other hand, incorporation of syllogistics into formal mathematics does contain a core of thought that has its original legitimacy; moreover this core alone made it possible not to lose continuity of thought with traditional analytics. Mathematicians, to whom such obscurities offer little hindrance in their work of fashioning deductive theories, have meanwhile generally accepted the unity of "logic" and "mathematics" (or, more precisely, formal analysis [1].

If we go more particularly into the problem of this unity here, naturally it is not for us a matter of the interests of a special science, whether they be the interests of formal mathematics or those of formal syllogistics, or even those of the possibily admissible positive science that effects a union of these two. That is to say, it is not merely a matter of taking the two theories, which were separate in their historical development, and connecting them in the right manner theoretically, within the systematic structure of the one deductive science where they are supposed to belong together; it is not merely a matter of recognizing and developing the deductive relationships between them and, with the resultant insight into their respective functions
<66> in the theoretical whole, / furnishing each one of them for the

[1] *Author's note:* Disciplines such as pure geometry and pure mechanics — likewise "analytic" geometry and "analytic" mechanics — are thus excluded, as long as they actually relate to *space* and *forces*.

first time with its correct theoretical form. Great as such an interest may be, it falls far short of the philosophic interest: the interest in uncovering the teleological structures immanent in the final idea of a theory of science; the interest in developing, in originary evidence, the other ideas included in the intentional sense of that idea — ideas of component logical disciplines — and the essentially united set of problems peculiar to each of them. The extent to which philosophic interests of actually the highest order come into play here cannot, it is true, become visible until later. Nevertheless it will be conceded beforehand that philosophy includes the science of principles, likewise the principles of all science as such, and therefore the questions that concern the principles of logic. That can suffice here.

We have already been following the method of systematically explicating the teleological structure of the idea of logic; and by it we have developed and brought to some degree of purity at least one such structure, namely the idea of formal analytics, which relates exclusively to judgments (as pure significations). Formal analytics — and not as a mere idea but as an elaborated theory — has already existed in a certain manner for a long time, for thousands of years. In its historically given state, however, having shown itself from the beginning with an embryonic undevelopedness of its peculiar sense and of its essentially necessary delimitation and stratification and having continued in this obscurity throughout all its transformations, it cannot suffice. Now, to be sure, with our intentional explication, we have made considerable progress in this respect. Tracing the structure of ideal significations, we were able to distinguish three strata in the sense that was, so to speak, innate in historically existing logic; and accordingly we could display the three disciplines founded one upon the other within the pure analytics of judgments. But something important to an insight into principles is still wanting. How important it is, and how much deeper we must push our intentional clarification, will be shown by a treatment of the problem set for us by Leibniz and the new mathematics.

§ 24. The new problem of a formal ontology. Characterization of traditional formal mathematics as formal ontology.

The essentially *new problem*, of which we could not become mindful up to now, guided as we were by traditional syllogistic logic, emerges when we let ourselves be guided by the unclearness, not of traditional logic, but rather of the new mathematics — the mathematics that combines syllogistic algebra with the rest of
<67> / "analysis". This enlarged formal mathematics too is already there for us beforehand, and still not yet there. It is not yet there for us, so far as the sense of its unity, as a sense brought out by fundamental clarification, is lacking: the idea of a unitary science, as a *final idea explicated in evidence* and enabling us to understand that what this mathematics unites, in the manner characteristic of a theoretical technique, belongs together of necessity, by virtue of a congruity of sense having its basis in that clarified idea. As soon as we seek to gain the idea in question (whether we start from the idea of a formal analytics, which has already become clear to us, and strive to reach the old disciplines of formal mathematics, which are yet to be clarified in the process, or start from these and move in the opposite direction), the *new problem* — that of a formal ontology — obstructs our path.

To develop this problem in advance, let us start from the fact that Aristotelian analytics was established as *apophantic* and therefore had, as the fundamental concept of its themes, as the fundamental concept delimiting its province, the concept of the apophansis: the predicative sentence (that asserts with certainty) — correlatively, the predicative judgment. The methodically perfect development of this analytics (as soon as it becomes concerned exclusively with the signified judgments) necessarily leads to a formal apophantic "mathematics": Once anyone has become acquainted with deductive technique, as practised in modern mathematics and mathematical analysis generally, he must see forthwith (as Leibniz was the first to see) that proposition-forms can be treated in the very same manner and that one can "calculate" with them, just as one can with numbers, quantities, and the like — nay more, that this is the one manner in which a universal theory of propositions (as essentially a deductive theory) can be built. As we pointed out above, this holds good even for a theory merely of the forms of propositions.

Now, over against apophantics, developed by this method in the style of an apophantic mathematics, we have *non-apophantic mathematics*, the traditional formal "analysis" of mathematicians: the mathematics of sets, of combinations and permutations, of cardinal numbers (the modes of how-many), of ordinal numbers belonging to various levels, of multiplicities with their well-known forms — which are also called numbers, but must nowise be confounded with the numbers mentioned first, since the forms of multiplicities derive their sense from the definitions of the multiplicities to which they belong. *In this province predicative propositions*, "judgments" in traditional logic's sense of the word, manifestly *are not present at all as thematic fundamental concepts.* |

At first, when one asks for the all-embracing concept that <68>
should delimit the unitary province of these disciplines (which obviously belong together), one is perplexed. But when one considers [1] the naturally broadest universality of the concepts set and number, and considers also the concepts element and unit which respectively determine their sense, one recognizes that the theory of sets and the theory of cardinal numbers relate to the empty universe, *any object whatever* or *anything whatever*, with a formal universality that, on principle, leaves out of consideration every material determination of objects; and, furthermore, that these disciplines are interested specifically in certain derivative formations of anything-whatever: one of them, namely the theory of sets, in sets as made up of any objects whatever that are taken together; and, similarly, the theory of cardinal numbers, in numbers as certain systematically generable differentiations of forms of sets. Going on from there, one recognizes that, like the theory of sets and the theory of cardinal numbers, the other *formal mathematical disciplines* are *formal* in the sense of having as fundamental concepts certain *derivative formations of anything-whatever*. This gives rise to the idea of an all-embracing science, a *formal mathematics in the fully comprehensive sense*, whose all-inclusive province is rigidly delimited as the sphere of the highest form-concept, any object whatever (or the sphere of anything-whatever, conceived with the emptiest

[1] *Author's note:* As I did already in my *Philosophie der Arithmetik*. [*I. Bd.* (Halle, 1891). *Cf.* Farber, *op. cit.*, Chap. II.]

universality), with all the derivative formations generable (and therefore conceivable) a priori in this field — formations that always go on yielding new formations as products generated in a constructing that is always reiterable. Besides set and cardinal number (finite and infinite), combination (in the mathematical sense of the word), relational complex, series, connexion, and whole and part, are such derivatives. Accordingly it is natural to view this whole mathematics as an *ontology* (an apriori theory of objects), though a *formal* one, relating to the pure modes of anything-whatever. In so doing, one would also acquire the guiding idea for determining the separate provinces of this ontology — this mathematics of all objectivities as such — by apriori structural considerations.

§ 25. Formal apophantics and formal ontology as belonging together materially, notwithstanding the diversity of their respective themes.

According to these deliberations, the province of this formal ontology, as formal mathematics enlarged to a universality consonant with its essence, seems to be ***sharply discriminated***
<69> from that of the / analytics of judgments — this discipline itself being taken as pure of any thematizing activity directed to the subjective, an activity that has, indeed, remained alien to the theory of sets, to arithmetic, and to the other branches of formal mathematics, from the very beginning. We must not let ourselves be deceived, it seems, by the fact that syllogistics also admits of being treated algebraically and, when so treated, has a theoretical appearance similar to that of an algebra of quantities or numbers — nay more: that, according to George Boole's brilliant observation, the calculus of arithmetic (considered formally) becomes reduced to the "logical calculus", if one thinks of the series of cardinal numbers as limited to zero and one. Apophantic analytics and formal ontological analytics seem to be two different sciences, separated by their provinces.

Nevertheless one need only remind oneself that judging is the same as judging about *objects*, predicating *properties* of them, or *relative determinations*; taking this into consideration, one cannot fail to note that formal ontology and formal apophantics, despite their expressly different themes, must be very intimately related

and are perhaps inseparable. Ultimately *all the forms of objects*, all the derivative formations of anything-whatever, do make their appearance *in formal apophantics itself*; since indeed, as a matter of essential necessity, determinations (properties and relative determinations), predicatively formed affair-complexes, combinations, relationships, wholes and parts, sets, cardinal numbers, and all the other modes of objectivity, *in concreto* and explicated originaliter, have being for us — as truly existent or possibly existent modes — only as making their appearance in judgments. Accordingly, in all formal distinctions pertaining to judgments, differences among object-forms are included (no matter what this "being included" and the above-mentioned "making their appearance" may turn out to be when further clarified [1]. After all, in the plural judgment, for example, the plural is to be found; in the universal judgment, the universal. To be sure, in the former the plural is not the object in the pregnant sense: it is not what is judged "about", not the substrate of determinations. And, in the other example, the same is true of the universal. But, in the formal theory of judgments, as a theory of pure forms, those "operations" are also to be found, by which the plural judgment-form can be transmuted into the form of the singular predication about the collection, and the form of the all-or-none judgment can be transmuted into the form of a judgment about the universal as a genus. Predicatively formed affair-complex and determination are object-categories; but any judgment, S is p, that judges about S and predicates p of S can / be converted, by <70>
"nominalization", into a judgment about the affair-complex, S is p, or into the judgment about the determination, p, with the form, p belongs to S.[2] In view of this, the problem of the unity or diversity of logical analytics and formal mathematics can by no means be regarded as already solved; indeed, the concept of them as united even receives some force from this quarter. But very penetrative considerations are necessary to the acquisition of actual insight.

[1] *Author's note:* About this, [Part I,] Chapter 4, [pp. 105–129, *infra*,] will give information.

[2] *Author's note*: *Cf. Ideen*, [§ 119,] pp. 248f.; [English translation, pp. 335f.]; and *Logische Untersuchungen, II. Bd., I. Teil, 5. Unters.*, §§ 34–36 [*cf.* Farber, *op. cit.*, pp. 367–373], and *II. Teil, 6. Unters.*, § 49.

§ 26. The historical reasons why the problem of the unity of formal apophantics and formal mathematics was masked.

a. Lack of the concept of pure empty form.

The problem in question could not confront the ancients; incipient logic and mathematics had to appear as undoubtedly separate sciences to them, because they had not yet advanced far enough to reduce any mathematical discipline to a pure form. Arithmetic for them is not yet essentially differentiated from geometry and mechanics (as it is for us, in accordance with our fundamental contrast between formal mathematics and mathematics with a material content). For not even their concept of cardinal number is emptied of all non-formal material; in the units thought of as counted, it is not yet related to the realm of the empty anything-whatever. Moreover, on the other side (as we noted earlier[1] ancient apophantics, with its object-relation to reality, had not yet been ultimately formalized. Accordingly Aristotle had a universal ontology of realities only; and *this* was what he accepted as "first philosophy". He lacked formal ontology, and therefore lacked also the cognition that formal ontology is intrinsically prior to the ontology of realities.

The genuine discovery of the formal was first made, at the beginning of the modern age, by way of Vieta's establishment of algebra — that is to say, by way of the reduction of the theory of numbers and quantities to a deductive technique — and then attained its pure sense through Leibniz, whose *mathesis universalis* obviously has thrust off completely every restriction to even the highest materially filled universality.

The philosophic logicians — I do not mean logicians who
<71> vied with mathematicians in the technical development / of logical algebra and who, like them, remained philosophically naïve — the philosophic logicians of the modern age, so far as the present problem is concerned, did not overcome the spell of the Aristotelian-Scholastic tradition. They did not understand the sense of *mathesis universalis*, which, to be sure, is hard to gather from Leibniz's brief indications. They did not see the problem raised by the new mathematics; and for this there were other and profound reasons.

[1] *Author's note:* See § 12, the closing paragraph, p. 42, *supra*.

b. Lack of knowledge that apophantic formations are ideal.

In the first place, Aristotle's establishment of analytics as apophantics, as a logic of the predicative statement and, correlatively, the predicative judgment, proved itself a hindrance. However necessary that was as a beginning, it involved a deeply rooted difficulty: the difficulty, namely, of abstracting thematically from the judging activity and, while remaining consistent in so doing, regarding the judgment-sphere theoretically as a specific Objective field of apriori ideality, just as the geometer regards the sphere of pure geometrical shapes and the arithmetician regards the sphere of numbers.

It is because of the intrinsic nature of the affairs themselves that the ideal Objectivity of judgment-formations could not gain recognition, and that even in recent times — after having been brought out systematically and vindicated by a critical refutation of empiristic psychologism — it has not yet won universal acceptance. Judgments are there for us originally in judicative activities. Every work of cognition is a multiple and unitary psychic activity in which cognitional formations originate. Now, to be sure, external Objects too are originally there for us only in our subjective experiencing. But they present themselves in it as Objects already factually existent beforehand (Objects "on hand") and only entering into our experiencing. They are not there for us, like thought-formations (judgments, proofs, and so forth), as coming from our own thinking activity and fashioned by it purely (not, perchance, out of materials already on hand and external to it). In other words: Physical things are given beforehand to active living as objects originally other than the Ego's own; they are given from outside. Contrariwise, the formations with which logic is concerned are given *exclusively from inside*, exclusively by means of spontaneous activities and *in* them. On the other hand, to be sure, after having in fact been generated they are still taken to be existent; one "returns to them" as the same formations, and does so repeatedly at will; one employs them in a sort of practice, connects them (perhaps as premises) and generates something new: arguments, proofs, or the like. Thus one does / actually deal with them as with real physical <72>
things, even though they are far from being realities. And so they

float obscurely between subjectivity and Objectivity. To accept them seriously as irreal Objects, to do justice to the evidences *on both sides* (which it may well have been illegitimate to play off against each other), and to fix one's eye on what is seriously problematic here and take it seriously *as* problematic — that is something one does not venture, old inherited fears of Platonism having made one blind to the doctrine's purifiable sense and the genuine problem implicit in this sense.

To be sure, the situation is essentially the same in the case of the other apriori sciences, those handed down historically under the name of mathematics; essentially the same, that is, in the case of geometry, arithmetic, and the rest — sciences that nevertheless appear as relating quite indubitably to *Object*-spheres of their own, to geometrical shapes, cardinal or ordinal numbers, and so forth; though these objectivities likewise accrue to the investigators in subjective actions, by the drawing of lines, by a geometrical generation of surfaces, and so forth, or, on the other hand, by collecting, counting, ordering, or mathematical combining. And yet here one hardly thought of subjectivizing the produced formations themselves. For here one had the continual support of the sensuous configurations, spatial and temporal, which furnished examples and drew attention to the Objective side from the start; though at the same time they masked the irreality of the mathematical configurations. The constructions, sets, number-formations, and so forth, made with real objects as representative examples, furnished products that might be taken as real (as real figures, real solids, real sets, real numbers); whereas the like is not the case with products of judicative actions.

This makes it understandable that the very advanced insight already expressed in the Stoic doctrine of the λεκτόν [1] did not win out in antiquity and that, in the modern age, even after the development of a formal mathematics and its enlargement to include the calculus of logic, most logicians were unable to see an internal connexion between the themes of mathematics and the themes of logic. Such a connexion could not emerge until the formations dealt with in formal logic were made thematic as

[1] *Translator's note:* See Carl Prantl, *Geschichte der Logik im Abendlande, I. Bd., VI. Abschnitt*, pp. 415ff.

parallels to the formations dealt with in formal mathematics, and made so with the same focusing in both cases, on that which is both Objective and ideal. In mathematics this abstractive focusing was a fixed tradition; from the very beginning it alone had determined the theoretical aim of mathematical theorization. In logic it had yet to be achieved. /

c. Further reasons, particularly the lack of genuine scientific inquiries into origins. <73>

In addition to that, the risky interpretations of judgments in terms of "extensional logic", which were advanced as being necessary to an incorporating of the apophantic sphere into mathematics, had a far from prepossessing effect on philosophically minded logicians. As a result only a very few of them espoused the mathematicians' thesis; and at bottom even they were moved either by a feeling for what is correct — as was Lotze [1] — or by their prejudice in favor of the suporiority of the mathematicians' insight — as Alois Riehl obviously was [2] — more than by a grounding of their position on actual investigation. As for mathematics, logicians did not sense the presence therein of what are in fact quite parallel difficulties, pertaining to the intermingling or togetherness of the ideal Objectivity of the formations and the activity (counting, combining, or the like) that constitutes them subjectively; because it never actually came to a serious philosophic exploration of the origin of the concepts fundamental to formal mathematics, precisely as concepts of subjectively constituted formations. Had such an exploration been made, it would necessarily have become manifest that judging and counting are closely kindred active spontaneities, which constitute their respective ideal correlates, judgments and numbers, in similar manners;[3] consequently, that a consistently one-sided focusing makes possible and demands, in the case of

[1] *Author's note:* See the statements in Lotze's *Logik* [(1874, 2d ed. 1881), *I. Buch,*] *I. Kap.* § 18, and *3. Kap.*, § 111, which can hardly be accepted as fully thought out — the less so because in them he speaks of mathematics universally and, as the context shows, he does not exclude material mathematics.

[2] *Author's note: Cf. Der philosophische Kritizismus* [*und seine Bedeutung für die positive Wissenschaft* (*The Critical Philosophy and Its Significance for Positive Science*)], *Bd. 2, I. Tl.*, [1879,] p. 228.

[3] *Author's note: Cf.* my *Philosophie der Arithmetik*, 1891, e.g., p. 91 (categorial objects as produced formations).

judgments as well as in that of numbers, a theory — a mathematical theory — that is Objective in one and the same sense.[1]

It is altogether understandable that a radical investigation concerning the essential sense that is, so to speak, innate in the two disciplines was, and always continues to be, equally necessary in the case of each, in order to break the spell of tradition and penetrate to an internal understanding of the unity of their themes — instead of contenting oneself, like the mathematicians, with a unity that comes from theoretical technique or else, like most philosophers, with a supposed separation, which cannot be made understandable by any insight into principles. /

<74>

d. Comment on Bolzano's position regarding the idea of formal ontology.

How hard it is to think the matter through to the end and penetrate, in this manner, either from logical analytics into formal mathematics or the reverse, and how highly Leibniz's achievement in this respect is therefore to be esteemed, one sees from the case of Bernard Bolzano. In his admirable *Wissenschaftslehre* [*Theory of Science*], published in 1837, he has already gone far enough to project systematically a theory of propositions in themselves and truths in themselves, as a self-contained apophantic analytics. On the other side, even in 1810, in his *Beiträge zu einer begründeteren Darstellung der Mathematik* [*Contributions to a More Grounded Exposition of Mathematics*], he makes an attempt at a fundamental definition of mathematics, which already approaches the idea of a formal apriori theory of objects — to be sure, without penetrating to its actual sense (as I shall show forthwith, at the close of this section). And yet Bolzano does not go far enough to think the two ideas, that of an analytics of propositions and that of a formal mathematical analytics, through to the end and discover their internal equivalence, nor even far enough to take into consideration the possibility of an algebraic theorization of the formations with which logic is concerned, parallel to that of the formations with which formal mathematics, in the usual sense, is concerned. In short,

[1] *Author's note:* To bring this out was the chief object of the first volume of my *Logische Untersuchungen.*

much as he has learned from Leibniz, he falls far short of Leibniz's insights.

One reads at first with surprise, in Heinrich Fels's meritorious new edition [1] of Bolzano's youthful essay, which previously was as good as inaccessible, the sentences introducing § 8 (p. 17), which, however much they provoke criticism of details, would seem to promise a definition of formal ontology:

> I think that one might define mathematics as a science that treats of the universal laws (forms) with which things must accord in their existence [Dasein]. Under the word thing I comprehend here not merely such things as possess Objective existence, existence independent of our consciousness, but also such things as exist only in our presentation [*Vorstellung*] and do so, more particularly, either as individuals (that is to say, intuitions) or as mere universal concepts; in a word then: everything that can be at all an object of our faculty of presentation.

Precise inspection shows that here Bolzano gives a definition (which needs improvement, to be sure) of a universal apriori ontology that comprises both a material and an empty-formal ontology, without drawing a distinction between them. He then attempts, it is true, the isolation of a "universal mathematics", in which "the theory of numbers, the theory of combinations, etc." are to be included. He emphasizes that disciplines such as geometry and chronometry must be considered, not as coordinate with those, but as subordinate to them; and he finds the distinguishing characteristic of the former disciplines in the circumstance that their laws "are applicable to all things without exception", while the laws of the other disciplines are not. But when he thinks of the universal, thing, as the highest genus, under which / the superordinate concepts belonging to <75>
geometry and coordinate disciplines stand as particular genera, resulting from division, it becomes plain that he has failed to see the difference between the *empty form, anything-whatever*, as the highest genus *whose subordinate differentiations are likewise empty forms*, and the *universal region*, the possibly *factually existent* [*des moglicherweise Daseineden*], (the real in the broadest sense), which is differentiated *into particular regions*; and that therefore he has also failed to see the difference between subsumptions of formal particularizations under formal universalities and subsumptions of regional particularizations (material-mathematical particularizations) likewise under formal universalities. Regional particularizations are by no means confined within the bounds of formal mathematics; formal particularizations, on the other hand, accrue by formalization of material mathematics. In a word, Bolzano did not attain the proper concept of the formal, the concept that defines formal ontology; though in a certain manner he touched upon it.

[1] *Author's note*: In Ferdinand Schöningh's *Sammlung philosophischer Lesestoffe*, 9. *Bd.*, Paderborn, 1926.

§ 27. The introduction of the idea of formal ontology in the *Logische Untersuchungen*.

To the best of my knowledge, the idea of a formal ontology makes its first literary appearance in Volume I of my *Logische Untersuchungen*, [1] in connexion with the attempt to explicate systematically the idea of a pure logic — but not yet does it appear there under the *name* of formal ontology, which was introduced by me only later. The *Logische Untersuchungen* as a whole and, above all, the investigations in Volume II ventured to take up in a new form the old idea of an apriori ontology — so strongly interdicted by Kantianism and empiricism — and attempted to establish it, in respect of concretely executed portions, as an idea necessary to philosophy.

The *Apriori of formal ontology* (*op. cit.*, in the final chapter of Volume I) turned out to be an Apriori connected inseparably with the *apophantic Apriori* (that of statement-significations); and this necessarily brought an awareness of the problem of how the inseparability should be understood. This problem of the relationship between formal ontology and apophantic logic, which has determined the course of our present investigation, is not yet propounded in the *Logische Untersuchungen*. It may be of use to trace the motivation that led to the statements in the chapter just mentioned, and then to let the chapter itself take up the word. The fresh clearing up of what is set forth there all too briefly will involve critical limitations and essential developments, which will bring us appreciably nearer to the goal of our present investigation. /

<76> #### *a.* The first constitutional investigations of categorial objectivities, in the *Philosophie der Arithmetik*.

I had already acquired the definite direction of regard to the formal and a first understanding of its sense by my *Philosophie der Arithmetik* (1891), [2] which, in spite of its immaturity as a first book, presented an initial attempt to go back to the spontaneous activities of collecting and counting, in which collections

[1] *Author's note*: *Logische Untersuchungen, I. Band, Prolegomena zur reinen Logik* ["Prolegomena to pure Logic"], first edition, 1900.

[2] *Author's note:* It is a mere literary elaboration of my Halle habilitation essay (1887), of which a fragment, *Über den Begriff der Zahl* [*On the Concept of Number*], appeared in order to satisfy the academic requirement but was not offered for sale.

("sums", "sets") and cardinal numbers are given in the manner characteristic of something that is being generated originaliter, and thereby to gain clarity respecting the proper, the authentic, sense of the concepts fundamental to the theory of sets and the theory of cardinal numbers. It was therefore, in my later terminology, a phenomenologico-constitutional investigation; and at the same time it was the first investigation that sought to make "categorial objectivities" of the first level and of higher levels (sets and cardinal numbers of a higher ordinal level [1]) understandable on the basis of the "constituting" intentional activities, as whose productions they make their appearance originaliter, accordingly with full originality of their sense. It can be seen a priori that, as often as these spontaneous actions are alike in form, the formations produced by them must also be, correlatively, alike in form. Therefore, if the concepts, set and cardinal number, are fashioned purely and with the broadest universality, no part of the material contents (the what-contents) of collected elements or counted units can enter into that universality; the material contents must remain variable with absolute freedom — which obviously corresponds thoroughly to the intention of the theories of sets and cardinal numbers. The formalness of these disciplines lies, then, in this relationship to "*any objectivity whatever*", "*anything whatever*", with a most empty universality, a universality that leaves every material determination indeterminately optional. Their fundamental concepts, however, are (in my later terminology) syntactical formations *in forma*, syntactical derivative forms of the empty Something.

It was a matter of course that, in my continued investigations, which embraced the whole of formal mathematics [2] and / aimed <77>
ultimately at a "theory of deductive systems", at the forms of deductive sciences as deductive, I went on forthwith to regard all formal mathematics under the unitary aspect of a science that has to do essentially with derivative formations of anything-whatever, and that therefore has the common basis for all its

[1] *Author's note:* With express reference to this work and citing the legal person as another example, Benno Erdmann, in his *Logik* (*I. Bd.*, 1st edition, 1892, p. 101), introduced the term "*Gegenstände hoherer Ordnung* [objects of a higher order]".

[2] *Author's note:* See the preface to *Philosophie der Arithmetik*. [*Cf.* also Farber, *op. cit.*, p. 25.]

disciplines, giving them an essential mutual coherence, in the empty region anything-whatever.

b. The way of the *"Prolegomena"* from formal apophantics to formal ontology.

We shall now consider the path that led, in the last chapter of the *"Prolegomena zur reinen Logik"*, from the systematic explication of the sense of a formal apophantic logic to formal ontology. The guiding idea in the case of the former discipline was that of the apriori theory of science, with its research directed exclusively to the Objective-ideal content of the sciences, a content that (no matter how it arose from subjective producings) is present ⟨in the case of each science⟩ as a system of true propositions, a unity of theory. More particularly, my preferential regard was directed from the beginning to the *theoretically explanatory* (*nomological, deductive*) sciences and to the *"unity of systematically perfected theory"* [1], of *"theory in the strict sense"*. It was therefore a question of the Apriori of theory as such, *understood in this manner*, and with a formal universality that leaves undetermined every material particularity of the objects or object-provinces to which a theory relates. Now, as a task for such a formal logic, there arose first of all the bringing out of the constituent concepts pertaining to the essence of a theory as such. This led [2] to the concepts, proposition (judgment) and concept, and to all the concepts that concern the structure of judgments, simple and complex, and naturally also to the concept of truth. This group of concepts was called the group of *"signification-categories"*. With them were contrasted, as correlative concepts appertaining to logical science, the group of *"formal object-categories"*: the concepts *object*, predicatively formed affair-complex, unity, plurality, cardinal number, relation, connexion, and so forth —
<78> all these concepts being kept free from the particularity of / the cognition-material.[3] In that connexion the task of determining

[1] *Author's note:* "*Prolegomena*", § 63, p. 232. [(*Cf.* Farber, *op. cit.*, p. 140.]

[2] *Author's note:* [*Op. cit.*,] § 67, 1st edition, pp. 243 ff.; pp. 242ff. in the 2nd edition, where only a few phrases have been altered. [*Cf.* Farber, *op. cit.*, pp. 142f.]

[3] *Author's note:* The concept of category and the related concept of "analytic" or formal laws as contrasted with synthetic or material ones, the difference between sensuous and categorial intuition, and so forth, were dealt with in comprehensive investigations, in the second volume of the *Logische Untersuchungen*. See particularly: *I. Teil, 3. Unters.*, § 11; and *II. Teil, 6. Unters.*, the entire *2. Abschnitt*, on "sensuousness and understanding". [*Cf.* Farber, *op. cit.*, pp. 293f. and 448–488.]

the appertinent *laws* was then [1] discussed; and the laws were *differentiated according to the same two groups* of categories, the signification-categories and the object-categories. *By that very procedure, formal logic was characterized* with the utmost sharpness as *both* an *apophantics* and an *apriori formal theory of objects.* It includes, as follows from the further exposition, not only syllogistics, as related to the field of ideal significations, but also the theory of cardinal numbers, the theories of ordinal and quantitative numbers[2], and likewise, naturally, all of formal quantity-theory, the theory of combinations and permutations, and other such theories.

[1] *Author's note: "Prolegomena"*, § 68. [*Cf.* Farber, *op. cit.*, p. 245.]
[2] *Author's note: op. cit.*, p. 25).

CHAPTER 3.

Theory of deductive systems and theory of multiplicities.

§ 28. THE HIGHEST LEVEL OF FORMAL LOGIC: THE THEORY OF DEDUCTIVE SYSTEMS; CORRELATIVELY, THE THEORY OF MULTIPLICITIES.

But, in consideration of the fact that a completely novel type of *mathematical analysis* had shot up in a mighty theoretical-technical development during the nineteenth century, and because of the need of making clear the still utterly confused logical sense of this analysis, I saw yet a third and highest task for a formal logic or formal theory of science. It is announced, in the title of § 69 [1], as the *theory of possible forms of theories* or (correlatively) the *theory of multiplicities*.

Since the concept of theory (according to what is said in the preceding section of the present essay) was intended to be understood in the pregnant sense — in conformity with the nomological or deductive sciences — that is to say, as ⟨the concept of⟩ a systematic connexion of propositions in the form of a system-
<79> atically / unitary deduction, a beginning was found here for a theory of deductive systems or, in other words, a logical discipline relating to the deductive sciences as deductive and considered as theoretical *wholes*. The earlier level of logic had taken for its theme the pure forms of all significational formations that, as a matter of apriori possibility, can occur *within* a science: judgment-forms (and the forms of their elements), argument-forms, proof-forms — correlatively (on the objective side): any objects whatever, any set and any set-relationship whatever; any combinations, ordered sets, quantities, or the like, with their appertinent formal essential relationships and connexions. Now, however, *judgment-systems in their entirety* become the theme — the systems, each of which makes up the unity of a possible deductive theory, a ⟨possible⟩ "theory in the strict sense" [2]. As

[1] *Author's note:* "*Prolegomena*", p. 247.

[2] *Author's note:* This is what is meant by the word "theory" as first introduced (*op. cit.*, § 64) and throughout.

the concept of a totality of objects (a concept understood throughout as formally universal), there appears here that which mathematics, without any explicative determination of its sense, has in mind under the name "*Mannigfaltigkeit* [multiplicity]". It is the form-concept of the province belonging to a deductive science, this science being thought of as a systematic or total unity of theory. I shall repeat here the strict characterization of the idea of a formal theory of theory-forms — correlatively, a formal theory of multiplicities. I cannot improve on it; but we must have its content in mind.

> "The objective correlate of the concept of a possible theory, determined only in its form, is the concept of *any possible province of cognition that would be governed by a theory having such a form*. Such a province, however, the mathematician (in his sphere) calls a *multiplicity*. It is a province, then, that is determined solely by the circumstance that it comes under a theory having such a *form*: the circumstance, in other words, that, among the Objects belonging to the province, *certain* connexions are possible, which come under *certain* fundamental laws having such and such a *determinate form* (here the only determinig condition). In respect of their matter, the Objects remain completely indeterminate — the mathematician, to indicate this, prefers to speak of "*Objects of thinking*". Thus they are determined, neither directly as individual or specific singularities, nor indirectly by their intrinsic [*innern*[1]] species or genera, but exclusively by the *form* / of the connexions ascribed to them. These connexions <80>
> themselves are accordingly as little determined in respect of content as the Objects connected; only their form is determined, namely by the form [2] of the elementary laws assumed to hold good for them: And these laws determine, then, both the province [or rather the province-form] [3] and the theory that can be built or, stated more correctly, the *theory-form*. In the theory of multiplicities "+", for example, is not the sign of numerical addition but the sign of any connexion whatever for which laws of the *form* "$a+b=b+a$", and so forth, hold good. The multiplicity is determined by the circumstance that the Objects of thinking that belong to it make possible these "operations", and others that can be proved to be compatible a priori with these.
>
> "The *most universal idea of a theory of multiplicities* is the idea of a science that develops in a determinate manner the essential types of possible theories [and correlative provinces] [4] and explores the manners in which those types are interrelated conformably to laws. All actual theories, then, are specializations or singularizations of corresponding theory-forms; just as all theoretically treated provinces of cognition are *single* multiplicities. If the relevant formal theory has been actually developed within the theory of multiplicities, then all the deductive theoretical work

[1] *Translator's note:* Changed to *materialen* (material) in the second edition.
[2] *Translator's note:* Changed to the plural in the second edition.
[3] *Translator's note:* Inserted in the second edition.
[4] *Translator's note:* Inserted in the second edition.

necessary to the building of all actual theories with the same form has been done."

So far, the "*Prolegomena*" ([§ 70, first edition,] pp. 249f.).

The new superordinate concept appertaining to the discipline here in question would therefore be: *form of a deductive theory*, or of a "deductive system". Naturally it is founded on the categorial concepts belonging to the lower level. Besides the task of formally defining that concept, there are the endless tasks, not only of differentiating the forms subsumed under it, of projecting, in their explicity systematic developed state, possible forms of deductive theories, but also of recognizing various deductive theory-forms of this sort as singularities subsumed under higher theoretical form-universalities, of differentiating in a systematic theory the particular determinate forms subsumed under each of those higher form-universalities — and ultimately under the highest idea itself, that of any theory-form, any deductive theory, whatever.

§ 29. The theory of multiplicities and the formalizing reduction of the nomological sciences.

The sense of these tasks was clarified more particularly [1] by
‹81› showing that the modern / mathematical theory of multiplicities and, ultimately, the whole of modern formal analysis are already a realization — partial, to be sure, but in process of living development — of this idea of a science of possible deductive systems. Precisely with that demonstration there was acquired for the first time an understandable and radically evident explication of the sense of modern formal analysis, which (taken in its full breadth) actualizes the Leibnizian idea of a *mathesis universalis* — just as the explicated sense of logic at its highest level, the universal logic of deductive systems, is at the same time a necessary explication of the sense that Leibniz had in mind.

Freely repeating the "elucidations" presented in the aforesaid § 70 [2], let us point out here that any nomologically explanatory theoretical science — for example, Euclidean geometry (as Euclid himself understood it, as the theory of intuited world-

[1] *Author's note: Op. cit.*, § 70.

[2] *Translator's note:* The heading of the section may be translated: "Elucidations pertaining to the idea of the pure theory of multiplicities".

space) — can be reduced to a theory-form. Naturally this is done by that peculiarly logical universalization called "formalization", as a result of which all the materially determinate What-contents of the concepts — in the case of geometry, all the specifically spatial contents — are converted into indeterminates, modes of the empty "anything-whatever". Consequently the materially determinate system of geometry becomes changed into an exemplary system-*form*: To each geometrical truth a truth-*form* corresponds; to each geometrical argument or proof, an argument-*form* or a proof-*form*. The determinate *object-province* made up of spatial data becomes the *form of a province*; it becomes, as the mathematician says, a *multiplicity*. It is not just any multiplicity whatever (that would be the same as any set whatever); nor it is the *form*, "any infinite set whatever". On the contrary, it is a set whose peculiarity consists only in the circumstance that it is thought of with empty-formal universality, as "a" province determined by the complete set of Euclidean postulate-forms — that is to say, determined in a deductive discipline having a *form* derived from Euclidean space-geometry by formalization.

§ 30. MULTIPLICITY-THEORY AS DEVELOPED BY RIEMANN AND HIS SUCCESSORS.

The great advance of modern mathematics, particularly as developed by Riemann and his successors, consists not in its having merely made clear to itself the possibility of going back in this manner to the form of a deductive system (that is, to the particular *forms* of deductive sciences), starting from geometry and then from other de facto sciences, / but rather in its having <82>
also gone on to view *such system-forms themselves as mathematical Objects*, to alter them freely, universalize them mathematically, and particularize the universalities — not, however, by obeying the rules for differentiating the species of a genus according to the Aristotelian tradition (such a differentiating being meaningless here), but rather in conformity with the superordinations and subordinations that present themselves in the province of the formal. To be sure, the usual locutions were and are unclear: Mathematicians talk, not about the categorial *form* ⟨of⟩ space,

but about *"Euclidean space"*.[1] In referring to universalizations, they talk about *n*-dimensional spaces, about Riemannian and Lobachevskian spaces, instead of about universalizations of that categorial *form* ("three-dimensional Euclidean multiplicity"), which yield *forms* of "multiplicity"-types having *n* dimensions and further defined thus and so in respect of form. Just as unclearly, they talk about axioms, instead of about axiom-forms, and then go on to speak of theorems, proofs, and so forth, in referring to a formally universal deduction in which *forms* of principles are presupposed and the theorem-*forms* included in the principle-forms are derived — in *forms* of arguments and proofs. This lack of differentiation, which was first removed by the evident (but not everywhere heeded) demonstrations in the designated sections of the *"Prolegomena"*, has caused much confusion among mathematicians and even among logicians under their misguidance; on the other hand it has provoked mistaken objections on the part of philosophers — for the genius of mathematics was right, as always, about the matters at issue, even though its logical self-understanding was faulty.

§ 31. The pregnant concept of a multiplicity — correlatively, that of a "deductive" or "nomological" system — clarified by the concept of "*definiteness*".

Mathematicians went on in the above-characterized direction without restriction. Unconcerned about theoretical sciences
‹83› that were already given, / they freely constructed "multiplicities" (forms of multiplicities) or, correlatively, forms of deductive sciences. To be sure, geometry and the Euclidean ideal evinced therein, did indeed provide ultimate guidance — as they had in antiquity and throughout the whole subsequent development of mathematics. The tendency toward a distinctive version of the mathematical concept of the multiplicity (and therefore toward one particular aim in the theory of multiplicities) was determined

[1] *Author's note:* We must not be led astray here by the Kantian concept of the space-form, a concept that concerns the regional form belonging to actual Nature and to any possible Nature. Here we are dealing with purely analytic forms, "categorial" forms belonging to objects and judgments and abstracted by completely emptying out all their material contents. "The form space", in the Kantian sense, is the space of Euclid's geometry, of space-geometry *per se*. This "space-form" is itself a singularity subsumed under the analytic form "Euclidean multiplicity".

by the Euclidean ideal. I attempted to give that version concrete formulation in the *concept of the definite multiplicity*.

The hidden origin of this concept, which, so it seems to me, has continually guided mathematics from within, is as follows. If the *Euclidean ideal* were actualized[1], then the whole infinite system of space-geometry could be derived from the irreducible finite system of axioms by purely syllogistic deduction (that is to say, according to the principles of the lower level of logic); and thus the *apriori essence of space could become fully disclosed in a theory*. The transition to form then yields the form-idea of any multiplicity that, conceived as subject to an axiom-system with the *form* derived from the Euclidean axiom-system by formalization, could be *completely explained nomologically*, in a deductive theory that would be (as I usually expressed it in my Göttingen lectures) "equiform" with geometry. If a multiplicity is conceived from the start, with indeterminate universality, as a multiplicity defined by such a system of forms of axioms — if it is conceived as determined exclusively thereby — then the wholly determinate system of the forms belonging to the theorems and component theories, and ultimately the whole *science-form* necessarily valid for such a multiplicity, can be derived by pure deduction. Naturally all the materially concrete multiplicities subject to axiom-systems that, on being formalized, turn out to be equiform are multiplicities that have the same deductive science-form in common; in their relationship to it, these multiplicities themselves are equiform.

In this connexion we are confronted with the following *problem*: Just what is it that, *purely formally*, characterizes a self-contained system of axioms as "*definite*", as a system by which actually a "*multiplicity*" *in the pregnant sense* would be defined? / For, as I <84> recognized, the intention of this concept includes a hidden intentional sense. Multiplicity meant properly the *form-idea of an infinite object-province for which there exists the unity of a theoretical explanation* or, in other words, the unity of a *nomological science*. The form-ideas, "theoretically explainable province" (province of a deductive science) and "definite system of axioms", are equivalent.

[1] *Author's note:* That is to say, the ideal suggested to mathematicians by the system-form of the *Elements*, though not formulated by Euclid himself.

It should be noted here that, to be sure, *every* formally defined system of axioms has an infinity of deducible consequences. But the idea of a *"nomological science"*, or correlatively the idea of an *infinite province* (in mathematico-logical parlance, a multiplicity) governable by an explanatory nomology, includes the idea that there is no truth about such a province that is not deducibly included in the "fundamental laws" of the corresponding nomological science — just as, in the *ideal Euclid*, there is no truth about space that is not deducibly included in the "complete" system of space-axioms. When, from such considerations of the peculiar nature of a nomological province, I went on to formalization, I obtained the distinctive characteristic of a *multiplicity-form in the pregnant sense* — that is: a multiplicity-form that can be explained nomologically. Such a multiplicity-form is defined, *not by just any formal axiom-system*, but by a *"complete"* one. Reduced to the precise form appropriate to the concept of the definite multiplicity, that implies:

The axiom-system formally defining such a multiplicity is distinguished by the circumstance that any proposition (proposition-form, naturally) that can be constructed, in accordance with the grammar of pure logic, out of the concepts (concept-forms) occuring in that system, is either "true" — that is to say: an analytic (purely deducible) consequence of the axioms — or "false" — that is to say: an analytic contradiction —; *tertium non datur.*

Naturally this raises extremely significant problems. How can one know a priori that a province (for example space, in respect of the spatial shapes belonging to it) is a nomological province, and that one's list of immediately evident space-axioms comprehends the essence of space completely and is therefore sufficient for a nomology? And then above all, when carrying out a pure formalization or when freely constructing forms of multiplicities, how can one know, how can one prove, that a system of axioms is definite, is a "complete" system?

Throughout the present exposition I have used the expression "complete system of axioms", which was not mine originally but
‹85› / derives from Hilbert. Without being guided by the philosophico-logical considerations that determined my studies, Hilbert arrived at his concept of completeness (naturally quite inde-

pendently of my still-unpublished investigations); he attempts, in particular, to complete a system of axioms by adding a seperate "axiom of completeness". The above-given analyses should make it evident that, even if the inmost motives that guided him mathematically were inexplicit, they tended essentially in the same direction as those that determined the concept of the definite multiplicity. In any case, it seems to me not unimportant even today (and not least important for the philosophic logician) to clarify, in accordance with the above-attempted trains of thought, the deep sense of a *nomology* and of a *definite (nomological) multiplicity*.

The concept of the definite multiplicity served me originally to a different purpose, namely to clarify the logical sense of the computational transition through the "imaginary" and, in connexion with that, to bring out the sound core of Hermann Hankel's renowned, but logically unsubstantiated and unclear, "principle of the permanence of formal laws".[1] My questions were: Under what conditions can one operate freely, in a formally defined deductive system (a formally defined "multiplicity"), with concepts that, according to the definition of the system, are imaginary? When can one be sure that deductions that involve such an operating, but yield propositions free from the imaginary, are indeed "correct" — that is to say, *correct consequences of the defining forms of axioms*? How far does the possibility extend of "enlarging" a "multiplicity", a well-defined deductive system, to make a new one that contains the old one as a "part"? The answer is as follows: If the systems are "definite", then calculating with imaginary concepts can never lead to contradictions. Without referring to these problems, I gave a detailed description of the concept of the definite in my *Ideen*, p. 135, [2] (on the basis of a double lecture for the *Göttinger Mathematische Gesellschaft*, Winter Semester, 1901–1902). In the first volume of the *Logische Untersuchungen*, which I projected as really no more than an introduction to the phenomenological investigations in the second volume, I abstained from pursuing questions of the theory of multiplicities any further; and therefore the references to the concept of the definite and to the imaginary — the concluding theme of my old philosophico-mathematical studies — are lacking.

§ 32. THE HIGHEST IDEA OF A THEORY OF MULTIPLICITIES: A UNIVERSAL NOMOLOGICAL SCIENCE OF THE FORMS OF MULTIPLICITIES.

When mathematicians proceeded, with mathematical freedom, to define forms of multiplicities and to do so exclusively by *forms* of propositions conceived as holding good for them, / they <86>

[1] *Translator's note: Cf.* Hermann Hankel, *Theorie der komplexen Zahlen* [*Theory of Complex Numbers*], 1867.

[2] *Translator's note:* English translation, pp. 204f.

ran into an infinity of multiplicity-forms. Each multiplicity defined by a system of axiom-forms presented them with the task of explicitly constructing the form of the corresponding deductive science itself; and the execution of the task involved precisely the same work of constructive deduction that is done in a concrete deductive science with concepts having material contents. It was impossible and pointless to construct divers forms of this kind unselectively, since, by viewing the forms produced from the factually existing sciences, one could see forthwith that the forms themselves of deductive systems combine to make up deductive systems. At this point there arises, therefore, the *idea* of an all-embracing task: to strive toward a highest theory, which would comprise all possible forms of theories (correlatively, all possible forms of multiplicities) as mathematical particularizations — accordingly, as *deducible*.

§ 33. Actual formal mathematics and mathematics of the rules of the game.

The danger of becoming lost in an excessive symbolism, such as has greatly hindered uncovering the properly logical sense of the new formal mathematics and kept its latently impelling total intention from evolving in the form of a comprehended task, is a danger that can be avoided only if the idea of this mathematics is built up — after the fashion of the expositions in the *Logische Untersuchungen* — within the total complex of the idea of a *logic*. Then this mathematics is recognized as an all-embracing theory of theory-forms (each closed as a system) and, correlatively, as an all-embracing theory of the possible forms of multiplicities. Thus it appears as the *highest level of logical analytics*, founded on the essentially preceding lower level, which (in view of the results of the fourth *Logische Untersuchung*) is divided into theory of pure forms and theory of validity (consequence-logic).

At first the mathematicians, entangled in their current theoretico-technical interests and cares, were little receptive to fundamental logical analyses such as are instituted in the *Logische Untersuchungen*; and only recently have they begun to note, in their own manner, something of this separation of levels. They are gradually seeing that a formal mathematics of the higher level, the multiplicity-level, can never enable us to do

without the specifically logical categories / (signification- <87>
categories and object-categories) and the actual axioms relating to these. To be sure, even now most mathematicians do not yet see that, logically considered, the arithmetic of cardinal numbers has an existence of its own, and that the same is true of the arithmetic of ordinal numbers, the arithmetic of quantitative numbers, and the rest.[1] And, on the other hand, they do not yet see that a theory of "real numbers" (which belongs in the formal mathematics of the higher level) can furnish none of those independently constructable disciplines from its own resources. Naturally the deceiving fact here is that we are dealing with equiform deductive disciplines, and that technically therefore it would be pointless to build each of them explicitly by itself, instead of deriving the relevant form of theories systematically from the common forms of axioms, once for all, at a higher level of formalization. Nevertheless, as already said, one can never spare bringing out in particular their respective *fundamental concepts*, within the complex of logical categories, and the *actual axioms* relating to those concepts.

This is true even if, instead of building a mathematical analysis *itself* or a serious theory of multiplicities itself, one builds only a *discipline comprising deductive games with symbols*, which does not become an actual theory of multiplicities until one regards the game-symbols as signs for actual Objects of thinking — units, sets, multiplicities — and bestows on the rules of the game the significance of *law-forms* applying to these multiplicities. Even in playing a game one actually judges, one actually collects and counts, one draws actual conclusions, and so forth.

§ 34. Complete formal mathematics identical with complete logical analytics.

The systematic order in building a full and entire "*mathesis universalis*" — that is to say, a formal mathematics that does not float in the air but stands on its foundations and is inseparably one with them — is naturally a great problem. According to our showings, however, it is none other than the problem of a full and entire *logical analytics*, a problem already implicit in the sense of the expositions in the *Logische Untersuchungen*. But then it

[1] *Author's note:* See the preface to my *Philosophie der Arithmetik*, [p. VIII].

is clear that an all-embracing theory of multiplicities, with its <88> free manner of defining this or that / form of multiplicities by forms of axioms or by the forms of any propositions that presupposedly hold good, must indeed have at its command the fundamental proposition-forms (which make their appearance systematically in the theory of judgment-forms) and the logical categories involved in those fundamental forms — must have *all* those forms and categories at its command, and must finally become conscious of what that signifies. In other words, it must *base itself consciously on a preceding theory of the forms of judgments* (categorial significations). Precisely here it is easy to be led astray by an inclination that arises from supposed needs for greater exactness: namely the inclination to put in the place of the actual theory of multiplicities its symbolic analogue — that is, to define multiplicities in terms of mere rules of the game.

In the definition of a multiplicity we must not define merely in terms of signs and calculational operations — for example: "It shall be allowed to manipulate the given signs in such a manner that the sign $b + a$ can always be substituted for $a + b$". Rather we must say: "There shall obtain among the *objects* belonging to the multiplicity (conceived at first as only empty Somethings, "Objects of thinking") a certain *combination-form* with the *law*-form $a + b = b + a$" — where *equality* has precisely the sense of actual equality, such as belongs to the categorial logical forms. Which logical categories are to be introduced by definitions is a matter of choice, though the choice is restricted by the requirement of non-contradiction; but in any case they must be meant, and designated, as those entirely determinate categories.

§ 35. Why only deductive theory-forms can become thematic within the domain of *mathesis universalis* as universal analytics.

a. Only deductive theory has a purely analytic system-form.

There is need of still another important supplementation, which will be made with critical reference to the exposition in the "*Prolegomena*":

By the ascent to the systematic theory of theories and multiplicities, the *problems of entireties* had been introduced into logic,[1] so far as they can be set as *formal* problems. / Whether this <89> completes formal logic (analytics in the broadest sense), as focused exclusively on the all-embracing field of signification- and object-forms, is admittedly something that should have been previously investigated or shown in that context. The fact that the whole inquiry into the sense of a "pure" logic (*sc.* as analytics) was guided by the ideal of specifically theoretical science — that is to say, nomological science (as exemplified by geometry and theoretical physics) — imposed an initial restriction in the "*Prolegomena*" that had not been justified: precisely the restriction of the universal concept, science as *theory in the broadest sense* (the self-contained system of propositions making up any science whatever), to the *particular* concept of *deductive theory* (nomologically "explanatory" science). Nevertheless, when one considers the *problem* that was involved and is now to be expressly formulated — the problem, namely, of what characterizes the form of a province and, correlatively, the form of a theory in the *broadest* sense — the restriction may admit of some justification after the fact.

To begin with, it should be obvious that, when we practise formalization on sciences of the type represented by psychology or phenomenology, or by history, and then ask what combines all the emerging proposition-forms to make up the unity of a system-form — or ask to what extent those forms, *as forms*, have at all the formal unity of a system — we come upon nothing

[1] *Author's note:* It is a fault of the exposition in the *Logische Untersuchungen* that this thought was not made central by repeated *emphasis*, despite the fact that it continuously determines the sense of the whole exposition. A more serious fault of the "*Prolegomena*" is, by the way, the following:

In connexion with the concept of truth the modalities of truth are not mentioned, and probability is not cited as one of them. When they are taken into account, an enlargement of formal logic becomes necessary: to the effect that, as universal formal possibilities, modal variants of judging and of judgments enter into certainty- or truth-logic — because any such variant can enter into the predicational content of the judgment and, when it does, it must not be regarded as extra-formal. In other words, only the content that goes beyond anything-whatever is the "matter" of judgments, in the sense proper to formal logic; all the forms in which one judges — not only with certainty but also in the mode of possibility, or in other modalities — belong to anything-whatever. A kindred enlargement results from taking into consideration the fact that emotions and volitions also bring modalities of anything-whatever, which are introduced in the same manner into the doxic sphere. (On this last point *cf. Ideen*, pp. 243ff. [English translation, pp. 531ff.]; also § 50, pp. 135 ff., *infra*.)

but the empty universality, that such a science is an open infinity of propositions that hang together *by virtue of their objects* and can be united with one another at least as analytically non-contradictory. In respect of their theoretical type, these sciences are set apart *essentially* from sciences that are "nomological" in our exactly defined sense.[1] In other words: Theirs is not the
<90> system-form of a definite / deductive theory; correlatively, their provinces are not definite multiplicities. Obviously we can become cognizant of the principle of *unity* in such sciences *only by going beyond the analytico-logical form. The system-form of the deductive theory*, on the other hand, is *itself a formation belonging in the analytic sphere.* Thus *deductive* or *nomological sciences are characterized by the fact that their system-principle is purely analytic.* The deductive theory has a systematic unity-form that belongs *within the province of formal logic itself*, one that can be constructed a priori in logic itself — and, more particularly, in its highest discipline, the theory of multiplicities — as part of the total system of those forms of deductive systems that are possible a priori.

b. The problem of when a system of propositions has a system-form characterizable as analytic.

Thus we have learned something very significant for the understanding of logic. It was still lacking in the *Logische Untersuchungen.* A correct exposition there would have omitted every anticipatory reference to the ideal of "theoretical" or "nomologically explanatory" science — an ideal that can by no means be accepted for every science. Rather, in the course of explicating the sense of a logic as a theory of science (and, more particularly, a theory with an exclusive regard for the formal moment in the result-components, those moreover of *any* science, chosen quite at will), a correct exposition would have brought out the corresponding *problem.*

This problem can be briefly outlined in the following manner. Any science whatever is a multiplicity of truths — not haphazardly thrown together, but combined and relating in any case to a unitary province. *When* does the whole that comprises the infinite multiplicity of propositions making up a science have a

[1] ***Author's note:*** See § 31, [pp. 94 ff.,] *supra.*

systematic unity-form that can be constructed a priori, on the basis of a finite number of pure axiom-forms, *by means of logical-categorial concepts? When* is the group of axiom-forms that defines a theory-form *definite* and the province-form, correlatively, a *"mathematical" or "definite" multiplicity*? If this condition is fulfilled, the unity-form of the whole is the system-form of a "deductive", a "theoretically explanatory", science.

Mathesis universalis (from now on the name is always equivalent to logical analytics) is, *for apriori reasons, a realm / of* <91>
universal construction; aside from the operative elements, it is entirely a realm of operational formations, which, despite their infinity, can be governed a priori. In it occur, as the highest level, the *deductive* system-forms and *no others*. Precisely this is the answer to the question of when a science or a scientifically closed group of propositions has, according to purely analytic (mathematical) principles, a unitary, mathematically constructable, system-structure.

It is to be noted that this question belongs only in a certain sense to formal analytics. About the name science formal analytics and we ourselves, so far as we have progressed up to now, know only this much: It means a certain universe of propositions that arose somehow from theoretical effort and have a systematic order wherein a certain universe of objects becomes determined. Thus logic, as analytics, is *not equipped with any ready-made distinction among sciences*, like the usual distinctions between concrete (descriptive) and abstract ("explanatory") sciences or any other distinction that may be proposed. By its own resources it can attain only the cognition that, conceived with formal universality, an open plurality, or "multiplicity", of objects is formally conceivable as having *this* particular determination: that it is a definite mathematical multiplicity and that, correlatively, the propositions conceived with formal universality as jointly holding good for it have a constructional (deductive) system-form.

On our present course, which, pushing far beyond the aim of the *Logische Untersuchungen*, advances toward an intentional explication of the idea of a theory of science, analytics has taken its place as a first stage of the explication; but there remains the open problem of what, beyond an analytics, can still be aspired to a priori under the name of ⟨theory of⟩ science — with a "formal" universality that no longer has the sense of being analytically formal.

§ 36. Retrospect and preliminary indication of our further tasks.

After this clearing up of the concluding part of the "*Prolegomena*" (a clarification that, in the present chapter, has indeed been also a supplementation and critical limitation), I believe that even now, almost three decades later, I can uphold that essay in its essentials, which still have not exercised their full effect. But it has also become apparent that, in one respect, we have made essential progress by our present investigation,
<92> namely / in that we were able to establish, in Chapter I, the fundamental triple stratification of logic, or the new separation of the formal "logic of non-contradiction" from the formal "logic of truth". On the other hand, we were still behind the *Logische Untersuchungen* in Chapter I, since consideration of the results obtained in that earlier essay has now required us to recognize a higher level of problems, the aforesaid entirety-problems or "multiplicity"-problems, and to regard them as the theme of a higher discipline, though one that is still formally logical (analytic). We already anticipate the possibility of *separating a stratum pertaining to non-contradiction and a stratum pertaining to truth also at this highest level*, and in precisely the sense previously established in detail. But we must first acquire the necessary preparation — by a detailed treatment of the problem from which we started, the problem of the *relationship between ontology and significational logic.* /

B. PHENOMENOLOGICAL CLARIFICATION OF THE TWO-SIDEDNESS OF FORMAL LOGIC AS FORMAL APOPHANTICS AND FORMAL ONTOLOGY. <93>

CHAPTER 4.

Focusing on objects and focusing on judgments.

§ 37. INQUIRY CONCERNING THE RELATIONSHIP BETWEEN FORMAL APOPHANTICS AND FORMAL ONTOLOGY; INSUFFICIENCY OF OUR CLARIFICATIONS UP TO NOW.

Let us return to our demonstration that the eidetic laws and possibly developed disciplines of the lower level are simultaneously and inseparably formal-ontological and apophantic, since they do indeed relate expressly not only to formal signification-categories but also to formal object-categories.[1] Naturally the very same is true of fully developed formal analytics, because *theory-forms*, according to their own sense, have as their correlates *objective multiplicities*. The consistently followed path of inquiry into the formal conditions for possible truth and finally for true science, the path starting from the *propositional* structure of a science (that is: from the significational side), led at the same time — precisely by virtue of the *sense-relation to objectivities that is involved in the propositions themselves* — to an all-embracing formal *ontology*, which at its highest level defines the name: theory of multiplicities.

We must now ask whether this essential double sense has already been made sufficiently intelligible. Is it already clear what this properly signifies: *to be focused sometimes on judgments as such and sometimes on objectivity as such*, with formal universality? Furthermore, is the / sense of a formal ontology, as <94>
contrasted with a material ontology, already transparent enough? (We do not say an ontology of realities, because we do not yet know what may fall under the second heading.) Is there not an objection to speaking at all of formal ontology? As a matter of fact, I felt difficulties on that score, even at the time of the *Logische Untersuchungen* and for a long time after. The greatly needed clarifications shall be our next task. In them we shall be assisted in part by insights that have already enabled us to make the three-fold division of analytics.

[1] *Author's note: Cf.* §§ 25 and 27, [pp. 78 f. and 86 ff., *supra*].

§ 38. Judgment-objects as such and syntactical formations.

Recalling at the same time our earlier exposition, [1] we can now ask: Can a *formal ontology* be at all distinguished from an apophantic logic, if only as the latter's correlate, yielded by a mere change of focus from propositions to objects?

The *province* of a formal ontology is said to be the "formal region" of the object as conceived universally; a formal ontology, therefore, should determine *objects* in apodictic truths and with the same formal universality that characterizes its province. When we look into the sphere ⟨of the universal category, object,⟩ and consider as examples no matter what single cases among determinable objects — perhaps this table here — we see that determination is effected first in the form belonging to *explication* of determinate single *properties* and then, at a higher level, in an unlimited sequence of new judgment-acts: acts in which new objects are brought in and *relative determinations* effected or *pluralities* are related to the same predicates in plural judgments; or else acts in which we judge universally, and *something universal* thus becomes the (higher) theme; and so forth. Here, in the course of our judicative determining, we are indeed directed to something objective: the table, whose objective sense, as a sense determined in respect of its content, leads to the different levels of materially filled concepts. But what if we wished to determine the table *purely* by concepts belonging to "formal ontology", like object, property, relationship, and plurality — that is to say, variational concepts pertaining to anything-whatever? Are these something other than *"categorial" concepts* — that is: concepts that have accrued through merely looking abstractively at the *syntactical forms* in which the object is apprehended at varying levels in syntactical actions, actions of judgment? /

<95> *In formal analytics*, then, *the object is thought of purely as an object of possible judgments* and purely as having the *judgment-forms* accruing to it through them; and, if that yields important results, precisely in the case of a thinking with apriori universality (whereas *in concreto* it would lead to ridiculously empty judgments), it does so because of the evidence that the free choice of syntactical fashionings is restricted, as long as the objects are possibly to exist in truth and, correlatively, the judgments are

[1] *Author's note:* See § 25, [pp. 78 f., *supra*].

possibly to be truths. The judgment-syntaxes, as formative, are governed a priori by laws that set forth conditions for possible truth. Naturally the forming done in the judgment (a forming from which all mathematical concepts in both the narrower and the narrowest sense — such as set, cardinal number, series, quantity, and multiplicity — also originate, though on the basis of judgment-formations of the highest level) is a forming executed, not upon the "transcendent" objects, but upon the objects *objectivated in the judgment itself*. So too, in the formal-apriori judgments of logic, the "empty core" Something (that is: the formal sense of the letters S, p, and so forth) is a component of the judgments themselves. How then have we gone beyond a formal judgment-theory? After all, do we not stand within the realm of formal judgment-theory whenever we make formal distinctions among judgment-objectivities?

§ 39. The concept of the judgment broadened to cover all formations produced by syntactical actions.

To be sure, in these considerations such activities as *collecting, counting, ordering, and combining mathematically*, have been accounted as *judgment-activities*; and their correlates have been accounted as judgment-formations. But is it not true that they are actually form-producing activities at different levels? Is it not true that their correlates are represented in predicative judgments themselves — judgments in the usual sense — by forms that no theory of the forms of judgments may ignore? We have already touched on this point: [1] Just as *property* designates a form that makes its first appearance non-selfsufficiently in the judgment and, on being "nominalized", yields the substrate-form property, so the *plural* makes its appearance in plural judging and, on being "nominalized", on being transformed into the object in the pre-eminent sense (the substrate, the "object-about-which"), yields the *set*. Here it is a matter of indifference, that one can collect and count without forthwith incorporating the produced formations into actual predications. Collecting and counting are "Objectivating" / ("doxic") activities like the <96>
predicative activities; they too, as believings, have doxic modalities — the same modalities that predicative activities

[1] *Author's note:* § 25, [pp. 78 f., *supra*].

have; they can be performed on the basis of any conceivable substrates (anything whatever), and consequently the formations produced by them are, in the same manner, ⟨exemplifications of⟩ formal categories.[1] Moreover the essential nature of these formations is such that all of them can be incorporated into predicative judgments and given additional forms in these. In an actually executed apophantics, as a theory of predicative judgments, *all the forms belonging to doxic "positings" and doxic posita* [*Sätze*] — all the forms that we ever call *formal-ontological* — must *also* occur in the course of that universal treatment of all apophantic forms which is demanded for a formal logic. But one must also heed this belonging-together ⟨that is, the circumstance that the above-mentioned non-predicative activities belong with the predicative activities⟩ and, on the other hand, this interconnexion ⟨between apophantic and ontological forms⟩ and not delimit apophantic logic in an inadequate fashion: as though, for example, set and the theory of sets, or cardinal number and the theory of cardinal numbers, were none of its concern.

§ 40. Formal analytics as a playing with thoughts, and logical analytics. The relation to possible application is part of the logical sense of formal mathesis.

The things just stated receive additional significance, however, when we take into account the *interest in cognizing*, which, as a ruling interest consistently directed to some province of cognition, incorporates into all doxic activities the intention aimed at cognition and, more particularly, cognition of the province in question. If our activities embody such an interest, we stand within the horizon of a science; and, in the case of a formally universal consideration, we stand within *logic*, whose two-sided theme is all possible sciences as such: on the subjective side, the possible forms of the actions productive of and cognitive of scientific cognitional formations; on the Objective side, these formations themselves. Logical analytics, as we have been conceiving it up to now, as purely Objective, naturally relates

[1] *Author's note:* Essentially the same statement was already made in my *Philosophie der Arithmetik*, p. 91. [*Cf.* Farber, *op. cit.*, p. 35.]

(with an abstractive one-sidedness) exclusively to the formations. But, as soon as we find ourselves within the frame indicated by the words "scientific *cognizing*" and "*province of cognition*", *every* sort of doxic activity is thought of necessarily as incorporated into the *predicatively* interconnected activities. Then, for example, one collects or counts, not for sport or because one is interested in it for any other non-epistemic reason, / but rather <97> in the interest of cognizing the province (for example, Nature): ultimately therefore in order to cognize, and *to determine predicatively* (apophantically), the collected elements or counted units as belonging to the province. *That is why logic*, which indeed is attentive exclusively to epistemic interests, those of science, *never speaks of anything but predicative judgments* — in which, however, the pluralities, the cardinal numbers, and so forth, make their appearance as *component formations* or are thought of as making their appearance in possible broader cognition-complexes.

A mathematics undergoing development in the manner characteristic of a special science, as an end in itself, may not care about such things: It may not concern itself with the fact that it is logic and logical method, that it must render service to cognition, that the formations it produces are called on to function as laws governing the forms of still-indeterminate cognition-complexes, pertaining to likewise indeterminate provinces of cognition. It need not care that the *relation to openly indeterminate ideally possible application belongs to its own sense as formal logic*: in such fashion, namely, that the sphere of this application is not restricted by any "cognition-material" and is thus a formal sphere. Accordingly it can remain indifferent to the fact that all the formations it produces have the sense of being called on to make their appearance within some *cognitional judgments* or other (which remain indeterminate in respect of their material) — as they do make their appearance in every case of actual application in "applied mathematics", since, for example, they function in theoretical physics as components of physical-scientific determinations. But the philosophic logician must care about these things. He cannot accept a mathematics conceived κατὰ μηδεμίαν συμπλοκήν, a mathematics that tears itself away from the idea of possible application and becomes an ingenious playing with thoughts — or even, as in the case of a mathematics developed merely calculatively, a playing with symbols that receive their sense from mere computational conventions. As a logician he must see that *formal mathematics is originally logical analytics*, and that consequently its own *logical* sense includes a sphere of cognitional functioning, established by the intention aimed at cognition — a sphere, that is to say, of possible *applications*, which, with all their indeterminateness, are part of the *mathematical sense*. And for this very reason we stand, as we have said, inside the sphere comprising apophantic judgments — in which, however, all mathematical formations find a place as components. /

<98> § 41. THE DIFFERENCE BETWEEN AN APOPHANTIC AND AN ONTOLOGICAL FOCUSING, AND THE PROBLEM OF CLARIFYING THAT DIFFERENCE.

If we now return to our difficulty, we find that the important insight brought us by this last exposition has obviously not removed it. The idea of formal logic and the idea of the "formal" are rigidly circumscribed by the doxic syntaxes, all of which can — and, from the standpoint of logic, must — enter as components into the syntactical unity of an *apophansis*, a judgment in the usual logical sense. To each cognition-objectivity, as a judgment-objectivity, there belongs a "categorial" form deriving from the κατηγορεῖν (or from its syntactical actions), a syntactical form. Formal logic determines objects with pure universality by that form. It is also true that nowhere but in the judgment does the empty concept Something make its appearance, the concept in which all objects are thought by logic. But does that signify that there is no difference whatever between *apophantic logic* and *formal ontology*; or that, because in making formal-ontological determinations we never step outside the judgment-sphere, the theme of formal object-theory is not objects after all, but judgments? Are the following not essentially different things: *being focused on judgments as one's theme* (and focused at the same time on the syntactical formations that make their appearance in the particular thematic judgment, with the sense of being judgment-components); and, on the other hand, being focused on *objects* and *their* syntactical forms — which, it is true, are thematic *in* the judging, but in such a manner that the judgments and *their* components are not thematic?

§ 42. Solution of this problem.

a. Judging directed, not to the judgment, but to the thematic objectivity.

We shall now attempt to clarify these two focusings and to justify originaliter the consequent distinction between apophantic logic (in the broadest sense) and formal ontology — a distinction, however, that is at the same time an equivalence, since it will remain true that the two disciplines, even down to the last detail, stand in perfect correlation throughout and, *for that reason*, must be held to be a single science.

Let us start from the fact that objects exist for us, and are what they are for us, exclusively as the objects of which we are at any time conscious: as objects / experienced (that is, perceived <99> and recollected) or as objects emptily objectivated but nevertheless meant believingly (as certain objects, uncertainly presumed objects, or the like), and thus somehow as objects meant in some modes or other of consciousness, including those belonging to the emotions and the will — regardless, moreover, of how such objects have acquired from our previous conscious living the sense that they now have for us. Here belong also the modes of consciousness proper to *thinking*, in the specific sense: the modes of comprehendingly judicative thinking, and naturally also those of "cognitive"-predicative thinking. Therefore, if we are busied with objects — and, in particular, if we are judging about them —, we stand inside our own consciousness; which is naturally not to say that our consciousness is what we are busied with, and most assuredly is not to say that those objects are nothing but states or processes of consciousness.

We need not give any transcendental philosophy here. We have only to explicate correctly what concerns us: at present, namely, that fact that, when we are judging, the relation to the object is effected in our judging itself. It must be noted in this connexion that the object can indeed be given already by experience, prior to the predicative judgment, but that the experiential judgment or the subsequent non-experiencing judgment that is nevertheless "based on experience" includes *in itself* either the experience (as the experiential judgment does) or (as the non-experiencing judgment "based on experience" does) a mode of consciousness derived somehow from the earlier experience and modifying it: and it is only by virtue of this inclusion that the judging, in its concreteness, is a judging about such and such. Now, in the current judging we have made a judgment; and we are well aware that the judgment made (or else being built member by member in the making activity) should not be confounded with the judging, the making activity itself.

We now note that this *"having the made judgment in the making of it"* is not at all the same as having that judgment *objectively*: as a *"theme"* and, in particular, as a *judgment-substrate*. In judging we are *directed*, not to the judgmeut, but to the *"objects-about-which"* (the substrate-objects) currently intended to, to the *predicates* (that is, the objectively determining moments) currently intended to, to the *relational complexes;* or, in causal judgments, we are directed to the *predicational affair-complexes* currently intended to as grounds and the correlative predicational affaircomplexes as consequences; and so forth. At any time, however, a *change of focus* is obviously possible, such that we make our *judgments*, their components, their connexions and relations, *the theme*. This happens in a new *judging at the second level*, a judging about judgments, a judging in which judgments /
<100> become objects undergoing determination. Naturally, without this change of focus we could not obtain any concept of the judgment or of the judgment-syntaxes belonging to it.

b. Identity of the thematic object throughout changes in the syntactical operations.

When focusing on no matter what *objects*, we perform judging operations having many forms, which vary according to circumstances. For example, if we have judged "S is p", we then can judge, while "nominalizing" and thereby giving a new form, "That S is p is regrettable", "— has its reasons", and so forth. Whereas originally S was the substrate-object and was determined as having the property p, now the substrate-object is "This, that S is p": the affair-complex which was indeed constituted before but was not then the object-about-which. The same operation, when exercised on p, changes it into the nominalized P, the P

that has become the judgment-substrate (the red, the quickness, or whatever it is). Accordingly these changes of form (syntactical changes), which are effected in the judging, do not in any respect alter the fact that we are directed to *something objective*. The new syntactical *forms* themselves make their appearance in the judgment as *forms shaping that which is objective*; though we, as directed to this itself, do not take them to be an intrinsic part of it. For example, we say: The same *predicatively formed affair-complex* is meant judgingly — only in different forms — as "S is *p*" and as "this, that S is *p*, . . ."; the same *property* is meant, now as the predicate "red" and again as the subject "this red".

The acts of identification performed here are syntheses that combine judgments with judgments, to make judgments of a higher level — syntheses with which the form "*the same*" enters in various manners (though often tacitly) into the significational contents. And so too in all other cases: for example, where "the same" plurality that was judged in the plural judging makes its appearance afterwards as the object "sum", as "this plurality", or the like. *In its essence the objective focusing, which is at all times an integral part of the judging itself*, is such that the judging makes these *identifications throughout changes of the judgment-modes* in which "the same" presents itself as differently formed. Precisely by this there becomes effected, throughout the judgment-concatenation, a *unitary determining* (and this, understood in the broadest sense, is after all what judging continuously is). No matter how much the determining may become — now and then and at different levels — a determining of nominalized substrates, it pertains ultimately to the / *lowest* and *primarily* ‹101›
thematic substrates (in the sciences, the objects belonging to their provinces); the determination of these substrates is the aim throughout all intermediary steps.

c. The types of syntactical object-forms as the typical modes of Something.

That which is objective and repeatedly identified throughout such courses of judgment (which, as relating to the unity of some thematic domain or other, effect a unity of determination) has, in respect of its possible categorial forms (*object-forms!*), a quite determinate set of types. They are the typical *modes of anything-*

whatever: as "property", relational complex, predicatively formed affair-complex, plurality, singularity, series, ordered set, and so forth. We call them [1] *derivative forms* of Something, of the fundamental formal category, object; and they are indeed derived from it — *by judging itself*, by all the doxic activities that determine the broader sense of judgment. *Property*, as a form, accrues originally in plain categorically determinative judgment, in the same way that, in collecting, *collection* originally accrues: naturally not as a really immanent psychic Datum, but as the intentional correlate of a positing. This correlate can then, in the course of a judicative determining, take on different judgment-syntaxes; and throughout the changes in these, as we have seen, it can become identified as the same property, the same predicatively formed affair-complex, the same collection, the same universality, and so forth.

d. The dual function of syntactical operations.

At first it is indeed confusing that *syntactical operations function dually*. On the one hand they function as *form-creating*: by creating objectivities that have different syntactical forms, the derivative forms of anything-whatever — which (*as* forms of anything) any conceivable object, having become the substrate (alone or with others), can take on in, and through the instrumentality of, the doxic action itself. On the other hand they function as the *changing* syntaxes that such a categorial objectivity (a substrate, a property, a relational complex, a species, or the like) can take on, and throughout whose changes it nevertheless remains identical, while functioning sometimes as a subject and sometimes as an Object, or sometimes as an original predicate and sometimes as a nominalized predicate, or sometimes as simply a predicatively formed affair-complex and sometimes as a predicatively formed affair-complex with the function of a / premise, <102> and so forth. It is easy to see that *all syntactical modes function in both manners* and that, in particular (as has already become important to us from the other side), all syntactical forms can enter into the form, "predicatively formed affair-complex", as components belonging to such an affair-complex itself. On the other hand, in the course of any more extensive syntactical

[1] *Author's note: Cf. Ideen*, [§ 11,] p. 24. [English translation, pp. 69f.]

activities that embrace it, the predicatively formed affair-complex can in turn receive (from outside, so to speak) a changing functional form, which is not taken to be an intrinsic moment of that complex itself. This form then belongs precisely within the predicatively formed affair-complex of a higher level, which is constituted by means of the new judging.

These relationships — intricate but, in their essential necessity, perfectly transparent — still do not in any respect alter what is most important for us here: *The judger is directed to something objective and, in being directed to it, he never has it otherwise than in some categorial* (or, as we also say, syntactical) *forms or other, which are therefore ontological forms.* Every new judgment in the coherent judgment-complex, every judgment-combination and ultimately the whole coherent complex as *one* judgment, only on a very high level, constitutes a new categorial objectivity.

e. Coherence of the judging by virtue of the unity of the substrate-object that is being determined. Constitution of the "concept" determining the substrate-object.

The progressive judging has *coherence* by virtue of the *unity* of one pervasive *"theme"*, in the first and most pregnant sense: the *substrate-objectivity* currently intended to, determination of which is the continual and final aim throughout the judging. Judging and again judging, the judger acquires for this objectivity the multiple "How it is", individually or universally; he acquires predicatively formed affair-complexes pertaining to it, in which it stands thus and so, and the like — ever new categorial objectivities into which the substrate-objectivity enters in consequence of his judgments, and which themselves become *relatively thematic* and thus in turn undergo determination; while at the same time, through them, the first substrate-objectivity, as the *ultimately thematic* one, becomes determined.

The judgment-process can progress as unitary *ad infinitum*; the substrate-objectivity can include infinities of single particulars within itself, as the sciences illustrate. For example, the yet-undetermined infinity of Nature / lies before the judger ‹103›
as a substrate for determination, when he goes on from mere experience to his judging endeavor. And then he constitutes the

determining formations, the new categorial fashionings of the substrate. All the various particular formations that he actively acquires in doing so have categorial coherence by virtue of the identity of the substrate-objectivity (itself constituted in a judging identification); and they progressively constitute for the substrate the *determining concept* accruing to it precisely from all these judicative performances — the current "How it is, all told", a concept always in progress, always being further fashioned, and also refashioned. For it must be taken into consideration that, in the course of actions of judging, convictions not only must become amplified, but also may undergo cancellation in particular: as "false" convictions, in whose place others then enter as the "correct" ones, determining the substrates in a new manner. Whether this happens on the basis of insight is beside the question for us here. It is enough that a process of fashioning the judgment-substrate which the judger "has in mind" takes place.

In this connexion it is to be emphasized that even ideas and differences among ideas belong to the unity of the production constituted in judging. I mention here, for example, such differences as that between "*Nature as it simply is*", as the idea of the true being of Nature or, equivalently, the idea of the concept completely determining Nature, as the concept that would be yielded in a (to be sure, impossible) complete and harmonized judging about Nature, and, on the other hand, *Nature as it is according to the judicative performance, which has gone so far and no farther, but which can be carried on without limit*, as the unity pertaining to the convictions acquired up to now. Within the proper sense-content of the judging directed to the unity of the yet-undetermined and to-be-determined province, the content that is being generated (and has been generated) in the judging itself, there lies the *idea of possible continuation of the determining categorial formings* — and likewise of possible consistent continuation of the aim at determining — *ad infinitum*. At first it lies therein implicitly as a horizon, which becomes predelineated as the judging actually goes onward and is drawn onward; but then, perhaps, it lies in a particular *judicial fashioning of the idea, as a categorial objectivity on a special level and having a special dignity*. And, in like manner, there lies within the sense-content

the first-mentioned idea of Nature: Nature "as it itself / is", and <104>
simply is — an idea that then enters into the idea of Nature as cognized currently by us and to such and such an extent: relatively and as a partial installment, subject moreover to possible correction. Evidently *"Nature itself"* thus acquires the value of a concept that is being constituted synthetically throughout the course of such partial installments (with their relative concepts of Nature), abandoned determinations being excluded and corrective ones inserted during the process: and, as so constituted, this concept is the categorial correlate of the idea of a process of judgment that can be prolonged harmoniously *ad infinitum.*

What has just been stated holds good for substrates of every kind, as scientific provinces (whatever the further particularizations may turn out to be) — if the processes of judgment carry within them an intention aimed at determination with insight, and if the idea of a genuine science is taken into consideration.

f. The categorial formations, which accrue in the determining, as habitual and intersubjective possessions.

Of course it must not be overlooked that categorial formations are objectivities for judgers, *not merely in and during the judging action: transcendence is implicit in their own being-sense.* What the judger has fashioned now in his active thinking, he possesses from now on as an abiding mental acquisition: The active acceptance changes for him into habitual acceptance. That which has once been given acceptance in an actually constituting activity can emerge again in memory; and it emerges not only as something that was once accepted but as something still accepted. This emerging is not an explicit repetitive recollection of the earlier process of constitution step by step; rather it is a one-rayed vague returning to what exists thanks to an earlier action. It involves, however, the certainty of being able to reactivate the constitutive process, to go back to it, with its continuing acceptance, and restore it — that is, to produce the same categorial objectivity as the same. Only thus are any advancing processes of judgment made possible — not alone the ones that can be resumed and continued after interruptions.

They all depend on *habitual and reawakable acceptance*, as a continuing acceptance throughout any number of reawakenings; what exists is what exists "henceforth" for the judger — as long as he does not give up his "conviction" and does not cancel the acceptance, which is at the same time a *continuing acceptance*. /

<105> It makes no essential difference in our exposition if we now take into consideration the *establishing of a community* of judgers, in respect of their thinking, and if we accordingly regard categorial objectivities as constituted in the judgment-community. In the case of Nature, for example, it is then a matter, not of Nature "for me", but of *Nature "for us"* — Nature, let us say, "for us natural scientists", "for the natural science of our times", or the like.

g. The objectivity given beforehand to thinking contrasted with the categorial objectivity produced by thinking – Nature as an illustration.

Of course one must not fall back on the Nature already given by sheer experience *before all thinking*. Nature as a judgment-formation — in particular, as a natural-scientific cognition-formation — will of course *have under it* Nature as an experience-formation, a unity pertaining to actual and possible experience, one's own and the pooled experience of a community that includes others: But *the under-it is at the same time an in-it*. Only the Nature-experience taken into the judging itself is an experience that determines the judgment-sense; and by the judger, qua judger, only *that* Nature is accepted which is *categorially formed* in the judging. With respect to the rest of experienced or experienceable Nature, this signifies an open, still unrealized, horizon of judgments to be made on the basis of experience. To be sure, we call the unity pertaining to an all-embracing experience Nature, and say that it *exists* and has such and such peculiarities *in itself* and that it is what or as it is, *"before"* our judging. A priori, however, it receives the "existing" and the "it is as it is", the "properties", the "predicatively formed affair-complexes", and the like, only from our judging, and has them only for possible judgers. Only if we are no longer engaged merely in our simple judicative doing on the basis of experience (the doing in which we acquire the categorial formations) — only if we go on synthetically to make our experiencing itself and its productions a theme of judgment, can we have original knowledge of the fact that this (harmoniously flowing) experiencing already bears "implicitly" in itself, "before" our thinking and the categorial formations produced by our thinking, the being-sense of Nature, as the same sense that thinking explicates.

All this too is anything but a piece of argumentative idealism. It is obtained not from any speculating "epistemology" or standpoint-philosophy, but from plain sense-investigation and discovery. /

§ 43. Analytics, as formal theory of science, is formal ontology and, as ontology, is directed to objects. <106>

What holds good for Nature as existing and for the natural science determining it, holds good, we said, *for all provinces* and their sciences. Therefore it applies *also to analytic logic* as formal theory of science. The theme of analytic logic is all categorial objectivities in respect of their pure forms — that is, as objectivities comprehended under the form-concepts that arise by virtue of formalization and pertain to them as categorial. Here the materially filled "cores" — which originate at the lowest level from experiential intuitings and then constitute, at the level of judgments, the concrete own-essentiality of the objects and provinces — remain indeterminately universal, are thought of with indeterminate universality as just anything, any This-and-What maintaining itself as identical throughout identifications. This "abstraction" from the material content, this dropping of it with the variability of the merely identifiable, signifies correlatively that *concept-forming in logic follows the categorial syntaxes exclusively*. We should therefore think of the logician as having the attitude or focus called for by an orientation according to the scientific judger, the scientist directed to his particular province in continuously determining it, who always winds up with new levels of theory. Accordingly the logician is like the scientist in that, when conceiving his own theme, he has thought also of a sphere of application comprising *some* substrate-objectivities or other, as objectivities that are to be <scientifically> determined, and *some* categorial objectivities or other, as the substrates included in

⟨the scientist's⟩ determination. The logician need not start out here by thinking explicitly of universal scientific provinces nor by speaking of them. Nevertheless, as he advances with his consideration of formal possibilities, he must come upon not only the fact that single judgments can cohere because of their substrates, but also the fact that infinite judgment-systems cohering in that same manner are possible; and then indeed, as happened above, the pre-eminence of deductive systems within the sphere of ideas belonging to logic itself (as analytically formal) will also come to light.

Our result is therefore as follows. Like the sciences themselves, *analytics as formal theory of science is directed to what exists* [*ontisch gerichtet*]; moreover, by virtue of its apriori universality, it is ontological. It is *formal ontology*. Its apriori truths state what holds good for *any objects whatever*, any object-provinces whatever,
<107> with formal universality, *in / whatever forms they exist* or merely *can exist* — as objects of judgments [*urteilsmässig*], naturally: since, without exception, objects "exist" only as objects of judgments and, for that very reason, exist only in categorial forms.

§ 44. The shift from analytics as formal ontology to analytics as formal apophantics.

a. The change of thematizing focus from object-provinces to judgments as logic intends them.

After we have advanced to this point, the question is whether the direct opposite of what we intended to show has not been made evident: since, indeed, we intended to show the *duality* inherent in the idea of logic, as both a formal ontology and a formal apophantics. But, as some might say, we have only one thing here. *All the objectivities* with which we ever busy ourselves or ever have busied ourselves, with all their formal-ontological configurations — all the objectivities of which we say or ever could say "They *are*" and (if we are set to cognize and verify) "They are in truth such and such" — are, it seems, *nothing at all but "judgments"*: judgments in our *amplified sense*, "posita" generated in activities of judgment, in doxic positings, themselves; they are the correlates of these as actual and then as habitual; they are produced formations, which in turn can themselves be enveloped by repeatedly new judgments and thus can enter into new judgments as parts. That which comes into being and has come into being as judged in the judicative producing, that which then, as an ideal objectivity, is always re-identifiable, is it not, by definition, a *judgment*? *Is it anything else but a categorial objectivity*?

Now, in order to justify our previously announced position (despite the evidence of our exposition up to now, an evidence that is unassailable when taken in a certain sense), we have to show that, *contrasting with the thematizing focus* with which we have been operating up to now, there is possible at any time such a *shift of thematizing interest* that what then lies *in the thematic field* is *not the particular object-province* and the categorial objectivities formed out of it at higher levels, but — *as something other* and sharply differentiated — *what we call the judgments* and *their* components, their combinations and other transmutations to make judgments at ever new levels. /

b. Phenomenological clarification of this change of focus. <108>

α. The attitude of someone who is judging naïvely-straightforwardly.

First it must be pointed out that, in the preceding exposition, we were *putting ourselves in the position of the judgers* and seeking exclusively for *what is "there" for them as judgers*. And this, we found, is, on the one hand, such and such substrate-objects or provinces and, on the other hand, such and such categorial objectivities (with ever new forms and at new levels), which accrue to the judgers, in their determinative judging, as the objectivities accepted by them. For judging is always believing something, having something "before one" as existent [*etwas als seiend "vor sich" haben*], whether one has it there intuitively or non-intuitively. Merely a different phrasing is: accepting it as existent [*es in Seinsgeltung haben*]. As we added immediately, that does not exclude the eventuality that, in the further course of judgment, this acceptance as existent by the judger will no longer stand firm. The existent becomes "modalized"; it becomes the doubtful, the questionable, the possible, the presumable, or even the null. The judgment-complex is called *harmonious* as long as nothing like that happens and the currently accepted objectivities continue to be simply accepted as existent: as long as, for the judger, they simply *are*. For the style of his further activities of judgment this signifies that each one of these objectivities, throughout its further syntactical changes, is posited over and over in connective identifications as "one and the same": that it is accepted — and *goes on being accepted* — in judgments, as the same objectivity.

β. In the critical attitude of someone who intends to cognize, supposed objectivities as supposed are distinguished from actual objectivities.

But the particular judger does not only give acceptance to objectivities as existent, cancel something here and there, give acceptance to something else instead, and in this way, passing through modalizations, end with a harmony that is free from unsatisfactory disturbances. There arise occasionally, even in everyday judging, interests in cognizing in the pre-eminent sense: interests in assurative "*verification*", needs to convince oneself "*by the affairs themselves*" of "how they *actually* are". The categorial formations which previously were simply existing objectivities for the judger, and simply the same ones while the process of identification continued, must be verified by going over to the evidence, the "categorial intuition", in which they would be given originaliter as they "themselves", verified, cognized as *truly and actually existing*. Thus a distinction arises /
<109> occasionally, even for the judger, between the supposed objectivities *as supposed* — purely as the ones that have become posited in such and such a categorial form in his actions of judgment, purely as what, throughout the synthetic course of his positings, is *positum qua positum* — and the corresponding "*true*" or "*actual*" objectivities, that is: the categorial formations accruing in the distinctive phenomenological form of insights, in the *judging that "gives them-themselves"*, step by step, formation by formation.

In general, when judging goes right ahead naturally, the process will be such that the judger goes on accepting the accepted objectivity, even while he is being guided by his need to verify; so that, when he ends with the evidently seen object "itself", he says: "*The* object is actual, is actually qualified thus, stands actually in these relationships", and the like. With the transition, there takes place here an *identifying coincidence* between, on the one hand, the objective affair (and ultimately the total judgment-complex, the syntactically formed affair-complex, or state-of-affairs) that was already believed-in previously and, on the other hand, the objective affair now given — as it itself, the fulfilling actuality — in the believing with evidence, the believing that fulfils the intention aimed at cognition. Thus it is, in the case of successful verification.

But the intention aimed at verification — that is, for the judger, the endeavor to get at the objective affair "itself" and be with it itself, to descry in it itself "what is actually there" — this intention can be *disappointed* instead of fulfilled. In that case, to be sure, it still becomes fulfilled in respect of component positings; but these are supplemented in the affairs themselves to yield the total positing of a categorial objectivity with which the one previously believed-in "conflicts" — a conflict that makes cancellation of the latter necessary originaliter. The judger now says, for example: "The state-of-affairs is not *as I supposed*". The added phrase, "as I supposed", expresses a *modification of sense*. For "the state-of-affairs as I supposed it to be" is not a state-of-affairs in which I have continued to believe, nor could it remain such: By virtue of the cancellation that has now gained acceptance, it is the "previously merely supposed" state-of-affairs.

Addendum. It can be seen that our reference to "verification" proper (which leads to trueness derived from an evidence that gives the object itself), like every other preference of an *ideal* case, was a simplification — one that is indeed privileged for the sake of our future exposition but not absolutely necessary, as though it were the only case in which there is a motive for distinguishing between something supposed, as supposed, and something actual. Eventually the imperfections of evidence are to be taken into consideration here; and then the concept of / verification <110>
proper could be adjusted to the ideal case, that of perfection, where that which offers itself to the judger as something itself-given and existent or true is subject to no reservations, no anticipative presumptions whose possible fulfilment (in further syntactically annexable evidences) would decide whether the ostensibly true is the definitively true. But we can also adjust the concept of verification proper in a different fashion: We can designate verification as "proper", as actually an *adequatio* (though perhaps an imperfect one), as long as it is effected by an intuition that

gives something-itself. Relative to this sense there is also a verification "improper" and a corresponding refutation (beyond which the conflict and the criticism expressed in everyday discussions ordinarily do not aspire): that is to say, the verification or refutation of something accepted by something that stands unshaken as sure and unassailable — which is far from saying that the latter has been established by insight. In such a refutation what was previously simply existent becomes changed into the corresponding mere belief [*Meinung*]. On the other hand, confirmation of what has perhaps become doubtful — its reconversion into a confirmed certainty in connexion with something "quite sure", as a conversion demanded by this — yields the "improper" predicate of being true and actual.

γ. The scientist's attitude: the supposed, as supposed, the object of his criticism of cognition.

Here we need not enter into more extensive investigations; what has already been said enables us to see that, *by differentiation between something supposed and something actual*, differentation between the sphere of *mere judgments* (in the amplified sense) and the sphere of *objects* is prepared for. In order to advance further, we direct our regard to the *sciences*. Instead of the everyday judger, with his only occasional focusing on cognition, we now take someone who judges scientifically. In so doing, he lives a *"theoretically interested" life, with vocational consistency.*[1] That is to say, his vocational judging is always ruled completely by *intentions aimed at cognition*; and these themselves have their synthetic unity: namely in the unity of the cognitional interest directed to the scientific province in question. In the strict sense (which, to be sure, is an ideal one), *cognizing* his province signifies,
<111> for the scientist, nothing else but / accepting no judgments as scientific results except those that have shown their *"correctness"*, their "truth", by an *adequation to the affairs themselves* and can be produced again originaliter, at any time, with this correctness — that is to say, by a reactualizing of the adequation. Not that the scientist does not judge at all before such a having of the "affairs" themselves — the objectivities "themselves" that belong to the particular categorial level. But he takes all prior judgments as

[1] *Author's note:* "Vocational consistency" relates to the division of a whole life into periods (vocational hours, days, and so forth) that are separated and yet connected internally by intentional synthesis, and appertain to a habitual "vocational interest". This interest is consistently operative in such vocational activities as create ever new rational acquisitions; and it maintains acceptance of the old ones — perhaps (this being the case in science) as structural members or as bases for new acquisitions.

only provisional; the categorial objectivities accepted in them, as only provisionally accepted, as merely supposed objectivities. The intention aimed at cognition passes clear through them, as supposed, and aims precisely at the affairs themselves, at the givenness of them themselves or at the evidence of them.

But yet another difference distinguishes the cognitional striving of the scientist from the naïve cognitional striving of the non-scientific thinker. The latter "merely looks and sees" whether it is actually thus; and, if he sees, he is satisfied. The scientist, however, has long been apprised, not only that evidence has its degrees of clarity, but also that it may be deceptive evidence. Consequently there exists for him the further distinction between *supposed and genuine evidence*. His judgments must be verified by genuine, by maximally perfect, evidence; and only as so verified shall they be admitted among the results of science as theory. This brings about a *peculiar judging procedure on the scientist's part*, a *zigzag* judging, so to speak: first making straight for the givenness of something itself, but then going back *critically* to the provisional results already obtained — whereupon his criticism must also be subjected to criticism, and for like reasons. Thus the scientist is guided by the *idea* of an evidence that is perfect or perfectible by systematic stages, and attainable by means of criticism, an evidence having as its correlate an attainable, or approachable, true being (an idea, incidentally, the sense and limits of which are not matters for positive science itself to explore).

The critical attitude, it should be added, concerns all judging activities with respect likewise to the *modalizations* occurring in them and the distinctions between evidence and non-evidence that are peculiar to such modalizations themselves; but the intention aimed at cognition tends clear through these modalizations — through the questionabilities, possibilities, probabilities, negations — toward evident certainties. These, when actualized, are the unqualified truths as themselves-given: cognitional acquisitions abiding from then on, capable of again becoming accessible to insight at any time, and / accessible in this manner to *everyone* <112>
as a rationally thinking subject, even as they were before their "discovery". Every "scientific statement" has this sense from the start. It is already addressed to this "everyone" and states

what the substrate-objectivities are in truth — as everyone can see.

§ 45. The judgment in the sense proper to apophantic logic.

Because of the *transition through the critical attitude* — a transition necessary to every scientific cognition and therefore one that every scientific judgment must undergo — the scientist has before him, in continual alternation, an *objectivity simpliciter* (as the actuality existing for him in his straightforward judging or else aimed at by him as a cognitive subject) and, on the other hand, a *supposed objectivity as supposed*: a supposed consequence, a supposed determination, a supposed plurality, a supposed cardinal number, or the like — each of them *as* supposed. With this *supposed as such*, the mere correlate of the "supposing" or "opining" (often spoken of as the opinion, δόξα), we have now laid hold of *what is called the judgment* (*apophansis*) *in traditional logic* and is the theme of apophantic logic.[1] Still, as we already know, apophantic logic — guided as always by what science does — prefers to frame here a *narrower concept*, one however that completely includes the broadest concept of a "supposed categorial objectivity as supposed", though of course not as a specific particularization. Scientific judging is aimed [2] at cognizing the particular province determiningly. Consequently the *predicative judgment* (the apophansis as a *self-contained unity of determination*) is always given pre-eminence. As we have already explained, all formable categorialia are called on to function within predicative judgments; and in the sciences (we are disregarding logic itself) they all present themselves as component parts within such judgments. In other words: judgments, in the sense proper to apophantic logic, are supposed predicatively formed affair-complexes as supposed; and, more particularly, they are self-sufficiently complete ones. All other categorial suppositions function as parts within such "judgments". /

[1] *Author's note:* It is the noema of the judging. On the concept of noema, see *Ideen*, [§ 88,] pp. 180ff., and, especially in the case of the judgment, [§ 94,] pp. 194ff. [English translation, pp. 257ff. and 272ff.]

[2] *Author's note: Cf.* § 40, [pp. 108 ff., *supra*].

§ 46. Truth and falsity as results of criticism. The double sense of truth and evidence. <113>

The *final result of criticism* — ideally speaking — is either a "*truth*" or a "*falsity*". Here a truth signifies *a correct critically verified judgment* — verified by means of an adequation to the corresponding categorial objectivities "themselves", as given in the evidential having of them themselves: given originaliter, that is, in the generating activity exercised on the basis of the experienced substrates "themselves". From this adequation — in other words, from the fulfilling transition to the having of the objectivity itself — and from the reflection on the *mere opinion or meaning* and its coincidence with the *meaning in its fullness* there originates the *concept of that correctness which is the sense of one concept of truth, the critical concept,* according to which the *judgment* is true — or false, or else (to do justice now to the other modalizations) questionable, presumable, or the like. Whereas falsity depends on the givenness of a predicatively formed affair-complex itself with which the supposed affair-complex as supposed — that is, the judgment — conflicts, so that the latter undergoes original annulment (which, with an appropriate change of focus, yields an evidential grasping of the nullity itself as an existent nullity), the situation is different in the case of the other modalities: That which is given originaliter is not the syntactically formed affair-complex or its negative, but at best a motivated alternative possibility "that argues against matters being thus", or else a number of such possibilities, or the like.

Here we have the basis for understanding the *pre-eminence of negation* among the modalities, and its usual situation beside and on a par with position, for the logician, with his critical attitude. At present, however, we must not go into this any further.

Besides the critical concept of truth, the concept of a judgment's correctness by virtue of its original (present or past) adjustment to the itself-given actuality, we have then the concept of *actuality, as the second concept of truth.* The true is now the *actually existent* or the *truly existent,* as the correlate of the evidence that gives the actuality itself. Naturally the actual [*das Wirkliche*] in the sense of the *real* [*des Realen*] is merely a particular case under this broadest, analytico-formal, concept of actuality.

The word *evidence* also takes on a *double sense* in connexion with these two concepts of truth: In addition to signifying the *original having* of a true or actual being *itself*, evidence signifies the property belonging to the judgment — as a supposed cate-
<114> gorial / objectivity (an "opinion" or "meaning") — when it fits, in original actuality [*Aktualität*], a corresponding actuality [*Wirklichkeit*]. Thus evidence involves, in the latter case, that *original consciousness of correctness* which arises in the event of actual adequation. That consciousness is itself evidence in the first sense, with regard to the correctness; it is a particular case under the broader concept of evidence as the having of something itself. Then, in a naturally amplified sense, a judgment is called evident, also with reference to the potentiality of bringing about its adequation.

As for the second (but at bottom the intrinsically first) concept of truth, that of *actuality* [*Wirklichkeit*] as trueness of being, we still have to take into consideration its peculiar *breadth*. The scientist speaks of actual or true being, not only with regard to predicatively formed affair-complexes — that is to say: those "truths" that govern the truth (as correctness) of predicative judgments — but also with regard to *all categorial objectivities* of whatever sort. The name actuality comprehends actual properties, actual relationships, actual wholes and parts, actual sets and connected complexes (for example, solar systems), and so forth. In the predicative judgments the supposed categorial objectivities that occur as judgment-components correspond to those actualities. Showing the correctness of whole judgments, or else "correcting" them, involves showing the corresponding correctness or incorrectness of these components.

The peculiar formal stamp of the intentionality ruling throughout the unity of scientific living and the formations it produces determines the particular stamp of *scientific reason*, as a reason that actualizes *"genuine"* cognition *by an unremittingly concomitant criticism of cognition*. Accordingly the systematic product of scientific reason — *science*, as a theory to be further developed *ad infinitum* — has the particular sense of being a system of judgments that, while undergoing an incessant criticism, are consciously made adequate to an evidential giving of the categorial objects themselves and that are, in this sense, truths:

originally correct judgments, adjusted to the truly and actually existent itself, ideally embracing and (with their "complete" system) exhausting all the true being of the province.

In this connexion the following is to be noted. Scientific judging indeed forsakes the naïvely straightforward cognitional directedness to objective actualities that come from the naïve having of them themselves in straightforward evidence, and *continually* | *makes the judgments thematic*, the supposed objectivities <115> as supposed. Consequently it always terminates in propositions for which the attached predicate "correct" or "true" has been originally acquired and established — even though, as present throughout all the theoretical results, it may usually remain unexpressed. But it is obvious, on the other hand, that this procedure is *subservient* to determining the province itself, and that therefore the *judged propositions are only intermediary themes*. The goal is cognition of the substrate-objectivities encompassed in the concept of the province. *Cognition in the ideal sense* is the title for the actually attained true being of the objectivities themselves, in respect of all the categorial formations in which their being shows its *true* being, the formations in which it becomes constituted originally as true; and so far as that has already occurred, just "so far" is there something truly existent from the standpoint of cognition. Actually progressing cognition of true being is followed by cognition in the sense of habitual possession in consequence of original acquisition, with the corresponding potentiality of actualization. None of this becomes altered by the method of criticism, which, on the contrary, is intended to make certain the attainment of true being or to diminish the gap between imperfect and perfect cognition.

Chapter 5.

Apophantics, as theory of senses, and truth-logic.

§ 47. The adjustment of traditional logic to the critical attitude of science leads to its focusing on the apophansis.

The result of these observations — which have concerned the manners of judging [*Urteilsweisen*] that belong to, and the intentionality that holds sway in, the sciences — will help us *to progress in our structural understanding of the idea of logic.* We recall that, from its inception, logic intended to be theory of science. Accordingly it always looked to the antecedent beginnings, or the extensively executed projects, of the sciences as its field of examples; and it understood reason and rational production according to that moment in scientific projects which, though not at hand as an actualization of the ideal, nevertheless evinced in itself the ideal final sense of scientific intentionality. This makes it comprehensible that, *for logic, the judgment-sphere purely as such* had to be set apart and first of all become *a*
<116> *thematic field by itself.* / Logic, as theory of science, therefore constituted itself, from the very beginning, as a science that intended to serve that criticism which creates genuine science. The cognitions, the sciences, which it looked upon as examples, it took as mere claims — that is: as *mere "judgments"* (suppositions) and judgment-systems, which must be submitted to criticism and which then, as determined with the aid of criticism, must be fashioned in such a manner that the predicate "truth" can be rightly ascribed to them. *Thus logic followed the attitude of the critic — who judges, not straightforwardly, but rather about judgments. Only mediately,* therefore, as long as it remained a logic of judgments, was logic directed *to the existent itself* as possibly making its appearance in activities that fashion and give something itself; *immediately* it was directed to *judgments, as suppositions* of something existent. As "formal logic", which was, after all, traditionally meant and developed entirely as a logic of judgments, it had as its theme those judgment-forms that, as

eidetic laws, are conditions for possible adequation to something existent itself.

After our earlier observations on the primacy of the predicative judgment in the sciences, it is quite comprehensible that *formal logic was constituted as apophantic* and that predicative judgment was accordingly its highest concept of its theme. But, as we have seen, if the execution had been systematically complete, that would not have signified any restriction (as it did in fact, to the great detriment of logic), because, as we know, the apophansis takes in all categorial suppositions. Along with judgments in the narrower sense, judgments in our widest sense are therefore themes of formal logic — of apophantics as understood in the full sense — and, more particularly, themes in the formal-logical disciplines of all levels.

§ 48. Judgments, as mere suppositions, belong to the region of senses. Phenomenological characterization of the focusing on senses.

Judgments are themes. In other words: *suppositions*, as suppositions, are *objects belonging to a region of their own*; they form a self-contained field of objects. Here we need a more penetrating phenomenological clarification, such as has already been partly attained by the analyses in Chapter 4. We now intend to deepen it yet further, from a more inclusive point of view.

Let us begin with a short summary of what has already been stated. Every judging is directed to something objective. Not only that the judger / always has his "*objects-about-which*", <117>
to which he directs himself in the pre-eminent sense while determining them; also, in a second sense, he directs himself to the *determining*; and furthermore he directs himself, in an "improper" sense, to the *predicatively formed affair-complex* — "improper" because, though he has indeed constituted the affair-complex with the aforesaid substrate-objects and the determinings, he requires a redirection of his thematizing regard in order to be directed (in the special sense) to the affair-complex. In this manner divers categorialia are "there" for the judger qua judger; and, as has been said, each becomes identified in the unity of a coherent judgment-process and, at the same time, has

its determinational *function* relative to the ultimate substrates that the judger intends to determine in the process. It is the same in cognitive judging; only that the categorialia are pervaded by the intention aimed at a having of them themselves in the form of so-called evidential judging — in connexion with which fulfilling identification takes place, if they are attained in the mode "they themselves".

This is *judging simpliciter* — a completely relative term, as will become apparent forthwith: It is essentially possible to convert any judging into a *judging at a second level,* in which what was judged straightforwardly, and was therefore an existing objectivity for the judger, is no longer posited, but rather *the judged as such* is posited in an act of reflection. Thus reflection is indeed what yields the novelty, but not such a relfection as makes the judicial action the theme[1] and therefore the object of a new judging (a new positing, which then tends to change into a predicatively determining positing). Not only a substrate-object, a determination, a predicatively formed affair-complex, or the like, but also *a supposed substrate as supposed,* a supposed determination *as* supposed, or the like, can be objective; and, as we have said above and are now about to establish, the latter are *objectivities,* which — despite this relation to something antecedent — do in fact indicate *a region of their own.* In the first place:

Naturally the transition from a judgment (a supposed objectivity simpliciter) to a judicial meaning or opinion (a supposed objectivity as supposed) can be repeated at any number of levels. It is a *reiterable process* of possible reflection and of constantly changing one's attitude or focus. At the same time it is evident that we get back to an *ultimate difference* here, the difference
<118> between / *objectivities that are suppositions and objectivities that are not suppositions.* It is precisely for this reason that we speak of different regions within the formal all-embracing region, "any objectivity whatever". All upper-level suppositions surely belong themselves to the region of suppositions, of "*opinions*" or "*meanings*". Instead of saying meaning, we may say *sense*; and,

[1] *Author's note:* That would be noetical reflection, reflection on the noetic multiplicities constituting the noematic unity. *Cf. Ideen,* [I, §§ 97f.,] pp. 201–207. [English translation, pp. 282–289.]

taking statements as our starting point, we may speak of their *significations*. To ask about the signification or sense of a statement and make its sense distinct to ourselves is manifestly to go over, from the straightforward stating-and-judging attitude in which we "have" only the pertinent objects, into the reflective attitude, the attitude in which the corresponding object-meanings and predicatively formed affair-complex-meanings become seized upon or posited. Hence we may *designate this region also as the region of senses*.[1] In the case of closed predicative judgments, we have affair-complex-senses (supposed predicatively formed affair-complexes as supposed); in the case of substrate-objects, we have precisely object-senses in the narrower sense; in the case of relational complexes, relational-complex-senses; and so forth.

We have said nothing here about whether the straightforward (unreflective) judgments and the reflective judgments about senses are evident, nor about whether they bear within themselves intentions aimed at cognition or ever occur as fulfilments of such intentions. Such variant modes can obviously occur *with a judicative attitude of either kind* — with the "straightforward" focusing or with the reflective focusing on senses — since they are modes belonging to all judgments as such, and therefore to judgments about senses. Accordingly, in the case of these judgments too, there is the difference between the evidential having of something itself and merely believing in it; there is modalization (in particular: possible cancellation, verification, evident refutation — as negative verification —, and so forth); and then, thanks to going back to the sense at a higher level, there is criticism.

Explication of sense *can* be evident; but it need not be; moreover it can deceive. If the objects called senses are actually other than objects simpliciter, then a coherent judging that, as coherent, returns identifyingly to the objects already posited — and consequently a *cognizing judging* in particular — *traverses respectively different paths when concerned with the two formal regions* and makes different identifications, different distinctions, and different eliminations by / cancellation. The sense called <119>

[1] *Author's note: Cf. Ideen*, [I, § 128,] p. 265. [English translation, p. 359.] For more about the relationship between sense and noema, see *op. cit.*, [§ 90,] pp. 185 and [§§ 129–131,] 266–273. [English translation, pp. 261f. and 361–368.]

"the judgment *S*-is-*p*" can never be identified with the simply judged *S*-is-*p*, nor with the predicatively formed affair-complex obtainable from the latter by nominalization. Furthermore, with the transition to evidence of being, it is clear that the actual being of the judgment, as a sense, does not suffer if *S is* not, or if *S* is not *p* — in a word, if the affair-complex, the one existing for the judger, does not exist. In that case the judgment is incorrect; but, *as* a judgment, it is something *existent, belonging to the region of senses*. Moreover, all forms of identification in possible judgment-continuities (of which those leading to evidence are a particular subdivision) enter, as modified, into the sphere of senses.

It need only be mentioned that senses, as objects, are ideal poles of unity, "transcending" the acts and subjects related to them, in quite the same fashion in which objects that are not senses do. After all, the same is true of all objects, without exception.

§ 49. The double sense of judgment (positum, proposition).

Casting another glance back at the *correlation between judging and judgment*, we see that the *double sense* that played the decisive rôle in all these clarifications should be expressly emphasized once more: Judging in the broadest sense is doxic "positing" [*doxisch "Setzen"*]; and what is posited therein is the "positum or proposition" [*der "Satz"*]. Specifically predicative judging [*Urteil*] posits the *predicative proposition*. This is *what* is judged. But is the proposition or judgment then what apophantic logic — the apophantic logic that criticizes with regard to correctness and falsity — conceives under the name proposition?

What is judged in a judging is the judged — the judgingly meant or supposed — *categorial objectivity*. As we have ascertained, not until there is a judging on a *second level* does the *proposition in logic's sense of the word* — the proposition as a sense, the supposed categorial objectivity *as supposed* — become the object; and, in this new judging, *it* is the judgingly supposed objectivity simpliciter. The sense of any judging, to be sure, "lies" within it; and we say, likewise with evidence, that the objectivity supposed straightforwardly in a judging need not always exist. But we can say such things with evidence, *only* by virtue of those judgments and evidences at a second level by which we "draw" from the simple judgments their suppositions, making these into *objects*. By this very process the suppositions have become cognitional goals in their own right and, when given in evidence, goals that are themselves / attained; whereas in the straightforward judging <120> the corresponding suposition is, to be sure, implicitly intended to, but is a mere "*passage*" traversed by the aim at cognition, which, for its part, terminates in the corresponding categorial objectivity itself and not in the mere judgment.

§ 50. The broadening of the concept of sense to cover the whole positional sphere, and the broadening of formal logic to include a formal axiology and a formal theory of practice.

Now it is instructive to note also that what we have said about judging and judgment-sense holds good for the *whole sphere of positional consciousness*. Every cogito has its cogitatum — for the phenomenology of intentionality that is a fundamental essential situation. Cogito can signify "I perceive", "I remember", or "I expect" — modes of consciousness that indeed belong in the doxic sphere, though not in the sphere of predicatively determining thinking. But it can also signify: I exercise "valuing" emotional activities in liking or disliking, in hoping or fearing, or volitional activities,[1] or the like. Carried on straightforwardly, every such cogito is always directed to the Objects of experience, to the concrete values and disvalues, of the ends and means, or the like. But each permits a reflection (with a change of attitude or focus) — a reflection directed to its *cogitatum qua cogitatum*, its "*intentional objectivity as intentional*". Such a reflection can be a doxic reflection; but it can also be a corresponding emotional or else purposefully endeavoring reflection.

Confining our attention to the doxic reflection possible in every case, we see that something new becomes posited in it, namely the sense [2] to which reflection is directed: the perceptual

[1] *Translator's note:* Reading *oder Willenstätigkeiten* instead of *oder in Willenstätigkeiten.*

[2] *Author's note:* This universal concept of sense, a concept extending to all intentional spheres, had already emerged in the *Logische Untersuchungen.* The "psychology of thinking" ["*Denkpsychologie*"] developed in our times has adopted it, but unfortunately without taking into consideration the deeper intentional analyses, particularly the much more extensive analyses presented in my *Ideen.* (*Cf. op. cit.*, [§ 124,] pp. 256ff. [English translation, pp. 345ff.])

sense, [1] the valuational sense, the practical sense, or the like — in short, the *supposed or meant as such.* Everywhere, moreover, *this sense must become thematic if "criticism" is to be instituted. All acts in a pre-eminent sense of the word,* namely all intentional mental processes that bring about "positions" (positings, theses, position-takings) [*"Setzungen" (Positionen, Thesen, Stellungnahmen)*], *are subject to a critique of "reason"*; and to each genus
‹121› of such / positions a *peculiar evidence* corresponds, [2] which, according to an eidetic law, can be transmuted into a *doxic evidence.* Therefore identifying synthesis in the sphere of judgment also has as its analogues identifying syntheses in the other positional spheres. Everywhere the straightforward themes (the word being taken now in a maximally broad sense, which relates to all genera of positionality) undergo a modification by the aforesaid reflection.

We spoke of the possible turning of any evidence into a doxic evidence. With greater universality it may be said here that any extra-doxic sense can at any time become the theme of a doxic act and thus enter the doxic sphere — and, in particular, the apophantic sphere. It is similar to the manner in which any modalized judgment can take on the form of a judgment made with certainty — a judgment in the normal sense. When this happens, possible, probable, or the like, makes its appearance within the judgment-complex; and the situation is similar in the case of beautiful or good. Thus the formal logic of certainties can not only be enriched by taking in the forms of the ⟨doxic⟩ modalities, but can also absorb, in a ccrtain manner, the modalities of emotion and volition.

These observations enable us to foresee that the spheres comprising extra-doxic acts can likewise be considered formally. This has great significance, because it opens up the possibility of broadening the idea of *formal logic to include a formal axiology and a formal theory of practice.* Accordingly there arises what might be called a "formal logic" of concrete values [*der Werte*] and a

[1] *Translator's note:* The preceding note is attached here in the text.

[2] *Author's note:* Emotional evidence was first brought to light by Franz Brentano. See the statements about "right love" and "love characterized as right" in his lecture, *Vom Ursprung sittlicher Erkenntnis* [*On the Origin of Moral Cognition* (1889)], edited and republished by Oskar Kraus (Leipzig, 1921), p. 17. [English translation, by Cecil Hague, under the title, *The Origin of our Knowledge of Right and Wrong*, Westminster, 1902.]

formal logic of ⟨practical⟩ goods [*der Güter*]. Each positional sphere has its "syntactical" categories, its own specific primitive modalities of "something" and of the derivative formations of "something"; and each has therefore its "formal logic", its "analytics".[1]

§ 51. Pure consequence-logic as a pure theory of senses. The division into consequence-logic and truth-logic is valid also for the theory of multiplicities as the highest level of logic.

Restricting ourselves once more to the judgment-sphere as the realm of apophantic senses, including all categorial senses, we must regard *pure formal analytics* as *a* / *self-contained systematic* ⟨122⟩
theory, the thematic sphere of which consists exclusively of just those senses. This follows when our clarification of the concept of the judgment as the predicational objective sense, the clarification gained in our present investigations, is connected with what we ascertained concerning the sense and structure of logical analytics in Chapter I — where, to be sure, the highest level of analytics, the theory of the forms of deductive theories, had not yet come within our sphere of vision. Analytics is a *pure* systematic theory of the region of what are strictly and properly *senses*, only in its two lower strata: as the *pure theory of forms* of senses (or significations) and as the *pure analytics of non-contradiction.* Since the latter stratum is founded on the theory of forms, it makes up a self-contained logical discipline only as united therewith; and, when thus understood, it is the all-embracing and pure science of apophantic senses, which includes nothing that goes beyond what appertains to their own essentiality. Its theme excludes all questions of truth; for precisely these, with the predicate "true" (and all its modifications), go beyond the Apriori that pertains purely to the proper essence of the sphere of senses, as is shown

[1] *Author's note:* In the summer semester of 1902 and subsequently, I attempted to develop systematically the ideas of a formal axiology and a formal theory of practice, not only in lecture courses and seminars devoted to this particular matter but also in the context of lectures on logic and on ethics. All expositions with a similar sense that have since appeared in the literature derive, I dare say, from those lectures and seminars — however considerable the modifications that the thoughts communicated may have undergone. Above all, Theodor Lessing's [*Studien zur*] *Wertaxiomatik* [(*Studies pertaining to Value-Axiomatics*), [*Archiv für systematische Philosophie,* XIV, 1908; 2d ed., Leipzig, 1914,] derives from them quite immediately.

by the fact that the signification of "true" is based on ⟨the idea of⟩ adequation.

The broader explications made above for purposes of clarification enable us to understand that, with the development of analytics into the theory of systematic theory-forms (correlatively, the theory of mathematical multiplicities) and thus into a full *mathesis universalis*, everything that we showed in the case of the lower levels must still hold good: in the first place, the distinction between one stratum as a pure *mathesis of non-contradiction* and another as *mathesis of possible truth* and then the interpretation of the former as a *mathesis of pure senses*. For, if we take any determinate systematic form of theories (or, correlatively, any determinate mathematical multiplicity) as it has been constructed a priori — for example, the *form* Euclidean geometry (or, correlatively, Euclidean multiplicity) — then, within the extension of this form (as a universal concept), single
<123> multiplicities are / thought of as single particulars, though with complete indeterminateness: in our example, merely as multiplicities having the Euclidean form. And they are thought of as built exclusively *out of categorial formations*, all of which therefore — up to and including each particular whole multiplicity itself — belong entirely within the sphere of apophantic logic, so far as their syntactical forms are concerned. *The whole mathesis universalis is accordingly the analytics of possible categorialia*, the theory of their essential forms and eidetic laws.

Let us now note that *the theory of multiplicities has no compelling reason* to include in any manner within its theme *questions about the possible truth* of its theory-forms or, correlatively, questions about *the possible actuality* (the possible true being) *of any single multiplicities* subsumed under its formal ideas of a multiplicity. Equivalently, the *mathematician as such* need not be at all concerned with the fact that there actually are multiplicities in concrete "actuality" (for example: such a thing as a mathematically cognizable Nature; or a realm, such as that of spatial formations, which can perhaps be apprehended as a *Euclidean* multiplicity); nor indeed need he be at all concerned with the fact that there *can* be something of the sort, that something of the sort with some material content or other is thinkable. *Therefore he does not need to presuppose possible multiplicities*, in the sense of multiplicities that might *exist concretely*; and — as a "pure" mathematician — he can frame his concepts in such a manner that their extension does not at all involve the assumption of such possibilities.

§ 52. "*Mathesis pura*" as properly logical and as extra-logical. The "mathematics of mathematicians".

To be sure, not only the lower level of logical analytics but also this higher level and finally analytics as all-embracing — as *mathesis universalis* — thereby lose the essential part of their properly logical sense, of their sense as theory of science; since logic, even where it intends to be a mere formal logic, still intends to relate to possible provinces and possible cognition of them, possible systematic theories, to lay down eidetic laws of possibility for them in advance and as norms. If, in this endeavor, it comes across the fact that conditions for possible truth and for truly existing theories and theorizable provinces of cognition can be exhibited even in the forms of "judgments" themselves, it naturally does not thereby relinquish its specifically logical sense. But perhaps it takes a step in that direction, if it becomes aware of the essential stratification / that divides it into an analytics of <124> non-contradiction and an analytics of possible truth, and accordingly recognizes:

Firstly, that *judgments, taken purely as senses* (and, included in them, all objectivities purely as object-senses), are subject to *a self-contained set of formal laws* — and, at the level of "distinctness", a set of laws of consequence, inconsistency, and non-contradiction — that *in themselves say nothing as yet about a possible being* of objectivities that perhaps correspond to the judgments, or about a possible truth of these judgments themselves; and if, in addition, it recognizes:

Secondly, that the *laws of non-contradiction* evidently take on *mediately* the value of *logical laws*, absolutely first and most universal laws of *possible truth*; as well as that, in accordance with the specifically logical intent, possible being and possible truth ought to be investigated with regard to eidetic laws governing their possibility, and senses (pure judgments) ought to be thought of in this connexion as related to such possibilities —

and these ought accordingly to be thought of as presupposed along with them.

If that has been made clear, one can set up a whole science that, freed from the specifically logical aim, neither explores nor intends to explore anything beyond the universal realm of pure apophantic senses. It becomes apparent that, when questions about possible truth are consistently excluded in this manner, and the truth-concept itself is similarly excluded, one has not actually lost any of this logical mathesis; one still has the whole of it: as *"purely" formal mathematics.* This purity in restricting the theme to objective senses in their own essentialness — to "judgments" in the amplified sense — can also be exercised as it were *unconsciously*: in that the mathematician, following the custom long-established in mathematical analysis, never asks about the possible actuality of multiplicities or about conditions for their possible actuality that are based on the mere sense-form, as apophantic *logic* does traditionally. A trace of impurity may remain, since the mathematically constructed forms of multiplicities are, as a rule, thought of also as forms of possible actualities: provided only that — as has always been in fact the case — this thought never exercises any function in mathematics itself. *Thus it is understandable that, for a* (consciously or un-
<125> consciously) *"pure" formal mathematics, there / can be no cognitional considerations other than those of "non-contradiction"*, of immediate or mediate *analytic consequence or inconsistency,* which manifestly include all questions of *mathematical "existence"*.

It is otherwise, to be sure, for the *logician*: Being interested in a theory of science even when, consistently broadening the traditional confines, he presses onward to *mathesis universalis* (as I myself did in the *Logische Untersuchungen*), he will not easily come upon the thought of making this reduction to an analytics of pure senses; and therefore he will acquire mathematics as only an *amplified logic,* which, as a logic, relates essentially to *possible* object-provinces and theories. Philosophically one needs here the fullest awareness and a radical cognition of the demarcations that must be made. To interpret and ask what the professional mathematician presumably means is not enough. One must see that a *formal mathematics, reduced to the above-described purity, has its own legitimacy* and that, for mathematics, there is in any case no necessity to go beyond that purity. At the same time, however, a great advance is made philosophically by the insight that such a restrictive reduction of *logical* mathesis (formal logic, when it has attained the completeness befitting its essence) — namely its reduction to a *pure analytics of non-contradiction* — is essentially its reduction to a science that has to do with nothing but apophantic senses, in respect of their own essential Apriori, and that in this manner the *proper sense of "formal mathematics"*, the mathematics to which every properly logical intention (that is: every intention belonging to a theory of science) remains alien — the mathematics of mathematicians — at last becomes *fundamentally clarified.* Here lies the *sole legitimate distinction between formal logic and mere formal mathematics.*

§ 53. Elucidations by the example of the Euclidean multiplicity.

In view of the importance of the matter, it might be useful to add some elucidations of the nature of the reduction of the theory of multiplicities to a pure sense-theory.

The theory of multiplicities, we said, presents itself to the logician, first of all, as a science of the apriori-constructable form-types of *possible* multiplicities (or, correlatively, / form- <126>
types of *possible* deductive sciences, systematic theories) that have *possible truth.* Here reduction to purity, when explicated in detail, yields the following: "Euclidean multiplicity", to begin with this handy example, signified in the first place a form for possible deductive sciences as possible systems of true propositions, a form exemplified in Euclidean space-geometry, taken now as one among an open infinity of possible deductive sciences having this same categorial form. The reduction that severs every relation to the presupposition of possible truths delivers the form (still that of the "Euclidean multiplicity") as the form of a *system of possible propositions (judgments) purely as senses*, and, moreover, of such propositions as can be framed — purely as judgments — in distinct evidence, not only singly, but as a systematic whole: in a word, propositions that make up a self-contained system of pure consistency ("non-contradiction"). Thus the Euclidean form now has as its extension, *not deductive sciences* relating to *possibly existing* provinces, but *non-contra-*

dictory systems of judgments. And it indicates a law of form, which says: Any group of judgments that is subsumable under the Euclidean group of forms of axioms is, a priori, unifiable without contradiction; and, a priori, all consequences that can be derived from that group of judgments according to the principles (genuine axioms) of the lower analytics of non-contradiction are unifiable with those initial propositions; they make up a non-contradictory system, and a definite one if we can prove that the Euclidean system of axioms is definite.[1]

As the correlate of a *possible* systematic theory, we have a *possible multiplicity*, a possible object-province that it theorizes systematically. When this possibility is left out of account, its
<127> place is taken by a multiplicity, / not of objects *simpliciter*, but of supposed objects as supposed — that is to say, *object-senses, as substrate-senses, that are adapted to function harmoniously in a judgment-system* as substrates of predications. The substrate-senses, however, are only fundamental object-senses belonging to that theory, which has itself been reduced to the pure *theory-sense*. It itself, in respect of all its single and combined judgments and all the categorial fashionings that occur in them, is, after the present reduction, a "supposed objectivity as supposed", an object-sense or a judgment in the amplified sense; only we are dealing here with categorial forms of a higher level than that of the forms imposed directly on the substrate-senses.

It is hardly necessary to repeat, with express reference to analytics as amplified to become pure mathesis, what we have already said about the analytics of the lower level. As a science, pure mathesis naturally aims at truths concerning its province — that is to say, truths about senses and their relationships of consequence or consistency. But laws of truth (of correctness,

[1] *Author's note:* Obviously there lies behind this the primitive fundamental law of the analytics of pure consistency: Two judgments (in the broadest sense) that follow as consequences from a harmonious judgment are compatible in the unity of one judgment; they may be "multiplied". "Multiplication" in the "logical calculus" signifies just this operation of the conjunctive combination of judgments, thought of as non-contradictory in themselves, to make up one judgment. The corresponding operational law (with a reiterational sense) enunciates as a principle: A priori, any judgment (any "*distinct*", internally non-contradictory one) can be united with any other such judgment ⟨that is an analytic consequence of the same internally non-contradictory antecedent⟩ to make up another non-contradictory judgment. In the sphere of consistency, the validity of judgments signifies their harmoniousness in themselves, the possibility of performing them distinctly, *sc.* as the possibility of phantasying such a performance.

of possible true being as such, and so forth) belong no more to the province of *pure* mathesis than to that of any other science except logic proper. Truth belongs no more among the "purely" mathematical predicates than among the predicates of Nature that are explored thematically by the natural sciences.

§ 54. Concluding ascertainment of the relationship between formal logic and formal ontology.

a. The problem.

In our last observations we separated from all logical interests the idea of *mathesis universalis,* as a science of apophantic senses belonging to all categorial levels, in order to grasp that idea quite purely in its peculiarity. We now bring the excluded interests into play again.

Mathematics therefore lies once more within the theory of science, where it exercises functions pertaining to criticism; and its theories themselves assume a corresponding functional sense. The laws that state the relation between non-contradiction and truth are pronounced in advance; and then, conformably with them, introduction of the truth-concepts (true predictive judgment, truly existing substrate-object, true predicate, true multiplicity, and so forth) is allowed and is effected accordingly. The laws of consequence and non-contradiction become laws of possible material truth. In / them the material contents (the cores) <128>
remain indeterminates <and accordingly the laws themselves retain their universality>; nevertheless, with this universality, they are thought of now as relating to <some> possible objectivity. Possible truth, as correctness, signifies after all a possibility of adequation to possible matters themselves, possible affairs themselves. Thus, for example, formal laws of the possible correctness of predicative judgments include, *ipso facto,* laws of the possibility of predicatively formed affair-complexes. In this manner the whole mathematical system of logic becomes related to any possible objectivity whatever.

We now ask the following questions. *Is formal logic to be regarded therefore as formal ontology*? And why is it that, in any case, the analytics of mere non-contradiction cannot be so regarded, even though it too relates to all judgments and therefore to anything whatever?

b. The two correlative senses of formal logic.

Speaking straightforwardly of just anything, of just any object or of objects universally, normally signifies speaking of them as actualities or possibilities — in the case of the apriori Any-Whatever, it normally signifies speaking of eidetic possibilities, possibilities that can be conceived in fully free phantasy. Therefore, if we call an apriori science of any objects whatever *formal ontology*, the name signifies forthwith *a science of possible objects purely as possible*. Naturally the thematic realm of that science includes all those categorial modifications of "any objects whatever" that can be conceived as possible. Any other apriori science would then be a non-formal ontology; it would be an ontology with respect to its objective province, as a particular province of possible objectivities.

Consequently we must say: *The aforesaid pure mathematics of non-contradiction*, in its detachment from logic as theory of science, *does not deserve to be called a formal ontology*. It is an ontology of pure judgments *as senses* and, more particularly, an ontology of the *forms* belonging to non-contradictory — and, in that sense, possible — senses: possible in distinct evidence. To any possible object there corresponds its object-sense. Every sense-form pertaining to possible objects naturally occurs among the possible sense-forms dealt with by "extra-logical" mathematics. But the just-mentioned possibility of a sense-form ⟨as distinctly non-contradictory⟩ does not contain, in and of itself, the least possibility of objects with a sense corresponding to it; and indeed even this "corresponding" itself takes us beyond the sphere of pure senses. /

<129> As soon as we introduce such correspondence and interrelate the two possibilities, that of non-contradictory object-senses and that of possible objects themselves, thus raising questions of possible correctness, we stand within logic proper; and in it the whole mathematics of judgments as senses forthwith takes on a formal-ontological *significance* — *but still we must not, without more ado, pronounce it formal ontology*.

Let us consider. Formal analytics, as the formal logic of possible truth, has (so we explained) a *critical* attitude. That is precisely why its theme is the total realm of judgments (always including the totality of categorial senses), considered in respect of their possible adequation. But as long as we regard *judgments as our exclusive theme* — even though we bring in the corresponding possible objectivities that they might fit, thus taking on predicates of "correctness", of truth — *our attitude is not yet properly formal-ontological.* On the other hand, just as in the sciences the continually resumed critical attitude and, with it, the repeated focusing on judgments are only a *means* serving the primary interest, the interest in the affairs themselves and how they are in truth: so the focusing on judgments is likewise only a means in the case of that logic which does not lose sight of its calling as a theory of science. *According to its final sense* such a logic is therefore *not a pure formal apophantic logic but a formal-ontological logic.* An apophantics *can,* it is true, be worked out purely as such, with a fixed and exclusive thematical focusing on judgments as senses and on the possibilitiesof their adequation; and it may be said that the tendency to such an elaboration was effective in the historical development of logic. But the deep sense of *formal analytics, the sense that measures up to its task as theory of science, is that of being the science of the possible categorial forms in which substrate objectivities can truly exist.*

Categorially formed objectivity is *not an apophantical concept; rather* it is *an ontological concept.* To be sure, the essence of such an objectivity consists precisely in being a *fulfilled* judgment having a corresponding sense-form. When the judger, with his focusing on what is objective, goes on to an evidential having of the objectivity itself, the synthesis of fulfilment is essentially a synthesis of coincidence. We indeed say (while reflecting on the synthesis and making a statement about it), and we say with evidence: The very same objectivity / that I just now meant and <130>
still mean is itself given. Let us take the ideal case. If the fulfilments are ideally perfect, then the substrate-objectivities with all their categorial formings are themselves given in the strictest sense; the evidence actualizes and seizes upon them themselves as they are in truth.[1] By virtue of the evident coincidence with the

[1] *Author's note:* It actualizes them, naturally, with the hierarchical structure that, in the particular case, belongs to them according to their sense; and therefore it actualizes them in a hierarchy of evidences founded one upon another, which, in their synthetic unity, make up precisely the one evidence of the one categorial objectivity, structured thus and so: the unity of the having of the objectivity itself in consequence of actualizing it itself.

mere judicial meanings — that is, the supposed substrates in the supposed categorial forms — it is evident that *each judicial meaning is contained in the truly existing objectivity*; the only difference being that here the judicial meaning is saturated with fullness of cognition.

That is precisely why we have the *double sense of evidence* — parallel to that of *judgement* — which we have already brought to light. In one sense evidence is equivalent to: truly existing predicatively formed affair-complex in the mode itself-givenness (truly existing substrate-objectivity with such and such truly existing properties, relationships, and so forth). In the second and correlative sense evidence signifies itself-givenness of the correctness of the judicial meaning, by virtue of its fitting the evidence, in the first sense: that is to say, the categorial objectivity as itself-given. As cognitive-judging subjects, we have (so we have already explained) no objectivities other than categorially formed ones — nor does it make any sense for us, in that capacity, to want something different. Truly existing Nature, truly existing sociality or culture, and the like — these have absolutely no sense other than that of being certain categorial objectivities, to press on toward which by scientific method, generating them by following that method, is the whole aim of science.

Let no one oppose us here with metaphysics. If metaphysics is the word for a science, and not for obscure thoughts and locutions, then there is ⟨no metaphysical, because there is⟩ *no rational problem of "a formal and a real significance of the logical"*.[1] If a science — for example: natural science — does not satisfy us, then (provided that the legitimacy of its evidences — that is: the perfection with which it has its objectivities themselves — remains unassailed and accordingly the science itself remains
<131> unassailed) that can signify only that the / science in question is somehow one-sided, and that still further cognitions relating to its province are necessary: new categorial formations, relating to the same substrate-sphere, which must be set as goals to be attained by following a method that brings corresponding evidences about. If, instead of such a determinate science, such a science with material content, we take formal logic, it is a formal-

[1] *Author's note:* See the criticism of Lotze's false problem in my *VI. Logische Untersuchung*, [§ 65, 2d and] 3d ed., pp. 199f. [*Cf.* Farber, *op. cit.*, pp. 474ff.]

ontological science, provided that it consciously makes the possible forms of categorial objectivities (not those of the corresponding object-senses [1]) its final theme. We have a more special case of formal-ontological science if logic explores those categorialia that make up the form of a deductive theory, and if a deductive theory is understood to be, not a system of judgments, but a system of possible, predicatively formed, affair-complexes and, in its entirety, a distinctively formed unity belonging to a categorial objectivity.

Obviously the two correlative senses of evidence and the two correlative senses of truth that we cleared up signify *two correlative senses of formal logic*: Starting with the traditional *focusing on judgments* as apophantic meanings or opinions — that is to say, giving preference to the attitude of criticism — we acquire an *apophantic logic,* which, when fully amplified (on the side where lie the categorial sense-forms) to include the apophantic sense-forms of theories, attains the status of *mathesis universalis*. If we give preference to the *focusing on possible categorial objectivities themselves* or their forms, we are pursuing consistently from the very beginning a *formal-ontological logic,* which however will obviously be forced, for reasons of method, to make judgment-senses into objects — though only as a means, whereas its final purpose concerns *the* objects.

c. The idea of formal ontology can be separated from the idea of theory of science.

After this investigation, we may consider that the double sense of logic and the sense of the two focusings that correspond respectively to the two sides of logic have been thoroughly clarified. Naturally the mathematician is rather indifferent to such clarifications. In his positivity, living entirely with a view to discovering new theoretical results, he is not in the least interested in changes of attitude or focus that convert an equivalent into an equivalent. Transitions from one thing to another that is evidently its perfect correlate yield "the same", in his sense of the phrase. But the logician who does not regret the absence of such clarifications or who declares them to be of no consequence is,

Translator's note: Reading *entsprechender gegenständlicher* instead of *entsprechenden gegenständlichen*.

in any case, no philosopher; since here it is a matter of *insights*
<132> *that grasp the essential structure* of a formal logic. Unless / the essential sense of logic is clear, it is manifestly impossible to take up the great questions that, within ⟨the sphere of inquiry prescribed by⟩ the idea of a universal philosophy, must be asked about logic and its philosophic function.

In conclusion let us note further that *the task of formal ontology can be undertaken directly from the very beginning, without starting from the idea of a theory of science.* In that case the question of formal ontology is: What can be stated within the limits of the empty region, object as such? Purely a priori, with this formal universality, the syntactical fashionings are available, by means of which an endless diversity of new categorialia can conceivably be generated from any objects (from any Somethings whatever) thought of as possibilities given beforehand. In that connexion, moreover, we shall come upon the distinctive character of those possible generatings which yield merely distinct meanings that are contradictory and therefore cannot lead to possible objects themselves; and so forth. Obviously the whole of formal mathesis will then accrue. *Afterwards,* to be sure, we can at any time make clear to ourselves the significance of this ontology for theory of science, a significance that it has because each science, within its own province, aims at "true being" — that is: at categorialia whose forms (if the science is genuine) must be among the forms that are formally-ontologically possible.

PART II. <133>

FROM FORMAL TO TRANSCENDENTAL LOGIC.

CHAPTER 1.

Psychologism and the laying of a transcendental foundation for logic.

§ 55. IS THE DEVELOPMENT OF LOGIC AS OBJECTIVE-FORMAL ENOUGH TO SATISFY EVEN THE IDEA OF A MERELY FORMAL THEORY OF SCIENCE?

In the first part of our investigation we explicated the sense predelineated for traditional formal logic by the Aristotelian analytics. Formal logic presented itself as a completely separate science. We brought to light the sharp essential delimitation of its province and likewise the strata-disciplines combined a priori within it by founding. We also learned to understand its perfectly correlated and therefore equivalent themes (as formal apophantics and as formal ontology), which allow us to speak of one logic treated in two attitudes.

It might now appear that, as philosophers, we were through with this logic and could leave its theoretical development to the mathematicians, who are already working on it anyhow, untroubled by the requirements of philosophic cognition. Consequently it might appear that, if we as logicians still had tasks to set ourselves, they could concern only an amplification of the idea of logic. The idea guiding us at the beginning was that of an all-embracing apriori theory of science. This theory was to deal with the (in the broadest sense) "formal" Apriori pertaining to all sciences as such: that which embraces them all with apriori universality; that by which they remain necessarily bound, so far as they are in truth sciences at all. In any case, form, in the sense proper to analytic or "formal" logic, is something of that sort: Every / science generates categorial formations and is <134>
subject to the eidetic laws of their form.

Therefore it might now be asked whether this analytico-formal theory of science completely fills out the idea of a universal theory of science, or whether the analytico-formal theory must be supplemented by a *material* theory. The peculiarity of analytics that determines its concept of form lies, as we know, in the circumstance that it takes the "cores" (the "cognition-materials") present in possible judgments and cognitions (and restricting these to definite object-spheres) and makes them into *optional* cores, thought of only as cores that are to be kept identical: modes of anything whatever. If we let fullness flow back into these cores, which have been kept emptily universal, can we not perhaps gain a material Apriori that has universal significance for the theory of science?

If we determine the *concept of the analytic Apriori* by means of pure formal analytics, taken in its full breadth, [1] then our question concerns a new Apriori, a "*synthetic*" or, more descriptively, a "nuclear" Apriori (an Apriori of the cores): a material Apriori and, more particularly, a *universal* material Apriori, one that *ties together all separate material-apriori provinces in one totality*. In other words, we are asking: Is not every existent — thought of concretely as materially determined and determinable — essentially an existent in a *universe of being*, a "*world*"? Is not every *possible* existent (as this word "essentially" indicates) something that belongs to its *possible* universe of being; accordingly, is not every material Apriori something that belongs to a universal Apriori, namely the Apriori that predelineates the apriori material form [*die apriorische sachhaltige Form*] for a possible universe of the existent? It seems therefore that we must now steer toward a material ontology, an ontology proper, which would supplement the merely analytico-formal ontology.

But, however obvious this whole line of thought may be, we have as yet no right to follow the newly emergent guiding idea. *For it is not the case that we were actually through with formal analytics* — we, not as mathematical technicians, but as philosophic logicians and therefore as seriously intent on doing justice to the final idea of an analytico-formal theory of science. Has this intention been perfectly satisfied by our earlier investigations? /

[1] *Author's note:* In any case, this is a fundamental concept of the analytic, the one delimited in the "*III. Untersuchung*" (*Logische Untersuchungen*, Vol. II). [See particularly §§ 11f. *Cf.* Farber, *op. cit.*, pp. 283–313, particularly pp. 293–295.]

§ 56. THE REPROACH OF PSYCHOLOGISM CAST AT EVERY CONSIDERATION OF LOGICAL FORMATIONS THAT IS DIRECTED TO THE SUBJECTIVE. <135>

Let us begin by considering the demand that logical researches be *two-sided,* a demand that we stated in our preparatory considerations, [1] but without a sufficient clarification of the thematizing activity directed to the subjective. This demand was stated as quite universal and therefore as valid in the case of the logic that is first in itself, namely analytic logic. *The sense and the legitimacy of this thematizing of the subjective by logic* — a thematizing that, to say it forthwith, will not claim the significance of a separate logical discipline, to be set apart from analytics as directed to the Objective and ideal — are now in question.

But here at the entrance stands the bogy of *psychologism.* Against the demand for logical researches directed to the subjective, an appeal is made to the first volume of my *Logische Untersuchungen* (which bears the significant title, "*Prolegomena zur reinen Logik*" ["Prolegomena to *Pure* Logic"]); and the objection is raised that the "*Prolegomena*" were intended to effect the radical elimination of everything psychological from the theme of logic, first from that of traditional logic and then from that of logic as amplified to become the full *mathesis universalis.* The empiricism that had become dominant (anti-Platonism in its historical origin) was blind to the peculiar Objectivity of all ideal formations; everywhere it re-interpreted them psychologistically as the concomitant psychic activities and habitualities: This was true, in particular, respecting those objectivities (irreal, according to their own sense) which — as statements, as judgments, as truths, as arguments, proofs, and theories, and as categorial objectivities that occur as formed within all these, — make up the thematic province of logic. The judgments of which logic speaks in its laws are not the mental judgment-processes (the judgings); the truths are not the mental evidence-processes; the proofs are not the subjective-psychic provings; and so forth.

The theory of cardinal numbers (which, as we know, is itself a part of logic) has to do, not with mental processes of collecting

[1] *Author's note:* See § 8, [pp. 33–36,] *supra.*

and counting, but with numbers; the theory of ordered sets and ordinal numbers has to do, not with mental processes of ordering, but with ordered sets themselves and their forms; and, in like manner, syllogistics does not have to do with the psychic processes of judging and inferring. The same is true of the other Objective / <136> sciences. No one would designate as the province of natural science the psychic processes of experiencing Nature and thinking about it, rather than Nature itself. Here the psychologistic temptations, to which recent logic had yielded almost universally, did not exist. And, according to all this, every thematizing of the subjective (instead of which most people will immediately say "psychological thematizing") seems to be excluded for logic, as it is for every other Objective science (except human and animal psychology). The subjective belongs in the province, not of logic, but of psychology.

But then what about our demand that correlative investigations of the subjective be included in logic? Is it not on a par with the corresponding demand in the case of any other science?

Soon after publication of the *Logische Untersuchungen* the reproach was cast that the phenomenological investigations demanded there under the name "clarification" of the fundamental concepts of pure logic, investigations which the second volume attempted to block out in broad outline, signified a relapse into psychologism.

It is noteworthy that readers regarded the "*Prolegomena zur reinen Logik*" as an unqualified overcoming of psychologism and failed to take notice that nowhere in that volume was psychologism pure and simple (as a *universal* epistemological aberration) the theme. Rather the discussion concerned *a psychologism with a quite particular sense*, namely the psychologizing of the irreal significational formations that are the theme of logic. The obscurity still generally prevalent today concerning the problem of a universal epistemological psychologism, an obscurity that affects the fundamental sense of the whole of transcendental philosophy (including so-called "theory of knowledge") is something that, at the time, I myself had not entirely overcome; though precisely the "phenomenological" investigations in the second volume, so far as they paved the way to a transcendental phenomenology, opened up at the same time the necessary avenues to the setting and the radical overcoming of the problem of transcendental psychologism. Clarifications pertinent to this problem will be attempted later in the present essay.[1]

[1] *Author's note:* See Chapter 6, particularly § 99, [pp. 250 ff., *infra*]. The reader is also referred in advance to more detailed expositions in publications that are to follow shortly. [*Cf.* Edmund Husserl, "*Phänomenologie und Anthropologie*," *Philosophy and Phenomenological Research*, Vol. II, No. 1 (September, 1941), pp. 1–14.]

Thus it is very necessary to go into detail again concerning the *particular problem of psychologism* treated in the "*Prolegomena*". But we intend, not to confine ourselves to our earlier presentations, which need improvement in particular points, but rather to give the problem a purer form and also set it in more general contexts, which will provide a transition to the clarification of the necessary sense of a "two-sidedly" inquiring logic, one that is, in the genuine sense, philosophic. / Our chief purpose is to show <137>
that a logic directed straightforwardly to its proper thematic sphere, and active exclusively in cognizing that, remains stuck fast in a naïveté which shuts it off from the philosophic merit of radical self-understanding and fundamental self-justification, or, what amounts to the same thing, the merit of being most perfectly scientific, the attainment of which is the raison d'être of philosophy, above all as theory of science.

§ 57. Logical psychologism and logical idealism.

a. The motives for this psychologism.

We have already [1] spoken of the difficulty of separating from psychological subjectivity the psychically produced formations making up the thematic domain of logic — the difficulty, that is, of regarding judgments (and likewise sets, cardinal numbers, and so forth) as anything other than psychic occurrences in the human beings who are doing the judging. What accrues originaliter in the judicative doing, as subjects and predicates, premise-propositions, conclusion-propositions, and so forth, does indeed make its appearance, member by member, in the field of the judger's consciousness. It is nothing alien to the psychic, nothing like a physical process, a physical formation accruing in physical action. On the contrary, the judgment-members and the whole judgment-formation make their appearance in the psychic activity itself, which goes on as a process of consciousness; they make their appearance in it without separation from it and not outside but inside. Indeed, the misled followers of English Empiricism do not even succeed in making a distinction here between the judging mental process and the formation that takes shape "in it", member by member. What is true of originally

[1] *Author's note:* See § 10, [pp. 38 f.,] *supra.*

generative actions of thinking is true also of the secondary modes of thinking — for example: having something come to mind confusedly and other processes of meaning "indistinctly" (and equally true of originally generative actions belonging to the parallel types of rational consciousness, rational emotional and volitional consciousness, and true also of *their* corresponding secondary modes). It is in the confused thinking consciousness itself, and not as something external, that these confused thoughts make their appearance. How then, in logic, have we stepped outside the field of "psychic phenomena", "phenomena of internal experience"? It would follow that all the Data for logic are real occurrences belonging to the sphere of psychology; and, as such, according to the usual view, they would be unambiguous-
<138> ly determined within the universal causal nexus / of the real world and explainable by causal laws.

But this latter point may be left out of consideration. Our main concern here is the *equating of the formations produced by judging* (and then, naturally, of all similar formations produced by rational acts of any other sort) *with phenomena appearing in internal experience*. This equating is based on their making their appearance "internally", in the act-consciousness itself. Thus concepts, judgments, arguments, proofs, theories, would be psychic occurrences; and logic would be, as John Stuart Mill said it is, a "part, or branch, of psychology".[1] This highly plausible conception is *logical psychologism*.

b. The ideality of logical formations as their making their appearance irreally in the logico-psychic sphere.

In opposition to this we say: There is an original evidence that, in repeated acts, which are quite alike or else similar, the produced judgments, arguments, and so forth, are not merely quite alike or similar but *numerically, identically, the same* judgments, arguments, and the like. Their "making an appearance" in the domain of consciousness is multiple. The particular formative processes of thinking are temporally outside one another (viewed as real psychic processes in real human beings, they are outside

[1] *Translator's note: An Examination of Sir William Hamilton's Philosophy*, Chap. XX.

one another in Objective time); they are individually different and separated. Not so, however, the thoughts that are thought in the thinking. To be sure, the thoughts do not make their appearance in consciousness as something "external". They are not real objects, not spatial objects, but irreal formations produced by the mind; and their peculiar essence excludes spatial extension, original locality, and mobility. Like other products of the mind, they admit, however, of a physical embodiment: in their case, an embodiment by the sensuous verbal signs; and thus they gain a secondary spatial existence (that of the spoken or written sentence). Every sort of irreality, of which the ideality of significations and the different [1] ideality of universal essences or species are particular cases, has manners of possible participation in reality. Yet this in no way alters the essential separation between the real and the irreal.

But more deeply penetrating clarifications are indispensable here. By studying and paralleling the evidence of the real and the irreal we shall gain an understanding of the universal homogeneity of objectivities — *as* objectivities. /

§ 58. The evidence of ideal objects analogous to that of individual objects. <139>

The evidence of irreal objects, objects that are ideal in the broadest sense, is, in its effect, quite analogous to the evidence of ordinary so-called internal and external experience, which alone — on no other grounds than prejudice — is commonly thought capable of effecting an original Objectivation. The identity and, therefore, the *objectivity* of something ideal can be directly "seen" (and, if we wished to give the word a suitably amplified sense, directly experienced) with the same originality as the identity of an object of experience in the usual sense — for example: an experienced object belonging to Nature or an experienced immanent object (any psychic Datum). In repeated experiences — before any repetition, in the continuous modification of the

[1] *Author's note:* The exposition substantiating this distinction, not yet made in the "*Prolegomena*", will be offered in my *Logische Studien* [*Logical Studies*], which will soon appear. [See Edmund Husserl, *Erfahrung und Urteil: Untersuchungen zur Genealogie der Logik* (*Experience and Judgment: Investigations pertaining to the Genealogy* of *Logic*) *ausgearbeitet und herausgegeben von Ludwig Landgrebe*, Prag, 1939, and Hamburg, 1948 and 1954, § 64, *c*), pp. 314–317.]

momentary perception in retention and protention, then in possible recollections, repeatable at will — there comes about, with their synthesis, the consciousness of The Same, moreover as an "experience" of this self-sameness. The possibility of such original identification belongs, as essential correlate, to the sense of *every* object of *experience* in the usual and pregnant sense, a sense determined to the effect that experience is an *evident seizing* upon and *having* of either an immanent or a real *individual* Datum *itself*.

In just the same fashion, we say, there belongs to the sense of an *irreal* object the possibility of its identification on the basis of its own manners of being itself seized upon and had. Actually the effect of this "identification" is like that of an "experience", except that an irreal object is *not individuated in consequence of a temporality belonging to it originally.*[1]

The *possibility of deception* is inherent in the evidence of experience and does not annul either its fundamental character or its effect; though becoming evidentially aware of ⟨actual⟩ deception "annuls" the deceptive experience or evidence itself. The evidence of a new experience is what makes the previously uncontested experience undergo that modification of believing called "annulment" or "cancellation"; and it alone can do so. Evidence of experience is therefore always presupposed by the process. The conscious "dispelling" of a deception, with the
<140> originality of "now I *see* that it / is an illusion", is itself a species of evidence, namely evidence of the nullity of something experienced or, correlatively, evidence of the "annulment" of the (previously unmodified) experiential evidence. This too holds for *every* evidence, for every "experience" in the amplified sense. Even an ostensibly apodictic evidence can become disclosed as deception and, in that event, presupposes a similar evidence by which it is "shattered".

§ 59. A universal characterization of evidence as the giving of something itself.

The continual obstacle that may have been sensed during this exposition is owing solely to the usual, fundamentally wrong,

[1] *Author's note:* Irreal objectivities can very well assume an extra-essential relatedness to time, likewise an extra-essential relatedness to space and an extra-essential reification.

interpretation of evidence, an interpretation made possible by the utter lack of a serious phenomenological analysis of the effective performance common to all forms of evidence. Thus it happens that evidence is usually conceived as an *absolute apodicticity*, an absolute security against deceptions — an apodicticity quite incomprehensibly ascribed to a single mental process torn from the concrete, essentially unitary, context of subjective mental living. The usual theorist sees in evidence an absolute criterion of truth; though, by such a criterion, not only external but also, in strictness, all internal evidence would necessarily be done away with. If, being unable to explicate evidence as a functioning intentionality, the theorist, by a kind of sensualistic substitution, falls back on so-called feelings of evidence, then their attainment of truth itself (an attainment he still ascribes to evidence) becomes a miracle, nay, at bottom a countersense.

Let no one upbraid us with the renowned evidence of "internal perception", as an instance counter to these statements. For internal perception's giving of its "immanent percept" itself — about this we shall have more to say [1] — is, by itself alone, the giving of something-itself which is only a preliminary to an object; it is not the giving of something-itself which is an object in the proper sense. Perception *alone* is never a full Objectivating performance, if we understand such a performance to be indeed the seizing upon an *object* itself. We accept internal perception as a seizing upon an object itself, only because we are tacitly taking into account possible recollection, repeatable at will. When
actualized, recollection gives for the first time original / certainty <141>
of the being of a subjective *object* in the full sense, a so-called psychic Datum, as something acquired originaliter and identifiable at will, something to which one can "always go back again" and which one can recognize in a reactivation as the selfsame. Naturally, the concomitant intentional relation to such a "*synthesis of recognition*" plays a similar rôle in the case of each external objectivity — which is by no means to say that it makes up the full performance effected by external experience.

Evidence, as has already become apparent to us by the above explanations, designates *that performance on the part of intentionality which consists in the giving of something-itself* [*die intentionale*

[1] *Author's note:* See § 107, [pp. 283–290,] *infra.*

Leistung der Selbstgebung]. More precisely, it is the universal pre-eminent form of "intentionality", of "consciousness of something", in which there is consciousness of the intended-to objective affair in the mode itself-seized-upon, itself-seen — correlatively, in the mode: being with it itself in the manner peculiar to consciousness. We can also say that it is the primal consciousness: I am seizing upon "*it itself*" originaliter, as contrasted with seizing upon it in an image or as some other, intuitional or empty, fore-meaning.

Still we must immediately point out here that evidence has *different* modes of originality. *The primitive mode of the giving of something-itself* is *perception*. The being-with is for me, as percipient, consciously my now-being-with: I myself with the perceived itself. An intentionally modified and more complicated mode of the giving of something itself is the memory that does not emerge emptily but, on the contrary, actualizes "it itself" *again: clear* recollection. By its own phenomenological composition, clear recollection is intrinsically a "reproductive" consciousness, a consciousness of the object itself as my past object, as (correlatively) the object which was perceived by me (the same Ego, but reproduced in the mode, "past"), and with which I (the active Ego as present for himself) am now "again" — with it itself.

Let us note here, because we might otherwise be misled, [1] that the modification of itself-giving as perception and recollection plays very different rôles for *real* and *ideal* objectivities respectively. This is connected with the circumstance that *the latter have no temporal loci to bind them individuatingly*. Merely because of an essentially possible alteration of attitude or focus, any clear
<142> explicit recollection of an ideal species changes into a / perception of it — something naturally excluded in the case of temporally individuated objects.

We are not opposing our universal characterization of evidence to the usual one as though ours were a new "theory", an attractive interpretation, which is yet to be tested, who knows how — perhaps in the end even by experiments on thinking. Rather we are presenting it as an evidence attained at a higher level, by the phenomenological explication of any experience and of any

[1] *Author's note:* As I was misled at the time of the *Logische Untersuchungen*.

actually exercised "insight" (something that others, without reason, have separated quite essentially from what are usually called experiences). This higher evidence, in turn, can be itself explicated and understood in respect of its effect only by means of an evidence belonging to a third level; and so *in infinitum*. *Only in seeing can I bring out what is truly present in a seeing*; I must make *a seeing explication of the proper essence of seeing*.

Precisely because it gives its objective affair as the affair itself, any consciousness that gives something-itself can establish rightness, correctness, for another consciousness (for a mental meaning process that is merely unclear or even one that is confused, or for one that is indeed intuitive but merely prefigurative, or that in some other manner fails to give the object itself) — and it does so, as we had occasion to describe, [1] in the form of *synthetic adequation* to the "affairs themselves"; or else it establishes incorrectness, in the form of inadequation, as the evidentness of nullity. Thus the givings of things themselves are the acts producing evident legitimacy or rightness; they are creative *primal institutings of rightness*, of truth as correctness [2] — precisely because, for the objectivities themselves as existing for us, they are the originally constitutive acts, originally institutive of sense and being. In like fashion, original inadequations, as givings of nullity itself, are primal institutings of falsity, of wrongness as incorrectness (*positio* changed: of the trueness of the nullity or incorrectness). They constitute, not objectivity simpliciter — that is: existing objectivity — but rather, on the basis of supposed or meant objectivity, cancellation of that "meaning" — that is: its non-being.

§ 60. The fundamental laws of intentionality and the universal function of evidence.

We have already touched on the fact that the giving of something-itself is, like every other single intentional process, a *function* in the all-embracing / nexus of consciousness. The effect <143>
produced by a single intentional process, in particular its effect as a giving of something-itself, its effect as evidence, is therefore not shut off singly, The single evidence, by its own intentionality,

[1] *Author's note:* See § 44, *b*, β, [pp. 122–124,] *supra*.
[2] *Author's note:* See § 45, [p. 126,] *supra*.

can implicitly "demand" further givings of the object itself; it can "refer one" to them for a supplementation of its Objectivating effect. Let us turn our attention to that which pervades all conscious life, in order to appropriate a significant cognition that concerns evidence universally.

The concept of any intentionality whatever — any life-process of consciousness-of something or other — and *the concept of evidence, the intentionality that is the giving of something-itself, are essentially correlative.* Let us confine ourselves to "positing" consciousness, positional consciousness. In the case of "neutral" consciousness everything that we shall now state becomes modified in an easily understood manner; the places of evidence, adequation, and the rest, are taken by their as-if modifications. The following obtains as a *fundamental law of intentionality*:

Absolutely any consciousness of anything whatever belongs a priori to an openly endless multiplicity of possible modes of consciousness, which can always be connected synthetically in the unity-form of conjoint acceptance (*con-posito*) to make one consciousness, as a consciousness of *"the Same"*. To this multiplicity belong essentially the modes of a manifold *evidential consciousness,* which fits in correspondingly as an evidential having, either of the Same itself or of an Other itself that evidently annuls it.

Thus *evidence is a universal mode of intentionality, related to the whole life of consciousness.* Thanks to evidence, the life of consciousness has an *all-pervasive teleological structure,* a pointedness toward "reason" and even a pervasive tendency toward it — that is: toward the discovery of correctness (and, at the same time, toward the lasting acquisition of correctness) and toward the cancelling of incorrectnesses (thereby ending their acceptance as acquired possessions).

It is not only with respect to this all-pervasive teleological function that evidence is a theme for far-reaching and difficult investigations. These concern also the universal nature of evidence as a single component of conscious life — and here belongs the property mentioned above: that in every evidential consciousness of an object an intentional reference to a synthesis of recognition is included. They concern furthermore the modes of originality of evidence and their functions, as well

as the different regions and categories of / objectivities them- <144>
selves. For though, in characterizing evidence as the giving (or, relative to the subject, the having) of an object itself, we were indicating a universality relating to all objectivities in the same manner, that does not mean that the structure of evidence is everywhere quite alike.

Category of objectivity and category of evidence are perfect correlates. To every fundamental species of objectivities — as intentional unities maintainable throughout an intentional synthesis and, ultimately, as unities belonging to a possible "experience" — *a fundamental species of "experience", of evidence, corresponds*, and likewise a fundamental species of intentionally indicated evidential style in the possible enhancement of the perfection of the having of an objectivity itself.

Thus a great *task* arises, the task of exploring all these modes of the evidence in which the objectivity intended to *shows itself*, now less and now more perfectly, of making understandable the extremely complicated performances, fitting together to make a synthetic harmony and always pointing ahead[1] to new ones. To declaim from the heights about evidence and "the self-confidence of reason" is of no avail here. And to stick to tradition — which, for motives long forgotten and, in any case, never clarified, reduces evidence to an insight that is apodictic, absolutely indubitable, and, so to speak, absolutely finished in itself — is to bar oneself from an understanding of any scientific production. Natural science, for example, *must* rely on *external experience*, only because external experience is precisely that *mode of the having of something itself which pertains to natural Objects*, and therefore without it there would be absolutely nothing conceivable to which believing about Nature (spatial things) might adjust itself. And again, only because imperfect experience is still experience, still a consciousness that is a having of something itself [*Bewusstsein der Selbsthabe*], can experience adjust itself to experience and correct itself by experience. For this same reason, moreover, it is wrong for a criticism of sensuous experience, which naturally brings out its essential imperfection (that is: its being at the mercy of further experience!), to end with rejecting it — whereupon the critic in his extremity

[1] *Translator's note:* Reading *vorweisenden* instead of *vorweisende*.

appeals to hypotheses and indirect arguments, with which he attempts to seize the phantom of some (absurdly) transcendent "In-Itself". All transcendental-realistic theories, with their arguments leading from the "immanent" sphere of purely "internal" experience to an extra-psychic transcendency, are attributable to a blindness to the proper character of "external"
<145> experience as / a performance that gives us something itself and would otherwise be unable to provide a basis for natural-scientific theories.

I do not find that sufficient attention has been paid to the clarification of evidence and of all the pertinent relationships between mere "*intention*" and "*fulfilment*", which was first effected in the *Logische Untersuchungen, II. Teil,* and deepened in my *Ideen.* It is certainly in great need of improvement; still I believe that I am right in seeing in this first clarification a decisive advance of phenomenology beyond the philosophic past. I am of the certain conviction that only by virtue of the resultant insight into the essence, and the genuine problems, of evidence has a seriously scientific transcendental philosophy ("critique of reason") become possible, as well as, at bottom, a seriously scientific psychology, conceived centrally as the science of the proper essence of the psychic, an essence that (as Brentano discovered) consists in *intentionality.* The new doctrine admittedly has one inconvenience: The appeal to evidence ceases to be, so to speak, a trick of epistemological argumentation; instead it raises tremendous reaches of evidently seizable and soluble problems — ultimately those of phenomenological constitution, which we shall develop in Chapters 6 and 7.

§ 61. Evidence in general in the function pertaining to all objects, real and irreal, as synthetic unities.

Returning now to irreal objectivities, particularly those belonging to the sphere of analytic logic, we recall that in Part I we became acquainted with the evidences that in their case, and according to their various strata, are legitimizing evidences, evidences that give something-itself. In the case of the irreal objectivities of each stratum such evidences, then, are the corresponding "experiences"; and they have the *essential property of all experiences* or evidences of whatever sort — that is to say: with the repetition of the subjective life-processes, with the sequence and synthesis of different experiences of the Same, they make evidently visible *something that is indeed numerically identical* (*and not merely things that are quite alike*), namely *the* object, which is thus an object experienced many times or,

as we may also say, one that *"makes its appearance" many times* (as a matter of ideal possibility, infinitely many times) in the domain of consciousness. If one substituted for the ideal objectivities those temporal occurrences in the life of consciousness in which they "make their appearance", then, to be consistent, one would have to do likewise in the case of Data of experience ⟨in the usual narrower sense⟩. For example, psychic Data, the Data of "internal experience", are experienced as in immanent time and thus as intentionally identical Data given in the flow of subjective temporal modes. We should therefore have to put the immanent / constitutive complexes of "original time-conscious- <146>
ness" [1] in their place.

But the constitutive that pertains to the identical of external experience is more easily accessible. Physical objects too make their appearance "in the field of consciousness"; and, in respect of what is most general, no differently than ideal objects — that is to say: as intentional unities (though in the mode: "itself given") making their appearance in the flow of multiple manners of appearance built one upon another. In this making-of-their-appearance within the mental experience-processes, they are, in a legitimate sense, "immanent" in these, but not in the usual sense, that of real immanence.

If one intends to understand what consciousness does and, in particular, what evidence does, it is not enough, here or anywhere else, to speak of the "directedness" of consciousness, particularly of experiencing consciousness, to objects and, at most, to distinguish superficially among internal and external experience, ideation, and the like. The *multiplicities of consciousness* coming under these headings must be brought to sight in phenomenological reflection and dissected structurally. One must then trace them with regard to their *synthetic transitions*; and, down to the most elementary structures, one must seek out the intentional rôle or function. One must make it understood how, in the immanence of the multiplicities of mental processes (or ⟨in the immanence⟩ of the changing modes of appearance

[1] *Author's note:* Regarding analysis of the constitution of temporal Data, see my *Vorlesungen zur Phänomenologie des inneren Zeitbewusstseins* [*Lectures on the Phenomenology of the Consciousness of Internal Time*], edited by Martin Heidegger, this *Jahrbuch*, Bd. IX [(1928; also reprinted separately, Halle, 1928]. [*Cf.* Farber, *op. cit.*, pp. 512–519.]

occurring in these multiplicities), their *being-directed-to* and that *to which* they are directed are *made*; and one must also make it understood wherein, now, *inside the sphere of vision belonging to the synthetic experience itself*, the transcendent object consists — as the *identical pole immanent in the single mental processes and yet transcending them by virtue of having an identity that surpasses them.* It is a giving of something-itself and yet a giving of something-itself that is "transcendent": an at first *"indeterminately"* itself-given identical pole, which subsequently displays itself, in "its" (likewise ideally identical) "determinations", throughout the giving of it-itself, a giving that can be continued in the synthetic form: "explication". But, in the manner of something instituted originally, *this transcendence lies in the proper essence of the experience itself.* What it signifies can be learned only by interrogating experience; just as what a legal property-right /
<147> signifies and what demonstrates it at any time (incidentally, a matter that itself belongs within our province) can be found out only by going back and examining the "primal instituting" of that right.

The following great, and so often neglected, truism must therefore be made the center of all investigations of essential sense [*aller prinzipiellen Besinnungen*]. Such an affair as an object (even a physical object) draws the *ontic sense* peculiar to it (by which it then signifies what it signifies in all possible modes of consciousness) *originally from the mental processes of experience alone* — from such processes as are intrinsically characterized as awarenesses-of in the mode "it-itself", as appearances-of a Something itself, and (in the case of physical objects) as our being confronted by something itself, the being of which is certain. The *primitive form* here is *showing-itself-as-present,* which belongs to perception, or *showing-itself-"again"*, which belongs to recollection in the mode of the past.

Experience is the primal instituting of the being-for-us of objects as having their objective sense. Obviously that holds good equally in the case of *irreal* objects, whether their character is the ideality of the specific, or the ideality of a judgment, or that of a symphony, or that of an irreal object of some other kind. Everywhere, and therefore even in the case of external experience, it is true that an evidential giving of something itself must be characterized as a process of constitution, a process whereby the object of experience arises [*ein Prozess . . . eines Sichbildens des Erfahrungsgegenstandes*] — though, to be sure, this constitution is at first restricted, since the object claims an existence extending beyond the multiplicities of actual present experience. (This moment of the object's being-sense also requires constitutional clarification; and, by virtue of the intentionality implicit in experience itself and always uncoverable, it permits such clarification.) Essentially in the continuous and discrete syntheses of manifold experiences, the experiential object, as such, is built up "visibly": in the varying show of ever new sides, ever new moments belonging to its own essence. And from this constitutive [*aufbauenden*] life, which predelineates its own possible harmonious flow, the sides and moments and the object itself (as showing itself only thus, variously) draw their respective senses, each as the Identical that belongs to possible and — after their actualization — repeatable shapings of something itself [*Selbstbildungen*]. Here too the identity is evident: The object is evidently not itself the actual and openly possible experiential processes constituting it; nor is it the evident possibility, connected with this process, the possibility, namely, of repetitive synthesis (as a possibility pertaining to "I can"). /

§ 62. THE IDEALITY OF ALL SPECIES OF OBJECTIVITIES OVER AGAINST THE CONSTITUTING CONSCIOUSNESS. THE POSITIVISTIC MISINTERPRETATION OF NATURE IS A TYPE OF PSYCHOLOGISM. <148>

Consequently a certain *ideality* lies in the sense of every experienceable object, including every physical object, over against the manifold "psychic" processes *separated* from each other by individuation in immanent time — the processes of an experiencing life, then too of potential experiencing life, and finally of potential and actual becoming-conscious of all sorts, including the non-experiencing sorts. It is the *universal ideality of all intentional unities* over against the *multiplicities* constituting them.

In it consists the *"transcendence" belonging to all species of objectivities over against the consciousness of them* (and, in an appropriately altered but corresponding manner, the transcendence belonging to this or that Ego of a consciousness, understood as the subject-pole of the consciousness.

If, in spite of this, we still *separate immanent from transcendent objects*, that can involve a division only *within* this broadest concept of transcendence. In no respect does it alter the fact that likewise the transcendence belonging to the real, and, at the highest level, the intersubjectively real (the Objective in a pre-eminent sense), is constituted in respect of its being and sense exclusively in the immanent sphere, the sphere of the multiplicities of consciousness, and that the *transcendence belonging to the real, as such, is a particular form of "ideality"* or, better, of a *psychic irreality:* the irreality of something that *itself*, with all that belongs to it in its own essence, actually or possibly *makes its appearance* in the purely phenomenological sphere of consciousness, *and yet* in such a manner that it is evidently *no real part or moment of consciousness*, no real psychic Datum.

Accordingly we find a *precise analogue of the psychologistic interpretation of logical*, and of all other, *irrealities* (we might say: the amplified region of Platonic ideas) in that well-known type of *positivism* which we could also designate as Humeianism. It is represented, for example, by the Machian philosophy and the "philosophy of as-if" — though in a manner that, so far as originariness and depth of problematics are concerned, falls far short of Hume. For this positivism, physical things become reduced to empirically regular complexes of psychic Data ("sensations"); their identity and therefore their whole being-
<149> sense become / sheer fictions. It is not merely a false doctrine, completely blind to the essential phenomenological facts; it is also countersensical, because of its failure to see that even fictions have their mode of being, their manner of evidence, their manner of being unities of multiplicities, and therefore carry with them the same problem that was to be theorized away by means of them.

§ 63. Originally productive activity as the giving of logical formations themselves; the sense of the phrase, their production.

We have often spoken of a *producing of logical formations* in consciousness. In connexion with this locution, warning must be given against a misunderstanding, which, *mutatis mutandis*, concerns all speaking of a constitution of objectivities in consciousness.

In other cases where we speak of a producing, we are referring to a *real* sphere. We mean thereby an active bringing forth of real physical things or real processes: Something real, already there within the sphere of the surrounding world, is suitably treated, is rearranged or transformed. In our case, however, we have before us *irreal* objects, given in real psychic processes — irreal objects that we treat and, by acting, form thus and so, with a practical thematizing directed to *them* and not at all to the *psychic realities*. Accordingly, it is not as though the statement might be weakened, that here, and *in all seriousness*, a *formative doing*, an acting, a practical directedness to aims or ends, took place; as though something new were not actually produced here, by purposeful action, out of something given beforehand as a basis for practice. As a matter of fact, *judging too* (and naturally, in a particular manner, cognitive judging with its originality) *is acting*; the only difference is that, by its essential nature, judging is not a treating of something real, no matter how self-evidently any acting whatever is itself something psychically real (Objectively real, where, with the psychological attitude, we take judging as a human activity). But, from the beginning and in all its formings at different levels, this acting has exclusively the irreal in its thematic sphere; in judging, something irreal becomes intentionally constituted. In the active formation of new judgments out of judgments already given beforehand, we are, in all seriousness, productively active. As in every other acting the ends of our action, the new judgments to be produced, are consciously intended to by us beforehand in modes of an anticipation which is empty, still undetermined in respect of content, or in any case still unfulfilled; we are conscious of them thus as the things toward which we are striving and the bringing of which to an / actualizing givenness of them-themselves makes up the <150>
action, as accomplished step by step.

Thus the objectivities "treated" here are no realities: The peculiar sense that ideal objectivities possess, in being (as we have said) exactly as originally certain to us in an evidence of their own as are the real objectivities coming from experience, is unalterable. Equally unalterable, on the other hand, is the fact that they too are producible ends, final ends and means, and that they are what they are, only "as coming from" an original production. But that is not at all to say that they are what they are, only *in* and *during* the original production. That they are "in" the original production signifies that they are intended to in it, as a certain intentionality having the form of *spontaneous activity*, and more particularly in the mode belonging to the *original objectivity itself. This manner of givenness — givenness as something coming from such original activity* — is nothing other than *the sort of "perception" proper to them.* Or, what is the same thing, this originally acquiring activity is the *"evidence" appropriate to these idealities*. Evidence, quite universally, is indeed nothing other than the mode of consciousness — built up, perhaps, as an extrordinarily complex hierarchical structure — that offers its intentional objectivity in the mode belonging to the original "it itself". This evident-making activity of consciousness — in the present case a spontaneous activity hard to explore — is the "original constitution", stated more pregnantly, the primally institutive constitution, of ideal objectivities of the sort with which logic is concerned.

§ 64. The precedence of real to irreal objects in respect of their being.

In concluding this investigation, let us add that much vehement opposition — which to be sure disregards our phenomenological findings — arises from a misunderstanding of the sense in which we put ideal objectivities and also categorial variants of realities (such variants as predicatively formed affair-complexes) on a par with realities themselves. For us it is merely a matter of the legitimacy of the *broadest sense, "any object whatever"* or "anything whatever", and, *correlatively, of the most universal sense of evidence,* evidence as the giving of something itself. Otherwise than with respect to the legitimate subsumption of ideas under the concept of object, and consequently under the concept of substrate of possible predications, there is no parity at all between real and ideal objectivities, as can be understood precisely on the basis of our tenets. *In respect of its being, reality has precedence to*
<151> *every / irreality whatsoever,* since all irrealities relate back es-

sentially to an actual or possible reality. "The attempt" to survey these relations on every side and attain systematic cognition of all that actually or possible exists, the realities and the irrealities "— that attempt" leads to the highest philosophic problems, those of a universal ontology.

§ 65. A MORE GENERAL CONCEPT OF PSYCHOLOGISM.

The extraordinary broadening and, at the same time, radicalizing of the refutation of logical psychologism, which we have effected in the foregoing investigation, have brought us an extreme *generalization of the idea of psychologism*, in a *quite definite* — but not the only — *sense.* Psychologism in this sense is to be distinguished by the circumstance that some species or other of possibly evident objectivities (or even all species, as is the case in Hume's philosophy) are *psychologized,* because, as is obvious, they are constituted in the manner peculiar to consciousness — that is to say: their being-sense is built up, in and for subjectivity, by experience or other modes of consciousness that combine with experience. That they are "psychologized" signifies that their objective sense, their *sense as a species of objects* having a peculiar essence, is *denied* in favor of the subjective mental occurrences, the Data in immanent or psychological temporality.

But it is not important here, whether these Data be regarded as real [1] Data for *psychology* (a science of men and brutes as Objective realities) or as Data belonging to something distinguished, no matter how, as *"transcendental" subjectivity* (a subjectivity antecedent to all Objective realities, including human subjects); nor, in the latter case, does it matter whether the Data be regarded as a bundle or collection of absolutely posited sensations or as intentional mental processes in the teleological unity of a concrete Ego and a community of Egos. Still the expression psychologism is more appropriate to any interpretation which converts objectivities into something psychological in the proper sense; and the *pregnant* sense of psychologism should be defined accordingly.

[1] *Translator's note:* Reading *reale* instead of *irreale.*

§ 66. Psychologistic and phenomenological idealism. Analytic and transcendental criticism of cognition.

This psychologism, conceived so universally and (purposely) in hybrid fashion, is the fundamental characteristic of every *bad* /
<152> *"idealism"* (*lucus a non lucendo!*) like Berkeley's or Hume's. Yet it extends far beyond the conception one usually connects with the word "idealism", as this conception usually fails to take into consideration precisely the genuine idealities of the amplified Platonic sphere (though the Humeian conception is indeed to be excepted here). But the *phenomenological idealism* developed by me should not be mistaken for this idealism, as it is, time after time, by superficial readers of my works (even phenomenological readers); it gets its *fundamentally different and novel sense* precisely by radical criticism of the aforesaid psychologism, on the basis of a phenomenological clarification of evidence.

The following is pertinent here and can help to characterize phenomenological idealism.

Every "seeing" and, correlatively, everything identified in "evidence" has its own legitimacy; likewise every self-contained realm of possible "experience", as the *province* of a science, as its *theme* in the *first* and most proper sense. At the same time, there belongs to each science a *secondarily thematic sphere,* the sphere of its *criticism*: This is a criticism of "cognition" in a first sense "of the term criticism of cognition" — that is to say: relating to the ideal cognitional results (those belonging to the "theory") and, on the subjective side, relating to what is ideal in a correlative sense, namely the acting (concluding, proving) that corresponds to these idealities. Through this criticism, which we may designate as *analytic criticism of cognition,* each science gets its relation to analytics as a universal science of theory conceived with formal universality and, correlatively, its relation to the correspondingly delimited analytic practical discipline.

Finally, however, every science has a *third thematic sphere,* likewise a sphere of criticism, but of a criticism *turned in a different direction.* This criticism concerns the *constituting subjectivity* corresponding to each province and to each scientific performance busied with a province. Over against criticism of the prior data, the actions, and the results, that make their appearance openly in the field of consciousness, we have here a

criticism of cognition that has quite a different nature: criticism of the constitutive sources from which the positional sense and the legitimacy of cognition originate; accordingly criticism of the *effective performances that remain hidden* during the inquiring and theorizing directed straightforwardly to the province. This is the criticism of *"reason"* (taken either psychologically or transcendentally); or, contrasting it with analytic criticism of cognition, we may say it is *transcendental / criticism of cognition.* ‹153›
What we have said holds good for logic as well as for every other science; and already, in our general preparatory considerations, we asserted it under the heading, the *two-sidedness* of logical thematizing, though not with the distinctness and precision that have been possible here.

§ 67. The reproach of psychologism as indicating failure to understand the necessary logical function of transcendental criticism of cognition.

Now the *reproach of psychologism* was, as we remember, directed against precisely that two-sidedness — with regard to the *Logische Untersuchungen* because, in the *"Prolegomena"*, they combatted psychologism and yet, in Part II, went over to investigations of phenomenological subjectivity, to investigations concerning the intentional structures of stating and signifying, of objectivation and the content (sense) of an objectivation, of perception and the sense of a perception, of judging and the supposed predicatively formed affair-complex, of categorial acts and the constitution of categorial objects as contrasted with sensuous ones, of symbolic-empty consciousness as contrasted with intuitive, of the intentional relationships between bare intention and fulfilment, of evidential consciousness, of adequation, of the constitution of true being and predicational truth, and so forth. Such "descriptive-psychological" researches in the psychology of cognition were said to be psychologistic transgressions of a pure logic. This was the objection; though it was not intended to involve the rejecting of epistemo-critical researches concerning all sciences (logic presumably included). On the contrary, such researches were highly regarded by everyone. But the opinion was that they should follow quite a different line; they must not take our concretely actual and possible cognitive living, they must not take its intentional analysis, as their problem. That was said to be psychology and to signify epistemological psychologism.

Such criticism and the whole ruling conception involve *separating science and the criticism of reason*; they involve granting science a separate existence in its own right and taking criticism of reason as a science of a new sort, relating to all science and enjoying a higher dignity, but not disturbing the rightful independence of the sciences. This is above all the case with analytic logic; it holds in advance as an absolute norm, which all rational cognition presupposes. The worth of my criticism of logical psychologism, and all similar criticisms before and / after
<154> mine, is seen to lie precisely in their bringing out a pure (analytic) logic, which is to be separated from all psychology as a *self-sufficient* science, like geometry or natural science in this respect. The criticism of reason may have questions to ask about pure logic; but they must not disturb its independent course and must on no account delve into the concreteness of logical conscious life, for that would be psychology.

As against this, let us first bear in mind that the war against logical psychologism was in fact meant to serve no other end than the supremely important one of making the specific *province* of analytic logic visible in its purity and ideal peculiarity, freeing it from the psychologizing confusions and misinterpretations in which it had remained enmeshed from the beginning. — Its "province": that is to say, its thematic field in the first and chief sense, such a field as any science has. But that does not preclude the possibility that secondarily — for the sake of cognition of the province — something that is not part of it, but is essentially connected with it, will also be made a theme. Indeed, this is already the case, as mentioned earlier, with respect to the field of "analytic" criticism indispensable to every science: the field comprising, on the one hand, its theory and all its judgments relating to the province and, on the other hand, the corresponding ideal actions.

And now cannot something similar be the case, and must it not be the case, with respect to the total field comprising the intentional acts, the manners of appearance, the modes of consciousness of every sort, in which the scientific province and

its objects and complexes of objects are given beforehand for the subject who judges, and comprising, in like fashion, those in which his whole theoretical living and striving relating to the province goes on intentionally, those in which the theory and the scientifically true being of the province are intentionally constituted? Should not this too be in fact a field for a criticism necessary to all sciences, a transcendental criticism — necessary, if they are to have any capability whatever of being genuine sciences? If this could be made evident and the great field of tasks awaiting this last and deepest criticism could be displayed, logic would naturally be served thereby; for, as the universal, and not the merely analytic, theory of science (not mere *mathesis universalis*), logic would relate not only to all genuine sciences, with respect to their universal essential possibilities, but also to any and all criticism pertaining to them and their genuineness, and here likewise with respect to its essential universalities. *Universal theory of science is ipso facto universal | theory of genuine* <155>
science as such, a criticism belonging to its own essence, whether as criticism of judgments as produced formations, ideal components of its ideal theories, or as criticism of the intentional life that constitutes province and theory.

It is not our present task to inquire about any traditional or now-accepted criticisms of reason, or about their paralyzing fears of a concrete consideration of cognitive subjectivity (a consideration interdicted under the name psychologism), their fears of every introduction of psychology into observations proper to a theory of science. We are asking only about what pertains to the essential possibility of genuine science. If the investigation of constitutive consciousness, the inquiry into the whole teleology of the intentionalities belonging to cognitive life, could be proved essentially necessary for making genuineness of the sciences possible, it would have to be accepted by us. And if, in this regard, a "psychologism" should still have to be obviated (a psychologism with a different sense from that of the phychologism which we have treated up to now, though allied to it), then we should have to learn this by considering the requirements themselves for logic. Without any commitment on our part, the thematizing of the subjective — more distinctly: of the intentional-constitutive — a thematizing whose essential function is still to be clarified, shall henceforth be designated as *phenomenological.*

§ 68. Preliminary view of our further problems.

The affair that we must clear up is complicated; because logic is itself a science and, as a science, should likewise need such criticism, and because, on the other hand, in its relation to the open range of possible sciences, logic should be the science that treats as a theme those critical investigations of the subjective which are necessary to all sciences (though logic's treatment of them would have a universality relevant to all the sciences at once). The two characteristics do not immediately coincide. Logic or, more particularly, formal analytics, which alone is now delimited for us certainly, has as its first thematic sphere the forms of produced categorial judgment- and object-formations and relates only extensionally to the formations themselves belonging to all the sciences and coming under these forms; and therefore, in the case of logic, we have precisely the constitutional problems peculiar to it, problems that concern the subjective forming of the universal categorial forms and, first of all, the highest regional concepts belonging to logic, like any-judgment-
<156> whatever or any-objectivity-whatever. / These problems, it is true, come into consideration also in the case of the single sciences, but only by way of logic as their method: Provided, namely, that it is indeed possible to show that a genuineness of science can only be a genuineness on the basis of a conscious squaring with the normative principles of logic, and that therefore — as was previously asserted in our "Introduction" but must yet be actually established in what will follow — logic is not only one science among others but at the same time a fundamental part of the method for every possibly feasible science whatever.

In any case, after all the investigations carried out up to now for the radical clarifying and critical safeguarding of the peculiar province of analytics and the provinces to be distinguished within it, our immediate task is to direct our further investigations first of all to *clarifying the nature and necessity of the investigations of the subjective demanded in the case of this analytics.* The further investigations that consequently become requisite for developing the idea of a formal ontology into the idea of an ontology of realities and, ultimately, into that of an absolute ontology will themselves lead us to the still-awaited actual clarification of the genuine sense of a transcendental psychologism — into which we have by no means lapsed already if we ground formal logic on intentional researches and likewise ground the positive sciences on a theory of cognition whose course lies in such researches.

Chapter 2.

Initial questions of transcendental logic: problems concerning fundamental concepts.

§ 69. Logical formations given in straightforward evidence. The task of making this evidence a theme of reflection.

Despite misinterpretations and disguisements of the analytic sphere, analytic logic has long been with us; with respect to those of its disciplines that are "formal-mathematical" in the narrower sense, it has been with us even in a highly developed form. Consequently there can have been no lack of evidence in the forming of logical categories and differentiated forms; indeed, such evidence has at all times been particularly esteemed. But, in spite of that, it is anything but exemplary. By using this word, we have already intimated that such evidence — that evidence of every sort — should be reflectively considered, reshaped, analyzed, purified, and improved; and that afterwards it can be, and ought to be, taken as an exemplary pattern, a norm. /

<157> The formations with which logic is concerned and their universal forms are given at first in a *straightforward evidence*; and this comes first necessarily. But now a *thematizing reflection on this evidence* is demanded: a reflection, that is, on the formative activity, which has heretofore been carried on straightforwardly and naïvely, without becoming a theme. The formations and universal forms (formations belonging to a higher level), which are "given" in the activity and are, at first, all that is "given", must now be "clarified" reflectively in order that, by clearing up the intentionality that aims at and actualizes its objective sense originaliter, we may rightly apprehend and delimit this sense and secure its identity against all the shiftings and disguisements that may occur when it is aimed at and produced naïvely. In other words: Every productive doing involves intention and actualization. One can consider this doing itself and what it involves, and assure oneself of the identity between its purpose and the actualization that fulfils its purpose. In naïve intending and doing, the aiming can shift, as it can in a naïve

repetition of that activity and in any other going back to something previously striven for and attained. It is thus in the thematizing that goes on in the complex of the logician's naïve actions. Turning reflectively from the only themes given straightforwardly (which may become importantly shifted) to the activity constituting them with its aiming and fulfilment — the activity that is hidden (or, as we may also say, "anonymous") throughout the naïve doing and only now becomes a theme in its own right — we examine that activity after the fact. That is to say, we *examine the evidence* awakened by our reflection, *we ask it what it was aiming at and what it acquired*; and, in the evidence belonging to a higher level, we identify and fix, or we trace, the possible variations owing to vacillations of theme that had previously gone unnoticed, and distinguish the corresponding aimings and actualizations, — in other words, the shifting processes of forming concepts that pertain to logic.

§ 70. The sense of the demanded clarifications as scientific inquiry into constitutive origins.

a. Shift of intentional aimings and equivocation.

It is often said in this connexion (and, at an earlier time,[1] I too expressed it thus) that the *danger of equivocation* must be averted. It / is to be noted, however, that here it is not a matter <158>
of explicit equivocations, which are such that one should, or could, merely follow up the words and the verbal significations. Rather it is a matter of *internal shiftings of intentionality* and its product, shiftings that are tied together, and demanded, by essential interconnexions. These shiftings then lead to verbal equivocations, which we cannot remove while confining our attention to the language itself and simply examining it with respect to the significations to which it points associationally. On the contrary, we can remove them, we can first formulate them as equivocations, only by the aforesaid reflective examination of the intentional aimings and of the original constitution of the formations, with the effectuation of those aimings.

An illustration of what has just been presented, but at the same time a supplementation that carries us further, is offered

[1] *Author's note:* See, for example, the introduction to the second part of the *Logische Untersuchungen* (in the second and later editions), p. 7.

by all the investigations we made in the interest of clarifying the province of logic. Their indispensability to a seriously scientific logic is beyond question. For how could such a logic become possible while the themes belonging to it originally remained confused? Not only was it necessary to put an end to the psychologistic reinterpretation of them; the sphere of logic, even when apprehended in its purity, stood in need of those difficult investigations which alone can make evident its division into three strata. Without exception these investigations were *directed phenomenologically to the subjective*; they concerned the contrasting of three different focusings in judging, with the interchanging of which the direction of actual and possible identification — the directedness to something objective — becomes altered, and the pointing out of three different evidences, three correspondingly different modes of empty expectant intention and of fulfilment, and three different concepts of the judgment, which become originally separated accordingly. Here it is a matter of a shifting of concepts and an equivocation that went on in the logicians' thinking, not for accidental but for essential reasons and that necessarily remained hidden, because they themselves pertained to the unity in respect of theme that characterizes the logicians' "straightforward" thinking, as directed to the critical evaluation of judgments according to the norm of *truth*. More precisely, they necessarily remained hidden because inquiry about the formal conditions for possibly *true* judgments necessarily proceeded on the systematic levels that we distinguished as theory of the forms of judgments, consequence-theory, and theory of truth.

We see here that it is not a matter of just any unnoticed change in sense, but rather of a change belonging to a quite distinctive
<159> and particularly important type: *the change | is at the same time an overlapping and a coinciding* — the latter, because the judgment-unity of the lower level enters at the same time into the higher level by identification, in such a fashion that the novelty belonging to the higher level (the distinctness, or properness, of the judgment; or else the filledness of the evidence) must be taken as a predicate in its own right. Within the unity of logical thinking, unities belonging to all levels exercise their functions for thinking and cognition; therefore the focus can change and,

with it, the sense of the unity that pervades the coinciding, yet changes ⟨from level to level⟩.[1]

b. Clarification of the separate fundamental concepts belonging to the several logical disciplines as an uncovering of the hidden methods of subjective formation and as criticism of these methods.

Thus the verbal equivocation is, in a certain manner, essentially necessary. On the other hand, to disentangle and master it, *fundamentally to distinguish the three judgment-unities* and the *fundamental concepts* relating to them, is an absolute necessity for a logic that intends to have its thematic spheres continually before it as essentially differentiated — as logic must in order to be a genuine science. It must be clear to the logician that judgments in the sense proper to the theory of forms — judgments for whose evident givenness originaliter a distinctness merely in the rhythmics of a verbal indication is sufficient — cannot found consequence-relationships. He must have made it clear to himself that the proposition understood only verbally, understood explicitly in grasping the definite rhythmics of a symbolic indication, is grasped as a unity of "signification" which is, precisely, the unity of a mere rhythmic indication; and that what is thus indicated is the judgment in the second sense, the new rhythmics of the judicial meaning or opinion (that is: the predicatively formed complex-of-affairs meaning) constituted in the judging proper, in the actually performed categorial action, — the new rhythmics which, on being subsequently performed, fulfilled the symbolic rhythmics. And, again, he must have made clear to himself that where aiming at cognition pervades the judging, the explicit judgment, now the proper or "distinct" judgment itself qua meaning or opinion, points to a fulfilling It-Itself: to the predicatively formed complex of affairs "itself", to its subject and predicate "themselves", and so forth.

But he must know all these things because for him they are method, and because for him there must be no naïve, instinctive, hidden doing, because, on the contrary, he must be able to render

[1] *Author's note:* See the more penetrating clarifications in Chapter 4, *infra*, above all §§ 89 and 90, [pp. 215-221].

<160> an account for every doing and its effect; / and therefore, as a logician, he must have reflected, with absolute universality, on the hidden *naïve method* and explicated it thematically, in order subsequently to put the *genuine logical method* into practice. This, the *most original* method, which produces judgments and judgment-forms as logical, is essentially different in the theory of forms from what it is in consequence-theory; and in each of these it is different from what it is in the theory of truth.

Indispensable to the logician in the same manner are, obviously, all the other investigations concerning the subjective which we conducted above, those in which the correlative senses of an apophantics and a formal ontology, and likewise the respective peculiarities of a pure mathematics and a logical mathematics, were made clear.

They all have the character of investigations fundamental to the *uncovering and criticism of the original logical method*; and indeed we can characterize them all likewise as *explorations of the method by which the "fundamental concepts" of analytics are produced originaliter*, in that evidence which assures us of their respective essences as identical and safeguarded against all shiftings.

The fundamental concepts are already familiar and at our free disposal; and, as products, they have been produced, and are produced again in renewed evidence, wherever the need for evidence is awakened. But this naïvely used "method" is not yet a genuine method. Therefore it is *not as though a mere "psychological analysis" were in question*, a reflective psychological consideration of how on occasion we form, or have formed, a particular concept. Only at the outset is constitutional inquiry such a reflection and progressive uncovering of the method used in fact and "unconsciously". As it advances, it is *"criticism"* — that is: *active fulfilment*, along the various lines of fulfilment, based on systematic separation of the intentional directions combined in the synthetic unity. But this signifies that here such criticism is *creative constitution* of the objectivities intended to each in the unity of a harmonious givenness of that objectivity itself, and creation of their respective essences and eidetic concepts. On the basis of a concomitant fixing of terminology, these concepts are then to persist as acquisitions in the realm of habit.

Every constitutional analysis is, in this respect, creative. *The creatively acquired unities of constitution are norms*; and the *creative acquiring of them is / a method that has itself become* <161>
thematic and, as thematized, a norm for future habitual practice according to method. Genuine logical method is possible only as coming from a thematizing exploration and a purposfully active shaping of the naïvely used method itself.

§ 71. Problems of the foundations of science, and constitutional inquiry into origins. Logic called on to lead.

That already projects a light on the much-discussed *problems of the foundations*, not only of mathematics, but of all the other Objective sciences. In the case of formal mathematics, as analytics itself, the sense of these problems has already been determined by our preceding considerations, and the usual confusion in setting them has been removed. Everywhere we observe, as in the setting up of other epistemological problems, the repeatedly cited error of accepting the sciences as something that already exists — as though inquiry into foundations signified only an ex post facto clarification or, at most, an improvement that would not essentially alter these sciences themselves. The truth is that sciences that have paradoxes, that operate with fundamental concepts not produced by the work of originary clarification and criticism, are not sciences at all but, with all their ingenious performances, mere theoretical techniques.

The creation of fundamental concepts is therefore, in the most literal sense, a *fundamental performance*, laying the foundations for all sciences, as we said beforehand. But first of all for *logic*, which is called on to be the essentially universal method for them all, to embrace all their special methods within the Apriori of any method whatever and consciously to govern the shaping of them according to principles. Only in a scientific life that submits itself to the radicalness of this inquiry is genuine science possible. How this requirement can be satisfied and, if not absolutely, in what sequence of methodical approximations — this problem, we see in advance, prescribes a chief part of the creative shaping of methods, a chief part of the logical work concerned with the subjective. But here we are only at the beginnings; and the beginning of these beginnings is *work on the concepts that are, in the strictest sense, fundamental* — the work that must bring them out of the confusion and lability of their naïve form, into the stability and definiteness of fundamental *scientific* concepts, by a method that is itself definite and can at any time be reactivated and, by reactivation, verified. /

<162> § 72. The subjective structures as an Apriori, correlative to the Objective Apriori. Transition to a new level of criticism.

The subjective structures in question in the already-described inquiries of a logic directed to the subjective have a congruity with the corresponding concepts pertaining to the theory of Objective logic which is obviously not a matter of accidental psychological fact. They indicate an *Apriori which is perfectly correlated with the Objective Apriori.* It is inconceivable, for example, that a process of evidence in which a judgment becomes itself-given explicitly should have an essential structure other than the one that reflective analysis brings to light. The formalizing universalization that converts a de facto judgment into a universal judgment-form is, in its subjective aspect, necessarily an essential — and, in the correlative sense, a formal — universalization of the evidence of the de facto judgment. This holds good, then, in a corresponding manner, not only for all the other fundamental concepts of pure analytic logic, but also for the pertinent fundamental and derivative laws of logical theory. *To every operational law of the theory of forms there corresponds a priori a subjective law concerning the constitutive subjectivity,* a formal law relating to every conceivable judger and his subjective possibilities of forming new judgments out of old ones.

The *fundamental concepts,* the primitive concepts, belonging to logic are the *highest concepts of the province itself that belongs to logic* and of the stratification of that province as divided into synthetically functioning component provinces. With the fashioning of these concepts there takes place an *initial criticism* of the necessarily first, the straightforward, logic and, at the same time, a criticism of *its mode of cognition,* the nature of its method. But is this initial criticism, with the resultant initial fashioning of the province-concepts, already a full and complete criticism — even when we disregard the new critical researches that will presumably be necessary concerning subsequent concepts?

CHAPTER 3.

The idealizing presuppositions of logic and the constitutive criticism of them.

Having made clear to ourselves the necessity of our first series of critical investigations, let us now make clear their insufficiency. We now require a criticism of analytic logic that can make us
<163> conscious of a number of *idealizing presuppositions* / with which logic operates as if they were truisms, not on the basis of a method that has become thematic, but again on the basis of a method used naïvely — presuppositions that we ourselves had consequently taken over without noticing them. This new criticism is a continuation of the one we practised at the first level, to clear up the division into three strata; and it therefore presupposes that criticism's investigations.

§ 73. Idealizing presuppositions of mathematical analytics as themes for constitutive criticism. The ideal identity of judgment-formations as a constitutional problem.

If we first observe *pure mathematical analytics* taken in its fullness, the mere logic of analytic judgment-consequence, we see that, with its universal forms, it relates to the openly infinite range of possible judgments and *presupposes their ideal identity.*

Let us consider in what sense one should speak here of a presupposition and what this presupposition includes. The forms are universal essentialities ("concepts"), gained in an evidence of their own on the basis of exemplificatory judgments, these themselves being drawn from the modes of evidence that we have described. As a mental occurence, the intentionality of the judging varies; but, where we speak nevertheless of the *same* judgment, there is maintained an intentional unity, directedness to one and the same judgment, which becomes itself-given in evidence as the same — the same that was at first a confused meaning or opinion and then became distinct. Everything that making distinct brings out productively, with its activity proper, was already confusedly "implied" beforehand as something meant; and this is true finally of the whole judgment, if making distinct is completely successful.

But *even "confused"*, "vague", judging is not dead and inflexible, but changeable; and, if we suppose that in it the same judgment — the same for the theory of forms, which needs no activity of production proper — becomes constituted as an identical objectivity, the question is: *What assures us of this identity*? And then the same question is to be asked about the judgment in its *"distinct"* properness. To be sure, while the evidence is alive we have the judgment itself, as the one judgment, offering itself throughout change in the mental processes as it-itself. But, if the process of thinking progresses, and we, connecting synthetically, *turn back* to what was previously given as One, then / this itself is no longer originally evident: We are <164>
conscious of it again in the medium of recollection and in a recollection that is not in the least intuitive. Recollection, succeeding as actual intuition proper, would indeed be restitution of each single moment or step of the original process. But, even if that takes place, even if a new evidence is thus brought about, is it sure that this evidence is restitution of the earlier evidence? And now let us remember that the judgments which, in living evidence, were constituted originally as intentional unities — constituted in the mode, having something itself — are supposed to have a continuing acceptance as objects *existing for us at all times*, avaliable to us at all times, — as convictions lasting for us from the time of their first constitution.

Logic relates, not to what is given only in active evidence, but to the *abiding* formations that have been primally instituted in active evidence and *can be reactivated and identified again and again*; it relates to them as objectivities which are henceforth *at hand*, with which, taking hold of them again, one can operate in thinking, and which, as the same, one can further shape categorially into more and more new formations. At each level they have their manner of evident identifiability; at each they can be made distinct, can be united in evidently consistent or evidently inconsistent complexes; out of them, by cancellation of inconsistencies or by suitable transformation, purely consistent complexes can be produced. Obviously logic, with its formal universalities and laws, presupposes judgments, categorialia of every sort and level, *whose being-in-themselves remains fixed as identical.* It presupposes what to every thinking subject and community of thinking subjects is a truism: What I have said, I have said; *I can at any time become certain of the identity of my judicial meanings or opinions*, my convictions, *after a pause in my thinking activity*, and become certain of them, in insight, as an abiding and always available *possession.*

Now everyone is of course acquainted with the fact that there are occasional deceptions in that respect, occasional *shiftings and confoundings of meaning*; and everyone is acquainted also with the possibility of *fixing* a confusedly vacillating sense and reducing vague judgments to distinct and definitely identifiable ones. The vague may have its multifarious determinability; when the thinking subject goes on to something definite, which
<165> he can identify repeatedly and evidently, it may be that / his affirmation, "*This* is what I mean", signifies at bottom a voluntary decision: "From now on I will always accept this definite ⟨judgment⟩ as my meaning". But it cannot be a mere momentary choice, varying according to circumstances. If someone who is proving something recurs, in the proof-complex, to an earlier judgment, it must indeed be actually the same judgment.

Traditional logic and naïvely, straightforwardly, theorizing mathematics do not trouble themselves greatly about this. They *presuppose* that an identity extends through all rightly performed thinking: an identity of objects, when thinking is focused on the existent; an identity of object-senses and of judgments, when it is focused on the apophantic. Thus, at bottom, they presuppose that, in the concrete case, *in the thinking done by the particular scientists, a producing of such identity has been rightly effected,* that the scientists have already provided for a fixing of strictly identifiable objects and senses, in contrast to the varying confusions and obscurities, and the shiftings of sense made possible thereby.

Naïvely straightforwardly it is easy to bring out the ideal being of judgments as always-identifiable senses and then, as logicians, to rely on it continually. But how is such a bringing out and ascertaining possible? After all, this ideal being can have a reliable validity for us, only if what such an ascertaining does can be made a matter of actual insight. This ideal being has a peculiar transcendence: *It transcends the current living evidence* in which the judgment, as this judgment, actually becomes itself-given. *This* evidence surely cannot be responsible for the required *new performance*, in which the itself-given supposedly acquires the *legitimate sense of an ideal transcendency*. And yet we were just saying that any thinker is simply sure of being able to make judgments as firmly identifiable judgments, on the being and accessibility of which he can count, even if he is not thinking of them. Now if this demands a particular evidence *supplementary to* the first, in which the ideal objectivity becomes itself-given, is there not a danger that *the problem will be repeated*, and so *in infinitum*?

Even if the method used naïvely to acquire these ideal identities (which logic actually *presupposes* as acquirable at any time) does perform what is demanded of it, and the presupposition made by logic has accordingly an original legitimacy, / still we <166>
cannot *legitimately* accept that presumed legitimacy, *as long as the method — being used naïvely — remains anonymous, and its intentional performance has not been made a theme and clarified.* Or do we propose to be satisfied perchance by appealing to the favored *empeiria* of the sucessful sciences, to the practice, that is to say, of scientists, who surely attain fixed judgments in their theories? But here we recall the ambiguity of the fundamental concepts used in the sciences, and the consequent ambiguity of all their theories, and shall have to say, therefore, that an actual attaining is not in question here, that accordingly it is a matter of an *ideal*, which has never been fulfilled in practice and which presumably can never be fulfilled. *But if it is a matter of an ideal*, which logic, as the first giver of norms for the possibility of any genuine science, presupposes, then we face the following *alternative*:

Either logic operates with a universal *fiction*, and is therefore itself anything but normative; or logic is indeed normative, and this ideal is indeed an *actual fundamental norm* pertaining inseparably to the possibility of genuine science.

If we must give preference, at least at first, to the latter conception and attempt to justify it, then *an essentially new part is added to our reflective logical problem of subjective methods* and, more particularly, to the problem of the subjective method whereby the *fundamental concepts* of logic are created. As a matter of fact, this ideal of the identity of statement-significations (in the manifold senses of the word) is involved in the sense of every fundamental logical concept. Consequently the universally formulable method for actualizing an identical signification — a method belonging, with formal universality, to all concretely logical (that is: scientific) thinking — is a *component of the method for forming the fundamental concepts of logic.* Taken separately, *the problem concerns the constitution of normative ideal Objective identity,* with the stages of approximation that, as we see in advance, are essentially involved in such constitution.

The problem of constitution is again broadened when we recall that *verbal expression,* which we excluded from our considerations of logic, is an essential presupposition for intersubjective thinking and for an intersubjectivity of the theory accepted as ideally existing; and that accordingly an ideal identifiability of the expression, as expression, must likewise raise a problem of constitution. /

<167> § 74. Idealities of And-so-forth, of constructable infinities, and the subjective correlate of these idealities.

The thematizing of subjective intentionality by an analytics that (with all its restriction to the analytically formal) intends seriously to be a theory of science, seriously to establish the possibility of a genuine science, seriously to make ready for the scientist the principles for vindicating genuineness, leads, as we see, into unsuspected phenomenological depths and breadths. But, even so, we have *not yet taken into consideration all the idealizations* that play a universal rôle for a pure analytics. I mention in addition only the *fundamental form "and so forth",* the form of *reiterational* "infinity"; never stressed by logicians, it has its subjective correlate in *"one can always again".* This is plainly an idealization, since de facto no one can always again. Still this form plays its sense-determining rôle everywhere in logic. One can *always return* to an ideal significational unity or to any other ideal unity — "and so forth" is thus a fundamental part of the problem of the preceding sections. One can, for example, always have another set, which is excluded from a given set, and join it to the latter by addition: Given any cardinal number, *a*, one can always form an $a + 1$; and in this manner, starting from 1, form the "infinite" series of cardinal numbers. In the theory of forms of analytic senses, we have none but reiterational laws; in all of them infinity — "always again", "and so forth" — is involved. Mathematics is the realm of infinite constructions, a realm of ideal existences, not only of "infinite" senses but also of constructional infinities. Obviously we have here a repetition of the problem concerning subjective constitutive origins: as the hidden method of constructions which is to be uncovered and reshaped as a norm, the method by which "and so forth", in various senses, and infinities as categorial formations of a new sort become evident (though even in the sphere of preconceptual objectivations they play a great rôle). Precisely this evidence, in all its particular formations, must now become a theme.

§ 75. The law of analytic contradiction and its subjective version.

Now let us go a bit further in laying bare the problems that relate to the subjective. In pure *consequence-logic* we have to do /
with laws of consequence and of contradiction and, at most, of the <168>
external non-contradiction that does not depend on consequence.[1] *Objectively* [*objektiv*], one judgment is called a contradiction of another if, with respect to this other, it is either an immediate contradiction or a mediate contradiction, a contradiction of one of this other's consequences.

The fundamental Objective-ideal law, then, is: *Every contradictory judgment is "excluded" by the judgment that it contradicts.* Every judgment that is an analytic consequence of another is "included" in it.

The latter signifies, on the *subjective* side: Whoever has a judicial meaning or opinion and, in explicating it to himself, sees any analytic consequence, not only judges the consequence in fact but *"cannot do otherwise"* than judge it. In paying attention

[1] *Author's note:* See §§ 19 and 20, [pp. 65–68], *supra.*

merely to the syntactical form and being conscious of the optionalness of the cores actually present, he becomes conscious also of the necessity, the inability to do otherwise — most perfectly conscious thereof with the actual transition to formal universality. The general evidence of the analytic consequence, united with the attempting and starting of its negation, shows, on the Objective side, the general impossibility of this unity <*sc.* the unity that would be produced by conjoining a judicial meaning and the negative of any analytic consequence of that meaning in "distinct evidence"> and, on the subjective side, the impossibility of the judicative believing, not only for someone who is in fact judging, but also for anyone at all who might be judging, with distinct evidence. No one at all can do otherwise than negate in such a connexion. In like manner, whoever thinks of two judgments as judged by someone, and, on making them distinct, recognizes that one contradicts the other, cannot do otherwise than deny the conjunctive judgment formed out of them. Therefore *the following subjective version of the fundamental formal law of pure analytics* holds universally:

Of two judgments that (immediately or mediately) contradict one another, only one can be accepted by any judger whatever in a proper or distinct unitary judging.

Here, naturally, acceptance connotes, not truth, but a mere judging in the distinct mode. The analytic law of contradiction, accordingly, is not to be confounded with the law of truth-logic enounced historically under the same name.

Correct as those subjective versions are, they do no more than *indicate* the actual underlying conformity to law, which comes to light with the actual uncovering of the correlative subjective /
<169> structures. Purely *Objectively*, the law of pure analytic contradiction is a proposition about ideal mathematical "existence" and coexistence — that is: about the compossibility of judgments as distinct. On the *subjective* side, however, there stands the apriori structure of the evidence and of the other effective subjective performances pertaining to it — a structure, the uncovering of which actually brings out the essential subjective situations corresponding to their Objective sense.

With the subjective evidence pertaining specifically to the ideal sphere of consequence and inconsistency there are combined, by essential necessity, ***evidences that belong to the theory of forms*** and relate to the confused modes and to the previously shown connexions of unity between intention and fulfilment.

All these evidences, with the essential structures belonging to them, must be explicated as functioning together in the subjective and hidden "methods" of intentionally constituting the various ideal unities and connexions that join the theory of forms with consequence-theory to make up the unity of mathematical analytics. All the subjective structures have an *Apriori pertaining to their function*. All of them must be brought out; and, on the basis of a clear self-understanding, this Apriori must be consciously fashioned, to become the originarily clear method for a radically legitimized theory of forms and a full analytics legitimately grounded in such a theory — an analytics for which there can be no paradoxes and the legitimate applicational sense of which must be beyond question.

§ 76. TRANSITION TO THE PROBLEMS OF THE SUBJECTIVE THAT ARISE IN CONNEXION WITH THE LOGIC OF TRUTH.

Up to now we have been speaking of analytics in the narrower sense, as "pure" ***mathesis universalis***, a science of infinite fruitfulness, which, as we already know, acquires no new disciplines, but only the specifically logical function, when the concepts of truth are subsequently introduced into its theme and it is extended by the inclusion of a few propositions relating to them. These propositions are the basis for the fact that the formal laws of mere non-contradiction become conditions for the possibility of truth and can be stated as such. Pure mathematical analytics then becomes, as we have said, what is properly an analytic theory of science or the equivalent of such a theory, a "formal ontology".

More exactly considered, a theory of science, or an ontology, of that sort, thought of as pursued straightforwardly once its province has been laid bare, is very little fitted to / perform its <170>
intended function, namely to offer norms, even merely formal ones, govering the essential possibility of genuine science. This especially touches the new fundamental concepts and laws, with the new sense-determinations that they infuse into pure mathematical analytics. If formal analytics, as thus enriched to become

a "formal" logic, remains faithful to its principle of leaving the syntactical stuffs indeterminately universal and being a mere syntactics of possible true being and possible predicational truth, then it is a question *how it ever brings this "true" into its formal universalities.* It seems at first that here, *for creation of the new fundamental concepts,* nothing different is to be done than in the case of those belonging to the preceding logical disciplines: As these draw their essential concepts of form from examples by eidetic universalization, so the formal theory of truth draws its essential concepts, by eidetic universalization, from *examples of true being and predicational truth.* There cognition of certain idealizing presuppositions compelled investigations of the subjective. The like is to be expected here; and thus it seems that a like path is indicated in advance and that the difficulties to be solved here are of a like nature.

But, when we penetrate more deeply, it becomes apparent that here we encounter not only similar but also novel *presuppositions and difficulties,* and that these *reach much further* than the ones with which we have already had occasion to become aquainted. To be sure, as soon as they come into view, they spread to the whole of analytics, as restricted to the purely mathematical: Because logic, in all its historical forms, has been essentially determined by its "innate" fundamental sense, the sense of an analytic logic, and because naïvely positive research is part of this sense, we find that, in all those forms, it is also afflicted with certain fundamental difficulties, which are hidden from it precisely on account of this naïveté. We shall discuss these difficulties here, as they arise in connexion with the purified idea of an analytics.

Our investigation finds a given point of departure in the *concept of truth* and the *"logical principles"* that explicate it axiomatically. We recall our analyses of the origins of the concepts, *true being* and *truth as correctness of a judgment,* with their respective references back to the giving of something itself (experience, in both the narrow and the broad sense) and to
<171> adequation.[1] Those analyses were sufficient for our purpose at the time, / to isolate a pure mathematical analytics (of mere non-contradiction) as contrasted with a formal logic of truth;

[1] *Author's note:* See Part I, § 16, pp. 56 ff.; and, for the "principles of logic", § 20, pp. 66 ff.

but only by fleeting indications — for example: those pointing to differences in the perfection of "evidence" (in both senses) — did they refer to some of the dark places from which, as soon as they are penetrated, very difficult questions come forth.

§ 77. The idealizing presuppositions contained in the laws of contradiction and excluded middle.

Let us begin with the problems concerning the evidence of the "principles of logic". Their evidence must indeed be grounded in the evidential creating of the concepts truth and falsity. The *law of contradiction* expresses the general impossibility of contradictory judgments being true (or false) together. If we ask for the evidence in which it is grounded, we see that this impossibility involves the following: If a judgment can be brought to an adequation in a positive material evidence, then, a priori, its contradictory opposite not only is excluded as a judgment but also can *not* be brought to such an adequation; and vice versa.

That is not yet to say that, without exception, every judgment can be brought to an adequation. But just this is involved in the *law of excluded middle* or, on the subjective side, its evidential correlate. *Every judgment can be confronted with "its affairs themselves"* and adjusted to them in either a positive or a negative adequation. In the one case, the judgment is evidently true — it is in fulfilling and verifying coincidence with the categorial objectivity meant in the relevant judging [*im jeweiligen Urteil*] and now offering itself as itself-given; in the other case it is evidently false because, united with the *partial* fulfilment of the judicial meaning (the meant categorial objectivity as meant), there comes out as itself-given a categorial objectivity that conflicts with the total judicial meaning and necessarily "annuls" it. As we already know, an essentially possible alteration of the judgment-formation then yields, in place of the annulling negation (as a striking out), the *positive judgment* with the altered predicational sense that contains the negative as a predicational form and accordingly declares the truth of the contradictory opposite.

Thus the law of excluded middle, in its subjective aspect, has *two parts*. It decrees not only that, if a judgment can be brought to an adequation, to a synthesis with / something itself-given <172>

that corresponds (in the amplified sense), then it can be brought to either a positive or a negative adequation; but — in case one has not stated this beforehand as a separate principle of evidence — it decrees also, as we have said, that *every judgment necessarily admits of being brought to an adequation.* — "Necessarily" being understood with an *ideality* for which, indeed, no responsible evidence has ever been sought. We all know very well how few judgments anyone can in fact legitimate intuitively, even with the best efforts; and yet it is supposed to be a matter of apriori insight that there can be no non-evident judgments that do not "in themselves" admit of being made evident in either a positive or a negative evidence.

We have not yet reached the end. The double principle of contradiction and excluded middle says, without qualification, that every judgment is either true or false. It contains no subjective word such as "evidence", though truth and falsity derive their sense and legitimacy originally from evidence. A judgment is not true at one time and false at another, but true or false *once for all*; that is to say, if it is evident at one time, if it is legitimated at one time in the evidence of a fulfilling adequation, then it cannot be shown at some other time, in the evidence of an "undeceiving adequation", to be false.

One can also give the much-interpreted *principle of identity*, A is A, this very sense: If A is true (where A stands for a judgment in our broadest sense), then it is true once for all — truth is a determination belonging permanently to the ideally identical judgment. One could then append the other two principles: If any A is true, its contradictory opposite is false; and every judgment is one or the other, true or false. However, it is a question whether this three-fold division is homogeneous, since "once for all" is a subjective locution, which does not belong in the purely Objective principles.

But we still have not given the sense of the logical principles its due. Already in pure mathematical analytics we could have related the identity of judgment-senses to "*everyone*": The same judgment is not merely an ideal unity pertaining, as *my* abiding meaning or opinion, to *my* manifold subjective mental processes; on the contrary, everyone can have the same opinion — and accordingly the problem of the universal intersubjective evidence

of this sameness should have been raised earlier. Since we have preferred to introduce the "everyone" here for the first time, there comes into question now, as something further, the opinion, on the part of logic, not only that an adequation effected by one subject / yields *him the* truth once for all as an ideal unity, but <173>
also that this ideality relates to everyone. Everyone can have every judgment; and for everyone the possibility obtains of bringing any judgment to an adequation, and likewise the pertinent laws of logic obtain. In this respect, everyone is in perfect harmony with everyone else.

The remarkable sense-determinations of the truth-concept that logic makes fundamental, the concept of an "Objective" truth — that is to say: an intersubjectively identical truth — extend to all the propositions that it erects in its theory: its axioms and also its theorems. They all claim, accordingly, to be valid once for all and for everyone.

§ 78. TRANSMUTATION OF THE LAWS OF THE "*MODUS PONENS*" AND THE "*MODUS TOLLENS*" INTO LAWS PERTAINING TO SUBJECTIVE EVIDENCES.

Like the dual principle of contradiction, the fundamental laws distinguished by the names *modus ponens* and *modus tollens*, among which only the principle of analytic consequence that belongs in pure consequence-logic has shown itself to be a genuine principle,[1] can be transmuted into laws pertaining to subjective evidences. In place of the pure consequence-principle, we then acquire as a law: *The possibility of distinct evidence of the analytic antecedent judgment necessarily entails the possibility of such evidence of the consequent judgment.*

The novelty in the transmutation of the corresponding law of truth-logic is that, when the syntactical (categorial) actions involved in judging the antecedent are performed on the basis of originality of "the affairs themselves" (on the basis of "experience"), the same possibility of *material evidence* must exist also for the actions involved in judging the consequent. Naturally, these laws pertaining to evidences are like the others in not themselves elucidating the problems they raise; moreover, all those difficulties of understanding apriori laws pertaining to

[1] *Author's note: Cf.* Part I, § 20, pp. 66 ff., *supra*.

evidences that can be brought to light in the case of the earlier principles concern also the principle now in question. They all demand a reflective study of these evidences, their origin, their structure, and what they actually do. /

<174> § 79. THE PRESUPPOSITION OF TRUTH IN ITSELF AND FALSITY IN ITSELF; THE PRESUPPOSITION THAT EVERY JUDGMENT CAN BE DECIDED.

Let us now go back to the first principles, the ones that, so to speak, define truth and falsity and, for that very reason, stand first. In them truth and falsity signify predicates of judgments but *not predicates included in their own essences* — in traditional phraseology, not "*constituent marks*" of judgments. One cannot "note" these predicates in judgments without more ado. To have judgments themselves given is not the same as to have one or the other of these predicates itself given.

It cannot even be said that, in the strict sense of the word, a *claim to truth* is included in the proper essences of judgments; and consequently it is incorrect to account this claim-concept part of the judgment-concept from the start. Subjectively stated, it is not necessary for the judger to co-objectivate truth, whether intuitively or emptily. One must guard here against the double sense of the word *assertion* [*Behauptung*], which people like to use in explaining judgments. The usual and, so to speak, emphatic sense of assertion is to the effect: I vouch for that; it is true; one can legitimate it at any time by an adequation. But the judgment that might at any time enter into an adequation precedes the possibility of an adequation. Judgment is categorial belief (verbally expressed predicative belief) — in the usual and narrower sense, it is non-modalized categorial certainty — and not *per se* a having-convinced-oneself by any witnesses or testimonies, in particular the ultimately decisive ones: the "affairs themselves". In their own essence, then, judgments have no claim whatever to truth or falsity; but any judgment can take up into itself the practical intention aimed at verification, at "that is right" or at decision whether it is right or wrong; subjectively, as a judgment in the judging process of meaning or opining, it can enter into more exactly distinguishable intentional complexes of confirmation and evidential verification, the clarification of which is another important task for the efforts that logic devotes to the subjective.

In accordance with the original sense of apophantic logic and the essential relation of this logic to *criticism of judgment*, the *logician*, as we have already had occasion to point out, thinks of every judgment from the beginning as *an assertion to be verified* (that is: as having the intention aimed at cognition) or as an assertion to be called in question; and consequently he thinks of every truth as a decision, reached either by direct legitimating evidence or by evidence belonging to a mediative method. Now, be- <175>
cause / the scientist, living in the will to cognize, strives to reach a decision regarding the correctness of every judgment not yet decided by evidence and because, in order to withstand renewed doubts or critical objections, the scientist must sometimes retest by evidence judgments already decided, a *fundamental conviction already awaits* the logician and logic in the state of positivity, the unspoken conviction that guides every scientist in his province: his settled belief in *truth-in-itself* and *falsity-in-itself*. For *us*, the legitimacy of many judgments remains undecided. And, for us, most of the judgments that are somehow possible can never be evidently decided *in fact*; but, *in themselves*, they can be. *In itself every judgment is decided*; its predicate truth, or its predicate falsity, "*belongs*" to its essence — though, as we have pointed out, it is not a constituent mark of any judgment as a judgment. This is very remarkable.

Naturally we have been referring throughout to rigidly identifiable judgments, producible by us and indeed by everyone (with the idealization mentioned above) and, as so identifiable, already at our disposal. But these fundamental presuppositions and the difficult questions and investigations (whether instituted or overlooked) relating to them are not what we intend to discuss now; though we must have them constantly in view as involved here throughout. In any case, as logicians we stand on the certainty of available identical judgments. But now they are supposed to be "decided in themselves". That surely signifies: *by a "method"*, by a course of *cognitive thinking*, a course existing in itself and intrinsically pursuable, which leads immediately or mediately to an adequation, a making evident of either the truth or the falsity of any judgment. All this imputes an astonishing

Apriori to every subject of possible judging and therefore to every actual or conceivable human being — astonishing: for how can we know *a priori* that courses of thinking with certain final results "exist in themselves"; paths that can be, but never have been, trod; actions of thinking that have unknown subjective forms and that can be, though they never have been, carried out?

§ 80. The evidence pertaining to the presupposition of truth, and the task of criticizing it.

But, after all, we do have de facto cognition; we have evidence and a truth attained or a falsehood rejected in it. We have had judgments as yet in fact undecided; we have in fact questioned them, and presupposed with assurance that they can be decided
<176> positively or / negatively; and often the decision has been reached, which, at the same time, fulfilled this never-formulated presupposition. Now, when we, as logicians, ascertained the laws of contradiction and excluded middle, did we not do so on the basis of an eidetic universalization, starting with such single cases as examples and perhaps with de facto attempts to think them otherwise — an apodictically necessary universalization, such that we grasped the unconditionally universal truth of these principles and, in our attempt at denial, the unconditionally universal impossibility of their being otherwise? Naturally we could have chosen, instead of actual, *possible* truths and falsehoods, along with the showing of them. That is to say: in pure phantasy we could have immersed ourselves in some judging or other and could have phantasied intuitionally explicit courses of positive or negative adequation to corresponding possible materialities. After all, eidetic universalization is not bound to the factual; and since, even when it starts with an actual fact, it must freely change that fact (into ideally possible facts), it can start just as well from the very beginning with free possibilities.

Naturally there is no immediate objection to all this. Above all, that there are indeed truths in themselves, which one can seek, and also find, by avenues already predelineated in themselves, is surely one of life's unquestioned truisms. One never asks *whether* there is a truth, but only *how* it can be reached or, at worst, whether it is not utterly unattainable by our factually limited powers of cognition or else unattainable only because of our temporarily insufficient previous knowledge and methodic resources. In this manner, though always within limits, we have, besides the domains of cognizable truths that make practical living possible, the infinite fields of cognition that belong to the sciences. The possibility of sciences depends entirely on this certainty that their provinces exist in truth, and that, concerning their provinces, theoretical truths-in-themselves exist, as actualizable by following explorable and gradually actualizable ways of cognition.

We do not intend to give up any of these truisms; they surely rank as evidences. But that must not keep us from submitting them to criticism and *asking them about their peculiar sense and their "range"*. Judgment-evidences can have *presuppositions* — not downright hypotheses, but presuppositions included in the domain of the evidence pertaining to the material / substrata <177>
and therefore having a share in the founding of truths and falsehoods — presuppositions that do not become fixed evidentially because cognitional interest does not lie in that direction, perhaps because they are truisms of such a sort that they always play their part in the particular province of cognition in the same manner and, therefore, uninterestingly.

Consider, for example, the vast realm of *occasional judgments*, which, in spite of being occasional, have their intersubjective truth or falsity. This truth-value obviously depends on the relatedness of the single subject's and the community's whole daily life to a *typical specific likeness among situations*, such that any normal human being who enters a particular situation has, by the very fact of being normal, the *situational horizons* belonging to it and common to all. One can explicate these horizons subsequently; but the *constituting horizon-intentionality*, without which the surrounding world of daily living would not be an *experienced world*, is always prior to its explication by someone who reflects. And *it* is the factor that *essentially determines the sense of occasional judgments* — always, and far beyond what at any time is, or can be, said expressly and determinately in the words themselves.[1] These horizons, then, are "presuppositions",

[1] *Author's note:* In the *Logische Untersuchungen* I still lacked the theory of horizon-intentionality, the all-determining rôle of which was first brought out in the *Ideen*. Therefore, in the earlier work, I could not finish with occasional judgments and their signification.

which, as intentional implicates included in the constituting intentionality, continually determine the objective sense of the immediate experiential surroundings, and which therefore have a character totally different from that of premise-presuppositions or from that of any of the idealizing presuppositions of predicative judging already discussed. Because of the formal abstractness and naïveté of the logician's thinking, such never-formulated presuppositions can easily be overlooked; and consequently a false range can be attributed even to the fundamental concepts and principles of logic.

All things considered, it has already become visible, from these pieces of a criticism of evidence, that evidence is at first a naïvely employed and "hidden" method, which one must examine concerning its performance, in order to know *what* one actually has as "it-itself", and with what *horizons* one has it, when one has something in evidence, as a consciousness in the mode: having something itself. The necessity and significance of this /
<178> deepest criticism of performance will, to be sure, become much more visible and understandable in the sequel. At the same time it will become understandable why the question, "What is truth?" is not the merely frivolous inquiry of a dialectic that argues back and forth between skeptical negativism or relativism and logical absolutism, but rather is a vast problem for work, a problem having a material basis of its own and pointing to most highly comprehensive investigations. It will become apparent, from aspect after aspect, that the chief reason why logic is incapable of satisfying the idea of a genuine theory of science — that is: incapable of actually sufficing as a norm for all sciences — is that its formal universalities stand in need of the intentional criticism that prescribes the sense and limits of their fruitful application.

§ 81. Formulation of further problems.

Our present theme, the sense of logical "truth in itself" or, as it is also called, "Objective truth" — correlatively, the criticism of the principles relating to it — has different problematic aspects, which, however, are so intimately interwoven that they present expositional difficulties.

We have already touched on the problematic sense of "true for everyone", which is combined with "true once for all"; but we have by no means fully uncovered and clarified it.

Furthermore there is the set of problems offered by *the relation of predicational truth to objects-about-which* and, finally, to "ultimate substrates", objects of possible "experience". These objects, the material [*das Sachliche*] in the ultimate sense, are, in the opinion of traditional logic, something *"Objective"*: Experience as such is *Objective experience*; truth as such is *Objective truth.* Truth is truth in itself concerning "Objects" — belonging to an *Objective world.* As such "Objects", these, for their part, *are* "in themselves" and can be judged about, not only somehow but, as already said, in such a manner that *every* judgment can be decided in truths (and falsehoods) in themselves.

Closely connected with this is the fact that, in traditional logic, this being of Objects has, as a rule, been thought of as an *absolute being,* to which the relation to the cognizing subjectivity and its actual or possible subjective "appearances" is non-essential. The absolute being of all Objects has as its correlate an *absolute truth,* which explicates it quite exhaustively in predications. /

For all these presuppositions we have the corresponding <179>
problems of evidence, which, because anything that we intend to state rationally should be drawn from evidence, must be raised concerning each point. But *traditional logic's concept of evidence* is involved here throughout, the evidence that, as the correlate of absolute truth and absolutely existing objects, is conceived as having the performance-sense of an *absolute evidence.* That raises the problem of clarifying the universally known differences between *imperfect and perfect* and, in some cases, between *spurious and genuine evidence.* Other points of importance, which do not so easily admit of understandable preliminary characterization, will find their motivation and description within the context of the exposition itself.

CHAPTER 4.

Evidential criticism of logical principles carried back to evidential criticism of experience.

§ 82. REDUCTION OF JUDGMENTS TO ULTIMATE JUDGMENTS. THE PRIMITIVE CATEGORIAL VARIANTS OF SOMETHING; THE PRIMITIVE SUBSTRATE, INDIVIDUAL.

We must start by *going back from the judgment to the judgment-substrates*, from truths to their *objects-about-which.*

In the first place, we require here an important supplementation of the pure logic of non-contradiction, a supplementation that, to be sure, goes beyond formal mathematics proper, but still does not belong to truth-logic. It is a matter, so to speak, of a *transitional link* between them.

As we remember, the formalization which analytics carries out, and which determines its peculiar character, consists in thinking of the syntactical stuffs, or "cores", of judgments as mere anythings whatever, so that only the syntactical form, the specifically judicial (including the core-forms, such as the forms substantivity and adjectivity), becomes determinant for the conceptual essences that, as "judgment-forms", enter into the logical laws of analytics. Here we must note the *relativity* in which these laws leave *the indeterminately universal cores.* For example, the forms of the categorical judgment, and more particularly of the adjectivally determining categorical judgment, says nothing about whether the subject or predicate of the
<180> judgment already / contains a syntactical form in the core itself. The subject S, taken as a form, is formally particularized equally well by "S, which is a", "S, which is a, b", "S, which has a relation to Q", or the like. Meanwhile it remains undetermined whether, in each of these forms, the S itself already has syntactical structures of the same sort within it. In the same manner, on the predicate side, the p may already bear within itself a categorial determination (perhaps "p, which is q" — for example: blood-red); and thus there may be forms within forms, to any degree of complexity. But it can be seen a priori that *any actual or possible judgment leads back to ultimate cores* when we follow up its

syntaxes; accordingly that it is a syntactical structure built ultimately, though perhaps far from immediately, out of *elementary cores, which no longer contain any syntaxes.* Also, in following up the sense of the *substantivized adjective*, we are led back to the *original adjective* and to the more original judgment of which it is a member and in which it occurs as an irreducible primitive form. In the same manner, a universality of a higher level (for example: the logical form-genus, judgment-form) leads us back to universalities of a lower level (in our example, the particular judgment-forms). And always it is clear that, by reduction, we reach a corresponding *ultimate*, that is: *ultimate substrates* — from the standpoint of formal logic, *absolute subjects* (subjects that are not nominalized predicates, relations, or the like), *ultimate predicates* (predicates that are not predicates of predicates, or the like), *ultimate universalities, ultimate relations.*[1]

But this must be understood correctly. In the logic of judgments, judgments (as we have explained) are senses, judicial meanings (or opinions) as objects. Consequently the reduction signifies that, *purely by following up the meanings*, we reach *ultimate something-meanings*; first of all, then, as regards the meant or supposed judgment-objects, *supposed absolute objects-about-which.* — Furthermore that, in the ultimate judgments, the ones on which the other judgments at different levels are built, we get back to the *primitive categorial variants of the sense, absolute something*: absolute properties, relations, and so forth, as *senses.*

For *mathesis universalis*, as formal mathematics, these ultimates have no particular interest. Quite the contrary for *truth-logic*: because ultimate substrate-objects are *individuals*, about which very much can be said in formal truth, and *back to which all truth ultimately relates.* / If one keeps to the formal of pure <181> analytics, if the evidence — the evidence serving this discipline — accordingly relates only to pure judgment-senses as distinct, one cannot establish this last proposition; it is by no means an "analytic" proposition. To have insight into it, one must *make ultimate cores intuited*, one must draw fullness of adequation, not from evidence of the judgment-senses, but instead from evidence of the "matters" or "affairs" corresponding to them. In analytic

[1] *Author's note:* See Appendix I, [pp. 294–312] *infra.*

logic one can go so far, and only so far, as to say that, in the sense, there must be certain sense-elements as the ultimate core-stuffs in all syntactical forms, and that one is brought back to judgment-complexes of ultimate judgments having "individual" substrates. *Analytically one can assert nothing about the possibility or the essential structure of individuals.* Even that, for example, a *time-form* necessarily belongs to them — duration, qualitative filledness of duration, and so forth — is something one can know only from a material evidence; and it can enter the judgment-sense only by virtue of an antecedent syntactical performance.

§ 83. Parallel reduction of truths. Relation of all truths to an antecedent world of individuals.

To the reduction of judgments to ultimate judgments with an ultimate sense, there corresponds a *reduction of truths*: of the truths belonging to a higher level to those belonging on the *lowest level*, that is: to truths that relate directly to their matters and material spheres, or (because the substrates play the leading rôle here) that relate directly *to individual objects* in their object-spheres — individual objects, objects that therefore contain within themselves no judgment-syntaxes and that, in their experienceable factual being, are *prior to all judging*. That judgments (not judgment-senses) relate to objects signifies that, in the judgment itself, these objects are meant as substrates, as the objects about which something is stated; and reductive deliberation teaches, as an *Apriori*, that *every conceivable judgment ultimately* (and either definitely or indefinitely) *has relation to individual objects* (in an extremely broad sense, real objects), and therefore has *relation to a real universe*, a "world" or a *world-province*, "for which it holds good". (The second thesis takes us further and is yet to be grounded.)

To ground the first thesis more strictly let us point out that universal judgments say nothing with definiteness about
<182> individuals, but that / extensionally, according to their sense, they bear an immediate or a mediate relation ultimately to individual singles. This is clear, first of all, in the case of universalities with a material content. However much, as upper-level universalities, they may relate extensionally to other universalities, they evidently must lead back by a finite number of steps to singles

with a material content that are themselves not universalities but individuals. But, if it is a case of formal-analytic universalities — numbers, for example, or multiplicities — then "everything and anything" belongs to their extension or that of their units. That involves their possible determination by any arbitrarily selectable objects whatever; and these could themselves be analytico-formal formations, with respect to whose units the same is true; and so *in infinitum*. But, according to their sense, it also involves their possible application to arbitrarily selectable objects with material content; which would take us back to the preceding case. Thus it is indeed true that absolutely every universality has an ultimate extensional relation of applicability to individuals that are either delimited by universalities with material content or else themselves left open to choice in this respect. Now, in accordance with its sense, formal logic — and therefore all forming of formal-analytic universalities, as a function of the theory of science — is intended to serve the ends of sciences that have material content. With all its freedom in the reiterative forming of forms, and with all its reflexive relatedness to its own scientific character, formal logic still intends — and even *in* these reiterations and this reflexiveness — not to remain a playing with empty thoughts, but to become an aid to cognition that has material content. Thus the ultimate applicability of formal anaytics to individuals is, at the same time, a *teleological* relatedness to all possible spheres of *individuals*. And therefore these spheres are, for logic, what is first in itself.

§ 84. The hierarchy of evidences; the intrinsically first evidences those of experience. The pregnant concept of experience.

Now, if truth is in question and, correlatively, an evidence by which it becomes one's own originarily, then what has just been stated is of obvious significance. The *hierarchy of evidences* goes with that of judgments and their senses; and *the truths and evidences that are first in themselves* must be the *individual* ones. A priori, the judgments made subjectively in the form belonging to the evidence which is *actually most original*, the evidence that seizes upon its substrates and predicatively formed affair-complexes originally and *quite directly*, must be *individual judgments*. /

<183> Individuals are given by experience, *experience in the first and most pregnant sense*, which is defined as a direct relation *to something individual*. In this connexion however, if we take as *experiential judgments* the group of judgments that have the most original evidence, then in a certain manner we must take experience in a broad sense: not only as the simple giving of an individual existence itself — that is: with certainty of its being — but also as extending to the *modalizations* of this certainty, which can, after all, change into likelihood, probability, and so forth. But, over against *all* these forms of "actual" (that is: positional) experience, there comes into question "neutralized" experience, "*as-if experience*", we can also say "*experience in phantasy*", which, with a suitable and freely possible alteration of one's attitude, becomes positional experience of a possible individual. Naturally, as-if experience has parallel as-if modalities of its primitive mode, as-if certainty of being.

§ 85. The genuine tasks of so-called judgment-theory. The sense-genesis of judgments as a clue in our search for the hierarchy of evidences.

The considerations just pursued give us access to an understanding of the *proper task of judgment-theory*, a discipline that, although much discussed, has remained rather fruitless, because it has lacked all understanding of the specific character of the investigations directed to the subjective that are necessary in the case of judgments, in the logical sense, and in the case of the fundamental concepts relating to these.

1. If the general confusion was reduced to the extent that (overcoming the psychologistic confounding of them) one distinguished *judging* and *the judgment itself* (the ideal formation, the stated proposition), it then was even less possible to set a senseful *problem concerning the subjective* as long as the peculiar essence of all intentionality, as a constitutive performance, was not understood and therefore judicative intentionality in particular was not understood as the constitutive performance in the case of ideal judgment-formations — and, still more particularly, the intentionality of evidential judging was not understood as the constitutive performance in the case of ideal truth-formations. Therefore, after the aforesaid distinction

between judging and judgment has been made, the *first judgment-problem* that must be set in logic, starting from there, is that of going back to the variously effective intentionality and carrying out the reflective phenomenological clarifications in which / *logic's different concepts of the judgment* become separated, <184> according to their origins, as *fundamental concepts* for its disciplines and become, as the same time, understandable in their interrelatedness.

2. If this first series of investigations has been carried out — the ones we attempted in the earlier parts of this book — then *reductive deliberations* such as were occupying us a little while ago [1] become necessary. They uncover the *hidden intentional implications* included in judging and in the judgment itself as the product of judging. *Judgments as senses accordingly have a sense-genesis.*

What that signifies can be understood from the phenomenological *pointing back* that, for example, a nominalized predicate (as expressible by such nouns as "red" and "the red") bears, in that it points back to a nominalizing activity, on the noetic side, and to the original predicate (as expressible by such adjectives as "red"), on the noematic side. Such phenomenological pointings-back are shown by every other nominalized sense-formation (like "the similarity" and "this, that S is p") — pointings back to the corresponding more original formation and, correlatively, to the pertinent nominalizing activities; likewise, each attributive determination in the subject points back to the originality of that determination as a predicate; and so forth.

This yields, *even for the theory of forms* and, subsequently, for procedure in *an analytics of consequence-relationships, a principle of genetic order*, which at the same time determines the specifically logical aim conferred on analytics with the concepts and laws of *truth*. With respect to the subjective, that signifies that the predelineated *order of judgment-forms involves a* predelineated *order in the process of making materially evident* and in the different levels of *true materialities themselves*.

Uncovering the sense-genesis of judgments signifies, more precisely, an unravelling of the sense-moments that are implicit in, and belong essentially to, the sense that has plainly come to

[1] *Author's note:* See §§ 82 and 83, [pp. 202–205, *supra*].

light. Judgments, as the finished products of a "constitution" or "genesis", can and must be asked about this genesis. The essential peculiarity of such products is precisely that they are senses that bear within them, as a sense-implicate of their genesis, a sort of historicalness; that in them, level by level, sense points back to original sense and to the corresponding noetic[1] intentionality; that therefore each sense-formation can be asked about its *essentially necessary sense-history.* /

<185> This wonderful peculiarity is concomitant with the universality of consciousness of every sort as effective intentionality. All intentional unities come from an intentional genesis, are "constituted" unities; and everywhere one can ask the "finished" unities about their constitution, about their total genesis, and particularly about the eidetically apprehensible essential form of this genesis. This fundamental fact, embracing in its universality the whole of intentional living, is what *determines the proper sense of intentional analysis, its sense as an uncovering of the intentional implications,* with which there come to the fore, as contrasted with the overt, the finished, sense of the unities, their *hidden* sense-moments and "causal" sense-relations. At any rate, we understand this so far as the judgment is concerned; and it now becomes understandable in particular that *not only the overt, or finished, but likewise the implied sense must always have its say,* and that it too exercises an essential function, particularly in the process of making evident — here, in our logical sphere, the process of making logical principles evident. But, as will be seen forthwith, that applies not only to the syntactical implications but also to the deeper-lying genesis pertaining to the ultimate "cores" and pointing back to their origination from experiences. Without being clear about all that, we cannot actually have the principles of logic at our command, we do not know what hidden presuppositions may lie within them.

§ 86. The evidence of pre-predicative experience as the intrinsically primary theme of transcendental judgment-theory. The experiential judgment as the original judgment.

The lowest level reached by tracing back the clue of sense-genesis brings us, as we already know, to *judgments about*

[1] *Translator's note:* Reading ***noetische*** instead of ***noematische.***

individuals; and consequently, in the case of evident judgments, in the sense of seeings of the predicatively formed affair-complexes themselves, it brings us to those evidences of something individual that belong to the simplest type. These are the pure and simple *experiential judgments*, judgments about data of possible perception and memory, which give norms for the correctness of categorical judicial meanings at the lowest level concerning individuals.

Let us utilize a proposition from the general theory of consciousness — more particularly, from the phenomenology of universal genesis in consciousness. It states that, for objectivities of every sort, *consciousness in the mode, giving them-themselves, precedes* all other / modes of consciousness relating to them, all these other <186> modes being genetically secondary. Consciousness that gives us something itself is indeed always passing over, by way of retention and protention, into consciousness that does *not* give us something itself: empty consciousness. Even recollection, though it can be intuitive, is the awakening of an empty consciousness and points back to earlier original consciousness. Accordingly, from these genetical points of view, *the intrinsically first judgment-theory is the theory of evident judgments, and the intrinsically first thing in the theory of evident judgments* (and therefore in judgment-theory as a whole) *is the genetical tracing of predicative evidences back to the non-predicative evidence* called *experience.* With suitable further intentional formings, the experience enters into the judging done at the lowest genetic level, and the product of experience enters into the judgment-formation itself.

Here one has indeed reached the intrinsically *first beginning of a systematic judgment-theory*, as a theory that traces the essentially determined systematic genesis pertaining to the judgment employed originally on the matters themselves (the "evidential" judgment) and then follows the predelineated ways leading upward from what is intrinsically first in this genesis.

This beginning, moreover, is the place systematically, *starting from the judgment, to discover* that certainty and modalities of certainty, suppositive intention and fulfilment, identical existent and identical sense, evident having of something itself, trueness of being (being "actual") and truth as correctness of sense — that *none of these is a peculiarity exclusively within the predicational sphere, that, on the contrary, they all belong already to the intentionality of experience.* Starting from there, one can trace them into the givings of things themselves, the evidences, on a higher level — for example: those of the *proximate variants of the individual* (property, relation, and so forth) and particularly the evidence of the *universal* (derivable from the experience of individuals), with its extensional sense as embracing individuals.

Thus one comes *from the experiential judgment* — more particularly, from the most immediate experiential judgment having the categorical form — *to experience* and to *the motive for that broadening of the concept of judgment* already indicated by Hume's concept of *belief*. Historically, to be sure, the apprehension of this broadest concept remains crude, even countersensical. Its inadequacy is shown by the mere fact that the identification of judgment and "belief" presently necessitates introduction of a "presentation [*Vorstellung*]" allegedly founding this belief. This is not the place to submit the doctrine to extensive criticism.
<187> Lockean / sensualism, which reaches completion in Hume and John Stuart Mill and becomes almost all-prevailing in modern philosophy, finds in this *belief a mere Datum of "internal sense"*, not much different from a Datum of "external sense", such as a sound-Datum or a smell-Datum. To those prepossessed by the *parallelizing of "internal" and "external" experience* — correlatively, the sphere of individual psychic being (the sphere grasped in its real being by immanent experience, so they supposed) and the sphere of physical being — it appeared to be without question that, at bottom, *problems concerning judgment* and psychic problems generally must have *essentially the same sense as problems concerning physical Nature* and should be treated by the same method: as *problems concerning reality*, problems for a psychology as the science of "psychic phenomena", of Data of "internal experience", including belief-Data. Because of this blindness to all intentionality and — even after intentionality had been insisted upon by Brentano — because of a blindness to its Objectivating function, *all the actual problems concerning judgment* were indeed *lost from view*. If their genuine sense is brought out, the intentionality of predicative judgments leads back ultimately to the intentionality of experience.

According to what was indicated above, the theory of the

evidence of the pure and simple categorical experiential judgment should be called the "intrinsically primary" judgment-theory because, in respect of intentional genesis, the non-evident judgment, even the countersensical judgment, points back to an origin from experiential judgments. It should be emphasized that this referring back, just like the predicational sense-genesis discussed a little while ago, is not inferred from an *inductive empeiria* on the part of the psychological observer, perchance the experimentalist in the "psychology of thinking"; on the contrary, as can be shown in phenomenology, it is an *essential component of the intentionality*, a component uncoverable among the intentional contents thereof in the corresponding productions of fulfilment. Accordingly it is the case that, *for us*, to be sure, as carrying on a philosophico-logical sense-investigation, *the non-evident and the evident judgment are presented on an equal plane* and the course of *naïvely positive logic* is therefore the *natural* one; whereas, considered in itself, the evident judgment — most fundamentally, *the experiential judgment — is nevertheless the original judgment.* From its syntaxes, the ones that are first in themselves, genesis of the higher syntaxes goes upward, the ones with which formal analytics is exclusively occupied in its theories, / concerning itself with the conditions for possible judicative <188>
evidence that are implicit in the apriori forms of distinct judgings and of their intentional correlates.

Now, even though formal analytics, in respect of its province and its theory, has to do only with the *forms* of possible judgments and truths, and even though no such thing as evidence or experience is to be found <as thematic> in its province or its theory, still, in its "epistemo-critical" investigations of the subjective, which concern the radical method of intentional performances, it must investigate the categorial mediacies of evidence and verification, and accordingly must clarify the *performance of the original judgments.* Through these all truth and all judicative evidence, so we see, are related back to the primitive basis, experience; and, because experience itself functions *in* and *not beside* the original judgments, *logic needs a theory of experience* — in order to be able to give scientific information about the legitimating bases, and the legitimate limits, of its Apriori, and consequently about its own legitimate sense. If experience itself is accounted as judgment in the broadest sense, then this theory of experience is to be characterized as itself the first and most fundamental judgment-theory. Naturally this explication of experience, as the activity that precedes the specifically categorial activities and takes on shape in them, must be restricted to a *"formal" universality* consistent with the purpose of formal logic — a universality that is "formal" in the sense that, on the subjective side, is the *correlate* of the sense in which analytics is formal. The relevant and by no means easy unravelling of the multiform experiential performance carried out in the experiential judgment, and the unravelling of this original judgment itself, will be done elsewhere.[1] Here let us mention in particular only the fact that even this founding experience has its style of syntactical performances, which, however, are still free from all the conceptual and grammatical formings that characterize the categorial as exemplified in the predicative judgment and the statement.[2] /

<189> § 87. Transition to evidences at higher levels. The question of the relevance of the cores to the evidence of materially filled universalities and to the evidence of formal universalities.

From the experience that gives individual objects one must ascend, in a systematic judgment-theory, to the possible universalizations built on that experience, and ask how the underlying experience functions for the evidence of them. There then appears a fundamental difference in the character of *essential* universalizations, as brought about, on the one hand, in conformity with the *material Apriori* and, on the other hand in conformity with the *formal Apriori*. In the first case, we draw from the individual example *contents included in its own essence*, and we acquire the materially filled essential genera and species and the eidetic laws that have a material content; in *formalizing* universalization, however, each *individual* must be *emptied to become*

[1] *Author's note:* In the studies in logic that were announced above [p. 115, n.]. [*See Erfahrung und Urteil, I. Abschnitt* and *II. Abschnitt.*]

[2] *Author's note:* In my *Logische Untersuchungen, II. Bd., II. Teil, 6. Untersuchung*, the concept of the categorial was first introduced with exclusive attention to that which is syntactical in the judgment. No separation was yet made between, on the one hand, the syntactical as such, which makes its appearance already in the pre-predicational sphere and, moreover, has its analogues in the spheres of emotion and volition and, on the other hand, the syntactical that belongs to the specific sphere comprising judgments.

anything whatever. Accordingly, every syntactical fashioning of an object out of individuals, and likewise every categorial formation made out of antecedently present categorial objectivities, must be considered similarly as a mode of the bare anything-whatever. In place of something individual, there enters everywhere the positing of "a certain substrate (of whatever sort) about which one can judge"; meanwhile the fashioning of universalities is concerned exclusively with the forms and the form-genera of categorial formations as such. Here every law remains in a state of relativity, which leaves it indeterminate whether and how the indeterminate substrates of the categorial forms lead back to something individual.

When we go on from judgments as mere meanings or opinions to truths, this essential difference between materially determinate and formalizing universalization gives rise to the *great corresponding differences among the problems of evidence and truth*, and therefore to *correspondingly different problems for the criticism of apriori cognition*. Every Apriori with a material content (every Apriori belonging within a discipline that is "ontological" in the normal sense, and ultimately within a universal ontology) demands a return to *intuition* of individual examples — that is: to *"possible" experience* — if criticism is to bring about genuine evidence. It demands the criticism of experience and, based on that criticism, criticism of the specific judicative performance, and therefore the actual making of the syntactical or categorial formations that can be produced on the basis of data themselves of possible experience. *The evidence of / laws pertaining to the* <190>
analytic Apriori needs no such intuitions of determinate individuals. It needs only *some examples or other of categorialia*; even categorialia having indeterminately universal cores will do (as when propositions about numbers serve as examples). They may indeed *point back* intentionally to something individual; but they *need not be further examined* nor explicated in this respect. One does not have to go into a materially filled sense that is placed before one, as one must in the case of the material Apriori, where the evidence depends entirely on going into and explicating the own-essentiality of some materially determinate affairs or other.

Nevertheless, the *sense-relation of all categorial meanings* to something individual, that is, on the noetic side, to evidences of individuals, to *experiences*, — a relation growing out of their sense-genesis and present in every example that could be used by formal analytics — surely *cannot be insignificant for the sense and the possible evidence of the laws of analytics*, including the highest ones, the principles of logic. Otherwise, how could those laws claim *formal-ontological* validity: united with their validity for every possible predicative truth, validity for *everything conceivably existing*? This conceivability surely signifies a possibility of evidence, which leads back ultimately, even though with formal universality, to a possible individual something or other and, correlatively, to a possible experience. The *logician*, while he is obtaining his logical principles originally and evidently, has before his view some judgments (categorialia) or other as examples. He varies them with the consciousness of free option, thus forming the consciousness of "some judgments or other"; and he intends to conceive with pure universality the insights, about truth and falsity, whose typical essential style persists throughout the variation. The examples stand before him as finished products of a genesis which, generally speaking, was none of his doing. In the naïve process of making the principles evident, there is no question of an uncovering of this genesis or its essential structure — to say nothing of eidetically bringing the essential content of the sense, *any judgment*, as constituted in a genesis of this nature, into essential connexion with what the principles presuppose as truth and falsity, and what they determine concerning these. Can we rest content in this naïveté? No matter how unquestioned the principles of logic may be, do they not need a critical determination of their genuine sense, starting from the sources that fashion it? And do they not need, therefore, the uncovering of the genesis of judgments?

As a matter of fact, criticism of the principles of logic, as the uncovering of the hidden presuppositions implicit in them, will
<191> show / that, even in the evidence of formal universalization, the cores are not wholly irrelevant.

§ 88. The presupposition implicit in the law of analytic contradiction: Every judgment can be made distinctly evident.

When we consider the principles of logic from the point of view of sense-genesis, we come upon a *fundamental presupposition* included in them and inseparably inherent in at least the law of excluded middle. On close examination, this presupposition is seen to derive from another, correspondingly unnoticed, presupposition, which belongs to the lower stratum of formal logic, the stratum that is prior to introduction of the concept of truth and became distinguishable for us in our earlier analyses. As we ourselves, in those analyses, began naïvely and followed only one line of interest, this presupposition remained hidden from us in the earlier context. We can bring this lower-level presupposition to light by attempting to formulate *as a truism*: *Any possible judgment* in the broadest sense — any judgment, that is, whose possibility becomes evident merely from an explicitly apprehended indication belonging to the verbal significations of a declarative locution — can (if the laws of analytic consistency are complied with) be *converted into a possible "distinct" or "proper" judgment* — a judgment, the possibility of which becomes evident only with the actualizing of the indications, by making the indicated judgment itself, in the performance *proper* of the appropriate syntactical acts. In other words: "*Non-contradiction*", taken in the broadest sense, which includes every case of analytic consistency, is a *necessary and sufficient condition for this performability proper of a possible judgment.*

Now this is *by no means so universally correct*, as we can easily convince ourselves. And yet the establishing (?) [*Installierung*] of a lack of consistency presupposes that any judgment, in the broadest sense, can be made distinctly evident, positively or negatively, and that the analogue of the law of contradiction applies to this effect. Therefore some *unclarified presupposition or other must have entered restrictively into the judgment-concept of consequence-logic,* so that only with this tacitly presupposed restriction does "every" judgment satisfy the regulative conditions for performability proper. /

§ 89. The possibility of distinct evidence. <192>

a. Sense as judgment and as "judgment-content". Ideal existence of the judgment presupposes ideal existence of the judgment-content.

Let us start with examples. If we put ourselves in the place of someone who is hearing or reading "without thinking", we can grasp it as a possibility that such a person, merely following the symbolic indications belonging to the words and perhaps being biased by a credulous acceptance of authority, passively judges what he hears — even, for example: "This color plus one makes three". Nevertheless we say that the sentence *"makes no proper sense"*: It is impossible, in actual thinking (that is: in actually producing the single members of the predication and their syntactical cumulation), to acquire the judgment as a possible one — not, however, because it contains an analytic or extra-analytic contradiction, but because it is, so to speak, *exalted above harmoniousness and contradiction in its "senselessness"*. The single propositional elements are not senseless; they are good honest senses. But the whole presents no unitarily concordant sense. It is *not a whole that is itself sense.*

We have, then, harmony and discordancy (conflict) in the "sense", and in such fashion that what sense and whole sense signify *here* is *not* a matter of judgments performed actually and properly, judgments as consequence-logic intends them; though it is indeed a matter of judgments and of truth-logic. *Now contradictory judgments have harmony, in the unity of a "sense"*; but contradiction and harmony, according to the concepts belonging to consequence-logic, are mutually exclusive opposites, and it is obvious that they *already presuppose a unity of this "sense"*.

If we ask what determines the concept of sense here, we become aware of one of those essential equivocations of which we were speaking earlier. To clear it up, we must go back to the distinction that was treated in the *Logische Untersuchungen* as the difference between "quality" and "material".[1]

As the *sense* of a statement, one can understand —

Firstly, the corresponding *judgment*. But, if the person who makes the statement goes on from the simple certainty, "*S* is *p*", ‹193› to the / uncertain presuming, the considering probable, the doubting, the affirmation or the denying rejection, or the assumption, of the same "*S* is *p*", there stands out —

Secondly, as the judgment-sense, the *"judgment-content"* as

[1] *Author's note*: See *op. cit.*, II. Bd., I. Teil, pp. 111ff. An essential radicalization of the idea of "judgment-material", and therefore of the whole exposition in this section, is offered in Appendix I, [pp. 294—312, *infra*].

something common, which remains identical *throughout the changes in the mode of being* (certainty, possibility, probability, questionability, "actuality", nullity) and, on the subjective side, the changes in the mode of doxic positing. This *identical What* in the judgment — throughout the changing modifications of the primitive mode, doxic certainty —, this that, in the particular case, "is", or is possible, probable, questionable, and so forth, the *Logische Untersuchungen* apprehended as a non-selfsufficient moment in the judgment-modalities.

Thus the concept of sense has, in the judgment-sphere, an essentially *double sense*, a double sense, moreover, that extends, in a similar manner, to all positional spheres and first of all, naturally, to the lowest doxic sphere, that of "objectivation [*Vorstellung*]" — that is: experience with all its variant modes, including the empty mode. *The possible unity of such a judgment-content*, thought of as a *unity that can be posited* in some modality or other, *is restricted by conditions*. The mere unitary grammatical understandableness, the *purely grammatical sensefulness* (according to yet a third and quite different concept of sense: grammatical sense), is *not the only sensefulness that logical analytics presupposes*.

As we see, the concept of the distinct judgment — the judgment that can be properly effected syntactically — which is presupposed in consequence-logic and therefore in the formal principles of truth, is in need of a supplementary essential determination and a correspondingly deeper clarification. *The unitary effectibility of the judgment-content is prior to*, and a condition for, *the effectibility of the judgment itself*. Or: *the ideal "existence" of the judgment-content is a presupposition for*, and enters into, *the ideal "existence" of the judgment* (in the widest sense, that of a supposed categorial objectivity as supposed).

b. The ideal existence of the judgment-content depends on the conditions for the unity of possible experience.

If we inquire now about the "origin" of the former evidence <*sc.* the evidence in which the ideal "existence" of the judgment-content is constituted originaliter> (with its opposite, which finds its expression only in the multisignificant word "senseless-

<194> ness"), we are / referred to the syntactical *cores*, which seem to be functionless from the formal point of view. That would imply, then, that the possibility of properly effectuating the possibility of a judgment (as a meaning) is rooted *not only* in the syntactical *forms* but also in the syntactical *stuffs*. This fact is easily overlooked by the formal logician, with his interest directed one-sidedly to the syntactical — the manifold forms of which are all that enters into logical theory — and with his algebraizing of the cores as theoretical irrelevancies, as empty somethings that need only be kept identical.

But how is one to understand the function of the syntactical stuffs or cores in making possible the existence of the judgment — that is: the proper effectibility of the indicated judgment? Here the clarification is to be found in the *intentional genesis*. Every judgment as such has its intentional genesis or, as we can also say, its essentially necessary *motivational foundations*, without which it could not at first exist in the primitive mode, certainty, nor be modalized thereafter. These foundations include the necessity that the *syntactical stuffs* occuring in the unity of a judgment *have something to do with one another*. That, however, arises from that fact that the genetically most original manner of judging — we are speaking of an *intentional* and, accordingly, an essentially determined genesis, not a psychophysical and inductively inferred genesis, which, by the way, can be intelligibly conceived only on the basis of the former — is evidential judging and, at the lowest level, judging on the basis of experience. *Prior* to all judging, there is a universal experiential basis. It is always presupposed *as a harmonious unity of possible experience*. In this harmony, everything has "to do" materially with everything else. But a unity of experience can become *discordant*, though, of essential necessity, in such a manner *that the conflicting parts have a community of essence*, so that, in the unity of a coherent experience — an experience that, even in the mode conflict, is still coherent — everything has an essentially necessary community with everything else. Thus, *in respect of its content, every original judging* and every judging that proceeds coherently, has *coherence by virtue of the coherence of the matters in the synthetic unity of the experience*, which is the basis on which the judging stands. We do not intend to say in advance that there can be only one universe

of possible experience as the basis for judgment, and that therefore every intuitive judgment has the same basis and all judgments / belong to a single materially coherent whole. To reach <195>
a decision about that would require a separate investigation.

Now, from original judgings what has been said carries over, by essential necessity, to all possible judging of whatever sort; in the first place, to all judgments possibly making their appearance for the *same* judger in *his* nexus of consciousness, and accordingly, as something new, to all the *non-intuitional* judgments that are possible for him. To make this a matter of insight on the basis of eidetic laws is an undertaking that belongs in the universal context of constitutional theories that clarify the manner in which original intentionality, as "primally institutive", entails the constitution of secondary intentional formations and furnishes them with an intentionality that, as secondary, points back essentially to the institutive intentionality as its actualizable analogue. In the same context belongs likewise the whole eidetic theory of the formation of "apperceptions".

The syntactical stuffs of non-intuitional judgments cannot be varied with complete freedom, for the indicated reasons, which pertain to the genesis of their being and sense; it is not as though one could collect such stuffs quite *ad libitum* and form possible judgments out of them. Apriori the syntactical stuffs of each possible judgment and of each judgingly combinable judgment-complex have an intentional relatedness to the unity of a possible experience — correlatively, to a unitarily experienceable materiality. Meanwhile the already-emphasized possibility of discordancies, illusions, necessary cancellations, has not been overlooked. For it does not destroy the unity of a coherence, precisely the unity that is the ultimate basis for the material congruity of the stuffs of possible judgments, and therefore of possible judgment-complexes, no matter how extensive. *Formal-logical considerations* and theory, with their focusing on what is Objective, have nothing to say about that; but every one of their logical forms, with their S's and p's, with all the literal symbols occuring in the unity of a formal nexus, *tacitly presuppose* that, in this nexus, S, p, and so forth, have *"something to do with each other" materially*.

§ 90. Application to the principles of truth-logic: They hold good only for judgments that are senseful in respect of content.

The important supplementation received by our earlier analysis of the judgment has a decisive *significance for the |*
<196> *criticism of logical principles* that we were previously considering. This criticism is now easy to complete. Logic quite obviously does not have in mind such judgments as we called *senseless in respect of content* — for example: The sum of the angles of a triangle is equal to the color red. Naturally it does not occur to anyone who engages in the theory of science to think of such a judgment. And yet every declarative sentence that fulfils only the conditions for unitary *purely grammatical* sense (every unity of a sentence that is at all understandable) is also *thinkable as a judgment* — a judgment in the widest sense. *If the principles of logic were to relate to judgments universally, they would not be tenable, certainly not the law of excluded middle.* For all judgments that are "senseless" in respect of content violate this law.

The principles, to make this evident first of all, *hold good* unconditionally *for all judgments whose cores are congruous in respect of sense* — that is: all judgments that fulfil the conditions for unitary sensefulness. For, in the case of these judgments, it is given *a priori*, by virtue of their genesis, that they relate to a unitary experiential basis. Precisely because of this, it is true of every such judgment, in relation to such a basis, either *that it can be brought to an adequation* and, with the carrying out of the adequation, either the judgment explicates and apprehends categorially what is given in harmonious experience, or else that it leads to the negative of adequation: it predicates something that, according to the sense, indeed belongs to this sphere of experience; but what it predicates conflicts with something experienced. We have shown, however, with regard to the subjective version of the principles, that part of their sense is precisely that *every* judgment can be brought to either a positive or a negative adequation. But, for the broader realm of judgments, to which belong also the judgments that are *senseless in respect of content*, this disjunction no longer holds good. *The "middle" is not excluded here*; and it consists in the fact that judgments with predicates having no senseful relation to the subject are, so to speak, *exalted above truth and falsity in their senselessness.*

§ 91. Transition to new questions.

One sees, then, how necessary an intentional judgment-theory is and how far down it must go in order even to *understand in an original manner what the proper and pure sense of the principles of logic is.* /

But, when we consider what our investigation has accomplished <197>
for such a theory, and consequently for the clarification of the idea of truth, we see that its accomplishment is no more than the exhibition of the necessity of *preliminary "epistemological" work* that does justice to the essentially necessary relatedness of all judicative evidences to spheres of experience. *Judicative evidence* "gives" *truth* in the sense, correctness of a judgment, and, correspondingly, in the sense, the existing syntactically formed affair-complex itself and the other categorialia themselves universally. *Experience,* which we regard as a pre-predicative evidence, gives *"realities [Realitäten]"*, this word being used here as unrestrictively as possible, accordingly as taking in everything "individual". Among realities belong, naturally, the Objects of the spatio-temporal world. But perhaps not all experience is a giving of something-itself that is worldly; and perhaps criticism of logic's presuppositions and of its concept *"truth"* will bring us to the point where we shall learn to frame this concept otherwise and more broadly, without the reduction to experience and to Objects of experience — "realities" — suffering thereby. And it may be that this amplified conception of truth will be owing to the very fact that we must take into consideration a more extensive concept of experience, though still (as here) within the pregnant concept of the giving of "individuals" themselves.

Suppose that what we have comprehended in principle, but not actually grounded in detail, were actually shown, namely that, thanks to an uncoverable intentional genesis of judgments, every judgment — understood not only as being an indication that is senseful from the purely grammatical standpoint but also as having a senseful material homogeneity among its cores — necessarily has such a relation to a unitary sphere of experience (a unitary material province) that it can be brought to either a positive or a negative adequation; then what we have set up as the subjective version of logical principles, the turning of them into principles concerning evidence, is indeed established. But *how is evidence related to truth*? Actually the relation is not so simple as that conversion let it appear.

CHAPTER 5.

The subjective grounding of logic as a problem belonging to transcendental philosophy.

§ 92. CLARIFICATION OF THE SENSE IN WHICH OBJECTIVE LOGIC IS POSITIVE.

a. The relatedness of historically given logic to a real world.

The problems of *what evidence does,* which confront us as logicians, are — since all judgments point back to experience — problems concerning experience / itself and problems concerning <198>
the categorialia deriving from experience. The two sets of problems are interwoven in the task of clearing up the lowest level of judging [*Urteilsstufe*], correlatively the lowest level of categorialia, those that still bear their experiential source immediately within them. The way to these problems leads us (since we are letting ourselves be guided toward a transcendental logic by a criticism of naïve logic and its positivity) first of all to a *criticism of the naïve concepts of evidence and truth,* or true being, that govern the whole logical tradition.

To mention the fact again, it was only in its first and unforgettable inception, in the Platonic dialectic, that logic, as formal theory of science, had the fundamental theme: the possibility of a science as such and an existent as such. For *that* logic, there was as yet no actual science and no actual world, as already accepted beforehand. Under the altered conditions of later times, the situation was reversed. Logic assumed the guise of a formal apophantic criticism of already-given science, already-given truth and theory; correlatively, the guise of a formal ontology for which, so far as their most general natures were concerned, existing objects and an existing world were fixed unshakeably beforehand. Not that the definite constituents of the world and the definite currently developed sciences were presupposed in logic; on the contrary, a criticism of these was to be made possible by bringing out apriori logical norms. But true being as such, predicational truth and "valid" theory as such, and the possibility of pressing forward by experience and theoretical cognition toward these affairs, presupposed, in respect of their generic natures, as existing, — these were matters of course, never examined in traditional formal logic. One can say (and, as will eventually be seen, in this lies something particularly important) that it is a *logic* — a formal apophantics and a formal ontology — *for a real world, thought of as given beforehand.* This world is of course in and of itself what it is; yet, on the other hand, it is accessible to us, to everyone, in our cognitive consciousness, and primarily through experience. — To be sure, very incompletely and altogether imperfectly; but, on the basis of experience, the higher work of cognition proper is built, which leads us to Objective truth.

All the judgments, truths, sciences, of which this logic speaks, relate to this existing world. The matter-of-fact truths and sciences concern matter-of-fact existence in the world or the matter-of-fact existence of the world itself; the apriori truths and
<199> sciences, in like fashion, concern possible worldly being. / To speak more precisely, the latter concern what is necessarily valid when the matter-of-fact world is freely varied in phantasy — necessarily valid as an essential form of any world whatever, and therefore of this given world. Thus the apriori theories of space and time (geometry, "chronology") relate to space and time as essential forms of this world as somehow a world. Accordingly even the apriori sciences that logic considers are worldly: Like the being-in-itself of the actual world, the possible being-in-themselves of its possibility-variants is presupposed; and it is presupposed that, by means of actual and possible experience and theory, science of the actual world and science of any apriori-possible world whatever are possible "in themselves" or have existence in themselves, and can for that reason be matter-of-course aims of an effort bent on actualizing them logically.

Now logic, to be sure, kept within the bounds of an *aprioriness* that must not assert facts of any sort, nor any *de facto* world, in its theories. On the one hand, however, we should bear in mind that, as formal ontology, logic presupposed at least possible worldly being, which, after all, it must have acquired as a possibility-variant of the undoubtedly actual world. On the other hand, wherever logic felt the inclination to clarify its fundamental concepts and engaged in investigations *directed to the subjective,* it took these as *psychological* in the usual sense: investigations concerning the objectivating and thinking life and the evidential consciousness of human beings in the world — regardless of whether psychophysics and "Objective" experiment or mere "internal experience" was resorted to. And similarly our earlier investigations of fundamental concepts, since we did not express ourselves on this point, will have been taken, as a matter of course, to be psychological in the usual sense. In any case, the already-given actual world is always there, in the background — though it sufficed us, after all, that the relation of logic to an apriori-possible world, no matter how that relation came into logic, signifies a presupposition, and one with no less importance to the critic than the presupposition of the *de facto* world.

b. Its naïve presupposing of a world ranks logic among the positive sciences.

We were saying above that logic, by its relation to a real world, presupposes not only a real world's being-in-itself but also the possibility, existing "in itself", of acquiring cognition of a world as genuine knowledge, genuine science, either empirically or a priori. / This implies: Just as the realities belonging to the world <200>
are what they are, in and of themselves, so also they are substrates for truths that are valid in themselves — "truths in themselves", as we said with Bolzano. Furthermore: In the cognizing subjects there are corresponding possibilities of cognition, of seizing upon these truths themselves in subjective evidence-processes, in absolute evidences as seizings upon of the absolute truths themselves, the very ones that are valid in themselves. All of that is claimed as an Apriori. The truths that hold for what exists in itself — for *what exists absolutely*, and not for what exists relatively to the subjective (what we are given as existing, what appears in experience as existing and as being thus and so) — are *absolute truths*. In the sciences, they are "discovered", brought out and grounded by scientific method. The success of this enterprise is, perhaps forever, imperfect; but the aim itself remains doubtless and tacitly accepted as a universal idea; as does the correlative idea of its attainableness, the idea of an *absolute evidence*. If logic itself did not make these presuppositions a theme, then epistemology, psychology, and metaphysics, did so all the more — yet only after the fashion of *ex post facto* sciences, with no intention of intruding on the absolute self-sufficiency of logic.

But such a sequence of disciplines is possible — we shall present the more detailed reasons shortly — only where utter obscurity masks their problems; and, so far as the above-named supplementary philosophic disciplines are concerned, it leads to a *naïveté of quite another order* than that of the naïveté characterizing simple positivity. Simple positivity, as a naïve devotedness, not only of practical but also of cognitive living, to the world that is indeed given beforehand, has in it a legitimacy — unclarified, to be sure, and therefore still undelimited, but nevertheless a legitimacy. A naïve criticism of experience, however, and of the experientially derived cognition of a world existing in itself, a criticism operating with modes of argument belonging to a habitual logic, which has not even investigated them to see whether by their sense they do not already presuppose the being of a world, nay, which has not even thought of investigating the performance that is peculiar to experience and the performances that are peculiar to the other components of the subjectivity relevant to the being-sense of a world — such a criticism has a naïveté that, from the start, excludes its seemingly scientific theories from serious consideration.

Naturally, the existence of possible absolute evidences, which is certain a priori to the logician, is thought of as being also an existence for *everyone* capable of cognition. Everyone is equal to
<201> everyone else in that respect. / Either the absolutely existent in its absolute trueness is actually seen, and seen into as being the way it is; or else such sight and insight are lacking. Thus the validity of truth for everyone, and once for all, offers no particular problem. This "*everyone*" is every human being or supposable quasi-human being in the actual world (or in a possible world, in the case of absolute truths about *it*), so far as such a being is at all capable of evidence as cognition of truth. What sort of psychological constellations in us human beings (about intelligent beings in other worlds we know nothing) are relevant to the fact that, in the causality ruling everything psychic along with everything else that is real, these evidences become really actual in us — that is something that concerns, not logic, but psychology.

With this exhibition of the presuppositions of traditional logic, the problem of truth in itself, which we introduced at the beginning, has acquired a more definite sense, one that relates to an actual and possible world. Thus logic, as Objective in this new sense, as the *formal logic of a possible world*, finds a place for itself in the multiplicity of "*positive*" *sciences*, since for all of them — for what are called sciences in ordinary discourse, which, indeed, is not at all acquainted with any other science — the world is an antecedent unquestioned matter-of-fact; and first of all to call in question its legitimate existence (to say nothing of the legitimate existence of possibilities of worlds) contravenes the style of positive science.

§ 93. Insufficiency of attempts to criticize experience, beginning with Descartes.

a. Naïve presupposition of the validity of Objective logic.

To be sure, part of Descartes' attempted epistemological reform of all the sciences and remaking of them into a *sapientia universalis*, which would give them unity in a radical grounding, is the requirement that, as a means to their foundation, a *criticism of experience* must precede the sciences, since experience is what gives them beforehand the factual existence of the world. This criticism, as we all know, led Descartes to the conclusion that experience lacks absolute evidence (evidence grounding the being of the world apodictically), and that consequently the naïve presupposition of the world must be annulled and all Objective cognition grounded on the only apodictic givenness of an existent, namely that of *ego-cogito*. As we also know, this was the *beginning* of all the modern / *transcendental philosophy* that forced its way up <202>
through ever new obscurities and aberrations. At once this Cartesian beginning, with the great but only partial discovery of transcendental subjectivity, is obscured by that most fateful and, up to this day, ineradicable *error* which has given us the "*realism*" that finds in the idealisms of a Berkeley and a Hume its equally wrong counterparts. Even for Descartes, an absolute evidence makes sure of the ego (*mens sive animus, substantia cogitans*) as a first, indubitably existing, *bit of the world*; and it is then only a matter of inferring the rest of the world (for him, the absolute substance and the other finite substances that, besides my own psychic substance, belong to the world) by using a logically valid *deductive procedure*.

Even Descartes operates here with a naïve apriori heritage, with the Apriori of causality, with the naïve presupposition of ontological and logical evidences, in the treatment of transcendental themes. Thus he *misses* the *proper transcendental sense of the ego he has discovered*, that ego which, from the standpoint of cognition, precedes the being of the world. Likewise he misses the properly transcendental sense of the questions that must be asked of experience and of scientific thinking and therefore, with absolute universality, of a logic itself.

This unclarity is a heritage latent in the pseudo-clarities that characterize all relapses of epistemology into natural naïveté and, accordingly, in the pseudo-clear scientificalness of contemporary realism. It is an epistemology that, in league with a naïvely isolated logic, serves to prove to the scientist, and thus to make him fully sure for the first time, that the fundamental convictions of the positive sciences about a real world and a method that deals with it logically are thoroughly correct, and that therefore he can properly dispense with epistemology, just as he has for centuries been getting along well enough without it anyway.

b. Missing of the transcendental sense of the Cartesian reduction to the ego.

But can positive science, logic, and epistemology, be left in such a mutual relationship? Even from what we had to set forth repeatedly in earlier contexts, incomplete and often merely pro-
<203> spective as it had to be, it is certain that this question / must receive a negative answer. A realism like that of Descartes, which believes that, in the ego to which transcendental self-examination leads back in the first instance, it has apprehended the real psyche of the human being — a realism that then, from this first real, projects hypotheses and probability-inferences to carry it over into a realm of transcendent realities, thus (expressly or implicitly) using the mathematics of probability, which is itself a part of logic, and perhaps using the rest of formal logic — such a realism *misses the actual problem and does so in a countersensical manner*, since everywhere it presupposes as a possibility that which, as a possibility, is itself everywhere in question.

Clarification of the validity of the principles of logic — including all its fundamental concepts and fundamental propositions — leads to *investigations directed to the subjective*; without them these principles are left hanging in the air, scientifically unsupported. After the fragmentary investigations that we have already carried out (and are pushing further and further), that is without doubt. But, if one goes back to the *ego-cogito*, as that subjectivity by whose pure consciousness and, in particular, by whose evidences everything is, which is for him something existing (or possible, conceivable, presumable, false, countersensical, and so forth) — *can one presuppose logic there*? What about those investigations of the subjective that alone, and in the strictest sense, lay the ultimate foundations for any logic? Can they be contested by means of a logic that must first be clarified by them, and that perhaps, with its worldliness, even though its worldliness be justifiable, brings in sense-components and an acceptance of propositions that inadmissibly go beyond the realm of these investigations of the subjective?

Furthermore, can these investigations of the subjective be contested by means of *psychology*, which depends entirely on this Objective logic and which, even if that were not the case, would still be based on the continual presupposition of the Objective world, to which all psychic processes belong, according to their sense, as real moments of real psycho-physical beings? For *a radical grounding of logic*, is not *the whole real world called in question* — not to show its actuality, but to bring out its possible and genuine sense and the range of this sense, the range with which this sense can enter into the fundamental concepts of logic? If the anything-whatever of formal logic, taken as Objective logic, ultimately involves the sense, worldly being, then this sense is precisely *one of logic's fundamental concepts*, one of those determining the whole sense of logic. /

c. The grounding of logic leads into the all-embracing problem of transcendental phenomenology. <204>

And how about the hypotheses, so easily available to the realists, by which they seek to attain a real outside world on the basis of the ego — the only existing basis that the Cartesian reduction leaves as indubitably evident and the intrinsically primary basis for all cognition? Is not this *outside*, is not the possible sense of a transcendent reality and that of an Apriori belonging to a transcendent reality and including the forms (space, time, and causality) that permit the inferences, the problem? Is not the problem how, in the immanence of the ego, this outside can take on and confirm that sense of transcendence which we have, and use, naïvely-straightforwardly? And should one not ask what hidden presumptions, coming from the sense-constituting subjectivity, limit the range of that sense? Does not all this make up the problem that would have to be solved before one could decide about the essential possibility, the sensefulness or countersensefulness of such hypotheses in the transcendental sphere of the ego? And in the end, when one has grasped the genuine problems that arise when one goes back to this ego, does not the whole scheme of "*explaining*" the purely immanent data by a hypothetically assumable Objective reality, causally connected with them, turn out to be a consummate absurdity, a perfect countersense?

That is in fact the case. And the countersense originates from the circumstance that, firstly, with the *Cartesian reduction* to my ego as the subject of my pure consciousness, a *new sort of possibility of cognition and being became the problem* — namely the transcendental possibility of something existing in itself, *as* something existing with this sense for me, exclusively by virtue of the possibilities of my pure consciousness — and, secondly, that this problematical possibility is mistaken for the totally different possibility of making inferences from one real, which one already *has* cognitionally, to other reals, which one does *not* have.

The *decisive point in this confusion*, which, to be sure, is possible only because one has never clearly seen the sense of the former possibility, is the *confounding of the ego with the reality of the I as a human psyche*. One does not see that the psyche (*mens*), which is accepted as a reality, already contains a *sense-moment pertaining to externality* (the spatial world), and that every externality, including the externality that one sought to appropriate only by
<205> hypotheses, / has its place from the very beginning in the pure internality of the ego — its place, namely, *as an intentional pole of experience*, which itself (with the whole stream of worldly experience and the existent that becomes harmoniously confirmed in worldly experience) belongs to the inside, just like everything

else ascribable to that pole by possible experience and theory. Do not all the problems that can be raised, starting from this ego, lie entirely in this ego himself, in his actualities and possibilities of consciousness, in his performances and their essential structures?

Thus, having been led from knowledge and science to logic as the theory of science, and led onward from the actual grounding of logic to a theory of logical or scientific reason, we now face the *all-embracing problem of transcendental philosophy* — of transcendental philosophy in its only pure and radical form, that of a *transcendental phenomenology*.

Chapter 6.

Transcendental phenomenology and intentional psychology. The problem of transcendental psychologism.

§ 94. Every existent constituted in the subjectivity of consciousness.

Let us make clear to ourselves the sense of transcendental problems. Every science has its province, and aims at the theory of its province. In that theory it has its result. But scientific reason is what makes those results; and experiential reason is what makes the province. This is true in the case of formal logic, with its higher-level relation to something existent and perhaps to any possible world; this is true in the case of its theory, as having a higher-level universality relating likewise to all particular theories. Something existent, theory, reason — these do not come together accidently; and they must not be presupposed as a trio assembled accidentally, even though "with unconditional universality and necessity". This very necessity and universality must be examined, as pertaining to the logically thinking subject, to *me* as a subject who can submit himself only to a logic that he himself thinks through, and has thought through, with insight. — To me, because at first here no reference is made to any other reason than mine, nor to any other experience or theory than mine, nor to any other existent than an existent that I legitimate by experience, and that, as something somehow meant or supposed, must be in my field of consciousness if I am to produce a theory with it, in my theoretic acting, in my evidence. /

<206> As in everyday life, so too in science (unless, under the misguidance of "realistic" epistemology, it misinterprets its own doing) experience is the consciousness of being with the matters themselves, of seizing upon and having them quite directly. But experience is not an opening through which a world, existing prior to all experience, shines into a room of consciousness; it is not a mere taking of something alien to consciousness into consciousness. For how could I make a rational statement to that effect, without seeing such a state-of-affairs and therefore seeing

not only consciousness but also the something alien to consciousness — that is: *experiencing* the alien affair? And how could I objectivate such a state-of-affairs as at least a conceivability? Would that not be immersing myself intuitionally in such a countersensical experiencing of something alien to experience? Experience is the performance in which for me, the experiencer, experienced being "is there", and is there *as what* it is, with the whole content and the mode of being that experience itself, by the performance going on in its intentionality, attributes to it. If what is experienced has the sense of *"transcendent" being*, then it is the experiencing that constitutes this sense, and does so either by itself or in the whole motivational nexus pertaining to it and helping to make up its intentionality. If an experience is *imperfect*, if it makes the intrinsically existent object appear only one-sidedly, only in a distant perspective, or the like, then the experience itself, as this current mode of consciousness, is that which, on being consulted, tells me so; it tells me: Here, in this consciousness, something is given as it itself; but it is more than what is actually itself grasped; there is more of the same object to be experienced. Thus the object is transcendent; and also in that, as experience further teaches me, it could have been an illusion, though it presented itself as actual and as itself seized upon. Moreover, it is again experience that says: These physical things, this world, is utterly transcendent of me, of my own being. It is an "Objective" world, experienceable and experienced as the same world by others too. Actuality becomes warranted, illusion rectified, in my concourse with others — who likewise are, for me, data of actual and possible experience. Experience is what tells me here: I have experience of myself with primary originality; of others, of another's psychic life, with a merely secondary originality, since another's psychic life is essentially inaccessible to me in direct perception. The currently experienced (physical things, I myself, others, and so forth), the current More that could be experienced, the self-identity with which the experienced extends throughout manifold experiences, the pointing ahead by every sort of experience on the different levels of originality / to new <207>
possible experiences of the same (first of all, possible experiences of my own and, at a higher level, possible experiences belonging to others), to the style of progressive experience, and to what this

would bring out as existing and being thus and so — each and all of these are included intentionally in the consciousness itself, as this actual and potential intentionality, whose structure I can at any time *consult*.

And I *must* consult it, if I intend to understand what is actually the case here: that nothing exists for me otherwise than by virtue of the *actual and potential performance of my own consciousness*. Here the potential performance is the certainty of "I can" or "I could", which is predelineated in the sphere itself of my consciousness, starting from the actually present intentionality — the certainty, namely, that I could bring into play synthetically connected sequences of consciousness, with the unitary effect that I should continue to be conscious of the same object. In particular that includes, a priori, the potentiality of intuitions actualizable by me — experiences, evidences — in which this same object would show itself, and become determined, in continuous harmony: thereby continuously confirming its actual being. *That* this object is not only accepted as existent by me but also actually existent for me because of "good", because of "indubitable" reasons; and *what* it is for me already, and what it still leaves open for me: all this indicates certain performances, which cohere synthetically thus and so, which are consciously predelineated, which I can explicate, and which I can also freely bring about. In other words: No being nor being-thus for me, whether as actuality or as possibility, but as *accepted by me* [*mir geltend*]. This acceptence by me is precisely a name for a multiplicity of my actual and possible performances, with essentially predelineated ideas of harmony *in infinitum* and of definitive being — not a multiplicity demanded or postulated from some superior standpoint, but one that, although hidden at first, can be uncovered. Whatever I encounter as an existing object is something that (as I must recognize when I systematically explicate my own conscious life, as a life of acceptance [*Geltungsleben*]) has received its *whole* being-sense for me from my effective intentionality; not a shadow of that sense remains excluded from my effective intentionality. Precisely this I must consult, I must explicate systematically, if I intend to understand that sense and consequently to understand also what I am allowed, and what I am not allowed, to attribute to an object — whether with formal

universality or with regard to it as an object belonging to its own category of being — according to the constituting intentionality from which, as just now said, its whole sense has originated. To explicate this intentionality itself is / to make the sense itself <208>
understandable from the originality of the sense-constituting performance.

So it must be when I philosophize. For when I am not philosophizing, when I live naïvely, there is no danger. The living intentionality carries me along; it predelineates; it determines me practically in my whole procedure, including the procedure of my natural thinking, whether this yields being or illusion. The living intentionality does all that, even though, as actually functioning, it may be non-thematic, undisclosed, and thus beyond my ken.

I said *illusion* as well as *being*. For naturally it is characteristic of the performance-of-consciousness effected by experience itself that, on the one hand, only harmonious experience has the style of performance predelineated as normal for experience and that, on the other hand, its harmony can be broken, that experiencing can fall to pieces in *conflict*, and that the initially simple certainty of experience can end in doubt, in deeming possible, in deeming likely, in negation (nullity-qualification) — all this under definitely requisite structural conditions, which are precisely what must be explored. Exploration must then be extended to why, after all, the open possibility of deception — that is: the non-being of what is experienced — does not abolish the universal presumption of normal harmony and to why a universe of being at all times remains for me beyond all doubt: a universe of being that I miss, and can miss, only occasionally and in details.

Needless to say, something similar applies in the case of *each and every consciousness*, in the case of every manner in which something existent, possible, senseful, or countersensical, is for us what it is for us; and every *question about legitimacy* that is, or could be, asked receives from the pertinent intentionality itself of consciousness a predelineation of sense and of the way leading to legitimation. Throughout all the continuities of consciousness that pertain to the legitimation and, in favorable cases, terminate in an evidence, there runs an identity of the supposed and eventually legitimated existent — the same that, from first to last, is an intentional pole of identity: *There is no conceivable place where the life of consciousness is broken through, or could be broken through,* and we might come upon a transcendency that possibly had any sense other than that of an intentional unity making its appearance in the subjectivity itself of consciousness.

§ 95. NECESSITY OF STARTING, EACH FROM HIS OWN SUBJECTIVITY.

To be correct, however, I must say expressly *in the first place*: *I myself* am this subjectivity, I who carry on sense-investigation
<209> concerning what / exists for me and is accepted by me and who now, qua logician, am carrying on sense-investigation with regard to the presupposed existing world and the logical principles related to it. In the first place, then, it is always I and I again: purely as Ego of that life of consciousness by which everything receives being-sense for me.

But still (we must not pass over this as quickly as in the preceding section) the world is the world *for us all*; as an Objective world it has, in its own sense, the *categorial form, "once for all truly existing"*, not only for me but *for everyone*: For what we asserted [1] as a logical characteristic of predicational truth is manifestly a characteristic also of the world of experience, prior to the truth and the science that explicate this world predicatively. *World-experience,* as constitutive, signifies, not just my quite private experience, but *community-experience*: The world itself, according to its sense, is the one identical world, to which all of *us* necessarily have experiential access, and about which all of *us* by "exchanging" our experiences — that is: by making them common —, can reach a common understanding; just as "Objective" legitimation depends on mutual assent and its criticism.

Despite all this, and no matter how prodigious the difficulties that may be encountered in actually uncovering effective intentionality and, quite especially, in distinguishing between the effective intentionality that is originally one's own and the effective intentionality that belongs to others — or the difficulties that may be encountered in clarifying just *that* intersubjectivity which functions as sense-constituting for the Objective world — what was said stands fast in the first place, with an insuperable

[1] *Author's note:* See § 77, pp. 193ff.

necessity. First of all, before everything else conceivable, *I* am. This "I am" is for me, the subject who says it, and says it in the right sense, the *primitive intentional basis for my world*; and, at the same time, it must not be overlooked that likewise the "Objective" world, the "world for all of us" as accepted with this sense by me, is also "my" world. But "I am" is the primitive intentional basis, not only for "the" world, the one I consider real, but also for any "ideal world" that I accept; and this holds, without exception, for anything and everything of which I am conscious as something existent in any sense whatever that I understand or accept — for everything that I show, sometimes legitimately, sometimes illegitimately, to be existent — including me myself, my life, my believing, and all this consciousness-of. Whether convenient or inconvenient, and even though (because of no matter what prejudices) it may sound monstrous to me, it is the *primal matter-of-fact* | *to which I must hold fast*, which I, <210>
as a philosopher, must not disregard for a single instant. For children in philosophy, this may be the dark corner haunted by the spectres of solipsism and, perhaps, of psychologism, of relativism. The true philosopher, instead of running away, will prefer to fill the dark corner with light.

§ 96. The transcendental problems of intersubjectivity and of the intersubjective world.

a. Intersubjectivity and the world of pure experience.

Even the world for everyone, then, is something of which *I* am conscious, something accepted by *me* as the world for everyone; in my intentionality it is legitimated, it receives its content and its being-sense. Naturally the world for everyone presupposes that, in my ego — the ego who says, with the universality in question here, *ego cogito*, and includes in his actual and possible *cogitata* everything actual and possible for him — it presupposes, I say, that, in this ego, every other ego receives sense and acceptance *as* an other ego. Someone "else", others — these have an original relation to me who experience them and am conscious of them in other manners. —With everything, naturally, that belongs to their sense (their sense for me): Such as that someone else is here "facing me", bodily and with his own life, and has me now, in like fashion, as *his* vis-à-vis; that I —

with my whole life, with all my modes of consciousness and all my accepted objects — am *alter ego for him,* as he is for me; and, in like fashion, everyone else for everyone else; so that "everyone" receives its sense; and, in like fashion, we and I (as "one among others") as included in "everyone".

Let us now attempt to develop the involved set of transcendental problems concerning intersubjectivity, and therefore concerning the constitution of the categorial form, "Objectivity", belonging to the world (which, after all, is our world). Thus we may gain at least some conception of the nature of the clarifications to be effected here, purely by a systematic uncovering of one's own intentional life and what is constituted in it.

When, within the universality of my *ego-cogito,* I find myself as a psychophysical being, a unity constituted in my *ego-cogito,* and find related to this unity, in the form "others", psychophysical beings opposite me, who, as such, are likewise constituted in
<211> multiplicities belonging to my intentional life, I become / aware of great difficulties — in the first place, even concerning myself. I, the "transcendental ego," am the ego who "precedes" everything worldly: as the Ego, that is to say, in whose life of consciousness the world, as an intentional unity, is constituted to begin with. Therefore I, the constituting Ego, am not identical with the Ego who is already worldly, not identical with myself as a psychophysical reality; and my psychic life, the psychophysical and worldly life of consciousness, is not identical with my transcendental ego, in which the world, with everything physical and psychic that belongs to it, is constituted for me.

But do I not say I in both cases: whether, in natural living, I experience myself qua human being in the world, or, in the philosophical attitude, starting from the world and myself qua human being, I go back and ask about the multiplicities of constituting "appearances", meanings, modes of consciousness, and so forth, doing so in such a manner that, taking everything Objective purely as a "phenomenon", as an intentionally constituted unity, I now find myself qua transcendental ego? And do I not find then that my transcendental life and my psychic, my worldly, life have, in each and every respect, a like content? How can it be understood that the "ego" has constituted in himself the whole of what belongs to his own peculiar essence as, at the same time, "his psyche", psychophysically Objectivated in connexion with "his" bodily organism and as thus woven into the spatial Nature constituted in him qua ego?

Furthermore, if someone "else", as is obvious, is constituted with a sense that points back to me myself, qua human Ego — in particular, his organism, as "another's", pointing back to my own; his psychic life, as "another's" phychic life, pointing back to my own — how can this constitution of the new being-sense, his sense as someone *"other"*, be understood? If even the self-constitution of the ego as a spatialized, a psychophysical, being is a very obscure matter, then it is much more obscure, and a downright tormenting enigma, how, in the ego, an *other psychophysical Ego* with an *other psyche* can be constituted; since his sense as "other" involves the essential impossibility of my experiencing his own essential psychic contents with actual originality, as I do my own. Essentially, therefore, the constitution of others must be different from that of my own psychophysical Ego.

Moreover it must be made understandable that I necessarily ascribe to someone else (in his mental processes, his experiences and the rest, which I attribute to him as processes other than mine), not a merely analogous experienced world, but the *same* world that I experience; / likewise, that I mean him as ex- <212>
periencing me in the world and, moreover, experiencing me as related to the same experienced world to which he is related; and so forth.

If it is certain to me and, thanks to transcendental clarification, already understandable that my psyche is a self-Objectivation of my transcendental ego, then the other psyche also points back to a *transcendental ego*, but, in this case, *another's*, as the ego that someone else, for his part, starting from the world given him beforehand in his experience and going back to ask about the ultimate constitutive life, would have to grasp in his "phenomenological reduction". Consequently the problem of "others" takes also the following form:

To understand how my transcendental ego, the primitive basis for everything that I accept as existent, can constitute within himself another transcendental ego, and then too an open plurality of such egos — "other" egos, absolutely inaccessible to my ego in their original being, and yet cognizable (for me) as existing and as being thus and so.

Nevertheless, these problems are not sufficient. They are beset with enigmas that must themselves become apprehended in definite problems; until finally the whole excessively involved set of problems has become evidently resolved into a fixed and necessary hierarchy, which maps out the course that must be taken in working out the solution.

Let us start from the fact that for us — stated more distinctly: for *me* qua ego — the world is constituted as "Objective" (in the above-stated sense: there for everyone), showing itself to be the way it is, in an intersubjective cognitive community. It follows that a sense of "everyone" must already be constituted, relative to which an Objective world can be Objective. This implies that the *first* and fundamental *sense of "everyone"* (and therefore of *"others"*) cannot be the usual, the higher-level, sense: namely the sense "every human being", which refers to something real in the Objective world and therefore already presupposes the constitution of that world.

Now someone else on the constitutionally lower level points back, by his sense, to me myself, but, as we were saying, not as a transcendental ego but as my *psychophysical Ego*. Similarly, then, *this* psychophysical Ego *cannot yet be I, the human being* in the Objective world, in the world whose Objectivity must first be made constitutionally possible by the psychophysical Ego here in question.

This, in turn, points back to the fact that my *bodily organism*, which is, according to its sense, spatial and a member of an environment made up of spatial bodies, a Nature (within which I encounter the bodily organism of someone else) — it points back, <213> I say, to the fact that *none* / of these can as yet have *Objective-world* significance. My intrinsically first psychophysical Ego (we are referring here to constitutional strata, not temporal genesis), relative to whom the intrinsically first someone-else must be constituted, is, we see, a member of an *intrinsically first Nature*, which is not yet Objective Nature, a Nature the spatio-temporality of which is not yet Objective spatio-temporality: in other words, a Nature that does not yet have constitutional traits coming from an already-constituted someone else. In the nexus of this first Nature, as holding sway in that body (within this Nature) which is called my bodily organism, as exercising psychophysical functions in that body in a unique manner, my psychic Ego makes his appearance, "animating" it as the unique animated body, according to original experience.

It is now understandable that this first Nature or world, this first, not yet intersubjective, Objectivity, is constituted in my ego as, in a *signal sense, my own,* since as yet it contains nothing other than my Ego's own — that is: nothing that, by a constitutional involvement of other Egos, would go beyond the sphere of actually direct, *actually original, experience* (or, correlatively, the sphere of what originates from such experience). On the other hand, it is clear that this sphere, the sphere of my transcendental ego's *primordial owness,* must contain the *motivational foundation* for the constitution of those *trancendencies* that are *genuine,* that go beyond it, and originate first of all as "others" (other psychophysical beings and other transcendental egos), the transcendencies that, thus mediated, make possible the constitution of an Objective world in the everyday sense: a *world of the "non-Ego",* of what is other than my Ego's own. All Objectivity, in this sense, is related back constitutionally to the *first affair that is other than my Ego's own,* the other-than-my-Ego's-own in the form, someone "else" — that is to say: the non-Ego in the form, "another Ego".

b. The illusion of transcendental solipsism.

It is hardly necessary to say that this whole many-leveled problem of the constitution of the Objective world is, at the same time, the problem of dissolving what may be called the *transcendental illusion* that from the outset misleads, and usually paralyzes, any attempt to start a consistent transcendental philosophy: the illusion that such a philosophy must lead to a *transcendental solipsism.* If everything I can ever accept as existent is constituted in my ego, then everything that exists does indeed seem to be a mere moment of my own transcendental being. /

But the solution of this enigma lies, firstly, in the systematic <214>
unravelling of the constitutional problems implicit in the fact of consciousness which is the world always existing for *me,* always having and confirming its sense by *my* experience; and, secondly,

in progressively advancing exhibitions that follow the hierarchical sequence of problems. The purpose of these exhibitions, however, is none other, and can be none other, than actually to disclose, as matters included in that very fact of consciousness, the actualities and potentialities (or habitualities) of life, in which the sense, world, has been, and is continually being, built up immanently. The world is continually there for us; but in the first place it is there for *me*. This fact too is there for me; otherwise there could be no sense for me in which the world is there for *us*, there as one and the same, and as a world having a particular sense — not a sense to be "postulated" as such and such (and perhaps even to be suitably "interpreted", in order to reconcile the interests of the understanding and the emotions), but a sense to be explicated in the first place, and with primary originality, out of experience itself. The first thing, therefore, is to consult the experienced world, purely as experienced. Immersing myself wholly in the flow of my world-experiencing and in all the open possibilities of its consistent fulfilment, I direct my regard to what is experienced and to its universal, eidetically apprehensible sense-structures. Guided by these, I must then turn back and seek out the configurations and contents of the actualities and potentialities that function as sense-constituting for this being-sense and for its different levels — and here too there is nothing to "postulate" or to "interpret suitably", but only something to bring to light. Thus alone can that ultimate understanding of the world be attained, behind which, since it is ultimate, there is nothing more that can be sensefully inquired for, nothing more to understand. Can the transcendental illusion of solipsism withstand this onward march of mere *concrete explication*? Is it not an illusion that can appear only *before* the explication, because, as already said, this fact — that others and the world for others have their sense in and from me myself — is a presented fact, and therefore there can be no other problem here than that of clarifying this matter-of-fact, clarifying it, that is, as what is implicit in me myself?

c. Problems at higher levels concerning the Objective world.

Naturally the lines of work indicated above are not exhaustive. Research must go further. First of all — and the researches indicated above are concerned exclusively with this — the world of naïve experience must be apprehended purely and submitted to a constitutional clarification, in order to make possible the asking of the higher-level questions (which must be sharply distinguished from problems concerning the world of naïve experience). Among the higher questions are those concerning the constitution of what we may call a theoretical world: the world truly existing in the / theoretical sense, or the world <215>
pertaining to an unconditionally and Objectively valid theoretical cognition. A particularly important and difficult problem in this connexion is that of clarifying the *idealizations* involved in the intentional sense of the sciences. With formal universality these idealizations are stated as "being in itself" and "truth in itself", in the *idealized* sense proper to formal logic and its "principles". But in their particularizations, as relating to world-regions, these idealizations become truly great problems — for example: as the idea of exact Nature (according to the "exact" natural sciences), the Nature characterized by the "ideal" space of geometry (with its ideal straight lines, circles and so forth), by a correspondingly ideal time, and the like.

d. Concluding observations.

We must rest content here with having made at least roughly understandable the confusingly involved problems of intersubjectivity and worldly Objectivity.[1] Now it is clear: Only by the aforesaid uncovering of the performance that constitutes the being-sense of the given world can we avoid every countersensical absolutizing of this world's being and know, universally and in every respect, what we (as philosphers) are allowed to

[1] *Author's note:* The chief points for the solution of the problem of intersubjectivity and for the overcoming of transcendental solipsism were already developed in lectures that I gave at Göttingen during the winter semester of 1910–11. But the actual carrying-out required further difficult single investigations, which did not reach their conclusion until much later. A short exposition of the theory itself will be presented soon in my *Cartesianische Meditationen* [*cf.* p. 7 n., *supra*, and *op. cit.*, "*V. Meditation*"]. I hope that, within the next year, I shall be able to publish the pertinent explicit investigations. [This hope was not fulfilled.]

assign to that sense, to Nature, to space, to space-time, to causality, and in what sense we can legitimately understand the exactnesses of geometry, mathematical physics, and so forth — to say nothing of corresponding, but specifically different, problems concerning the moral sciences.

No matter how far all this takes us beyond the sphere of formal logic, we must have it in our field of vision beforehand, so that we can avoid wrong claims concerning validities belonging to formal logic. We must grasp the whole breadth and magnitude of the problems concerning the "range" of cognition. Indeed, only now do we understand properly what the old epistemological phrase, "the extent of knowledge", was aiming at; or at least what it should have been aiming at. /

<216>

§ 97. Universal philosophic significance of the method that consists in uncovering constitution in consciousness.

No philosopher can be spared the path of thorny investigations that we have tried to open. That *absolutely everything* of which an Ego can think is related to his life of consciousness has, to be sure, been generally recognized, since Descartes, as a fact that is fundamental for philosophy; and, particularly in recent times, it has again become the theme of much discussion. But there is no use in philosophizing about it from on high and veiling it even in the finest-spun thoughts, instead of forcing one's way into its huge concretenesses and making it actually fruitful philosophically. He who philosophizes must make clear to himself from the beginning what we, with good reason, have emphasized so strongly and so often: Anything that can exist, and be this or that, for him (accordingly, that can have sense for him and be accepted by him as existent and as being this or that) must be something of which he has consciousness in the shape of an appertinent intentional performance, which *corresponds to the particularity* of that existent; it must be something of which he is conscious by virtue of an appertinent *"sense-bestowing* [*Sinngebung*]", as I expressed it in my *Ideen*. He must not stop short with the empty generality of the word consciousness, nor with the empty words experience, judgment, and so forth, treating the rest as though it were philosophically irrelevant and leaving it to psychology, this psychology whose heritage is blindness to intentionality as the own-essentiality of the life of consciousness or, in any case, blindness to intentionality as a teleological function — that is: a constitutive performance. Consciousness can be methodically uncovered in such fashion that one can directly "see" it in its performing, whereby sense is bestowed and is produced with modalities of being. One can follow the way in which an object-sense, the particular *cogitatum* of the *cogitationes* in question, becomes fashioned into a new sense in the changing flow of these *cogitationes* with its functioning motivational coherence; one can see how what is already at hand has been previously fashioned out of a foundational sense, which originated from an earlier performance. If one has done bits of such intentional explication with selected examples, one recognizes immediately that one can in no way evade the tremendous task of uncovering this effective life in its universality, and thereby making whatever makes its appearance therein as "existing" understandable in its all-embracing ontic unity — all the sense-formations of natural life, of scientific life, of the higher cultural life in its entirety — and, indeed, *ultimately* understandable, as issuing from the sources that constitute it. /

To be sure, the method of intentional explication had first <217> to be developed, owing to the remarkable fact that Brentano's discovery of intentionality never led to seeing in it a complex of performances, which are included as *sedimented history* in the currently constituted intentional unity and its current manners of givenness — a history *that one can always uncover by following a strict method.* In consequence of this fundamental cognition, every sort of intentional unity becomes a "*transcendental clue*" to guide constitutional "analyses" and these acquire a wholly unique character: They are *not analyses in the usual sense* (analyses into really immanent parts), but *uncoverings of intentional implications* (advancing, perhaps, from an experience to the system of experiences that are *predelineated* as possible).

§ 98. Constitutional investigations as a priori.

But that fundamental insight would nevertheless have remained comparatively sterile, were it not for the cognition, already mentioned occasionally, that, in constitutional investi-

gations, *inductive empirical inquiry is not one of the first things*, but rather becomes so much as possible only by virtue of an antecedent *inquiry into essences*. The truly fundamental cognition in this connexion — a cognition foreign to all previous psychology and all previous transcendental philosophy — is that *any straightforwardly constituted objectivity* (for example: an Object belonging to Nature) *points back, according to its* ***essential sort*** (for example: physical thing *in specie*), to a *correlative* ***essential form*** *of* manifold, actual and possible, *intentionality* (in our example, an infinite intentionality), *which is constitutive for that objectivity*. The multiplicity of possible perceptions, memories, and, indeed, intentional processes of whatever sort, that relate, or can relate, "harmoniously" to one and the same physical thing has (in all its tremendous complication) a quite definite *essential style*, which is identical in the case of any physical thing whatever and is particularized only according to the different individual things constituted in different cases. In the same fashion, the modes of consciousness that can make one aware of some ideal objectivity or other, and can become united as a synthetic consciousness of it, have a definite style, essential to *this* sort of objectivity. As my entire life of consciousness — even in its entirety, and
<218> without prejudice to all / the manifold separate objectivities that become constituted in it — is an all-embracing unity of effective life, with a unitary performance, the *whole life of consciousness is governed by a universal constitutional Apriori, embracing all intentionalities* — an Apriori that, on account of the intrinsic nature of the intersubjectivity constituted in the ego, becomes extended as an *Apriori pertaining to intersubjective intentionality* and its production of intersubjective unities and "worlds". Exploration of this entire Apriori is an exceedingly great task, but is by no means unassailable or incapable of progressive, step by step, accomplishment. It is the *task of transcendental phenomenology*.

In that connexion, one must bear in mind that *effective subjectivity is necessarily more* than *actual* intentional life, with its in fact co-ordinating intentional processes; it consists also, and continually, in its *abilities*. These are not, perchance, hypothetical explanatory constructs; on the contrary, they can be brought to light, in single pulses of "I can" and "I do", as continually productive factors. And, going on from there, one can likewise bring to light all the universal abilities, single-subjective and intersubjective. It should be expressly emphasized that they too fall within the scope of the phenomenological Apriori, as drawn from corresponding intuitions of essences — such a source being universally implicit in the sense of phenomenology.

For the sake of a better understanding of the *method of inquiry into essences*, let us add the following brief indications.

Everything that we have stated in our observations concerning constitution can, in the first place, be made a matter of insight on the basis of no matter what *examples* of no matter what sorts of already-given objects — that is: in a reflective explication of the intentionality in which we simply and straightforwardly "have" a real or an ideal objectivity. We have made a significant advance when we recognize that what obviously holds good for *de facto* single cases of actuality or possibility still holds good necessarily when we vary our examples *quite as we please* and then inquire retrogressively for the correlatively varying "objectivations" — that is: the constituting mental processes — ⟨and⟩ for the "subjective" manners of givenness, which change, sometimes continuously and sometimes discretely. Primarily we must inquire here for the manners of "appearance" that are constitutive in the *pregnant* sense, the ones that are *experiences* of the exemplary objects in question or of their variants; and we must look for the *manners in which* the objects / take shape as synthetic <219>
unities in the mode "they themselves", in those experiences. That, however, is nothing other than inquiring for the systematic universe of possible experiences, possible evidences; or for the *idea* of a complete synthesis of possible harmonious experiences, as whose synthetic product the object in question would be intentional as itself absolutely given and absolutely verified, "all-sidedly", with the totality of determinations belonging to it: In this inquiry, the variation of the necessary initial example is the performance in which the "eidos" should emerge and by means of which the evidence of the indissoluble eidetic correlation between constitution and constituted should also emerge. If it is to have these effects, it must be understood, not as an *empirical variation*, but as a variation carried on with the freedom of pure phantasy and with the consciousness of its purely optional cha-

racter — the consciousness of the "pure" Any Whatever. Thus understood, the variation extends into an open horizon of endlessly manifold free possibilities of more and more variants. Now, in such a fully free variation, released from all restrictions to facts accepted beforehand, all the variants belonging to the openly infinite sphere — which includes the ⟨initial⟩ examplei tself, as "optional" and freed of all its factualness — stand in a relationship of synthetic interrelatedness and integral connectedness; more particularly, they stand in a continuous and all-inclusive synthesis of "coincidence in conflict". But, precisely with this coinciding, what necessarily persists throughout this free and always-repeatable variation comes to the fore: the *invariant*, the indissolubly identical in the different and ever-again different, the *essence* common to all, the universal essence by which all "imaginable" variants of the example, and all variants of any such variant, are restricted. This invariant is the ontic essential form (apriori form), the *eidos*, corresponding to the example, in place of which any variant of the example could have served equally well.[1]

But, when one turns one's regard reflectively from the ontic essential form (highest of them all, the "category") to the possible experiences that do the constituting, the possible manners of
<220> appearance, one sees that these / necessarily vary concomitantly ⟨with the constituted objects⟩, and in such a fashion that now an essential form with two correlative sides shows itself as invariant. Thus it becomes evident that an ontic Apriori is possible, as a concretely full possibility, only as the correlate of a constitutional Apriori that is concretely united with it, concretely inseparable from it. This holds good, not only for systems of possible *experience* of objects (systems that are constitutive in the pregnant sense), but also for systems that are constitutive in the broader sense, as systems embracing all, even the non-intuitional, modes of consciousness that are possible in the case of any objects "of the sorts in question".

[1] *Author's note:* It should be noted here that object [*Gegenstand*] is always understood by me in the broadest sense, which comprehends likewise all syntactical objectivities. Accordingly, the concept *eidos* is also given a maximally broad sense. At the same time, this sense defines the only concept belonging to the multisignificant expression, *a priori*, that I recognize philosophically. That concept alone is meant wherever the locution *a priori* occurs in my writings.

Finally, ascending to the broadest, the analytico-formal universalities, one sees that any object (no matter how indeterminately it is thought of, nay, even if it be conceived as void of content), any object thought of as a "wholly optional" Anything Whatever, is thinkable only as the correlate of an intentional constitution inseparable from it. This constitution is indeterminately empty, and yet it is not variable without restriction; that is to say: with each particularization of "Something", and with each ontic category thus substituted (the eidos that can be brought out by ontic variation of a suitable example), the constitution must become correlatively particularized. Accordingly, any intentional and constitutional analysis performable on the basis of factual data is to be looked upon from the start as an analysis of examples, even though the analyst does not understand it in that manner. All its results, when freed from factualness and thereby transposed into the realm of free phantasy-variation, become eidetic, become results that (as is apodictically evident) govern a universe of conceivability (a "pure" allness), in such a manner that the negation of any result is equivalent to an intuitable eidetic impossibility, an inconceivability. Accordingly that applies in particular to all the observations conducted just now. They have themselves been conducted as eidetic. To explicate the eidetic method is not to describe an empirical fact, a method that can, as a matter of empirical fact, be repeatedly followed at will. The universal validity of the eidetic method is unconditionally necessary; it is a method that can be followed, no matter what conceivable object is taken as an initial example; and that is the sense in which we meant it. Only in eidetic intuition can the essence of eidetic intuition become clarified.

It is very necessary to lay hold of this genuine sense, and this universality, of the Apriori and, in so doing, to grasp in particular the already-described relatedness of every straightforwardly derived Apriori to the antecedent Apriori of its constitution; accordingly, to understand also the apriori apprehensibility of the correlation between object and constitutive consciousness. Those are cognitions of unexampled philosophic significance. They create an essentially new and strictly scientific style / of philoso- <221>
phy, as contrasted with even the Kantian transcendental philoso-

phy, in spite of the many other great intuitions included in the latter.

Though the constitutional problems pertaining to all regions of objectivity open up vast fields here of apriori and the same time subjective research, we can already foresee that the fields for such research must be even more extensive than those included at first in the scope of methodical analysis. That is to say: if everything subjective that is factual has its genesis in immanent time, it is to be expected that this genesis also has its Apriori. In that case, ⟨inquiry into⟩ the *"static" constitution* of objects, which relates to an already-"developed" subjectivity, has its counterpart in ⟨an inquiry into⟩ *apriori genetic constitution,* ⟨a subsequent inquiry,⟩ based on ⟨the results of⟩ the former, which necessarily precedes it. Only by virtue of this genetic Apriori does what was already said in advance [1] become evident (and evident in its profounder sense): that, in what analysis uncovers as intentionally implicit in the living sense-constitution, there lies a sedimented *"history"*.

§ 99. Psychological and transcendental subjectivity. The problem of transcendental psychologism.

Neither a world nor any other existent of any conceivable sort comes "from outdoors [θύραθεν]" into my ego, my life of consciousness. Everything outside is what it is in this inside, and gets its *true being* from the givings of it itself, and from the verifications, within this inside — its true being, which for that very reason is something that itself belongs to this inside: as a *pole of unity* in my (and then, intersubjectively, in our) actual and possible multiplicities, with ⟨their⟩ possibilities as ⟨my (and our)⟩ abilities: as "I can go there", "I could perform syntactical operations", and so forth. Whatever the modalizations of being that may also come and go here, they too belong in this interior, where everything constituted therein is not only an end but also a beginning, perhaps a thematic end that also functions for a new thematizing. And, above all, it is thus with respect to the *ideas* constituted in the ego — for example: the idea of the *absolutely existing* Object belonging to Nature and the idea of the *absolute "truths in themselves"* about that Object. In connexion with the

[1] *Author's note: See* § 97 [pp. 244f., *supra*].

constituted relativities, the constituted unities at a lower level, such ideas have a "regulative significance".

The relation of my consciousness to a *world* is not a / matter <222>
of fact imposed on me either by a God, who adventitiously decides it thus, or by a world accidentally existing beforehand, and a causal regularity belonging thereto. On the contrary, the subjective Apriori precedes the being of God and world, the being of everything, individually and collectively, for me, the thinking subject. Even God is for me what he is, in consequence of my own productivity of consciousness; here too I must not look aside lest I commit a supposed blasphemy, rather I must see the problem. Here too, as in the case of the other ego, productivity of consciousness will hardly signify that I invent and make this highest transcendency.

The like is true of the world and of all worldly causation. Certainly I am in psychophysical causal connexion with the outside world — that is to say: I, this human being, a man among men and brutes, among other realities too, all going together to make up the world. But the world with all its realities, including my human real being, is a universe of constituted transcendencies — constituted in mental processes and abilities of my ego (and, only through the mediation of mine, in mental processes and abilities belonging to the intersubjectivity that exists for me); accordingly, this constituted world is preceded by my ego, as the ultimately constitutive subjectivity. The world's transcendence is a transcendence relative to this Ego and, by virtue of this Ego, a transcendence relative to the open community of Egos as this Ego's community. There comes to light in this connexion the difference already descried by Descartes, despite all the obscurity: that *this* Ego — that I, understood as the ultimately constitutive subjectivity, *exist for myself with apodictic necessity* (without prejudice to my infinite horizons of undisclosed and unknown determinations); whereas the world constituted in me, though it always exists for me in the stream of my harmonious experience, and exists quite without doubt (I could never summon up a doubt, where every new experience confirms existence), — this world, I say, has and, by essential necessity, retains the sense of only a *presumptive existence*. The real world exists, only on the continually delineated presumption that experience will go on continually in the same constitutional style.

It may be that profound and difficult investigations are necessary here, in order to attain perfect clarity. But there is no need of them in order to convince oneself that this difference emerges, which we turned to legitimate account earlier and which ranks as the most fundamental difference of all for the theory of cognition, the difference namely between —

Firstly, *transcendental-phenomenological subjectivity* (seen, through *my* transcendental subjectivity, as transcendental/
<223> intersubjectivity), with its constitutive life of consciousness and its transcendental abilities, and —

Secondly, *psychological or psychophysical subjectivity,* the human psyche, the human person and community of persons with their psychic mental processes (in the psychological sense), component parts of the Objective world, in psychophysical, inductively determined, connexion with physical organisms, which are also parts of the world.

It was because of this difference that all attempts to establish the existence of an Objective world by causal inferences from an ego given in the first place all by himself (in the first place as *solus ipse*) were characterized by us as involving a countersensical confounding of psychophysical causation, occurring in the world, with the correlation, occurring in transcendental subjectivity, between constitutive consciousness and the world constituted in consciousness. For ⟨an understanding of⟩ the true and genuine sense of transcendental philosophy it is decisively important to lay hold of the fact that *human being,* and not only *human organism* but also *human psyche* (no matter how purely the human psyche may be apprehended by internal experience), are *worldly* concepts and, as wordly, ⟨apply only to⟩ objectivities of a *transcendent apperception,* which therefore are included, as constitutional problems, within the universal transcendental problem, the problem of the transcendental constitution of all transcendencies, nay, all objectivities of whatever sort.

The radical separation of psychological from transcendental subjectivity (in which the former becomes constituted as having a worldly and therefore transcendent sense-content) signifies a *radical separation of psychology from transcendental philosophy* —

in especial: from the transcendental theory of transcendent cognition. It will not do to engage in any shifting of the concept of psychology, in spite of what may be called the essentially rooted temptations implicit in the circumstance that a pure analysis of consciousness, even though made in the first place as psychological, can be turned into a transcendental analysis, without altering any of its own essential contents.

It must never be lost sight of: that the only sense that *psychology* has now, or has ever had, is that of being a *branch of "anthropology"*, a positive worldly science; that, in psychology, "psychic phenomena" — more precisely, psychological Data: the mental processes and the dispositions (abilities) — are Data within the already-given world; that "internal experience" is a species of worldly, "Objective", experience, as truly as any experience of others, or any / experience of something physical; and that it is a <224>
falsifying dislocation, if one mistakes this psychological internal experience for the internal experience relied on transcendentally as an evidential experiencing of ego-cogito. To be sure, it is a falsification that could not become noticeable before the rise of transcendental phenomenology.

We by no means deny that every mode of intentionality, including every mode of evidence and every mode of the fulfilling of meanings by evidence, can be found by experience *also when one takes the psychological attitude*, and can be treated psychologically. We do not deny that *all our intentional analyses, whether carried out or merely indicated, are valid also when intentional life is apperceived psychologically*; but we do contend that psychological apperception is a particular worldly apperception, and that only a parenthesizing of it yields the concretions of transcendental subjectivity and their concrete parallels. Psychological theory of cognition has a legitimate sense — when understood simply as a name for work done on the manifold problems that cognizing, as a function in human psychic life, sets for psychology as the science of this psychic life. Such a theory of cognition becomes a countersense, only if it is expected to perform the transcendental tasks — that is: if psychologically apperceived intentional life is passed off as transcendental, and an attempt is made to effect the transcendental clarification of everything worldly by psychology — with the circularity that, in psychology, with its "psychic life", with its "internal experience", the world has already been naïvely presupposed.

And yet it can be said that, if this psychology of cognition had ever gone to work with a consciousness of its aim and had consequently been successful, its results would also have been work accomplished directly for the philosophic theory of cognition. All insights into structure that had been acquired for the psychology of cognition would also have benefited transcendental philosophy. Even if the latter had remained involved in a confounding of results attained in the psychological attitude and results attained in the transcendental attitude (a confounding hardly avoidable at the outset), this fault could have been remedied later by revaluation, without changing the essential core of the insights already gained. The interpenetration that is decisive here, and that necessarily remains hidden at first, is the very thing that causes such great difficulty — and defines the *transcendental problem of psychologism.* /

<225> And here attention must be paid to the following, as a misleading moment connected with the peculiar nature of so-called "descriptive" psychology — the psychology that considers the psyche abstractly, purely in and by itself, and is based on a correspondingly purified experiencing of it: *Pure psychology* (as had already become evident from the case of the *Logische Untersuchungen*) can be developed as *apriori,* just as transcendental phenomenology can be so developed. The restriction of psychological judging to intentional mental processes (those given in pure "internal" experience), to their essential forms (which become themselves-given in internal eidetic universalization), and likewise to purely psychic abilities, — this restriction yields a *psychologico-phenomenological* judging. It may even be said that the result is a self-contained *psychological phenomenology,* having the same method of intentional "analysis" that is used in transcendental phenomenology. But, in this psychologico-phenomenological judging, a *psychological* apperception is performed, though what is intentionally co-posited by this apperception, namely *the relation to the organism* and thus to something worldly, *does not enter expressly into the conceptual content* of the judging. Still the psychological apperception has its *determining effect on the sense* and must be consciously "pa-

renthesized", in order for that content (which is not itself altered by the parenthesis) to *acquire transcendental significance.* Insight into this parallelism between purely immanental and apriori psychology (psychological phenomenology), on the one hand, and transcendental phenomenology, on the other, and the showing of its essential necessity are the radically ultimate clarification of the problem of transcendental psychologism and, at the same time, its solution.

§ 100. Historico-critical remarks on the development of transcendental philosophy and, in particular, on transcendental inquiry concerning formal logic.

The way leading to the whole inquiry concerning origins, an inquiry that must be taken collaterally, as belonging to pure psychology and transcendental philosophy, and includes, in its essential universality, all possible worlds with all their essential regions of real and ideal objectivities and all their world-strata (therefore, in particular, the world of ideal senses, of truths, theories, sciences, the idealities / of every culture, of every <226>
socio-historical world) — that way remained for centuries untrod. This was an entirely understandable consequence of naturalistic and sensualistic aberration on the part of all modern psychology based on internal experience. This aberration not only drove the transcendental philosophy of English empiricism into that well-known development which made it end in countersensical fictionalism; it also arrested the transcendental philosophy of Kant's Copernican revolution short of full effectuation, so that the Kantian philosophy could never force its way through to the point where the ultimately necessary aims and methods can be adopted. If the *pure* concrete ego, in whom all the objectivities and worlds accepted by him are subjectively constituted, is only a senseless bundle or collection of Data — which come and perish, cast together now in this way and now in that, according to a senselessly accidental regularity analogous to that of mechanics (the sort of regularity ascribed to association as it was then interpreted), — the result is that only surreptitious reasons can explain how even as much as the illusion of a real world could arise. Yet Hume professed to make it *understandable* that, by a blind matter-of-fact regularity, purely in the mind, particular

types of fictions having the names "objects with continued existence", "identical persons", and so forth, arise for us. Now illusions, fictions, are produced *sense-formations*; the constituting of them takes place as intentionality; they are *cogitata* of *cogitationes*; and only from intentionality can a new intentionality arise. Fictions have their own sort of being, which points back to actualities, to what is existent in the normal sense. Once productive intentionality has been discovered, everything, being as well as illusion, becomes understandable in its essential Objective possibility; the subjectiveness of anything is then for us its constitutedness. And that is not the bad subjectivizing that, in Hume's case, turns both being and illusion into a solipsistic illusion; rather it is a transcendental subjectivizing, which is not merely compatible with genuine Objectivity but the apriori other side of genuine Objectivity.

Hume's greatness (a greatness still unrecognized in this, its most important aspect) lies in the fact that, despite all that, he was the first to grasp the universal *concrete problem* of transcendental philosophy. In the concreteness of purely egological internality, as he saw, everything Objective becomes intended to (and, in favorable cases, perceived), thanks to a subjective genesis. Hume was the first to see the necessity of investigating the Objective itself as a product of its genesis from that concrete-
<227> ness, in order to make the / legitimate being-sense of everything that exists for us intelligible through its ultimate origins. Stated more precisely: The real world and the categories of reality, which are its fundamental forms, became for him a problem in a new fashion. He was the first to *treat seriously the Cartesian focusing purely on what lies inside*: in that he began by freeing the soul radically from everything that gives it the significance of a reality in the world, and then presupposed the soul purely as a field of "perceptions" ("impressions" and "ideas"), such as it is qua datum of a suitably purified internal experience. Within this "phenomenological" realm, he outlined for the first time what we call "constitutional" problems; for he recognized the necessity of making its possible to understand how it happens that, purely within this phenomenologically reduced subjectivity and its immanent genesis, this same subjectivity can find, in a supposed "experience", transcendent Objectivities — realities

with the ontological forms (space, time, continuum, physical thing, personality) that we already take for granted.

Such a description of Hume's general intention can be made with assurance from the position attained by present-day phenomenology. We must add, however, that by no means did Hume consciously practise — to say nothing of thinking out radically — the method of phenomenological reduction, which prepares the ground for phenomenology; furthermore, that he, the first discoverer of constitutional problems, completely *overlooked the fundamentally essential property of mental life* as a life of consciousness, the very property to which those problems relate; and that consequently he overlooked the method appropriate to them as problems concerning intentionality, a method that, on being carried out, immediately confirms its own power of actual clarification. Because of his naturalistic sensualism, which could see only a collection of data floating in an unsubstantial void and was blind to the Objectivating function of intentional synthesis, Hume fell into the countersense of a "philosophy of as-if".

As for *Kant*, on the other hand: With the dependence on Hume implicit in his reaction against that philosopher, Kant took over the constitutional problem, at least so far as it concerns Nature; but without the full sense of even the problem of Nature, as only one component in the universal complex of constitutional problems to which Hume's re-conception of the Cartesian *ego-cogito*, as concrete "mental" being, had pointed. Kant did not set up a genuine intentional psychology, in opposition to *sensualistic* "psychology" (which, as we have said, was in truth a transcendental phenomenology in Hume's case, even though its sensualism made it countersensical); *a fortiori*, he did not set up such a psychology as, in our sense, an apriori eidetic theory. He never submitted the psychology of Locke and his school to a radical / criticism, one that would affect the under- <228>
lying sense of that psychology's sensualism. His own dependence on Lockean psychology was still too great. And, connected with this dependence, there is the additional fact that he never worked out the profound sense of the difference between *pure psychology* (solely on the basis of "internal experience") and *transcendental phenomenology* (on the basis of transcendental experience, which

originates from "transcendental-phenomenological reduction") and therefore did not work out the deepest sense of the transcendental problem of "*psychologism*". And yet one must say that his doctrine of synthesis and of transcendental abilities — that *all of his theories* relating to the Humean problem — are *implicitly theories of intentional constitution*; only they are not erected on the ultimate basis nor developed from there by a radical method.

But for us, who are striving toward a radical logic, the attitude of Kant's transcendental philosophy toward formal logic is of particular interest. Moreover, as we shall see, it is of interest in connexion with the modern motivation that has barred access to phenomenological transcendental philosophy.

However greatly Kant surpassed his contemporaries, and however much his philosophy remains for us a source of profound stimulations, the half-way character of his advancement of a systematic transcendental philosophy is shown by the fact that, although to be sure he did not, like English empiricism, regard *formal logic* (taken as syllogistics, Kant's "pure and universal" logic) as mostly a worthless scholastic survival or, again like empiricism (with respect to the parts of logic it accepted), rob that discipline of its peculiar genuine sense by a psychologistic reinterpretation of its ideality, still he *asked no transcendental questions* about it, but rather ascribed to it an extraordinary apriority, which exalts it above such questions. Naturally it will not do to cite here as an objection Kant's idea of a transcendental logic, which is something entirely different from that (transcendental-phenomenological) inquiry concerning the subjective which we have in mind.

Pure logic has as its thematic sphere ideal formations. But they would have had to be clearly seen, and definitely apprehended, as such ideal objectivities, before transcendental questions about them and about pure logic could have been asked. The eighteenth century and the age that followed were so strongly actuated by empiricism (or better, by anti-Platonism) that nothing was remoter from them than recognition of ideal formations as being objectivities — in the manner and in the good
<229> and never-relinquishable sense whose legitimacy we / have established in detail. For the recent history of transcendental philosophy and for the present, which is still so strongly swayed

by the old prejudices, that is a point of great significance. Nothing else hindered a clear insight into the sense, into the proper questions and methods, of genuine transcendental philosophy so much as did this anti-Platonism, which was so influential that it actuated all parties, and even the thinking of a Kant, struggling to free himself from empiricism. Leibniz, who figured as an exception (and had no transcendental problems, in our sense), we leave out of consideration here. In his own times he was unable to prevail in these respects, as in many others that are essential.

We shall emphasize here some of the chief moments that throw light on the historical development. Let us return to Hume, who demands our attention not only because of the intrinsic significance that, as already indicated, we ascribe to him but also because of his effect on Kant.

Hume did not raise, along with the transcendental problem of the constitution of the world, the transcendental problem of the *constitution of ideal objectivities*; thus he failed to raise, in particular, the transcendental problem of the constitution of logical idealities, of the categorial formations, the judgments, that make up the theme of logic. It ought to have been raised in connexion with those "*relations of ideas*" that, as the sphere of "reason" in the pregnant sense, play so great a rôle for Hume. Those relations *take the place of* the ideal eidetic relationships and laws. But neither these relationships and laws themselves nor any other ideal objectivities were introduced — not even as de facto data of a *supposed "experience"* or of some similar consciousness *supposedly giving objects themselves*, in the way that the data belonging to "Objective" Nature were introduced, as given in the experiencing of Nature. Accordingly, the corresponding Humean problem is missing; and also the corresponding theory, with the function of "explaining" the "experience" of such supposed ideal objects as being likewise an internal producing of mere fictions.

As a substitute, to some extent, for the transcendental problem of ideal objectivities, we have Hume's famous section dealing with *abstraction*. There, as we were saying, it is not a matter of converting abstract ideas, as the data of an experience, into fictions by showing that, although "perceptions" that we always

consider to be an experience of them are indeed encountered, nevertheless, as psychological analysis teaches, these perceptions
‹230› have only the value of pseudo-experiences — as / Hume tried to show with respect to external experience and its datum. Rather the aim of that section is to show that we have no abstract "perceptions" at all, that abstract "ideas", as data of some "experience" or other, are not encountered at all; but only particular individual ideas and the attendant habits, by which our general thinking is supposed to be explained as merely a thinking upon individual ideas.

Thus *Kant's position regarding logic* also becomes understandable. *According to the words*, beginning with the definition and throughout the exposition, Kant's logic is presented as a science directed to the subjective — a science of thinking, which is nevertheless distinguished, as apriori, from the empirical psychology of thinking. But *actually*, according to its sense, Kant's purely formal logic concerns the ideal formations produced by thinking. And, concerning them, Kant fails to ask properly transcendental questions of the possibility of cognition. How does it happen that he regards a formal logic, with its apriority, as self-sufficiently grounded? How is it comprehensible that he never thought of asking transcendental questions about the sphere of formal logic, taken as a sphere in and for itself?

That can be understood as a consequence of the above-mentioned *dependence on Hume implicit in Kant's reaction* against him. Hume directed his criticism to experience and the experienced world, but accepted the unassailableness of the relations of ideas (which Kant conceived as the analytic Apriori). Kant did the same with his counter-problem: He did not make his analytic Apriori a problem.

For the succeeding age this meant, however, that *those investigations in the psychology of cognition, or rather those transcendental phenomenological investigations, that are the thing actually needed for a full and, therefore, two-sided logic were never seriously undertaken.* But that was because no one ventured, or had the courage to venture, to take the *ideality of the formations with which logic is concerned* as the characteristic of a separate, self-contained, *"world" of ideal Objects* and, in so doing, to come face to face with the painful question of how subjectivity can in itself bring forth, purely from sources appertaining to its own spontaneity, formations that can be rightly accounted as ideal *Objects* in an ideal "world". — And then (on a higher level) the question of how these idealities can take on spatio-temporally restricted *existence*, in the cultural world (which must surely be considered as real, as included in the spatio-temporal universe), real existence, in the / form of historical temporality, as theories and sciences. Natu- <231> rally this question becomes universalized to concern idealities of every sort.

As for Kant himself: clearly as he recognized (in the nuclear components of the Aristotelian tradition) the apriori character of logic, its purity from everything pertaining to empirical psychology, and the wrongness of including logic in a theory of experience, he still did not grasp the peculiar sense in which logic is ideal. Otherwise that sense would surely have given him a motive for asking transcendental questions.

The overlooking of the objectivity of the ideal, in all its forms, has had its effect, beginning with Locke, in the theory of cognition — which was originally intended as a substitute for the disdained traditional logic — and, to state matters more precisely, its effect, beginning with Hume, in the famous *problem of judgment* and the attendant judgment-theories, which at bottom have never changed their style. What a genuine, clear-purposed, judgment-theory must perform we have already [1] attempted to set forth in detail. Here, with a critical consideration of history, the contrasting theory first comes into view.

The psychological naturalism that became generally dominant and that, beginning with Locke, was looking for describable psychic "Data", in which the origin of all concepts was supposed to lie, saw the describable essence of the judgment in "belief" — a psychic Datum, not differing as such from any Datum of sensation, a red-Datum or sound-Datum. But is it not peculiar that, after this discovery, Hume and, later, Mill speak in words of emotion about the enigmas of belief? What sort of enigmas can a Datum have? Why is it, then, that red and the other Data of sensation present no enigmas?

Naturally, everyone has intentionality really immanent in his mental life and has its performance before him; but, in the

[1] *Author's note:* See §§ 85 *et seq.*, [pp. 206ff., *supra*].

naturalistic attitude, one cannot lay hold of the very matter that is most important. This state of affairs was *not essentially changed even by Brentano's discovery of intentionality*. There was no consistently correlative observing of noesis and noema, *cogito* and *cogitatum qua cogitatum*. There was no unravelling of the intentionalities involved, no uncovering of the "multiplicities" in which the "unity" becomes constituted. Because this unity was not taken as the transcendental clue; because, in judgment-theory,
<232> the aim was not directed, from / the very beginning, at an examination of the judgment, in the logical sense, as the *ideally identical* affair, with a view to the noetic and noematic multiplicities, which enable us to understand its original accruing to us in its ideality: the whole theory lacked a proper goal. Such a goal would have presupposed recognizing the ideal judgment as ideal and as given in tangible evidence. But the theories stuck to their psychic "Data".

Likewise the more specifically developed logical theories of judgment-formation got lost in the turbid obscurities of the psychologies in the Lockean tradition, which exercised an unceasing influence — psychologies that, as we have explained, were failures in spite of the most zealous pursuit of "internal experience", since all the genuine problems of a pure psychology, including the judgment-problems, have the same style, that of "*constitutional*" problems in our phenomenological sense. As constitutional, the judgment-problems *cannot be isolated and treated under the restrictions imposed by traditional logic's narrow concept of the judgment*. Intentionality is not something isolated; it can be observed only in the synthetic unity that connects every single pulse of psychic life *teleologically*, in the unity-relation to *objectivities* — or rather in the double polarity, toward Ego-pole and object-pole. The "Objectivating" performance — to which all single intentional processes at a multiplicity of levels and in relation to various objects (which nevertheless combine sensefully to make up "worlds") are subservient — makes it ultimately necessary to have the whole universality of psychic life in view, as correlated with the ontic universality (the universality of the intrinsically unitary All of the objects). This teleological structure of intentional life, as a universally Objectivating life, is indicated by the fact that object and judgment (in the widest sense) belong together, and by the universality with which we can freely submit any already-given object to our categorial actions. For that reason moreover (and this is another index of that same teleology), the predicative judgment gains universal significance for psychic life.

Nevertheless, this field of genuine problems concerning judgments had to remain inaccessible: as long as, on the one hand, the objectivity of the ideal of every sort and, on the other hand, the sense and the method of intentional research had not yet been uncovered and the countersense of naturalistic psychology (including the naturalistic treatment of intentionality, once it had regained acceptance) had not yet been overcome. As long as that situation remained, neither psychology nor the / "normative" <233>
philosophic disciplines (logic, ethics, aesthetics), which concern ideals and need "psychological" clarification, could enter on a development that is certain of its aim or acquire their true method.

For logic, therefore, and likewise for the parallel philosophic disciplines, that points out the direction that their essentially necessary reform must take. Logic must overcome its phenomenological naïveté; even after having learned to recognize that which is ideal, logic must be more than a merely positive science of logico-mathematical idealities. Rather, with a continuously two-sided research (results on either side determining inquiries on the other), logic must go back systematically from the ideal formations to the consciousness that constitutes them phenomenologically; it must make these formations understandable, in respect of their sense and their limits, as essentially products of the correlative structures of productive cognitive life, and it must thereby fit them, like each and every other Objectivity, to the broader, the *concrete*, nexus of transcendental subjectivity. The ideal Objectivity of the formations with which logic is concerned — like the real world — is in no way altered in the process.

As we said above, the definite aim could not be attached to the obscure need for logical inquiries directed somehow to the subjective until after the ideal Objectivity of such formations had been sharply brought out and firmly acknowledged. For only then was one faced with the unintelligibility of *how ideal objec-*

tivities that originate purely in our own subjective activities of judgment and cognition, that are there originaliter in our field of consciousness purely as formations produced by our own spontaneity, *acquire the being-sense of "Objects"*, existing in themselves over against the adventitiousness of the acts and the subjects. How does this sense "come about", how does it originate in us ourselves? And where else could we get it, if not from our own sense-constituting performance? Can what has sense for us receive sense ultimately from anywhere else than from us ourselves? These problems, once they are seen in one sort of Objects, immediately become universal: Is not each and every Objectivity, with all the sense in which it is accepted by us, an Objectivity that is winning or has won, acceptance within ourselves — as an Objectivity having the sense that we ourselves acquired for it?

Accordingly the *transcendental problem* that *Objective logic* (taken no matter how broadly or narrowly) must raise concerning its field of ideal objectivities takes a position *parallel to the transcendental problems of the sciences of realities*, the problems
<234> that must be raised concerning the / regions of realities to which those sciences pertain, and, in particular, the transcendental problems concerning Nature, which were treated by Hume and Kant. It seems, then, that the immediate consequence of bringing out the world of ideas and, in particular (thanks to the effectuation of impulses received from Leibniz, Bolzano, and Lotze), the world of ideas with which pure logic is concerned, should have been an *immediate extension* of transcendental problems to this sphere.

But the historical development could not assume such a simple form. The Kantian problems and theory were fashioned as a whole, and were so rigidly closed off inside the hard shell of their systematic formation that any possible extension of them to the sphere of ideas with which logic is concerned was utterly out of the question. This was the case, then, not merely because such a thought had never occurred to Kant himself, for reasons already discussed. His transcendental problems, in their historically restricted form, are not raised — as such problems must be, in order to have ultimate clarity — within the primal realm of all transcendental research: phenomenological subjectivity. The fact is that, as soon as this realm has been attained, the *totality* of

transcendental problems and their uniform sense throughout are already given. Kant's problems, from the very beginning, were set in a form belonging on too high a level for them to be of possible use to *logicians* interested in the theory of cognition. Perhaps it can be said that the greatest hindrances, obscurities, and difficulties, with which Kant contended within his sphere of problems — and which make it so hard to find in his theories the satisfactoriness of full clarity — are directly connected with his having *failed to recognize the transcendental problem of logic as antecedent to that sphere.* For, if the transcendental possibility of Nature in the natural-*scientific* sense and therefore natural science itself are Kant's problem, his problem already includes, as an essential presupposition, the formal-logical problem of science as theory, and includes it as a transcendental problem. But Kant is satisfied in resorting to formal logic in its apriori positivity or, as we should say, its transcendental naïveté. Formal logic is, for him, something absolute and ultimate, on which philosophy can be built without more ado. If he had proceeded radically, he would first of all have had to divide the problems into two groups: those concerning pre-scientific Nature and those concerning scientific Nature. At first, he would have been free to ask transcendental questions (like Hume) *only about pre-scientific Nature,* as it itself becomes given exclusively in experiential intuition (that is to say: *not* in / "ex- <235>
perience" in the Kantian sense); and only after a transcendental-formal logic would he have been free to ask such questions about natural science and about the Nature to which *it* pertains. At the same time, the following is clear: Only if the transcendental philosophy of Nature had been at hand, in the first place, as worked out under an essential restriction to intuited Nature, would that philosophy have been suited (after the idealities had been uncovered) to motivate the origination and development of a transcendental logic.

At all events, it seems certain that the historical forms of Kantian and neo-Kantian transcendental philosophy, no matter how significant as preliminary stages of a genuine transcendental philosophy, were not suited to promote the transition to a transcendental consideration of ideal worlds — in particular: the world of idealities with which logic is concerned. Nay more, it was implicit in the nature of the historical development, at the stage reached with the uncovering of the sphere belonging to logic, as a realm of ideal objectivities, that it was, as it still is, *easier* to start *from these* objectivities — constituted by spontaneous activities — and *penetrate to the pure sense of all transcendental inquiries*, than to do so by a critical reform of the Kantian modes of inquiry and starting from their particular thematic sphere. Thus it was not at all accidental that phenomenology itself, when it first arose, took the way leading, from the uncovering of the ideality of the formations with which logic is concerned, to exploration of their subjective constitution, and only from there to grasping constitutional inquiry as universal and not concerned with those formations alone.

After this historico-critical degression, let us return to our main theme.

CHAPTER 7.

Objective logic and the phenomenology of reason.

§ 101. THE SUBJECTIVE FOUNDATION OF LOGIC IS THE TRANSCENDENTAL PHENOMENOLOGY OF REASON.

It was the evidence-problems connected with the fundamental concepts and laws of logic that led us (since it is evidence that is constitutive for truth, and for what truly exists in every sense accepted by us) to the most universal constitutional problems and the radical nature of the method appropriate to them. If logic, as having originated from a naïve evidence, is not to remain suspended sky-high above any possible application, these problems, in their hierarchical sequence, must / be set and solved. <236>
For *only a clarified sense prescribes the sphere of its legitimate application*. The formal theory of science should enounce an Apriori for possible science as such: the great problem, *How is science possible?*, is not removed, analogically speaking, by "*solvitur ambulando*". The possibility of science cannot be *shown by the fact* of sciences, since the fact itself is shown only by ⟨their⟩ subsumption under that possibility as an idea. Thus we are led back to logic, to its apriori principles and theories. But now logic itself is in question with regard to *its* possibility; and, in our progressive criticisms, it is continuously and very seriously called in question. These criticism lead us, *from logic as theory, back to logical reason* and the new field of theory pertaining to it. At the beginning of this essay, ***reason*** eventually appeared among the significations of the word logos; and the logic that investigates the subjective, in order to ground Objective logic radically, is a science of logos in that sense too.

Are we not drawn into a game of endless questions? Does not a new question immediately become urgent [1]: *How is a theory of logical reason possible?* But this question is answered by our last investigation [2]: *Such a theory is radically possible as the phe-*

[1] *Translator's note:* Reading ***unabweisbar*** for ***unbeweisbar*** [unprovable].
[2] *Author's note:* In [Part II,] Chapters 5 and 6, [pp. 223ff., *supra*].

nomenology of logical reason, within the frame of transcendental phenomenology as a whole. If this science is then, as may be expected, the ultimate one, it must show its ultimacy by showing that it can answer the question of its own possibility, therefore by showing that there is such a thing as an *essential, endlessly reiterated, reflexive bearing* ⟨of transcendental phenomenology⟩ upon itself, in which the essential sense of an ultimate justification by itself is discernibly included, and that precisely this is the fundamental characteristic of an essentially ultimate science.

§ 102. The relatedness of traditional logic to the world, and the inquiry concerning the character of the "ultimate" logic, which furnishes norms for its own transcendental clarification.

Let us leave these problems aside, since they are still too distant, and confine ourselves to the level of inquiry on which our previous investigations have placed us. /

‹237› The first things we have to consider are the relatedness of naïve logic to the world and the problems of evidence that are connected with that relatedness. Here again, deriving advantage from our observations concerning phenomenology, we shall have to say that this worldliness and the nature of its matter-of-course ascription — which was necessarily far-removed from any thought of the possibility that it assigns to logic a *particular* sense, and not the only possible one — were inevitable, as long as a transcendental horizon had not been opened up to men of science. Only discovery of the field of transcendental problems makes possible the distinction (without which a radical philosophy could not even begin) between the world — the actual world and any possible world whatever —, on the one hand, and, on the other hand, transcendental subjectivity, which, as constituting within itself the being-sense of the world, precedes the being of the world and accordingly bears wholly within itself the world's reality, as an idea constituted actually and potentially within this same transcendental subjectivity. To be sure, only the disclosure brought by transcendental-phenomenological reduction, with its universal epoché respecting all worldly affairs that are given beforehand, all transcendencies that make their appearance with the claim to existence "in themselves", — only that disclosure could lay bare the sphere of concrete transcendental being and, with it, the way to constitutional problems, particularly [1] those in connexion with which the "parenthesized" *transcendencies* have to function *as "transcendental clues"*. Proceeding within the transcendentally reduced ego, clarification of the constitution of "others" then led to the extending of the phenomenological reduction and the transcendental sphere to transcendental intersubjectivity (the universe of transcendental Egos).

This has a very important bearing on the *evidential problems* — or, to state it more inclusively, the *constitutional problems — of logic*. For, as has been shown, all the investigations of the subjective that pertain to logical reason are without question transcendental-phenomenological, and not psychological, when they are meant and carried on in the sense prescribed for them as investigations of the originary sense of the foundations of logic. But, if those investigations of origins which pertain to logic are transcendental and are themselves scientific, we come upon a surprising / fact, which has a fundamentally essential bearing <238>
on the sense of logic and the sense of science. All positive sciences presuppose the world; transcendental science does not presuppose the world. Naïvely natural logic, the logic that could be concerned only with positive sciences, presupposes the world: *What about the logic that furnishes norms for the transcendental investigations that clarify positive logic?* One conceives concepts, one forms judgments, drawing them from transcendental experience (experience of the data belonging to *ego-cogito*); one has empty and fulfilled judgments, one strives for truths and attains them by adequation, one deduces too, and it may well be permissible to proceed inductively: What about *truth* and *principles of logic* there, where true being is "merely subjective"? Truth, at least in the province of the most fundamental — the "purely egological" — phenomenology (almost the only phenomenology that could be discussed in Book I of my *Ideen*, the *only part published*), is no longer *"truth in itself"* in any normal sense, not even in a sense that has relation to a *transcendental* "everyone". To make this statement understandable, I may

[1] *Author's note:* The "immanent" sphere also has its constitutional problems. See, for example, the already-cited essay in this *Jahrbuch* (*IX. Bd.*). [Detailed reference, p. 163 n., *supra.*]

mention again that other subjects, as transcendental, are not given, within the bounds of my ego, in the manner in which my ego itself is given for me, in actually immediate experience, and that, at its first and fundamental level, the systematic structure of a transcendental phenomenology is free to lay claim to other egos solely as parenthesized, as "phenomena", and not yet as transcendental actualities. Thus, at this *fundamental level,* a remarkable transcendental discipline arises as the *intrinsically first transcendental discipline,* one that is actually *transcendental-solipsistic*: with eidetic truths, with theories, that hold good exclusively *for me,* the ego — that is to say: truths and theories that can rightfully claim to hold good "once for all", but without relation to actual or possible other egos. And with that discipline there also arises, then, the *question of a subjective logic* with an Apriori that can hold good only *solipsistically.*

Here, as elsewhere, and with respect to the single particular as well as to the ideal universalities of logic, naïve evidence and the naïve claiming of eidetic universalities precede the phenomenological clarification of their sense by penetrating to the next lower level and explicating the sense-bestowing. Should we, can we, disregard these problems, if we intend to understand logic, to master the possibilities and limits of its application and the sense of every level of what exists? Can we disregard them, if we intend to be philosophers (even metaphysicians, in
<239> the right way), if we intend, / not to "speculate" about what exists and about a theory applying to it, but to let ourselves be guided by the graded levels and depths of the sense itself? Here one thing inevitably leads to another. All that we actually wanted was a "formal logic" that would go just a little further than pure mathematical analytics. But now our questions about evidence take us into a phenomenological subjectivity, and the examples used in logical ideation take us into the concretenesses of the existing world and, from there, to the existing transcendental subjectivity. What looked so simple in its unquestioned obviousness now becomes exceedingly complex. The investigations take on a painful and yet unavoidable relativity, a *provisionalness,* instead of the definitiveness for which we were striving: Each investigation, *at its own level,* overcomes some naïveté or other, but is still accompanied by the naïveté of its level — which must

then be overcome in turn by more penetrating investigations of origins. The presuppositions of being, as they are uncovered at each level, become indices of problems concerning evidence, which lead us into the vast system of constitutive subjectivity. *Objective* [*objektive*] *logic*, logic in the state of natural positivity, is the *first logic for us, but not the final logic*. Not only does the ultimate logic reduce all the principles of Objective logic, as theory, to their originary and legitimate — their transcendental-phenomenological — sense, and confer the dignity of genuine science upon them: By the very fact of doing so or beginning to strive, level by level, toward that goal, it necessarily becomes amplified. A *formal ontology of any possible world*, as a world constituted in transcendental subjectivity, is a non-selfsufficient *part of another "formal ontology", which relates to everything that exists in any sense*: to what exists as transcendental subjectivity and to everything that becomes constituted in transcendental subjectivity. But how the latter science can be developed; how the most universal idea of a formal logic, as formal ontology and formal apophantics, can be satisfied within the absolute realm; how a logic satisfying that idea becomes constituted within the absolute and ultimate all-embracing science, within transcendental phenomenology, as a stratum necessarily belonging to it; what being-sense and what rank on that basis the logic that grew up naturally can claim as formal ontology; and what presuppositions of method restrict the legitimate application of that logic: these are very profound philosophic questions. They immediately become involved with new ones. /

§ 103. Absolute grounding of cognition is possible only in the all-embracing science of transcendental subjectivity, as the one absolute existent. <240>

Formal ontology, conceived as analytics, relates with empty universality to any possible world whatever; but, unlike *ontology in the sense, ontology of realities*, it does not explicate the idea, any possible world whatever, in respect of the *structural forms* essentially necessary to a world — forms in a new and very different sense: as the *"form"*, *allness of realities*, with the allness-*"forms"*, space and time; or such as the *"formal"* articulation of a world as comprising regions of realities; and so forth. What about the true *relationship between these two apriori sciences of whatever exists as worldly — each of them "formal" in a different sense —* their relationship when they both become grounded by virtue of original sources in transcendental subjectivity? For such a grounding is now the incessant demand; everywhere it is what makes a scientific purpose specifically philosophic; everywhere it makes the difference between *genuine science, which is nothing other than philosophy,* and *science in naïve positivity* (which can be accepted only as a stage preliminary to genuine science and not as genuine science itself).

A reduction to transcendental subjectivity must set us upon the systematic way to ultimate clarifyings of the possible sense and ultimate groundings of the legitimate sense. There must be a free development of those paths of fulfilment that, by virtue of the uncovering of hidden intentionality, show themselves to be the actually, though at times only relatively, fulfilling paths. — In addition to that, a free development of the essential forms belonging, on the one hand, to the goal-ideas and, on the other hand, to the relative fulfilments that, of essential necessity, lead toward the goal-ideas by corresponding stages of approximation. The *original grounding of all the sciences,* and of the formal ontologies of both sorts exercising in their behalf the function of a theory of science, the normative function, *gives all of them unity, as branches of a constituted production from the one transcendental subjectivity.*

In other words, *there is only one philosophy, one actual and genuine science*; and particular genuine sciences are only non-selfsufficient members within it.

Furthermore, the all-embracing science of transcendental subjectivity, in which all conceivable sciences, in respect of their
<241> actuality / and their possibility, are essentially predelineated transcendental formations — predelineated as actualizable by free action —, gives a legitimate sense, and indeed the only conceivable one, to the *ideal of grounding cognition with an absolute freedom from presuppositions.* Every existent (that ever had, or can have, sense for us) stands, as intentionally constituted, in a hierarchy of intentional functions and of existents already constituted intentionally, which, for their part, are involved in intentional functions for a new constituting of being. Contrary

to the false ideal of an absolute existent and the absolute trueness of an absolute existent, *every existent* is ultimately relative; not only everything that is relative in any usual sense, but *every* existent is *relative to transcendental subjectivity*. Transcendental subjectivity alone, on the other hand, exists "*in itself and for itself*"; and it exists, in itself and for itself, in a hierarchical order corresponding to the constitution that leads to the different levels of transcendental intersubjectivity. First of all, then, as ego I am absolutely existent in myself and for myself. I exist for another existent, only in so far as it is *someone* else, another ego, himself a transcendental subjectivity — who, however, becomes necessarily posited in me as the ego already existing beforehand for himself. In a similar fashion, transcendental intersubjectivity (in the amplified sense), which is constituted (in me, and hence relatively to me) as a plurality of "egos" — each of whom is legitimately accepted as intentionally related to the *same* intersubjectivity along with me — this intersubjectivity, according to its sense, also exists, *mutatis mutandis*, "in itself and for itself": with the mode of existence that belongs to something "absolute". *An absolute existent* is existent in the form, an intentional life — which, no matter what else it may be intrinsically conscious of, is, at the same time, consciousness of itself. Precisely for that reason (as we can see when we consider more profoundly) it has at all times an essential ability to *reflect* on itself, on all its structures that stand out for it — an essential ability to make itself thematic and produce judgments, and evidences, relating to itself. *Its essence includes the possibility of "self-examination"* — a self-examination that starts from vague meanings and, by a process of uncovering, goes back to the original self.

§ 104. Transcendental phenomenology as self-explication on the part of transcendental subjectivity.

The whole of phenomenology is nothing more than / *scientific* <242> *self-examination on the part of transcendental subjectivity*, an examination that at first proceeds straightforwardly and therefore with a certain naïveté of its own, but later becomes critically intent on its own logos; it is a self-examination that goes on from the fact to the essential necessities, the *primal logos* from which everything else that is "logical" originates. All prejudices necessarily fall away here, because they themselves are intentional formations, which become uncovered in the nexus of the systematically progressing self-examination. *All criticism* of logical cognition, not only the cognition that produces logic but also the cognition already mediated by logic — the criticism of cognition in sciences of every sort — is, as a phenomenological performance, *a self-explication on the part of subjectivity, as it investigates the sense of its own transcendental functions.* All Objective being has in transcendental subjectivity the grounds for its being; all truth has in transcendental subjectivity the grounds for the cognition of it, and if a truth concerns transcendental subjectivity itself, it has those grounds precisely in transcendental subjectivity. Stated in greater detail: if this subjectivity carries out self-examination systematically and universally — and therefore as transcendental phenomenology — then, as is clear from our earlier exposition, it finds, as constituted within itself, all "Objective" being and all "Objective" truth, all truth legitimated in the world. Something Objective is nothing other than the synthetic unity of actual and potential intentionality, a unity belonging to the proper essence of transcendental subjectivity. Because of the manner in which the open plurality of other egos is constituted in my apodictically existing ego,[1] this synthetic unity is relative to the universal community of the transcendental egos communicating with me and with one another, the transcendental egos existing "for one another"; that is to say, it is a synthetic unity of the intentionalities belonging to this community as part of its own essence. On the other hand, all truth concerned with this transcendental intersubjectivity as its theme is, so to speak, all the more relative to this intersubjectivity, correspondingly to this intersubjectivity's mode of being, which is being-for-itself, "absolute" being.

Thus the ultimate grounding of all truth is a branch of the universal self-examination that, when carried through radically, is absolute. In other words, it is a self-examination which I begin with the transcendental reduction, and which leads me to the grasping of my absolute self, my transcendental ego. As this

[1] *Author's note:* See § 96, pp. 237ff., [*supra*].

absolute ego, considering myself henceforth as my exclusive fundamental thematic field, I carry on all my further sense-investigations, those that are specifically philosophic — that is: purely phenomenological. I reflect upon what / I can find purely <243>
"in" myself; as indicated earlier, I separate that which is primordially my own (that which is constituted as inseparable from myself) and that which is constituted in me at different levels (on the motivating basis of what is primordially my own) as something "alien": that which is constituted, in me, as real or else as ideal; constituted, in me, as Nature, as psychophysical being, as a human community, as a people or as a state, as reified culture, as science, — also as phenomenology and, in the first place, by the effort of my own thinking. All this becomes a theme for phenomenological reflections, which are two-sided: uncovering the "subjective" constitution of the formations given beforehand straightforwardly in the particular case. When I proceed thus, reflecting and fixing my discoveries, the theoretical formations of transcendental phenomenology and this phenomenology itself, as an infinite open unity of science, are generated from myself by virtue of sources belonging to my own passivity (association) and activity, at first with a sort of naïveté. If transcendental phenomenology itself then becomes a theme for constitutional and critical inquiry at a higher level, for the sake of conferring on it the highest dignity of genuineness, the ability to justify itself down to its roots, then naturally I still move within the realm of my absolute subjectivity or within that of the absolute intersubjectivity derived from myself; for it is still the case that, as a philosopher, I will, and can will, nothing but radical self-examinations, which, of themselves, become self-examinations on the part of the intersubjectivity existing for me. The transcendent world; human beings; their intercourse with one another, and with me, as human beings; their experiencing, thinking, doing, and making, with one another: these are not annulled by my phenomenological reflection, not devalued, not altered, but only understood. And, in the same manner, positive science, as achieved by labors in common, becomes understood — and ultimately phenomenology, as having also been achieved by such labors, a phenomenology that finally understands itself as a reflective functional activity in transcendental intersubjectivity.

As a human being (as living in the natural attitude), I am "in" the world, I find myself as being "in" it and, accordingly, as determined in many different respects from the outside (a spatio-temporal externality). Likewise as a transcendental ego (as living in the absolute attitude), I find myself as determined from the outside — now, however, not as a spatio-temporal reality determined by an external reality. What do "external to me" and "being determined by something external" signify now? It is obvious that, transcendentally speaking, I can be conditioned by something "external", by something that goes beyond my self-contained ownness, only if it has the sense, "someone else", and, in a thoroughly understandable manner, gains and legitimates in me its acceptance as being another transcendental ego.
<244> Starting from here, the possibility and the sense, not only / of a plurality of *co-existing* absolute subjects ("monads"), but also of subjects who *affect one another* transcendentally and, in cooperative acts, constitute community-products as their works, becomes clear. — But none of this is hypothesis. These are the results of systematic sense-investigations concerning the world, which, as a "phenomenon", lies within me myself and gets its being-sense from me; results of a systematic inquiring back for the genuine, unclouded, sense of my own sense-bestowing and for all the presuppositions appertaining inseparably to that sense and lying within me, beginning with the absolute pre-positing [*Voraus-Setzung*], which gives sense to all presuppositions [*Voraussetzungen*]: the antecedent positing of my transcendental ego.

Actually, then, it is only self-examination — self-examination, however, that does not break off too quickly and turn into naïve positivity, but remains, with absolute consistency, just what it was at the beginning: self-examination. —Except that, as it progresses, it takes on the form of transcendental intersubjective self-examination, without any essential change in its style.

Accordingly *the radicalness of this philosophic self-examination*, the radicalness that sees in everything given beforehand as existing an index for a system of uncoverable constitutive performances, is indeed the most extreme *radicalness in striving to uproot all prejudice*. Every existent given beforehand, with the straightforward evidence thereof, is taken by it to be a "prejudice". An already given world, an already given province of ideal being, like the realm of cardinal numbers, — these are "prejudices" originating from natural evidence, though not "prejudices" in the disparaging sense. They require a transcendental criticism and grounding, guided by the idea of an absolutely grounded cognition, which could furnish knowledge and science in the strict sense — in other words, they require such criticism and grounding under the guidance of the idea of a *philosophy*, in which they must find their places.

This holds good, moreover, with respect to the formal universality with which they enter into a natural *logic*. But logic — and, in particular, modern logic since Locke's *Essay*, as a logic that has been intent on clarification of origins from sources revealed by "internal experience" — is continually hampered by prejudices, in the usual bad sense; and here the worst of all prejudices are those concerning evidence. They are connected with another prejudice, which we have already considered: the belief in an absolute world, a world existing in itself, as the substrate of truths in themselves, which, without question, pertain to it. In view of these prejudices, our transcendental criticism of logic still requires a final supplementation. /

§ 105. Preparations for concluding our transcendental criticism of logic. The usual theories of evidence misguided by the presupposition of absolute truth. <245>

There is, as we know, an extraordinarily wide-spread interpretation that eschews all phenomenological investigation of the intentionality of an evident judging and *construes evidence* conformably to a naïvely presupposed truth-in-itself. According to this interpretation, there "must" be an evidence that is an absolute grasping of truth (the naïve argumentation is often explicit), since otherwise we could neither have nor strive for truth and science. This absolute evidence is then taken to be an — indeed very wonderful — psychic characteristic of many processes of judgment, one that absolutely guarantees that the judicative believing is not mere believing, but rather a believing that makes the truth itself actually given. But what if truth is an *idea*, lying at infinity? What if it can be shown, in evidence, that, with respect to world-Objectivity in its entirety, this is no

accidental matter of fact, resulting from our unfortunately limited human cognitive powers, but an *eidetic law*? What if each and *every* truth about reality, whether it be the everyday truth of practical life or the truth of even the most highly developed sciences conceivable, remains involved in *relativities* by virtue of its essence, and referable to *"regulative ideas"* as its norms? What if, even when we get down to the primitive phenomenological bases, problems of relative and absolute truth are still with us, and, as problems of the highest dignity, *problems of ideas* and of the *evidence of ideas*? What if the relativity of truth and of evidence of truth, on the one hand, and, on the other hand, the infinitely distant, ideal, absolute, truth beyond all relativity — what if each of these has its legitimacy and each demands the other? The trader in the market has his market-truth. In the relationship in which it stands, is his truth not a good one, and the best that a trader can use? Is it a pseudo-truth, merely because the scientist, involved in a different relativity and judging with other aims and ideas, looks for other truths — with which a great many more things can be done, but not the one thing that has to be done in a market? It is high time that people got over being dazzled, particularly in philosophy and logic, by the ideal and regulative ideas and methods of the "exact" sciences — as though the In-itself of such sciences were actually an absolute norm for objective being and for truth. Actually,
<246> they do not see the woods for the trees. Because of a / splendid cognitive performance, though with only a very restricted teleological sense, they overlook the infinitudes of life and its cognition, the infinitudes of relative and, only in its relativity, rational being, with its relative truths. But to rush ahead and philosophize from on high about such matters is fundamentally wrong; it creates a wrong skeptical relativism and a no less wrong logical absolutism, mutual bugbears that knock each other down and come to life again like the figures in a Punch and Judy show.

To judge in a naïve evidence is to judge on the basis of a giving of something itself, while continually asking what can be actually "seen" and given faithful expression — accordingly it is to judge by the same method that a cautiously shrewd person follows in practical life wherever it is seriously important for him to "find

out how matters actually are". That is the beginning of all wisdom, though not its end; and it is a wisdom we can never do without, no matter how deep we go with our theorizings — a wisdom that we must therefore practise in the same fashion when at last we are judging in the absolute phenomenological sphere. For, as has already been mentioned on several occasions, it is essentially necessary that naïve experiencing and naïve judging come first. And, when the reflecting is serious, their naïveté is not that of light-mindedness, but the naïveté of an original intuiting, with the will to confine ourselves to what the intuiting actually gives. Though further reflective inquiry always follows — and finally the inquiry concerning ultimate transcendental essential structures and transcendental eidetic laws concerning all-embracing essential interconnexions — still this pure intuiting and a faithfulness to its pure contents are involved again and again, are continual fundamental characteristics of the method. (Eventually however, the inquiry must end with a cognition — itself intuitive — of results and methods as always repeating themselves, always having an identical essential style.) When we follow this procedure, we have continuously anew the *living truth from the living source, which is our absolute life,* and from the self-examination turned toward that life, *in the constant spirit of self-responsibility.* We have the *truth* then, not as falsely absolutized, but rather, in each case, as within its *horizons* — which do not remain overlooked or veiled from sight, but are systematically explicated. We have it, that is to say, in a living intentionality (called "evidence of it") whose own content enables us to distinguish between "actually itself-given" and "anticipated", or "still in our grip" retentionally, or "appresented as alien to the Ego's own", and the like — a content that, with the uncovering of the attendant intentional / implications, leads to all those relativities <247>
in which being and validity are involved.

§ 106. Further criticisms of the presupposition of absolute truth and the dogmatistic theories of evidence.

The upshot of a philosophic economy that operates with an absolute existent assumed beforehand in a completely empty manner — completely empty, since there has been no inquiry whether an absolute existent can properly be conceived — is already shown by Descartes' *Meditations*. How can the subjective-psychic characteristic of *clara et distincta perceptio* (which is nothing other that what later theorists "describe" as the evidence-characteristic, as the evidence-feeling, the feeling of strict necessity) — how can it guarantee an Objective validity, without which there would be no truth for us? With respect to the evidentness of *ego cogito*, the theorist is reassured, perhaps somewhat quickly, by the "evidence of internal perception". But even what goes beyond the momentarily living present given in internal perception (to say nothing of the concretely full ego) raises a doubt. Perhaps this leads him to accept inferior but still serviceable evidences; perhaps he resorts, already at this stage, to the logic of probabilities. In the case of the "outside world", it is true, he rejects the original Cartesian procedure (by way of the proof of the existence of God) for making comprehensible the transcendence characteristic of experience and of the experiential belief in being; but the same countersensical *type* of procedure (by way of inferences) for making this transcendence comprehensible — a type that we have already criticised — still persists. And likewise the whole underlying thought in the conception of evidence: Evidence "must" somehow be an absolute grasping of being and truth. In the first place, there "must" be an *absolute experience*; and that we have in the case of internal experience. Then there "must" be *absolutely valid universal evidences*; and we have them in the case of the evidences of apodictic principles, the highest of these being the principles of formal logic, which, moreover, govern deductive inferences and thereby make truths evident that are apodictically without question. Further aid is then given by induction, with its probability-inferences, which themselves come under the apodictic principles of probabilities, such as Laplace's famous principle. Thus an Objectivity valid cognition has been excellently taken care of.

But unfortunately this is only *theory from on high*. For what the theorist has meanwhile forgotten to say to himself is this: Since the actuality and likewise the possibility — the conceivability — of something existent of any sort derives the
<248> originality / of its sense only from actual or possible "experience", I must ask experience itself, or clearly phantasied possible experiencing, what I have in it as something experienced. Here

"experience" signifies, with the necessary universalization (in accordance with our earlier exposition): giving of something-itself, evidence as such — of which an outstanding particular case is experience in the usual, and equally indispensable, sense; and a very instructive case it is for the theory of evidence, once its peculiarity has been seen. Let us then examine this evidence of ordinary experience, to see what it itself can teach us. For everyone except confused philosophers it is absolutely without question that the thing perceived in perception *is the physical thing itself,* in its own factual being; and that, when perceptions are deceptive, that signifies that they are in conflict with new perceptions, which show with certainty what is actual *in the place of* the illusory. Whatever further questions should be asked here must, in any case, be directed to the experiences concerned; by an intentional analysis of them, we can gain an (essentially universal) understanding of how an experience can, in itself, give an existent itself as experienced, and yet this existent can become cancelled — how, of essential necessity, experience of this sort points ahead into horizons of possible further, confirmatory, experiences but also, of essential necessity, leaves open the possibility that conflicting experiences may supervene and lead to corrections, in the form of a determining as otherwise or else in the form of a complete striking out (as illusion). But something similar obviously holds good in the case of every sort of evidence, with the particular differences that can be gathered from the evidences themselves.

Investigations of such intentionalities were first taken in hand by phenomenology. *Experience, evidence, gives something existent,* and gives *it-itself*: imperfectly, if the experience is imperfect; more perfectly, if, according to its essential sort, the experience becomes perfected — that is: amplified in a harmonious synthesis. What the situation is with respect to the possibilities of such a perfecting, and also with respect to the possibilities of undoing and correction — whether in a particular case there are relative, or perhaps even absolute, optima, whether ideal perfections should be presupposed and striven toward — cannot be ascertained from prejudices or even from naïvely evident idealizations; rather, with genuine original legitimacy, it can be established only by an eidetic consultation of the experiences themselves

and those systematic possibilities of experience that are included a priori in the relevant essential sorts of experiences (and sorts of objects of experience) and can be made evident by intentional
<249> explication. — Naturally, / within the ultimate transcendental realm, which phenomenological reduction procures for us.

Already, in Descartes' first meditations (which substantially determined the development of transcendental phenomenology), right away with the criticism of external experience, this fundamental defect is conspicuous: Descartes gives special prominence to the possibilities of deception that are always inherent in external experience, and by doing so he wrongly cuts off his view of the fundamental sense of experience, namely as *an original giving of something-itself*. But that happens only because it never occurs to him to ask what actually determines the conceivability of a worldly existent, the conceivability with which worldly existence acquires legitimate sense; it happens only because, on the contrary, he has worldly existence beforehand, as an existence floating above the clouds of cognition. Or, as we can also say: It does not occur to Descartes to attempt an intentional explication of the stream of sensuous experience within the whole intentional complex of the ego, in whom the style of an experienced world becomes constituted, and quite understandably constituted, in the form: a world whose being, despite confirmation, is a being "until further notice", subject to always-possible and often-occurring correction — a world that, even as the All of being, exists, as a world for the ego, only on the basis of a *presumption* deriving its legitimacy (and yet only a *relative* legitimacy) from the vitality of experience. Therefore he does not see that the essential style of experience stamps on the being-sense of the world, and of all realities, an essentially necessary *relativity*, and that, accordingly, the attempt to remedy this relativity by appealing to the veracity of God is a countersense.

In what follows we intend to show, *in concreto*: on the one hand, how, ascending level by level from sensuous experience, one can acquire an understanding of *evidence as an effective performance* [*als Leistung*], and, on the other hand, what self-existent truth, as its performed effect [*als ihre Leistung*], signifies.

§ 107. Delineation of a transcendental theory of evidence as an effective intentional performance.

a. The evidence of external (sensuous) experience.

The phenomenological uncovering of sensuous experience — more precisely: experience purely of Nature, the experience in which mere physical Nature becomes given to us (in abstraction from all apperceptual strata of social or private significance) — is a great task / and requires extraordinarily far-reaching <250> investigations, as its actual execution shows.[1] Here the eidetic consideration of single Objects belonging to Nature and of our perception — or even our entire experience — of *them* is insufficient. One must explore the intentionalities implicit in the entire, synthetically unified, *world*-experience, extending throughout the life of the single ego and throughout the life of the transcendental community, one must explore the intentionalities implicit in its *all-embracing style*; and subsequently one must explore its constitutional genesis together with ⟨the genesis of⟩ this style. In such concrete studies one learns to understand, in *one* sphere, the *essence of evidence, evidence as an effective performance* [*als Leistung*], which, like other effective intentional performances, takes place as woven into systematically built performances and abilities. And naturally that is also the best way to learn the complete insignificance of the usual information about evidence and of the usual manners in which it is investigated.

Naturally, if one is guided by the delusion of a feeling of evidence that absolutely guarantees something presupposed, in empty prejudice, as existing absolutely, then external experience is not evidence; and that is indeed the general opinion. But the world, it is generally thought, still *is* what it is and, as what it is, is also accessible to an evidence. Few would hesitate to ascribe this absolute evidence to the infinite intellect (even if they had

[1] *Author's note:* My own concrete investigations, which have been continued through a number of years, and from which excerpts have often enough been communicated in courses of lectures, I hope to be able to publish within the next few years. A first elaboration, intended at that time for publication, was presented in the draft of the second book of the *Ideen*, which was written in connexion with the first book of that work, in 1912. In the redaction made by Dr. Edith Stein, this draft has been made accessible to a number of my students and colleagues. In the meantime, the concrete problems that must be solved have turned out to be much more difficult and extensive than I expected. [See Edmund Husserl, *Ideen zu einer reinen Phänomenologie und phänomenologischen Philosophie, zweites und drittes Buch, herausgegeben von Marly Biemel*, Haag, Martinus Nijhoff, 1952.]

recourse to the infinite intellect only as a limit-idea in epistemology), though that would not be one iota better than wanting to see divine omnipotence express itself in the mathematical sphere by the ability to construct regular decahedrons, or by any other theoretical countersense. The being-sense of Nature has the essential form absolutely prescribed for it by the essential style of the experience of Nature; and therefore even an absolute God cannot create a "feeling of evidence" that absolutely guarantees the being of Nature — or, in a better formulation, a self-contained process of ⟨external experience that, no matter how different it⟩ might conceivably be from "our" sensuous experience, would give something-itself apodictically and adequately. /

<251> *b.* The evidence of "internal" experience.

Internal experience has been a very misleading theme in the theory of evidence. Though much simpler than Nature-experience, since it enters into every phase of this, as it does into each and every evidence, internal experience too demands an uncovering of its intentionality; and it has surprising implications. We need not again call attention to the grave oversight that led to the general confusing of internal perception as psychological with internal perception as epistemological — that is: as transcendental-phenomenological, as the ego's perception of his cogito. Psychological experience, including internal experience, is an experience of something worldly; it is intimately combined, in its intentionality, with experience of Nature. It becomes phenomenologically pure experience, only if one "parenthesizes" the transcending apperception. But, in phenomenologically pure experience too, something existing (here something existing "immanently", in the phenomenological sense) is, to be sure, itself given: in perception, as itself present; in memory, as past. Yet even here, even in this most simple mode of constitutive performance, the itself-given, the immanently objective, becomes constituted in a very complicated manner: in the flux of original presentations, retentions, and protentions, — in a complicated intentional *synthesis*, the synthesis belonging to consciousness of internal time. Much as this evidence-structure remained unexplored, at least here the *actual having of something itself* was given prominence, though it was not thought of as present in

every other experience and evidence. But, even here (where it may be said, in a certain sense — which must be more precisely described and restricted —, that the immanent Datum makes its appearance really in the constituting mental process), we must be warned against the *error* of believing that already, with *this real occurring*, the Datum is *fully constituted* as an object. We said earlier that evidences are performings [*Funktionen*] that function in the intentional complexes to which they belong. If there were no ability to recollect, no consciousness that I can always come back again to what I am seizing upon even if it is no longer perceived, or if the memory in which I just had it has itself passed away, speaking of the Same, the object, would have no sense. To be sure, the first "evidence", the original occurring of the Datum and the original duration of, for example, an immanently apprehended Datum of sensation in its identity throughout this duration, has, as it were, an apodictic uncancellableness — throughout this duration. / But the original unity, <252>
which is coming into being in the continuous identification throughout this duration, is not yet an "object": it is an "object" only as existing in temporality (immanent temporality in the present case) — that is: existing with evidentness of being recognizable as the Same throughout all the changes in the subjective modes of the past ⟨as it recedes from the present⟩. The form of this self-identity of an object is the locus in time. Thus the *single perception*, along with the retention and the recollection of it, is indeed *never a complete evidence with respect to something existent*; it is still necessary to ask what constitutes the existent as an *identical* existent ("persisting" after its fashion) within the identical ego.

Now the situation is manifestly the same in the much more complicated case of external perception; and ultimately it is *the same*, with only particular differences, *for every evidence*. Indeed, we ourselves have already been brought back repeatedly to the *"always again"* and the problem of clarifying the evidence of it.[1]

[1] *Translator's note: Cf.* § 73 and § 74, pp. 4ff. *supra.*

c. Hyletic Data and intentional functionings. The evidence of Data occurring in internal time.

The Data-sensualism that is generally prevalent in psychology and epistemology and, for the most part, biases even those who verbally polemicize against it, or against what they mean by the term, consists in constructing the life of consciousness out of Data as, so to speak, finished objects. It is actually a matter of indifference here, whether one thinks of these Data as separate "psychic atoms" swept together into more or less cohesive bundles according to unintelligible matter-of-fact laws, like those of mechanics, or talks about wholes and *Gestalt*-qualities and regards the wholes as antecedent to the elements distinguishable within them; likewise whether, within this realm of objects already existing in advance, one distinguishes between sensuous Data and intentional mental processes as Data of another sort.

Not that the latter distinction should be completely rejected. As ego, one can focus on immanent objects as objects of immanental experience — that is: as objects in immanent time; and obviously that is the first thing that the beginner in phenomenology should do. In my *Ideen*, accordingly, I consciously and expressly excluded[1] problems concerning the consciousness of immanent time or (these being the same) problems concerning
<253> the constitution of these objects / belonging to egological temporality, and attempted to mark out a large field of connected problems for possible descriptions in this sphere, some of which I attempted. In this sphere there then emerges necessarily, as a radical difference, the difference between *hyletic Data* and *intentional functionings*. But, even in the immanent "internality" of the ego, there are *no objects beforehand* and no evidences that merely take in what already exists beforehand. The evidences, as functionings that (in union with all the other functionings and abilities that play their uncoverable rôles) constitute what exists, bring about the performance whose result in the sphere of immanence is called an *existing object*. That is already the case here; and it is the case everywhere else.

In this connexion various matters already touched upon to some

[1] *Author's note:* See *Ideen*, p. 163. [English translation, p. 236.] On these problems themselves, see the essay in this *Jahrbuch* (*IX. Bd.*), which has already been cited several times. [Detailed reference, p. 163 n., *supra*.]

extent should be noted again. If we take evidences in an extremely broad sense, as the giving (conversely, the having) of something-itself, then not every evidence necessarily has the form, specific *Ego-act*: directedness from the Ego (here this word dignates the Egopole) to what is itself-given (a "noticing", seizing, directedness — or perhaps a valuing directedness, or a volitive directedness — from the Ego to something that is itself given). The constituting of Data in immanent time, a constituting that goes on with rigid regularity, is a continuous evidence, in an extremely broad sense; but it is anything but an active directedness of the Ego to them.

Furthermore, *evidence, as the giving of something-itself, has its variant formations, its degrees of perfection in giving something-itself* — it has many diversities, which fall under *essential types* and must be explored. The variant formations of originality do not abolish the giving of something-itself, though they do modify it. The evidence of the absolutely original *present* of a sounding tone in the momentary now-point (naturally we are not referring to a mathematical point) functions, of essential necessity, in connexion with an evidence of the "*just gone*" and an evidence of the originally "*coming*". Likewise, every clear recollection is an evidence, a giving of something-itself with respect to the recollected past as such: not with respect to the past original, which, as an original, would be something present; but with respect to *what is past as, past.*

This evidence also affords examples for the *gradations of clarity* and, for the *idea of perfect clarity*, an *idea* derivable from these gradations: I "can" approach ideally perfect clarity; / and <254>
this I-can has its own evidentness. As we have already stated with respect to external experience, so here, in the primitive case of recollecting something immanent, illusion is not excluded. But the essential form of the uncovering of illusion here is also evident; and, as in the other case, it presupposes recollective evidence — in the form: evidence of other recollections.

Furthermore, just as in even the simplest case of a living experience of something internal, the essential form of the experience's flowing constituting is such that *evidences*, succeeding one another continuously and undergoing continuous modifications, *function together* — so it is universally in the great sphere of transcendental (or of psychological) inner life as a whole.

As we have already indicated, *the manifold object-categories that become constituted* are, of essential necessity, combined with one another. Accordingly *it is not only the case that for each object there is a peculiar evidence*: the evidence of it and the object itself, as evident, exercise *functions that overlap* ⟨those of other evidences and objects⟩. Any cultural object is an example. The ideality in which its peculiar being consists becomes "embodied" in a material objectivity (which, for its part, becomes "inspirited" by the cultural object); and consequently the evidence of the Objective cultural determination is founded on an evidence relating to Nature, and intimately combined with this evidence.

Or, the most universal example: All objects, as constituted, stand in essential relations to immanent objects, these relations being such that *the evidence of any particular objectivity whatever* must contain immanental evidences of the [1] functioning immanent mental processes. Everywhere, it is *as* functioning that whatever is functioning receives its particular intentional character — and with this are connected extremely important differences in the manner in which constituted objects can function "affectively", as "stimuli" for possible active turnings to them on the part of the Ego. If a physical thing is constituted, even in the unheeded "background", various implicated objectivities are constituted at the same time — for example: the perspectives and, ultimately, the particular Data of sensation that are "construed" as Objective colors and sounds. But it is *not* the case that all these *objects, existing "relative" to consciousness*" for the transcendental ego, are *on a par with respect to the possible affecting*. The physical thing is the first to affect ⟨the Ego⟩; and only with a reflectional diversion ⟨of the Ego⟩ from the thing does the perspective or, further back, the sensational color affect ⟨him⟩. Thus the sequence is determined by the founding relationships among the evidential functions. /

⟨255⟩ But we have said enough to establish a contrast to the tradition's empty talk about evidence and afford some conception of how much that comes under this heading must be explored — *if the sense and the feasibility of a criticism of evidence* are to become at all clear. It was very late before I recognized, not only that the entire criticism of evidences, and particularly of ju-

[1] *Translator's note:* Reading *die* instead of *sie*.

dicative evidences (more precisely, the evidences included among categorial activities) should be carried on within the frame of phenomology — in the present exposition this is a matter of course —, but also that this whole criticism leads back to an *ultimate criticism*: a *criticism of those evidences* that *phenomenology at the first, and still naïve, level* carries on straightforwardly. But that implies:

The intrinsically first criticism of cognition, the one in which all others are rooted, is transcendental self-criticism *on the part of phenomenological cognition itself.*[1]

d. Evidence as an apriori structural form of consciousness.

Another point is important. Traditional epistemology and psychology regard *evidence as an uncommon special Datum*, coming into the nexus of an internal psychic life in accordance with some inductive, or causal, *empirical law*. Usually they deny as a matter of course that anything of the sort occurs in brute animals.

As against this, the foregoing has already made it evident that a life of consciousness *cannot exist without including evidence* — if only by virtue of the sphere of immanent time — and also that, if we think of such a life as a consciousness relating to Objectivity, it cannot exist without including a stream of external experience. Another fact should be pointed out however: Not only does evidence having the structure appropriate to any level combine with other evidences to make up higher evidential performances; it is also the case that all evidential performances stand in more inclusive coherent complexes with non-evidences, and that essentially necessary *modifications* are continually taking place: the sedimentation of retentions, which gives them the form of "sleeping" consciousness; the essentially necessary forming of associational empty intentions, of meanings, empty aimings that / tend toward fullness; and so forth. "Evidence", or <256>
the giving of something-itself, as fulfilment, confirmation, verification, cancellation, falsity, practical failure, and so forth —

[1] *Author's note:* I attempted an actual carrying out of this ultimate criticism in a course of lectures given four hours weekly in the winter semester of 1922–23. A copy of these lectures has been made available to my younger friends.

all these are structural forms belonging a priori to the unity of a life; and the investigation of this unity, an investigation paying heed to and clarifying them all, is the immense theme of phenomenology.

CONCLUSION.

In this essay we have attempted to map the way from traditional to transcendental logic — which is not a second logic, but only radical and concrete logic itself, which accrues by phenomenological method. Yet, to speak more precisely, what we had in mind as this transcendental logic is only the traditionally limited logic, analytic logic, which, to be sure, by virtue of its empty-formal universality, embraces all spheres of being and objects and, correlatively, all spheres of cognition. Nevertheless, under the necessity of outlining the sense and the breadth of transcendental research, we acquired also a preliminary understanding of those "logics" (in another sense) that should be established: the *material* theories of science, among which the highest and most inclusive would be the *logic of the absolute science*, the logic of transcendental-phenomenological *philosophy* itself.

Naturally there is a legitimate sense in which the name logic, or the equivalent name ontology, likewise applies to all the establishable material-apriori disciplines — disciplines belonging in the one *mundane ontology*, which should at first be established straightforwardly, with the "naïveté" of a transcendental positivity. In the context of our expositions, it has already become apparent that this material ontology explicates the all-embracing Apriori of any purely possible world whatever, the Apriori of the eidos *world* — an eidos that must arise concretely by virtue of the method of eidetic variation, which starts with the world that is given us in fact and takes it as the directive "example". This thought is the basis from which arise, at successive levels, the great *problems* pertaining to a *world-logic* that is to be grounded radically, a genuine mundane ontology — some parts of which have already been indicated.

"Transcendental aesthetics" — in a new sense of the phrase

(which we use because of an easily apprehensible relationship to Kant's narrowly restricted transcendental aesthetics) — functions as the ground level ⟨in a world-logic⟩. It deals with the eidetic problem of any possible world *as a world given in "pure experience"* and thus precedes all science in the "higher" sense; accordingly it undertakes the eidetic description of the allem-
<257> bracing / Apriori, without which no Objects could appear unitarily in mere experience, prior to categorial actions (in our sense, which must not be confounded with the categorial in the Kantian sense), and therefore without which the unity of a Nature, the unity of a world, as a passively synthetized unity, could not become constituted at all. One stratum of that Apriori is the aesthetic Apriori of spatio-temporality. Naturally this logos of the aesthetic world, like the analytic logos, cannot become a genuine science without an investigation of transcendental constitution — and even from the constitutional investigation required here an exceedingly rich (and difficult) science accrues.

As a level founded on the logos of the aesthetic world, there rises the logos of Objective worldly *being*, and of *science, in the "higher" sense*: the logos of the science that investigates under the guidance of the ideas of "*strict*" being and strict truth, and develops correspondingly "*exact*" theories.[1] As a matter of fact, there grows up — first in the form of exact geometry and then in the form of exact natural science (Galilean physics) — a science with a consciously new style, not a science that reduces "observable and describable" (that is: aesthetic) formations, data of pure intuition, to types and comprehends such formations in concepts, but an idealizing-logicizing science. Historically, as we all know, this science first took shape as, and was afterwards guided by, the Platonizing geometry, which talks, not about straight lines, circles, and the like, in the "aesthetic" sense, nor about *their* Apriori, the Apriori of what appears in actual and possible *appearances*, but rather about the (*regulative*) *idea* applying to a space that so appears, about "ideal space" with its "ideal straight lines" and the like. The whole of "exact" physics operates with such "idealities"; thus, beneath actually experienced Nature, beneath the Nature dealt with in actual living, it places a Nature as idea, as a regulative ideal norm, as

[1] *Author's note:* See § 96, *c*, p. 243.

the logos, in a higher sense, belonging to actually experienced Nature. What that signifies, what it can do for the cognition and control of Nature, every undergraduate "understands" with naïve positiveness. But, for a radical self-understanding and a transcendental criticism of "exact" cognition of Nature, vast problems are implicit here — problems, of course, for a phenomenological inquiry, which, by following the clue offered by an explication of the noematic sense, ⟨exactly cognizable Nature,⟩ must uncover, on the noetic side, the "subjective" constitution of that sense and, going on from there, answer the ultimate questions about it and critically determine its "range".

To what extent similar, though certainly not the same, intentions can enter into the sense of the moral sciences, what regulative ideas are necessary in these and / must be consciously <258>
taken by them as guides to their methods, not perchance in order for them to acquire the exactness of natural science, but to impress on them concepts growing out of themselves and normative for their "higher" logicality — these are yet further new questions, indicating new fields of research for a "logic".

And so we have defined the essence of only a formal theory of science and brought only such a theory into its transcendental form; whereas the full idea of a theory of science, a logic, an ontology, has acquired only its outer frame, and refers the reader to future expositions, which will tell how far we have been able to advance in this respect.

SYNTACTICAL FORMS AND SYNTACTICAL STUFFS; CORE-FORMS AND CORE-STUFFS.

To deepen our insight into the essence of the *judgment-form*, let us further elucidate the distinction, so often employed in the text, between syntactical forms and syntactical stuffs and supplement it with other distinctions essentially connected with it. They all belong in the *form-theory of pure logic* ("the grammar of pure logic"); and, accordingly, wherever we use grammatical expressions like predication, sentence, and clause, we are thinking exclusively of the signification-formations. With this restriction of theme, our concern under the heading *syntax*, and related headings, will be a *descriptive exhibition* of previously unexplored *eidetic structures belonging to the judgment-sphere* — which are obviously relevant, on the other hand, for the grammarian.[1]

§ 1. The articulation of predicative judgments.

First let us take predications of the simplest categorical form, *A is b*. Each is *articulated*, in such a manner that it obviously has two parts; each has, so to speak, a *caesura, A // is b*, between the substrate-member, that "about which" something is predicated, and that which is predicated of it; and here let us take each of these two precisely in the manner in which it stands out observably and describably as a member in the significational unity, *A is b*. Naturally then articulation does not signify division into pieces; since the word "pieces" indicates parts, each of which can also be detached as something self-sufficient. Now it is obvious that at least the predicate-member is not detachable as

[1] *Author's note:* In its essentials the content of this appendix derives from my Göttingen lectures on formal logic — more particularly from their ultimate formulation during the winter semester of 1910–11. In them I attempted, while focusing purely descriptively on the noematic aspect, to project the systematic lines of a theory of the pure forms of predicative significations, as the theoretical basis for an analytics proper.

something self-sufficient. That the same is true of the subject-member will soon become apparent. /

Let us consider a case of more complicated articulation: for <260>
example, the hypothetical judgment, *If A is b, then C is d.* It is sharply articulated as having two parts; it too has a "caesura": *If A is b* // *then C is d.* Each of these members is, in turn, articulated. The hypothetical antecedent and likewise the consequent present themselves, each in respect of its own sense-content, as "modifications" of simple categorical propositions — modifications that, as differing from one another, receive expression, on the one hand, in the form *if A is b* and, on the other hand, in the form *then C is d.* Conformably to the unmodified categorical judgment to which it "refers us", any such modified judgment has a caesura between its modified subject-member and its modified predicate-member. The *A* in the original categorical form, or in any modification of that form, can, in turn, have members within itself, perhaps in the shape of attributive adjuncts. When that is the case, we have a caesura inside *A* itself: a principal member and an attributive collateral member (which may itself have the form of a relative clause).

Thus a unitary proposition can be more or less highly articulated; and we see that it is *not necessary for all members to be on an equal level.* The hypothetical proposition, for example, is articulated immediately as having its antecedent and its consequent. These immediate members, or members on the first level, have, in turn, their own immediate members, which are members on the second level, second-degree members, relative to the whole. And it can go on in this way, to articulations of the third degree, the fourth degree, and so forth. In any proposition, however, we come to *ultimate articulations* and ultimate members, the latter indicated symbolically in our example by *A, b, C,* and *d.*

All members, in the present sense of the word, are *non-selfsufficient* under all circumstances; they are what they are in the whole; and different wholes can have members that are quite alike, but cannot have the same member. If we say, *A is b,* and continue, *A is c,* the two propositions do not have an identical member. The same object *A* is meant twice, but in a different How; and this How itself appertains to the noematic meaning, the opinion (not the meaning act, the opining); it belongs to the

meant as meant, which we call the proposition. Occupying the corresponding places in the two propositions, we have differents, each with a content, *A*, that is quite like that of the other; and these contents are formed differently. Though not expressed, the form, "the same" occurs in the second proposition; and (as we see when we consider the sense closely) it establishes a connexion between the two, which moreover forms them differently. In other words, we have here the unity of an unstated total proposition: *A is b, and the same A is c.* The twice-occuring *A*-that-is-meant has a relational form in each ⟨clause⟩: The second
‹261› ⟨*A*⟩ has identity-relatedness to the / first; from that, however, the first receives a correlative identity-relatedness to the second, as we can learn by examining the sense of the first itself, as it occurs in the total proposition. Such analyses can be made wherever "the same" member occurs (the same "subject", predicate, or object, the same hypothetical antecedent, and so forth).

§ 2. Relatedness to subject-matter in judgments.

In the members of the concrete predicational unity of signification, and likewise in the judgment or proposition as a whole, we can distinguish moments of two kinds. Any self-sufficient proposition relates to some affairs or other and to something or other that they have. In the judged proposition a state-of-affairs is "meant". It will become apparent that this relation to objectivities, the *relatedness* of the proposition to *subject-matter*, as we shall say, is tied to definite moments in the proposition, which we shall call the *stuffs*; whereas this relation is possible — concretely and as a significational relation to something objective — only by virtue of other moments, the moments of *form*.

When we ask how the proposition as a whole brings about its relation to something objective, we observe more particularly, in the first place, that it must always have parts, each of which itself has relation to something objective. *All members* have such a relation; and, in case members are themselves articulated, so do all *their* members, down to the ultimate or intrinsically first members. With these we have what are, *from the point of view of articulation*, the types of partial significations that have ultimate relatedness to subject-matter. They are differentiated as subject-significations, which relate to substrate-objects (objects that become determined), as partial significations relating to properties, and as partial significations relating to relationships. On the other hand, even in the normal verbal expression, it is easy to distinguish parts (we are using "part" in an extremely broad sense, which extends even to non-members), like *is*, *or*, and *because*, that represent moments of signification essentially necessary to the proposition in which they occur, but that *contain in themselves no relatedness to subject-matter*. Naturally this is compatible with the fact that, by virtue of their functions in the proposition, or in a particular member, which as a whole has a relatedness to subject-matter, they participate in this relatedness. But, taken purely as they are in themselves, they involve nothing of the sort. On closer examination we see that every member, including every primitive member, contains such moments, even if, unlike the examples given above, these moments are not expressed by particular words in the complete sentence. /

§ 3. Pure forms and pure stuffs. ‹262›

From this there results, as a contrast to its articulation, a remarkable and totally heterogeneous "partition" of any predicational signification, any "concrete" proposition or proposition-member. On the one hand, we can pick out in these concretions, level by level, the obviously quite non-selfsufficient, quite abstract, moments that *lack* intrinsic relatedness to subject-matter. They are called *moments of pure form*. Then we have left, in every member, and finally in every ultimate member, a nuclear content, likewise something quite abstract, but the very thing that confers upon the member its relatedness to subject-matter. These contents we shall call *stuff-moments*. An example will make everything clear forthwith. If we take, say, subjects of sentences, like *the paper* or *the centaur*, and think of other sentences in which "the same" expressions have a modified function (a different grammatical case) — designating relative Objects, instead of the subjects that become determined — then, when we look at the significational side, something identical does in fact stand out for us. It is the identical something appertaining to the relatedness to subject-matter and maintaining, throughout all such changes of form, the relation to the Same, to *paper*, to *centaur*. Thus we arrive at two limit-concepts: "*pure forms*" and "*pure stuffs*". Both belong necessarily to the concretion; and in such a manner that we shall say: The pure stuffs ultimately make the relatedness to subject-matter possible by being formed at different levels, so that the formation at any particular level always exhibits *relative* stuffs and *relative* forms in its members. The relativity of stuff and form will occupy us further.

The forming, of course, is not an activity that was, or could have been, executed on stuffs given in advance: That would presuppose the countersense, that one could have stuffs by themselves beforehand — as though they were concrete objects, instead of being abstract moments in significations. Nevertheless, by following different lines of abstraction and at the same time varying the propositional formations (with the freedom of a judicative and quasi-judicative phantasying and phantasying-otherwise), we can, as it were, trace the function that the forms and their changes have with respect to the sense-fashioning exercised upon the relation to something objective. In other words, we can gain insight into the manner in which, by means of the essential structures of propositions and proposition-members, their relation to something objective and their differentiation into analytic-formal types are brought about. /.

<263> § 4. Lower and higher forms. Their sense-relation to one another.

Forms are differentiated as *forms of a lower level and forms of a higher level*: as those forms that belong to the lowest members and those that embrace already-formed members and make them into higher-level concretions, shaping them into more complex members or into fully concrete unities, self-sufficient propositions. According to their sense, the higher-level forms relate to the lower-level forms (which does not preclude the fact that, in respect of a universal sense-content, they may be like the lower-forms); and, in this backward relation, they function with respect to the relatedness to subject-matter. The proposition as a whole has forms appertaining to wholeness; and, by their means, it has a unitary relation to the meant as a whole, to what is categorially formed thus and so: the predicatively formed affair-complex. Obviously this relatedness to subject-matter is a founded one, since it presupposes the relatedness of the members to subject-matter and, on the other hand, the functioning of the particular forms belonging to their relatedness to subject-matter. I say "particular" forms, and intend to indicate thereby that, by virtue of the forming of the whole, each member is *formed as entering into* the whole: Its relation to something objective receives the form of a component in the relation of the whole proposition to something objective.

But there is also a second manner in which significational relations of forms to one another become apparent, along with differences (connected with such relations) between an immediate and a mediated relatedness to subject-matter. By virtue of the form, a member intrinsically related to subject-matter sometimes receives an extrinsic relatedness to subject-matter, namely one related to the intrinsic relatedness of another member to subject-matter. For example, if I judge, *This paper is white*, then, as in every categorically determining proposition, the predicate acquires, over an above its own material content, a relation to the subject, *paper*, and engages significationally with the relatedness of the subject to subject-matter. If I judge *bluish white*, instead of just *white*, the previously simple predicate *white* now has, in itself, a secondary determination, one that therefore concerns the primary subject even more mediately.

§ 5. The self-contained functional unity of the self-sufficient apophansis. Division of the combination-forms of wholes into copulatives and conjunctions.

As we had to recognize even in our first analyses, forms are of different sorts and determine the total sense in very diverse manners. Within the significational whole of the proposition, they stand in the / self-contained unity of one function: ⟨the <264>
word⟩ proposition [*Satz*] itself (not as ⟨signifying⟩ a member but as ⟨signifying⟩ the "self-sufficient", self-contained proposition) expresses (among other sense-moments) this functional unity,

with formal universality. In this unity, then, the members are functioning members and accordingly have their functional forms, which can be brought to light in the members themselves.

Yet, along with these forms, the moment of form *combining the members in the whole* also comes to the fore — in most cases, even in the verbal expression. But great differences in the mode of this combination-form also become apparent.

On the one hand, we have combination-forms like *and* and *or* — in short, the ones that are "*conjunctive*" in the amplified sense of the word. They combine; they bring about categorial unity. But in their own sense there lies no trace of that relation which is so exceptionally important everywhere, and particularly for the scientist and the logician: the relation to the judgment (or "proposition") in the pregnant sense, the *predicative,* the "*apophantic*", *judgment.* They themselves do not set up a categorial unity of that sort; nor do they point back to such a unity, whether by some "modification" thereof or otherwise — as they would if what they combine and the combination itself could occur only within a predication (within an apophansis).

On the other hand, we have the mode of "combination" that makes the specific unity-form belonging to a predicative proposition: in traditional phraseology, the form of the copula. We have, so to speak, the *copular unity-form*; and this is what gives unity to the members of the predication — first of all, the members of a simple predication. It is the *is-form* in the various structures wherein it occurs: in the structure of the categorical judgment (the determining judgment); but also in other structures, since obviously it is involved in the unity-structures of hypothetical and of causal judgments, and likewise in every identifying annexation.[1] It is the functional form that, in imposing membership-form on the members, makes them members of the propositional whole, in such a manner that the form of the whole can be abstractively disengaged as the form of their combination.

[1] *Translator's note: Cf.* Appendix I, § 7, Par. 2, p. 303, *infra.*

§6. Transition to the broadest categorial sphere.

a. Universality of the combination-forms that we have distinguished.

When we said that no trace of the copular form is included in the sense proper to those other combination-forms, we did not exclude the possibility that, for reasons external to that sense, they may take on something pertaining to the copular form, either because of *associational apperception* — since we are continually busy / incorporating categorial formations of every <265>
other sort into predications — or because we *combine judgments themselves conjunctively* (or disjunctively, or in some other manner) — as we always can. The combination, as the unity-function uniting the predications categorially, then has a necessary, sense-determining, influence on them as copular wholes and on their copular forms; while, reciprocally, the *and* (for example) in such a function has taken up into its sense something pertaining to the copular formations that it combines. It is clear that, when we observe the full extent of categorial formations (which we have good reason to characterize also as *syntactical*), we must find that the modes of combination here distinguished, the copular and the non-copular, have equal universality, as modes of the combinative forming of categorial objectivities to make new ones.

b. The distinctions connected with articulation can be made throughout the entire categorial sphere.

It is also clear that what we said about articulation, with an exclusive regard to apophantic judgment-formations, applies, with only a slight modification, to *all* "syntactical" formations — for example: to numbers and to "combinations" in the mathematical sense. Thus we have, also with respect to these other formations and their forms, a reduction to ultimate articulations, and a building — partly on a single level, partly on any number of levels — of categorial wholes out of ultimate members. The universality of the forms, which also function as combined with one another — on the correlative subjective side, the universality of the forms of actual or conceivable productive actions (conjunctive, disjunctive, identifyingly copulative, and so forth — precisely this universality results in the ideally reiterable construction of forms *ad infinitum*.

c. The amplified concept of the categorial proposition contrasted with the concept of the proposition in the old apophantic analytics.

All these formations fall under the broadest concept of the proposition as the analytic formation — a formation called "the proposition" ["*Satz*"], not qua correlate of a copulative combining, but qua correlate of a positing, namely the positing of a sense-content having categorial form. Here positing [*Setzung*] is understood as doxa, as belief in being but precisely as positing being [*als Seinssetzung*] — that is: at the same time setting down
<266> in an "utterance", accessible always and to everyone / and giving reason to expect that everyone can share the belief. Therefore the "posited" *being* has here a sense other than the copulative *is*, which belongs only to copulative propositions. In the case of copulative propositions, there combines with the copulative function another sense-fashioning, mediated by the mode of belief inseparable from that function, namely the sense-fashioning peculiar to the positing of being: existent — always and for everyone.[1] Guided by the Aristotelian concept of apophansis (which turns out to be, in fact, a radically fundamental concept), and impelled by motives with which we become acquainted in the main text,[2] traditional apophantic logic, in its judgment-theory, considers under the heading "judgment": *in the first place*, none but categorical propositions (including existential propositions), in all the doxic modalities (these being incorporable into the sense of categorical propositions). In the *second* place, it orders under that heading all conjunctive formations, and other formations, made out of categorical propositions — all the formations that are called on to make a unity of predicative theory.

Though our further investigation will be confined exclusively to this domain (and, indeed, was originally carried out with only this domain in view), let us emphasize beforehand that it can take in a greater universality, such that it would relate to the categorial sphere in its entirety (to the entire sphere of the judgment in the broadest sense and then also to the parallel syntactical formations belonging to the axiological and practical

[1] *Author's note:* For this reason, and also because I regard existential propositions as categorical propositions with anomalously altered subject-significations, I cannot adhere to Brentano's theory of judgment.

[2] *Author's note:* § 47, pp. 131f., *supra*.

spheres). This fact points to very important tasks of description in the total domain of such ideal noematic formations. Nor shall we deny ourselves every glimpse of that greater universality.

§ 7. Syntactical forms, syntactical stuffs, syntaxes.

In consideration of what we presented above concerning the unity-form of a proposition or "judgment" (in the domain of apophantic logic), and also concerning the correlative forming necessary to the members of the unity-form, there result — first of all for the theory of forms of doxic significations (the grammar of "pure logic") — important distinctions that can be shown, purely descriptively, in the propositions themselves (without asking anything about constitutive complexes or about sense-relations that these enable us to make out).

Given any judgment, we can think of others as connected with it copulatively,[1] after the fashion of, let us say, *This paper is white,* / and *This wall is whiter than this (same) paper*. An Aristote- <267>
lian formalization then yields the following: *This S is p,* and *This W is in the relationship ϱ to this (same) S*. Upon closer consideration of such annexations of new judgment-forms having suitable members that are "the same" — annexations that are always possible, given any judgment-form in the sphere of the grammar of pure logic — we can discriminate with eidetic universality, in judgments of any form and in all their members, not only describable differences of form but also describable *stratifications of form.* These we now intend to follow up.

In the first place, we shall be able to comprehend what stands out describably and *immediately* with the concepts we have used up to now: form and stuff. That is to say, we shall separate forthwith *subject-form* and *form of the predicate,* as the form of that which determines the subject in question; and, on the predicate side, "adjectival" *property-predicate* and *relationship-predicate.* Furthermore, when we compare our examples or their forms, and note that *this paper,* or the form *this S,* makes its appearance one time as <the subject or> the subject-form, the form of the substrate that is being determined, and another time as <the Object or> the Object-form within the relatival predicate, we can separate (as we did in § 3 of this appendix):

[1] *Translator's note: Cf.* Appendix III, § 2, pp. 335 f. *infra.*

on the one hand, the same *stuff-content*, which makes its appearance one time in the subject-form and the other time, in the predicate, in the Object-form and, on the other hand, these two *forms themselves*. The latter obviously are pure forms and belong immediately to the unitary functional form of the predication. But we see also that, *at first*, in making this separation between form and stuff, we have had to take the concept of stuff only as *relative* — that is to say: not as ⟨the concept of⟩ pure stuff; since, even in such simple examples, more form (*pure* form) can be distinguished in the same content that enters into the different functional forms.

At all events, we may say regarding the *pure total form of the apophantic unity*, as a form *including the pure part-forms belonging to it*: It is the *unity of the syntaxes* by which the identical *stuffs remaining after the syntaxes have been abstracted* (*this paper*), ⟨adjectival⟩ *white*, and the like) are *syntactically formed*. Accordingly subject-form, object-form, and so forth, are *syntactical forms*. It should be heeded that *these* stuffs — the *syntactical stuffs*, as we say — are such moments of the judgment as become distinguishable by abstraction from the above-mentioned *functional forms*, the syntactical forms. Thus among *syntactical stuffs are included*, for example, the substantive, as identical throughout changes in its syntactical form, and the "adjective", as identical regardless of the different syntaxes in which it occurs. /

<268> § 8. SYNTAGMA AND MEMBER. SELF-SUFFICIENT JUDGMENTS, AND LIKEWISE JUDGMENTS IN THE AMPLIFIED SENSE, AS SYNTAGMAS.

When we again take the syntactical stuffs in their forms, accordingly as concretely united with their forms, we call the unity of syntactical stuff and form the *syntagma*. It is the unity of the proposition-member, which is formed stuff; and for members in propositions the following eidetic law obtains: *Different members* can have *the same form but different stuffs*; and, conversely, they can have *different forms but the same stuff*.

This law holds good for members of a predication, no matter how complicated its structure or how many other propositions may make their appearance within it, in the syntactically modified shape of proposition-members.

But the law holds good also *for self-sufficient propositions* — whatever their structure and the degree of their complexity may be — on account of the eidetic law that, in formal universality and according to definite types, any proposition can undergo modifications that convert it into a syntactical member of higher-level predications. Thus every whole proposition is, so to speak, itself a "member", since it has the essential structures, and admits of the syntactical modifications, proper to a member as such. In a word, *the complete proposition too*, as a self-sufficient predicational whole, *is a syntagma*, a unity of syntactical stuff in a syntactical form.

And now let us take it into consideration, that meant categorial objectivities of whatever sort are rightly called so because they either are themselves predications or can occur in predications, and that their analytic forms and the analytic forms of possible predications stand in a corresponding relationship. Hence it follows that the universe of possible predications must include the universe of all categorialia of every sort. And, in consideration of this, it is clear that *judgments in the amplified sense* — all meant categorial objectivities whatever — are *syntagmas*, and come under the structural laws indicated by that name.

§ 9. The "judgment-content" as the syntactical stuff of the judgment qua syntagma.

For the sake of elucidation, particularly of the conception of whole predicative propositions as syntagmas, let us cite examples.

Wherever we have a complex proposition that can be divided into "pieces" — for example the judgment, *Because foggy weather set in, the military / operations were hindered,* — each <269>
piece in the whole is given as a syntactically formed piece, a member. If one piece — the first, let us say — is made self-sufficient, the member, as it is, does not become self-sufficient; rather, a self-sufficient proposition having the same "*judgment-content*" is made: the proposition, *Foggy weather set in*. Contrariwise, a syntactical change, such as is possible in the case of *any* self-sufficient proposition, could begin with the proposition just

stated — a change, namely, into a member of some other proposition. When a change of this sort has taken place, the proposition that has now become non-selfsufficient retains the same "content"; we simply say, *"the same proposition"*, on one occasion as a *proposition by itself*, on another occasion as an *antecedent proposition*, a *consequent proposition*, or the like. Being self-sufficient must itself be regarded as a syntactical form. Throughout the change of the functions in which "the same" proposition takes on various forms, as antecedent, as member in a disjunction, and so forth, there stands out, as something identical, the same "proposition-material" or "judgment-material" — that is to say: the same predicational *syntactical stuff*, which takes on different syntactical forms: proposition by itself, antecedent, consequent, and so forth. What we have been saying holds good with formal universality; it holds good, accordingly, for the corresponding proposition-forms, as forms of syntagmas. Consequently we can subject any proposition-form to a free variation — and do so reiteratively, without limit, — a variation in which we vary the syntactical forms while conserving the entire predicational stuff, as conceived *in forma* (while conserving what is, in an important sense, the form of their "material"); and we can do likewise with the member-forms; in short, we can do so with all the forms of self-sufficient or non-selfsufficient syntagmas.[1] /

<270> § 10. LEVELS OF SYNTACTICAL FORMING.

It is clear that, in contrast to the infinity of identical syntactical stuffs, the number of syntactical forms (subject, predi-

[1] *Author's note:* If we turn back from here to § 89, *a*, pp. 215ff., of the main text of this essay, the section concerning the possibility of distinct evidence, we recognize that, although everything stated there is correct, its significance becomes much deeper when the more radical concept of judgment-material, which we have now worked out, is brought into service. It is clear, namely, that, if a judgment-material having its unity of identity throughout changes in the "qualities" (that is: in the modalizations of certainty) can acquire distinct evidentness, then it is essentially possible for any of its syntactical variants to attain such an evidentness. (Here we are still using the word "judgment-material" in the sense that it has in the section referred to above, its sense as used in the *Logische Untersuchungen, II. Bd., I. Teil*, pp. 426 ff. [*Cf.* Farber, *op. cit.*, pp. 356f.]) The possibility of making any one of *these* variants distinct makes it certain in advance that all other such variants can be made distinct. But obviously that signifies that, in an extremely deep sense, the possibility of distinct evidentness is attached to the "judgment-material" in the more radical sense of the word: the total syntactical stuff of the judgment (or of the syntactical variant of a judgment) that is under consideration. — Naturally this radical concept of judgment-material applies throughout the sphere of judgments in the amplified sense.

cate, Object, attribute, the mentioned total predicational forms, and others) is restricted. And, though any syntactical stuff can take on manifold forms, naturally that is not to say that every stuff can take on every form; that this is not the case can be seen forthwith when we consider the members of a simple categorical predication.

When we penetrate more deeply, it becomes apparent that syntactical forms are separated according to *levels*: *Certain forms* — for example: those of the subject and the predicate — make their appearance *at all levels* of compositeness. Thus a whole proposition can function as a subject just as well as a simple "substantive" can. *Other forms*, however, such as those of the hypothetical antecedent and consequent, ***demand stuffs that are already syntactically articulated in themselves.***

Thus it is clear also that, within a total member, forms can make their appearance that are unlike the syntactical forms of of the members subordinate to it. Let us further elucidate this by another example: The conjunctive combination, *the philosopher Socrates and the philosopher Plato*, or, in the same fashion, the disjunctive combination, *the philosopher Socrates or the philosopher Plato*, can make its appearance in a proposition as a single member, perhaps in the syntactical form of the subject-member of a unitary, conjunctive or disjunctive, predication. But, in that unitary member, other members make their appearance: *the philosopher Socrates, the philosopher Plato*; and each of these has, in turn, its syntactical form, which, however, is not like the form of the whole.

§ 11. NON-SYNTACTICAL FORMS AND STUFFS — EXHIBITED WITHIN THE PURE SYNTACTICAL STUFFS.

The concepts of form and stuff that we have treated up to now are concepts relating to syntagmas. Thus, syntactical forms are forms of proposition-members and of propositions themselves (since a functional change can turn propositions into members of other possible propositions). A separate proposition, we were saying, is the unity of a self-contained function; and all the member-forms are essentially the partial forms belonging to the total function. The stuffs entering into the member-forms, and presupposed by them, likewise have (as we are about to show)

a certain *forming*; but it is of *quite a different ultimate sort.*
<271> In other words: / the forms belonging immediately and syntactically to the unity of the predication, as an is-unity, a copular unity, presuppose *forms of an entirely new style* in the ultimate stuffs. These forms do *not* belong to the *syntax* of the proposition itself.

To make this clearer, our best course is to follow directly the natural sequence of levels at which propositions are articulated: to proceed, that is, from their immediate members to the members of these members, and so on in the same manner until we come to the ultimate members, the ones that cannot be further analyzed into members. The syntactical stuffs of these ultimate members are distinguished by the fact that they are pure stuffs, free, that is, from syntactical forms. Among them are included, for example, substantives like *paper* and *man* — abstracted from the subject-form, the Object-form, the this-form, and so forth — and likewise adjectives such as *white* and *round*. If we now compare *different pure or ultimate syntactical stuffs such as these*, as they make their appearance in different propositions, in no matter what syntactical forms, we note that, *despite their difference*, they can still have *a distinguishable identical moment in common*. If, for example we compare the pure stuff *paper*, the pure stuff *man*, and so forth, an essentially universal moment of form comes to the fore for us — in formalizing universality: something or other which is "substantival" form. In the same fashion the "adjectival" form stands out for us, as does the form of the "relative", which can be grasped in such relatives as *like*, *similar*, and *greater*. Infinitely many contents can be put into one and the same form: Single substantives, for example, differ in content but have the same form. We thus arrive at a restricted group of utterly novel — that is: non-syntactical — forms; and all the ultimate syntactical stuffs, each of which presents itself as a unity of form and content, are grouped according to the *novel categories of pure grammar*: *substantivity* and *adjectivity* — the latter being divided into the category of *properties* and the category of *relationships* [*Adjektivität als Eigenschaftlichkeit und als Relationalität*].

§ 12. The core-formation, with core-stuff and core-form.

The place of the syntagma has now been taken by a *specifically different unity of stuff and form*: this or that substantive itself, property[1] itself, or relative itself, as included in the syntactical stuff. And every syntactical stuff must, as a matter of essential necessity, include such a unity; which means that we have reached a *deeper structure* of any predication whatever, a structure present in all its syntaxes and, specifically, in the syntactical stuffs. We call that unity the *core-formation.* /

Up to now, therefore, we had not penetrated to the ultimate <272>
formal structures. To make this plain, a new step in our descriptive analysis is needed.

When we compare the core-formations, *similarity* and *similar,* or *redness* and adjectival *red,* we see that, in every such pair, *core-formations belonging to different categories* are contrasted, but they have, in their stuff-aspects, *an essential moment in common. Redness* and adjectival *red* have a community of "content" within the different forms belonging to them respectively as core-formations, the forms that define the categories of substantivity and adjectivity. To the ideally identical something called the core-formation there belongs unchangingly its particular category; the core-formation is, after all, the syntactical stuff, which persists throughout changes in the syntactical function, which comes under fixed categories, and which admits of changes in its content while the category itself remains identical. The fully determined substantive, adjective, and relative, are syntactical stuffs; and we designate them according to the corresponding categories, which pertain to them by virtue of their essences. On the other hand, it is now apparent that such syntactical stuffs, when taken as core-formations belonging to different categories, can still have something identical in common, something that is therefore more deeply enclosed within these stuffs. We call it the *core-stuff* of the particular core-formation or, as we can also say, the core-stuff of the syntactical stuff. The correlate of this core-stuff — called the *core,* for short — is the core-form. It is what forms the core into a core belonging to its definite category; it is thus what makes the unitary core-formation

[1] *Translator's note:* Reading *Eigenschaft* instead of *Prädikat.*

or syntactical stuff: The essential something that *similarity* and *similar*, for example, have in common is formed, in the one case, in the category of substantivity and, in the other case, in the category of adjectival relationality. And thus, in each case, it is formed into a definite syntactical stuff.

§ 13. Pre-eminence of the substantival category. Substantivation.

We have not yet added the eidetic law in which a notable *pre-eminence of the substantival category* becomes expressed. Every adjective and every relative has as its counterpart a corresponding substantive, the "substantivized" adjective or relative. But there is no adjectivation (in a proper sense) of no matter what substantives. Such substantives as *similarity* and *redness* offer themselves as, according to their own sense, "modifications"; their senses are secondary, referring us to the original,
‹273› non-substantival senses. With this characteristic / there is connected an essential possibility of transforming certain propositions syntactically — for example: transforming the proposition *This roof is red,* into the proposition, *Redness is a property of this roof,* or else into *The redness of this roof* .... On the other hand, this is not a merely syntactical transmutation; it is, at the same time, a transmutation of the core-formations, taking place in a different stratum.

§ 14. Transition to complications.

Thus, in the sphere of predicative significations, we have attained a *reduction to the ultimate "elements"*, namely the *"stuffs" in the most ultimate sense of all,* such stuffs as have no significational forms of any sort and underlie all the formings of different sorts and at different levels. These ultimate elements have the *ultimate forms,* the core-forms.

All our considerations have been directly aimed at the ultimately elementary; but consideration of the higher complications will yield something else of importance: The structural distinction that we made apparent within the ultimate syntactical stuffs obtains in the case of all other syntactical stuffs without exception; and it can be made apparent in them all, in a quite similar manner, by putting suitable examples together and bringing out the ideally identical essential contents. Any categorial formation that does not already have "nominal" or "substantival" form can, as the *Logische Untersuchungen* expressed it, be *"nominalized"*; and here too, speaking more precisely, it is not the concrete formation, but its total syntactical stuff, that receives a substantival form — "substantival" in the amplified sense. We shall have to say that, here, a proposition-material (in the sense: "proposition" as syntactical stuff) has, as alternative core-categories, the category of substantivity and the category of proposition existing by itself — the latter designating, on the one hand, a syntactical form and, on the other hand, what this form has essentially in common with forming in ⟨the category of⟩ "substantivity". With this forming, as in the case of any other substantivation, a syntactical alteration goes hand in hand.

But the more detailed development of these questions, and their deeper treatment, will be left to future researches.

§ 15. The concept of the "term" in traditional formal logic.

Traditional logic has worked out as good as nothing pertaining to these distinctions, though they do occasionally / crop out in it. <274>
Indeed, it is clear forthwith that the concept of core-stuff, which we have fixed, coincides in the essentials with what traditional logic has designated as the *term* — quite vaguely, without attempting more precise definition and, moreover, without using the concept beyond a narrowly limited sphere. Use of the word terms is adapted, that is to say, to the traditional syllogistics. The judgment-forms of universal, particular, singular, and other such judgments are expressed symbolically by *All A's are b*, *Some A's are b*, and so forth. In like manner the form of the hypothetical proposition is expressed by *If M is, then N is.* When we ask ourselves what the letters indicate here, it seems at first to be a matter of syntactical stuffs. But when we note, for example, that in the argument, *All men are mortal, All mortals are perishable*, and so forth, *mortal* and *mortals* are taken to be the same term, from the standpoint of syllogistics, and are designated by the same letter, it becomes apparent that the differences among the core-forms are disregarded. Therefore term cannot be

understood here as designating the syntactical stuff; rather it must be understood as designating the *core-stuff*, which remains identical when the core-form changes.

Instead of term, people very often say *concept*. But the word concept is loaded with a multiplicity of ambiguities; and therefore we cannot use it in this sense without more ado. At all events, by means of the concept of core-stuff, one of the significations of the word "concept" is scientifically fixed.

Regarding this concept of the term or concept, we should note that, in conformity with the whole sense of analytics, the extension of this concept is not confined to ultimate core-stuffs. It is essentially broadened by our broadening of the concepts, substantive and adjective [1] — and consequently of the concept core-stuff — which raises them above the level of the primitive concepts suggested by our memory of the grammatical word-forms ⟨called by the same names⟩. Thus, for example, a proposition having the form, *That S is p implies that Q is r*, presents two substantives — that is: two "substantivized" propositions — in the forms, "antecedent" and "consequent". Analytics, which, in respect of its theme, aims at the system of laws governing formal consequence-relationships and consistency [*formale "Konsequenz"*], does not seek out ultimate cores; in its proposition-forms, analytics leaves undecided the question of whether the terms are substantivized categorial formations or not.[2] /

[1] *Author's note:* See the preceding sections.

[2] *Author's note:* See Appendix III.

PHENOMENOLOGICAL CONSTITUTION OF THE JUDGMENT. ORIGINALLY ACTIVE JUDGING AND ITS SECONDARY MODIFICATIONS.

§ 1. Active judging, as generating objects themselves, contrasted with its secondary modifications.

Active judging is a generating of "objects of thinking", categorial formations. Its essence involves the possibility (a word that signifies here subjective ability, "I can") of progressing to higher and higher levels — the possibility, ideally speaking, of a reiteration *in infinitum*. Any judging generates a supposed predicatively formed affair-complex. A simply determining ("categorical") judging, for example, generates a supposed predicatively formed affair-complex, *S is p*, in which the determinable substrate, *S*, becomes determined as *p*. This same judging also generates, simultaneously, the categorial result, *Sp*. That is to say, the *p* has entered, as a "precipitate", *into the sense* of the *S*, which is determined by it from now on. At the next level, the *S is p* (for example) may become the foundation of a new judging: Taking on new categorial forms, it may become a member in conjunctive, hypothetical, and other judgments. Or the judging may proceed differently, perhaps in such a fashion that the *Sp* becomes the determinable substrate of the new judgment, *Sp is q*. And in such manners the process can continue. Every newly generated judgment can thus become the foundation for new judgments, *in infinitum*. The same thing is true, obviously, if we take as our basis the amplified judgment-concept that predominates in the later parts of the present essay — and coincides with the concept of the (doxic) categorial objectivity, taken universally and as such.

Active judging is not the only, but it is the original, form of judging. It is the sole form in which the supposed categorial objectivity, as such, becomes actually and properly generated. It is, in other words, the only form of judging in which the "judgment" becomes itself-given originaliter. All the other manners of givenness of the same judgment are characterized intrinsically as *intentional modifications* of the actively generative, the original manner. We have here a particular case of the precedence that belongs to originality, according to an eidetic law, which has validity for *every* object-constitution, whether passive or active. /

<276> From here let us first of all digress into the general theory of intentionality, where we can gather cognitions that will enable us subsequently to gain deeper insights into our present theme.

§ 2. From the general theory of intentionality.

a. Original consciousness and intentional modification. Static intentional explication. Explication of the "meaning" and of the meant "itself". The multiplicity of possible modes of consciousness of the Same.

One and the same object can, *a priori*, be intended to in very different modes of consciousness (certain essential types: perception, recollection, empty consciousness). Among them the "experiencing" mode, the original mode of consciousness of the object in question, has a precedence; to it all others are related as intentional modifications.

But *intentional* modifications have, quite universally, the *intrinsic* property of *pointing back* to something unmodified. The modified manner of givenness, when, so to speak, we interrogate it, tells us itself that it is a modification *of* an original manner of givenness, to which it points. For the subject of the consciousness (and consequently for everyone who puts himself in that subject's place and understands such modes of consciousness in following him), that makes it possible, starting from the particular non-original manner of givenness, to strive toward the original one and perhaps make it explicitly present to himself in phantasy, at the same time making the object-sense "*clear*" to himself. The fulfilling clarification takes place with the transition to a synthesis in which the object of a non-original mode of consciousness becomes given either as the same as the object of consciousness in the mode "experience" (the mode "it itself") or else as the same object "clarified" — that is to say: as it "would" be itself-given in a "possible experience". In the event of, so to speak, negative clarification, clear countersense is brought out by the synthesis.

Every manner of intentional givenness, as a "consciousness-of", can be ***explicated "statically"*** in this fashion — not taken to pieces, but spread out intentionally and asked about its clear sense; and, with synthetical transitions that lead to possible self-givenness, this sense can be either produced or brought to clear self-annulment.

If it is a matter of those modes of consciousness whose original form is a generating by *synthetic activity*, it turns out that, as the text shows specifically in the case of judicative activity, two intentionalities and givings of something itself are in question here; and that the activity of / judging, as originally generating <277>
the judgment itself (merely *as* a judgment), combines, of essential necessity, with the activity of originally shaping (of making evident) the categorial objectivity itself, the corresponding predicatively formed affair-complex itself: the predicatively formed affair-complex in the mode, experience. This holds good for every sort of activity, since these two stand in mutual contrast quite universally: the activity of generatively constituting the *meaning*, merely as a meaning, and the activity of constituting the corresponding "It Itself". But ultimately something similar holds good, with the broadest universality and as a matter of essential necessity, for *every* intentionality — with respect to the giving of the mere meaning (sense) itself and the giving of the object "itself".

The property essential to any non-original consciousness, its property of "referring" intrinsically, as a "modification" of a corresponding original consciousness, to possible "experiences", possible modes of original consciousness of the Same — and, in case these, as "imperfect", are mixtures of originality and non-originality, its property of referring us to synthetical chains of possible progressive experience — this essential property has a counterpart. It lies in the fact that, conversely, every manner of original givenness carries with it its possibilities of transition to "corresponding" manners of non-original givenness, which can be united with it synthetically and belong to a fixed set of types. To be sure, we cannot speak of a *counterreference* here, as a reference in the proper sense, such as we find in the "intentional modifications". But, at all events, *every consciousness* has, of essential necessity, its place in a particular *multiplicity of conscious-*

ness that corresponds to it, a synthetic open infinity of possible modes of consciousness of the Same — a multiplicity that has, so to speak, its teleological center in the possible "experience". That betokens, in the first place, a horizon of *fulfilling* evidence, with It Itself anticipated as "to be actualized". At the same time, however, there remains essentially open the counter-possibility of an undeceiving *annulment* of the anticipated, with the form, "instead of that, something else" — a possibility that indicates a counterform of the centered multiplicity. — This prescribes for all "intentional analysis" the most general nature of its method.

b. Intentional explication of genesis. The genetic, as well as static, originality of the experiencing manners of givenness. The "primal instituting" of "apperception" with respect to every object-category.

"*Static*" *analysis* is guided by the unity of the supposed object. It starts from the unclear manners of givenness and, following the
<278> reference made by them as intentional modifications, / it strives toward what is clear. *Genetical intentional analysis*, on the other hand, is directed to the whole concrete nexus in which each particular consciousness stands, along with its intentional object as intentional. Immediately the problem becomes extended to include the other intentional references, those belonging to the *situation* in which, for example, the subject exercising the judicative activity is standing, and to include, therefore, the *immanent unity of the temporality* of the life that has its "*history*" therein, in such a fashion that every single process of consciousness, as occurring temporally, has its own "history" — that is: its *temporal genesis*.

In this connexion it becomes apparent — and this too is an all-pervasive essential peculiarity of intentional life — that the *original form* of consciousness, "*experience*" in the broadest sense (which is treated of in detail in the present essay), has not only a static but *also a genetic priority* to its intentional variants. *Genetically too the original* [*die originale*] *manner of givenness is* — in a certain fashion — *the primitive one* [*die ursprüngliche*]. It is genetically primitive, namely, for every fundamental sort of objectivities, in the sense that no mode of non-original consciousness of objects belonging to a fundamental sort is essentially possible, unless there has previously occurred, in the synthetic unity of immanent temporality, the corresponding mode of original consciousness of the Same — as, *genetically*, the "*primally institutive*" mode of consciousness, back to which every mode of non-original consciousness points genetically (as well as statically).

That is not to say that we cannot be conscious of any objectivities in a non-original manner unless we have previously experienced them originally — as the same ones. In a completely empty anticipation, for example, something can be indicated for us that we have never seen. But the fact that we objectivate physical things, and even see them at a glance — and here it must be taken into consideration that every perception of a physical thing includes empty anticipations of what is not itself seen —, refers us back, in the course of our intentional genetical analysis, to the fact that the *type*, experience of a physical thing, had its rise in an earlier, primally institutive, genesis, and that the category, physical thing, was thereby instituted for us with its initial sense. But, as becomes evident, that holds good, as a matter of essential necessity, for any object-category whatever, in the broadest sense, even for the category, "immanent" Datum of sensation, and, on the other hand, for every objectivity at the level of objectivities produced by thinking, of judgment-formations and furthermore of truly existing theories — also at the level of axiological and practical formations, of practical projects and the like. /

This is connected with the fact that every manner of original givenness has a *double genetic after-effect. Firstly*, its after-effect in the form of possible recollective reproductions, *via* retentions that attach themselves to it quite immediately by a process of original genesis; and, *secondly*, its "apperceptional" after-effect, which is such that anything (no matter how it is already constituted) that is present in a similar new situation will be apperceived in a similar manner. ‹279›

This makes possible a consciousness of objects that have themselves never yet been *given* in a consciousness, and a consciousness of objects as having determinations that they were never given as having — but precisely on the basis of the givenness of similar objects, or similar determinations, in similar situations. These are *facts pertaining to the intentional essence of empeiria* and the "association" constituting it; but they are *not empirical facts*. Static analysis takes the object-sense and, starting from its manners of givenness, follows up and explicates the "proper and actual" sense, consulting those manners of givenness as intentional references to the possible "It Itself". In like fashion, the intentionality of the concrete nexus, the *temporal nexus*, in which everything static is involved, must be consulted, and its *genetical references* must be intentionally explicated.

c. The time-form of intentional genesis and the constitution of that form. Retentional modification. Sedimentation in the inconspicuous substratum (unconsciousness).

The all-embracing essential form of intentional genesis, to which all its other forms relate back, is that of the constitution of immanent temporality, which governs each concrete life of consciousness with a rigid regularity and gives all processes of conscious-ness an abiding temporal being. Stated more precisely: a life of consciousness is inconceivable, except as a life given originally in an essentially necessary form of factualness, the form of the all-embracing temporality wherein each process of consciousness has its identical temporal locus, which it receives throughout the flowing changes in its typically modifed manners of givenness within a living present, and then retains abidingly by virtue of essential sources pertaining to habituality.

To select only one main point: Each mental process that makes its appearance in the primitive mode, immanent presentness, (and, *as* making its appearance thus, is itself also an object of consciousness) is followed, with inalterable necessity, by a „retentional" consciousness, as an original modification by virtue
<280> of which the primitive mode, "given at present", / goes over, in a continuous synthesis, into the modified form, the Same that "just now" was. As now present, this modified consciousness functions, in accordance with the same law, as the primitive mode relative to a new modification (a modification of the modification); and so on, continuously.

In itself, every such modification obviously refers us back, either immediately or medicately, to its absolute primitive mode

— to a consciousness that, to be sure, becomes modified forthwith but is not itself a modification. This undergoing of continuous retentional modification is the essential initial part of the constitution of an identical object, one that, in the broadest sense, persists. Instead of investigating this constitution any further here in its universality, we shall, in the next section, study it more closely in its particularity as the constitution of persisting categorial formations.

Continuous retentional modification proceeds up to an essentially necessary *limit*. That is to say: with this intentional modification there goes hand in hand a *gradual diminution of prominence*; and precisely this has its limit, at which the formerly prominent subsides into the *universal substratum* — the so-called *"unconscious"*, which, far from being a phenomenological nothing, is itself a limit-mode of consciousness. The whole intentional genesis relates back to this substratum of sedimented prominences, which, as a horizon, accompanies every living present and shows its own continuously changing sense when it becomes "awakened".

After this digression into the general phenomenology of intentionality, and accordingly into the methodological horizons pertaining also to our particular problem, that of the judgment, let us go back and, in treating this problem, utilize the extremely general insights that we have acquired.

§ 3. Non-original manners of givenness of the judgment.

a. The retentional form as the intrinsically first form of "secondary sensuousness". The livingly changing constitution of a many-membered judgment.

Over against the originally generative manner of givenness of the judgment, we have first as non-original, as not actually generative, its *retentional* manner of givenness. Among the modified manners of givenness this is *intrinsically the first*, the one from which all the others derive. Naturally, by virtue of the described regularity of time-constituting consciousness, / the judicative <281>
action in its original flow (like every other mental process) is followed continuously by its retentional modifications. More generally, this modification, as the modification of an *active generation* (other such processes being the activities of "emotion and volition",

with their constitutings of concrete values, ends, means), can be characterized as follows: Wherever an original constitution of an objectivity of consciousness is effected by an activity (perhaps a many-membered synthesis of co-ordinated and subordinated component actions), the *original action* changes, with retentional continuity, *into a secondary form*, which is no longer an activity; that is to say, it changes into a passive form, the form of a "*secondary sensuousness*", as we call it. By virtue of the continuous identifying synthesis, the passive consciousness is a consciousness of the same that was constituted "just now" with an active originativeness. Specifically, then, in the judgment-sphere this signifies: The judgment does not exist only in and during the active constitution, as being livingly generated in this process; rather it becomes the continuously abiding selfsame judgment, as a preserved *acquisition* dependent on functionings of passivity, these being involved everywhere in the constitution of identically persisting unities, including formations produced actively. So far we have seen only that the acquisition, as an abiding one, is constituted, in the first place, during the living progression of retentional modification, up to the limit where the acquisition is no longer prominent.

Without this sort of preservation in a passive continuous identification, advancing judgment-processes — as a living further-forming and connecting of meant catgorialia to make the unity of continually new judgments at higher and higher levels — would not be possible. The retentionally subsiding component formations remain, with this modification, within the scope of the judger's unitarily thematizing regard; he can reach back and seize them again, each as having its identical sense; also, in consequence of the new judgment-steps, they can undergo further accretions of sense in new formings. Only thus can the process of synthetic judgment-formation consciously conclude with the unity of something that has come into being as a complicated many-membered formation, which, upon its completion, no longer includes in their originality *any* of the originally generated products belonging to its various levels and members. Only their modifications are left, as greatly changed in the generating; but, throughout the passively flowing changes, the intentional unity of each component formation is preserved by the continuous identification. In this living constitution the component formations pertain to that primitive activity which makes given, in an original producing, the judgment-formation at the upper level and which has *finished* that formation at the point of its own conclusion. / That "finished" formation itself <282> undergoes in turn retentional modification; a subsequent judging can begin with it and shape it further.

b. Passive recollection and its constitutional effect for the judgment as an abiding unity.

Nevertheless, when we say that, because of the manner in which active genesis changes in accordance with laws of passive modification, every categorial activity leads to an *abiding acquisition*, we can mean something else too, and normally we always do mean something else: Every judging leads to a judgment-result that is, from then on, and not merely during its living retention, an *enduring "result"* for the judger, an intellectual acquisition that is at his free disposal whenever he pleases. Thus we are referred here to something beyond the already-described, first and living, acquisition by original generation and ensuing retentions. The universal eidetic laws of passive genesis are involved here and, along with them, the universal eidetic laws of object-constitution (as a constitution of "existing objects", with identity for me, for us, and accessible as the same ones at any time): the *eidetic* laws of *"association"* and of associative constitution. They include the eidetic laws governing the formation of *apperceptions*. The laws of passive genesis encompass the total sphere of consciousness, *as the sphere of immanent temporality*, in which every active operation of consciousness (every mental activity emanating from the Ego-pole) also has its temporal position and temporal form — it and what it produces originally as a syntactical formation. Consequently the active operation and its product enter forthwith into associational awakenings; and, on the other hand, when they sink down into the substratum through the medium of retention, they have their apperceptive after-effect and can accordingly participate variously in new object-constitutions, not only those that are passive but also those that are actively generative.

This is true, then, of categorial acts and, correlatively, of categorial formations. A proposition, a proof, a numerical formation, or the like, can come to mind because of associations, long after the original generating has disappeared; and, though given after the fashion of something that comes to mind memorially, it can play a part in new originative actions of judgment. The "result" of the earlier originative activity is picked up again, and something new is made with it; but picking it up does *not* involve *repeating the activity*. /

<283> **c. The emergence of something that comes to mind apperceptionally is analogous to something coming to mind after the fashion of passive recollection.**

But other formations can come to our mind, formations that, to be sure, are analogues of those that come to mind memorially, but are not themselves things coming to mind memorially, not formations that we ever produced actively, in an original manner. Yet we have indeed produced analogous ones and, precisely because of the analogy, these other formations can make their appearance after the fashion of modifications, as things coming to mind: as analogues of passive recollections and as, in fact, pointing back accordingly to their own genesis from earlier, similarly formed, judgments. All this can be made understandable on the basis of associative intentionality and the eidetic laws governing it. If we could speak of these things that come to mind as making their appearance apperceptionally, we could certainly speak thus, and in a more normal sense, wherever sensuous Data of perception, or their reproductions, awaken the categorial formations referred to, which then make their appearance in a manner quite analogous to that in which the formations that come to mind make *theirs* — though we are not in the habit of expressing ourselves in that manner.

For this there are understandable grounds: As soon as the *sign, expression,* or other perceptual object, that awakens something associatively and, on the other hand, the objects that makes its appearance apperceptionally because of an awakening or analogue thereof — as soon, I say, that these two become *thematic as a unit* and there consequently takes place a bilateral-unitary object-constitution (in the pregnant sense: constitution of a thematic object), the perceptually awakened does not affect in and of itself, nor does it become a thematic object by itself. Rather the awakened now has the character of a component, though a component that "matters", one that is signified or designated. The *preferential* thematizing regard goes "through" the sensuously given sign to what the sign designates. At the same time, however, the sign itself is a transitional theme; with the thematic telos, the sign makes up a closed, unitarily prominent objectivity, already given as a unit before being turned to; and therefore the sign is also ready to become thematic and may indeed become so, even contrary to its normal function.

§ 4. The essential possibilities of activating passive manners of givenness.

In all the secondary manners of givenness encountered in our last considerations — retentional manners of givenness, recollections proper (which, by the way, / can arise also in immediate <284>
connexion with retentions, involuntarily or voluntarily but, in either case, as associatively conditioned), and, finally, things that come to mind apperceptionally, whether in a seemingly free manner or as combined with outstanding "perceptions" — in all of these we have to do with "modifications", which, as such, point back phenomenologically to original activity.

It is to be noted furthermore that here, as everywhere else that references of this sort are present, there is included the consciousness of a freedom, of a practical possibility of restoring the sort of givenness that pertains to original activity, the sort that gives the formations properly, that gives them-themselves. If the restoration succeeds, a synthesis of fulfilling-identifying coincidence necessarily takes place: the consciousness of going, from the passively supposed, back to the meant *itself*. If, by means of a reawakening, in the form of passive recollection, in the form of a passive coming to mind, I re-encounter my old conviction with which I judged *S is p* and thereby acquired *Sp*, then *Sp* stands there, reawakened for me, in a manner similar to that in which it was "still given in consciousness" and "still in my grip" with the passive retention that followed my judging on the previous occasion; except that now the having in my grip, or rather the laying hold once more, has the phenomenological mode, Again: seizing upon something again, and seizing upon it, moreover, as still accepted by me, still remaining with me, *still my own conviction*.

But, instead of letting the matter rest with this passive re-emergence, this passive becoming re-aware of my judgment, I can *actually reactivate* it, seriously reproduce it, generate it, the same one, in a renewed and actual activity; I can change the emerging *Sp* back into *S is p* and at the same time constitute *Sp* in renewed activity — that is: originally. In the same fashion, to every other modification as something coming to mind, there belongs for consciousness the possibility of activation proper (at the same time, then, the possibility of a fulfilling access to "It Itself") — the consciousness of the ability to carry out an actual activity, which, naturally, like every other practical intention of consciousness, can have its modes of success and failure.

§ 5. The fundamental types of originally generative judging and of any judging whatever.

Let us apply this, first of all, to the important differentiation that the concept of *actively* judicative generating of supposed categorial objectivities (active judging in the broader sense) can undergo, as can the concept of any judging whatever. /

<285> *Originally generative* ("explicit") judging, as a process that begins and goes on in the form of synthetic unity, as a judging at higher and higher levels, can —

Firstly, be original activity "through and through". In this case, every categorial part-objectivity making its appearance in the formed and further formed categorial objectivity, functioning in it as a foundation for higher formations, has been originally generated in the active aliveness of the judgment-process; and consequently the highest whole itself that has come into being has, through and through, the originality of something that is itself given — itself given as a "supposed or meant categorial objectivity", a judgment in our amplified sense.

Secondly: The other case, which is usual, is the one in which the activity of judgment starts with old judgment-acquisitions, categorial objectivities that re-emerge and are received passively as given in this modified manner. For example, "long-known" propositions are again turned to account; or else substrate-objects that become themes of determinations carry, as sedimentations within their sense, their abundant determination-contents received from earlier determinative judgments and are taken up passively as having those contents. In such a case, an explicit judging is done, since new shapings are performed with a certain, relative originality; but they are performed on the basis of "old" shapings. We must, in this connexion, think at the same time of "things that come to mind apperceptionally": Very often we judge on the basis of judgment-apperceptions, passively received categorial thoughts that come to our mind, but do so indirectly, on the basis of our similar earlier formations — that come to our mind as *judgments* which "go down with us", in just our motivational situation, without further ado. Like things that come to mind memorially, they are formulated by us, for our action of predicative judgment, at first in words that offer themselves associationally, without our performing, on that account, the explicit action of judgment implicitly referred to. Or from the very beginning, it is a matter of signs, of expressions — and, indeed, normally functioning expressions, leading us to make the significational formations our theme. These formations — without regard to their functional form as significations — make their appearance just like things that come to mind, namely as purely passive presentiations, analogues of passive memories; and there the matter usually rests: They are not in the least reactivated. As thus appearing, they are used in a new judgment activity. That which we possess passively, the affair on the significational side that we accept (with certainty, normally) as something existentially valid, is what we start from; in our freely generative action new categorial meaning-formations accrue to us, united with appropriate signs or words. We forego entering into the not unterinteresting intentional / complications arising <286> from the fact that two-sided locutions themselves can make their appearance as things coming to mind and, as such, "imply" in their sense, in a secondary manner, everything that is already secondary in the case of the original locutions; so that we have something secondary that is intentionally wrapped "inside" what is secondary. We see here nothing but intentional implications (no real inclusions as parts!) in the emerging and likewise in the modes of the actualization — the actualization of the signs that come to mind with their referrings and the actualization of their significations themselves, which are referred to.

On the whole, according to this exposition, we have in some cases wholly "confused", thoroughly inexplicit, judgments. At best they are formulated in words, verbally articulated; and still nothing is originally, actively, judged in such cases. In extreme contrast to these, we have the *perfectly distinct,* fully explicit, judgments, those produced originally in respect of each and every categorial component: exceptional cases, to be sure, but exceptionally important. Between the two groups fall the rest of our explicitly made judgments, those that work up an old inherited stock, the cases of *incomplete distinctness.*

§ 6. Indistinct verbal judging and its function.

In both groups falling under the heading of incomplete distinctness a great rôle is played by language, with its articulated outstandingnessses and the outstandingnesses of its significational indications. (This was briefly explained in the main text of the present essay.[1] Every simple sign indicates a signification and, more particularly, a positing of some appertinent sense-content or other; and this indication is an associational one. Signs combine to make up the unity of one sign — in particular, single words combine to make up the unity of one locution —, because of the fact that the indications combine to make up the unity of one indication, over and above the fact that sensuous signs combine to make up the unity of one sensuous configuration — something that, after all, conglomerations of (significationally) "unconnected" words also do. The combination of the words to make up the unity of the locution (accordingly the connexion of the indications, belonging to the words, to make up the unity of one indication) is the unity of an apperception that originated associationally: namely, from analogous modes <of combination> belonging to a former, primally institutive constitution of categorial formations of that sort or else to such a constitution of
<287> already two-sided formations of judicative speech. /

Likewise, in voluntarily forming sentences and unitary discourses, we can, and very often do, follow the accustomed style

[1] *Author's note*: See § 16, pp. 56—62, *supra.*

of sense-forming; we can let new formations originate from elements and formations of a typically familiar form, without in the least actually carrying out categorial actions and acquiring the categorial formations in an original manner. Thus, without being noticed, not only material countersense, the senselessness of a unification of what is "totally unrelated" (matters that "have nothing to do with each other") can come about, but also analytic countersense, which is the main theme in the text of this essay: Unity of the "judgment" comes about, as a unity of judgment-positing; but the judging is "confused", inexplicit, not a judging "proper". It is an associative passivity, springing from associative motivations, but carrying within it, as an intentional implicate, a spontaneous activity converted and transmuted into passive sensuousness — a passivity referring us to this activity as something that can be activated.

Precisely because of that, such passivity has important functions in the sphere of reason, which yields categorial evidence of each sort only in the active producing — evidence as giving the supposed categorial objectivities themselves, which as merely associationally indicated, in no way have already that "existence" (of "distinctness") which is, in turn, the presupposition for adequation of the supposed categorial objectivities, the judgments themselves, to the categorial objectivities themselves, the categorial truths. Precisely because, in any case, association (in the usual sense of the word) only indirectly indicates and anticipates, and does not itself give (unless it becomes united simultaneously with the giving of the associated itself), "blind" judging, judging that has originated merely associationally, faces questions ot "existence" or "non-existence" — namely concerning the "existence" or "non-existence" of the indicated judgment itself and consequently the "existence" or "non-existence" of the categorial objectivities themselves, there being a consciousness "beforehand" of "them themselves" with the indicating of the adequation. When the mathematician, on the basis of the structure and sequence of formulas that he finds in his thinking-situation, anticipates a new theorem and a proof for it with an appropriate style — being guided, obviously, by association, which has obscurely awakened earlier similar situations, formulas, and combinations of formu-

las —, he has not yet found, as he very well knows, any actual cognition, any actual theorems or proof; and that signifies for him, as an analytic mathematician, that he has not yet made those actual judgments and combinations of judgments, in the actual activity of which each thing would spring to the fore from analytic relationships belonging to it originally. That is why he
<288> now strives for the / explicit action which is his rational activity proper — no matter how necessary the associatively indicative action may remain, as pointing ahead to goals and ways for his rational practice.

This then is the character of associative verbal (or otherwise symbolic) judging — including its more complicated and, understandably, more fruitful form as a "two-sided" judging: Following, in general, the associational indications ot the <verbal> expressions (or other symbols), it is an associational anticipation of judgments, of categorial objectivities, suppositions and adequations, which, as thus indirectly indicated, are ways for the "properizing" explicit practice that makes the actual judgments, and perhaps cognitions, themselves — or else ways to show their non-actuality.

§ 7. The superiority of retentional and recollectional to apperceptional confusion; secondary evidence in confusion.

There becomes apparent here, to be sure, a significant difference of those confused manners of judging from the inactivity of retentions and recollections, however much these are also open to, and in need of, justification by means of "properization". For, little as these give something-itself in an original manner and, therefore, little as they are evidences proper, they do have the *significance of secondary derivatives of evidence*, derivatives in which (as a criticism of cognition shows) *there still remains*, though indirectly, *something of evidence*. Without them there would be no science. If living retention were without value, thinking could never reach any result at all. As soon as legitimation begins, retention comes into play, and its acceptance-value is presupposed. Similarly in the case of *reproductive memories*. They have evidence, not only as *clear* recollections, the evidence belonging to experience of the past — to be sure, an imperfect evidence, but essentially perfectible in approximations to an ideal limit — but a *secondary evidence* also *as still unclear memories*. Without them, there would be no possible justification for the confidence that science is a store of permanent cognitional acquisitions, as evidences that can be reactivated as any time.

THE IDEA OF A "LOGIC OF MERE NON-CONTRADICTION" OR A "LOGIC OF MERE CONSEQUENCE".

§ 1. The goal of formal non-contradiction and of formal consequence. Broader and narrower framing of these concepts.

Traditional formal logic had long been designated as *Logik der* blossen Widerspruchslosigkeit [logic of *mere non-contradiction*] and also as blosse Konsequenzlogik [logic of *mere consequence*]; and I could say that my demonstration that, in respect of its essential theoretical content, it can be defined, and indeed exactly delimited, as a "pure analytics" results at bottom in the justifying of these old characterizations on essential grounds but also, to be sure, in the bringing out of a genuine and purified sense for them. Now the manner in which I have frequently used the same expressions and, in particular, the words *Widerspruchslosigkeit* [non-contradiction] (also *Verträglichkeit* [compatibility]) and *Konsequenz* [consequence] — with a universality that was partly determined by those traditional locutions — can give occasion for misunderstandings, as Professor Oskar Becker brought to my attention while this essay was in the press. Perhaps I have allowed myself to be carried somewhat too far — in my mode of expression — by the satisfaction of being able to provide an honorable status for the traditional locutions by new insights. It might be useful to add here some justifying elucidations, which, at the same time, take us further.

The old logic was called a logic of (formal) non-contradiction; though it did not direct itself merely to questions of the formal compossibility of judgments, merely to questions of their not contradicting one another. Questions of analytically necessary consequence [*Folge*], of syllogistic consequence [*Konsequenz*], were indeed its chief theme. At the same time, the old phraseology had a legitimate sense. With the old logic's normative atti-

tude, even the principle of contradiction was meant as normative: as the norm of a contradiction that should be avoided. Thus the whole intention of that logic may be distinguished by the question: <290>
In the first place, before any inquiry into their material themes, how can we, in our judgments, avoid falling into "contradictions", incompatibilities, that depend on mere form? And how can we find the pertinent normative laws of form? Now every negation of a formal necessary consequence is a contradiction. Thus the whole of formal consequence-logic, the the logic of analytic necessities, can be seen from the point of view of non-contradiction. To be sure, the intention to acquire a system of "formal truth" can become severed from the intention to avoid contradictions and equipped exclusively with a positive sense. Somewhat like this: If we already have judgments that are non-contradictory and cohere without contradiction, what further judgments are prejudged *through* those judgments, purely on the basis of form; what ones are included in them as analytic necessities of inference? In any case, however, universal inquiry for the essential forms and the norms pertaining to a universe of *non-contradiction* in particular leads at the same time, and necessarily, to inquiry for the essential forms of the analytic *necessities* according to which other judgments are included in judgments already given. The universal formal laws of non-contradiction thus include those of consequence in drawing conclusions; formal logic of non-contradiction is also formal consequence-logic, just as the concept of consequence is, of course, subordinate a priori to the most universal concept of non-contradiction.

Conversely, however, it is likewise an obvious procedure to relate the whole of logic to *Konsequenz* [consequence or consistency] and, in so doing, to take this concept very broadly. To abandon a judgment, to "cancel" it by negation or, more generally, to modalize it in any fashion — something that, after all, is not a matter of free choice —, I must have particular motives. What motives lie within the judgment-sphere itself and, more particularly, in the mere judgment-form? As one who judges, I remain faithful to myself, I remain self-consistent [*mir "konsequent"*], just as long as I stick to my judgments; in the opposite case I am inconsistent. But, even without knowing it, I have been inconsistent and, more particularly, formally inconsistent, when

I subsequently recognize, on more precise inspection of the forms in which I judge (on making them distinct), that my later judgment contradicts my earlier one.

Thus any judgments whatever make up a system of *Konsequenz* — in this sense — if on "more precise inspection" they go together, for the judging subject, to form the unity of a combined judgment within which no judgment contradicts any other.

We can now see that analytics, as the universal system of eidetic laws of possible formal non-contradiction, is also analytics
<291> as the system of eidetic laws of possible formal "*Konsequenz*". / Here too the concept of "*Konsequenz*" is a very general one, which comprises not only "logical" consequence, *Konsequenz* in the pregnant sense of necessary analytic consequence [*Folge*], but also consistency, *Konsequenz* in the sense of unitariness in, so to speak, accidental temporal *sequence* [*Folge*], namely of judgments meant in succession but yet *unitarily*, judgments that (as we see when we pay precise attention to their form) are mutually compatible — without any modalizing influence of one upon another.

Now all this holds good, but grows deeper, when we take into account the insights gained in the main text under the heading "distinct evidence or evidence of distinct and proper judgment-performance". Then only does it acquire its due significance. Our "pure analytics", in its purity, is indeed both an analytics of non-contradiction and an analytics of *Konsequenz*; and — in view of the naturally suggested broader significations of the words in question — we have so characterized it in the text. "*Konsequenz*" that has this broader sense then becomes divided *eo ipso* into the consequence that has the customary logical sense, analytic necessity of consequence [*Folge*], and the "trivial non-contradictoriness", or compatibility, of judgments "that have nothing to do with one another". As a result of the investigations in Appendix I (with the newly brought-out concept of judgment-material as "syntactical stuff"), these judgments become defined by the scientific expression, "judgments that have no component of their syntactical stuffs in common".

The fundamentally essential part of the doctrine stated in the main text is, in my opinion, the thesis that, as they function in the whole of analytics, compatibility, contradiction, formal

Konsequenz, in every sense that is in question here, can and must be precisely defined in a pure sense, one that contains no reference to the truth or falsity of the judgments — that is to say: the judgments meant at any time as thematic in respect of analytic relationships. In other words, *pure* analytics asks about judgments purely as judgments, purely about the judgment-relationships that affect the possibility or impossibility of a proper performing, and does not ask at all about whether such relationships have a relevance to the possible truth of judgments. Thus, in contrast to the case in traditional logic, compatibility and contradiction in *pure* analytics do *not* have the sense of compatibility and incompatibility in a possible truth; in the same fashion, consequence [*Folge*] does not have the sense of consequent truth (not even of supposed consequent truth); and so forth. There is a compossibility of judgments purely as judgments — compossibility within the unity belonging to an explicit and proper / judgment-performance; and this is the only <292>
compossibility that figures as a thematic concept for pure analytics. Stated subjectively, it is here exclusively a matter of the set of formal eidetic laws governing the ability to judge, and to judge together, explicitly and properly. There is no need of adding "and governing the *necessity* of judging together": The set of eidetic laws governing formal "compossibility" already includes those governing formal "connecessity".

The manner of expression in the main text frequently gives rise to an appearance of incorrectness, because, in various passages, this "connecessity" is not mentioned expressly, and furthermore because pure analytics is called, now simply consequence-logic and again logic of non-contradiction, and, in the latter connexion, non-contradiction is even designated as its sole and all-embracing theme. But the thought expressed by such passages is quite correct, as becomes apparent from the explanations given above, particularly those concerning the essential connexions between the all-embracing themes and laws of formal non-contradiction on the one hand and the all-embracing themes and laws of formal *Konsequenz* (in the broader as well as in the pregnant sense) on the other hand.

Let it also be pointed out expressly that, with those explanations, the characterization of the Euclidean multiplicity as a system of "non-contradiction' (p. 141, *supra*) — a word instead of which, by the way, the word "*Konsequenz*" is used a little earlier — becomes understood. Furthermore, it should be noted that there we are indeed speaking of a "multiplicity" and that previously, in [Part I], Chapter III, [§ 31,] (pp. 94ff., *supra*), the exact concept of the multiplicity, as a system arising purely from analytic necessity, had been clarified in detail.

§ 2. Relation of the systematic and radical building of a pure analytics, back to the theory of syntaxes.

With reference to those investigations concerning syntaxes that we communicated in Appendix I, the following application to pure analytics may be added.

Let us give the all-embracing task of this analytics the following simple formulation: to explore the eidetic laws of judgment-form, which are the conditions for the possibility that any judgment with some arbitrarily specified form is a "properly existing" judgment, one that can be made explicitly — that is to say: in the sense proper to distinct evidence.

Judgment is to be conceived with the broadest analytic universality, that of any supposed categorial objectivity whatever, as it was conceived predominantly in the later chapters of this essay.

The inquiry concerns also the judgment-forms themselves, as purely conceptual universalities pertaining to judgments; and, as concerning them, it can be stated as follows. When can judgment-forms be grasped in original insight as eidetic uni-
<293> versalities / pertaining to judgments that can be made actually and properly? When do they, as such universalities, have ideal "existence"?

Given the breadth of our concept of the judgment, any arbitrary conjunction of judgments, or any arbitrary categorial whole that, so far as pure grammar is concerned, can be constructed out of judgements (as supposed categorial objectivites), is one judgment; and the question of "existence" relates to the judgment in this sense. It therefore includes every question of the compossibility of any judgments whatever, which, as compossible, naturally function always as partial judgments, even when the whole is a mere conjunction.

Now it became clear in Appendix I that what a formal consideration conceives as quite indeterminately variable but self-identical — the terms — is precisely the "core-stuffs"; and that the formal regularities we are seeking are exclusively regularities of *syntax* and, at a deeper level, regularities in the change of core-forms — that is to say: in substantivation ("nominalization").

Therefore, when we attack our question systematically, we must trace the regularities of syntaxes and of the structure underlying them. In the first place, we must start from the syntactical articulation, with the pertinent distinctions between syntactical forms and stuffs, and from the forms of the "material". We should then have to turn back and seek out the "primitive" or primal forms and their primal articulation; furthermore the equally primitive modes of syntactical combination — how it is that primitive "elements" become united by them in a primitive manner to make judgments, and how it is that judgment-unity becomes possible at the various levels of complexity, either by means of the same modes of combination, as possible at any level of complexity (like the conjunctive combination), or by means of modes of combination peculiar to higher levels. As the primitive, the original, in the syntactical construction of forms, we can rightly account only self-sufficiency (which is changed by incorporation as a member, such incorporation being already a syntactical forming) and certainty of being (which becomes variously modalized in formally universal manners).

To them pertain laws of analytic existence — in the first place the law of analytic primitiveness: Primitive forms are a priori "existent" — that is: properly effectible. Every modalization, considered in and of itself, keeps this existence; yet it no longer does so unconditionally in complexes, since that which in and of itself has possible "existence" can become dependent on something else that is also possible in and of itself — dependent in the only manner that comes into question here, namely according to form-laws of possible coexistence or, equivalently stated, laws of possible syntactical unity. Furthermore: *Mere* conjunction, / without any copulative combining at all, yields new forms of <294>
possible existence. In this connexion it is to be heeded that any combination of forms by virtue of their having a term in common has the significance of a copulative combination belonging to that term; there belongs to that term an "it is the same". Judgments possible in themselves, which are somehow inserted syntactically — that is: made into members — do not always yield a whole that is possible according to its total syntax. Wherever the

possibility of coexistence (the compossibility, so far as it depends on pure form) can become *questionable*, it is because of combinations by copular forms (the copular forms that unite identifyingly, in an extremely broad sense). Consequently it can be said that unity by virtue of copulative combining defines a quite *distinctive concept of the judgment* and the very one that traditional logic has exclusively in view, since this logic leaves out of account "unconnected" conjunctions of judgments.[1] When considering the syntactical complexes belonging to this copular sphere, one naturally comes across, in the most universal fashion, all the analytic necessities and the contradictions that are their reverse.

These things are only indicated here, in order to show that it is well, and indeed necessary, to lay down beforehand a theory of forms, thoroughly developed as a systematic theory of syntactical structures, to serve as the foundation on which we can build an analytics having a systematic character, and an original genuineness, established by insight. This pure analytics, as contrasted with the "purely grammatical" theory of judgment-forms, which raises no questions about producibility proper, can be characterized as a *higher theory of forms*, the theory of the forms of possible explicitly producible judgments (naturally, with its correlate, the theory of the forms of negatively producible judgments, contradictory judgments). The forms, as eidetic universalities, are eidetic laws. Pure analytics, we can say according to all this, is a science that seeks out systematically the primitive forms of judgments that can be judged in a complete activity proper, the "primitive operations" whereby such judgments can be varied syntactically, and the original modes of their connective (copulative, conjunctive) combination. Starting from these forms, operations, and modes of combination, and guided by the purely grammatical reiterations in the constructing of forms, pure analytics must trace, level by level, the resultant possibilities of constructing forms of judgments "proper", and in this fashion it must bring under laws the whole system of judgment-possibility within the sphere of distinctness — ideally speaking, by systematic construction of the existent forms. /

[1] *Author's note*: Cf. Appendix I, § 6[c], pp. 302f., *supra*.

§ 3. The characterization of analytic judgments as merely "elucidative of knowledge" and as "tautologies". <295>

Let us further consider the peculiarity of analytics with respect to the rôle that the "terms" play in this discipline. From the constitutional point of view, the syntaxes and the "substantivations" that become involved in them are the noematic correlates of the specifically judicial activities and of the rhythmics of the repeated completing of these activities in the form of self-contained copulative combinings. As for the cores, they refer us to the fact that judicial action continually presupposes things given beforehand. These can be formations originating from earlier judgings; but finally we come to something corresponding to the ultimate stuffs and their substantival and adjectival forms, namely to the passive and subsequent active experience that gives us something individual beforehand, and to the prior formings brought about here by a merely experiencing-explicating process of taking cognizance. These are themes for a separate investigation.[1] Analytics, even when it goes back and inquires into its own correlate in the sphere of productive subjectivity, does not ask about them. Analytics regards its terms as openly indeterminate and does not ask whether they, as making their appearance in its form-universalities, are ultimate substantives and adjectives originating from experience or formations originating from syntactical actions. Thus its formally distinct evidence concerns only the properness of the syntactical forming; while the terms remain, as it were, floating freely, so far as their origin and therefore their possibility are concerned. To this state of affairs there corresponds the fact that, even in the case of a material exemplification or application of analytics, nay, even in looking to see whether an inference is analytically evident (without appealing to laws of form), the thematizing interest does not penetrate into the material terms but, while merely keeping them identical, concerns itself exclusively with the syntaxes.

[1] *Translator's note*: See Edmund Husserl, *Erfahrung und Urteil: Untersuchungen zur Genealogie der Logik [Experience and Judgment: Investigations pertaining to the Genealogy of Logic], ausgearbeitet und herausgegeben von Ludwig Landgrebe*, Prag, 1939, and Hamburg, 1948 and 1954, *I. Abschnitt, Die vorprädikative (rezeptive) Erfahrung* [Part One, Predicative (Receptive) Experience].

"Analytic judging" and the judging done with formal universality by analytics itself can of course be characterized as analytic also in the sense that Kant sought to formulate as "merely elucidative of knowledge", rather than "amplifying knowlege". For this formulation can signify only that the analytic interest is directed purely to the possibility of distinct evidence (a possibility consisting in the proper performability of the judgment-acts at all the syntactical levels) and that the evidence of whatever is given beforehand in a particular case is irrelevant to this possibility. This is of use to logic: The self-
<296> contained set of laws of "non-contradiction" founds / the self-contained set of laws of possible truth. Knowledge is not "enriched"; in all our analytic doing we never get beyond what we already "had" judicially or cognitionally; everything accruing analytically is "included" in it. Only it is so often necessary to call in the help of the mathematician's genius, in order merely to "make distinct", to „elucidate". If we think of the whole aim of analytics, ideally, as related to just any openly infinite sphere of prior givenness, we have, at all levels of analytic performance, "always the same" — the same affairs, the same stock of predicatively formed affair-complexes. What we infer is something already there; materially it is identical with the totality of, or with part of, our presuppositions. Obviously this determines the concept-forming that comes to the fore in modern logistics, and the logistical doctrine of "*tautology*" as including every closed analytic complex.

Professor Oskar Becker has very kindly put at our disposal the following interesting remarks, which give that doctrine a place within a "pure" analytics.

§ 4. Remarks on "tautology" in the logistical sense, with reference to §§ 14—18 of the main text. (By Oskar Becker.)

From the logistical point of view, a tautology can be conceived as the negative of a contradiction; and, conversely, any negative of a contradiction is a tautology. The purely analytic character of such tautologies follows from this "definition". They are, so to speak, self-sufficient consequence-systems, requiring no premises outside themselves. The peculiar character of tautology stands out as strictly analogous to that of contradiction, if at first we leave the province of pure analytics and take into consideration the possible truth or falsity of judgments (see § 19 of the main text):

"Any contradiction ... excludes from the start all questions of adequation; it is *a limine* a falsity." (P. 66, *supra*.) In precise correspondence with this: Any tautology excludes from the start all questions of adequation; it is *a limine* a truth.

If we take the judgments, $p_1, p_2, \ldots p_n$, and construct the complex form, $P(p_1, p_2, \ldots p_n)$, by logical operations — as a form that itself represents a judgment by virtue of its purely grammatical structure —, then P is a tautology (or else a contradiction), if, and only if, P is true (or else false) *regardless of whether the judgments, $p_1, p_2, \ldots p_n$, are true / or false.*[1] The <297>
question of the adequation of the judgment-senses of $p_1, p_2, \ldots p_n$, to any formal-ontological — to say nothing of material — predicatively formed affair-complexes is therefore quite irrelevant.

Now these definitions can also be set up correspondingly in the purely analytic sphere — that is to say: strictly without making any use of a concept of truth or falsity:

"P is a tautology (or else a contradiction)" signifies: "$P(p_1, p_2, \ldots p_n)$ is compatible (or else incompatible) with either p_1 or non-p_1, with either p_2 or non-p_2, ..., with either p_n or non-p_n." (That is to say, according to whether P is a tautology or a contradiction, it is either compatible or else incompatible with any logical product that arises from $p_1, p_2, \ldots p_n$, when any p_i is replaced by its negative.)

This process of converting a "truth-logic" formulation into a "consequence-logic" formulation can obviously be applied also in the more general case where we intend to say that $P(p_1, p_2, \ldots p_n)$ is true (or else false), if certain of the p's, the p_i's, are true and othe p's, the p_j's, are false. Then the purely analytic formulation is: The negative of P (or else P itself) is incompatible with a certain logical product of statements, which arises from $p_1, p_2, \ldots p_n$, when the above-mentioned p_j's (and they *alone*) are replaced by their negatives. (Strictly, we must also assume that the law

[1] *Author's note*: This characterization of tautology is derived from Ludwig Wittgenstein (*Tractatus Logico-Philosophicus*, [New York and] London, 1922; also in the *Annalen der Natur- und Kulturphilosophie*, Bd. 14, 1921.)

of excluded middle holds good in the case of those judgments of which we form negatives. Otherwise, in each instance, we should have to replace the incompatibility of the negative of q with r by a positive includedness of q in r.) — Thus the possibility of avoiding the concept of truth in the whole of logistics would seem to have been shown in its essentials.

Just as truth is a predicate that can belong only to a distinct (<and> non-contradictory) judgment (p. 66, *supra*), so falsity is a predicate that can belong only to a non-tautological judgment — that is: a judgment that is not already self-evident within the sphere of mere distinctness.

Just as the discordancy [*Unstimmigkeit*] of the "component senses" (the "component propositions or posita") in a complex judgment excludes truth, so the "self-correctness [*Selbststimmigkeit*]" (the tautological structure) of the component senses excludes falsity — and the exclusion is *a limine* in both cases. Possible truth and possible falsity are alike open only to judgments that are harmonious [*einstimmig*] but not "self-correct [*selbststimmig*]" and distinct but not "self-distinct". /

<298> As we said at the start, negatives of tautologies are contradictions, and *vice versa*. With this is connected the fact that, throughout the whole sphere of either tautological or contradictory judgments, the *law of excluded middle* holds good, as is well known *not* to be the case universally in the purely analytic sphere (see § 90, [pp. 220f., *supra*]; *cf.* § 77, [pp. 193ff., *supra*]). Obviously this depends on the fact that — as soon as the idea of possible truth or falsity is included — the question of whether the truth-value of a judgment belonging in the sphere of tautologies and contradictions can be *decided* is answered *a limine* in the affirmative (*cf.* § 79, [pp. 196ff., *supra*]).

Lightning Source UK Ltd.
Milton Keynes UK
17 May 2010

154291UK00001B/27/A

9 789024 720521